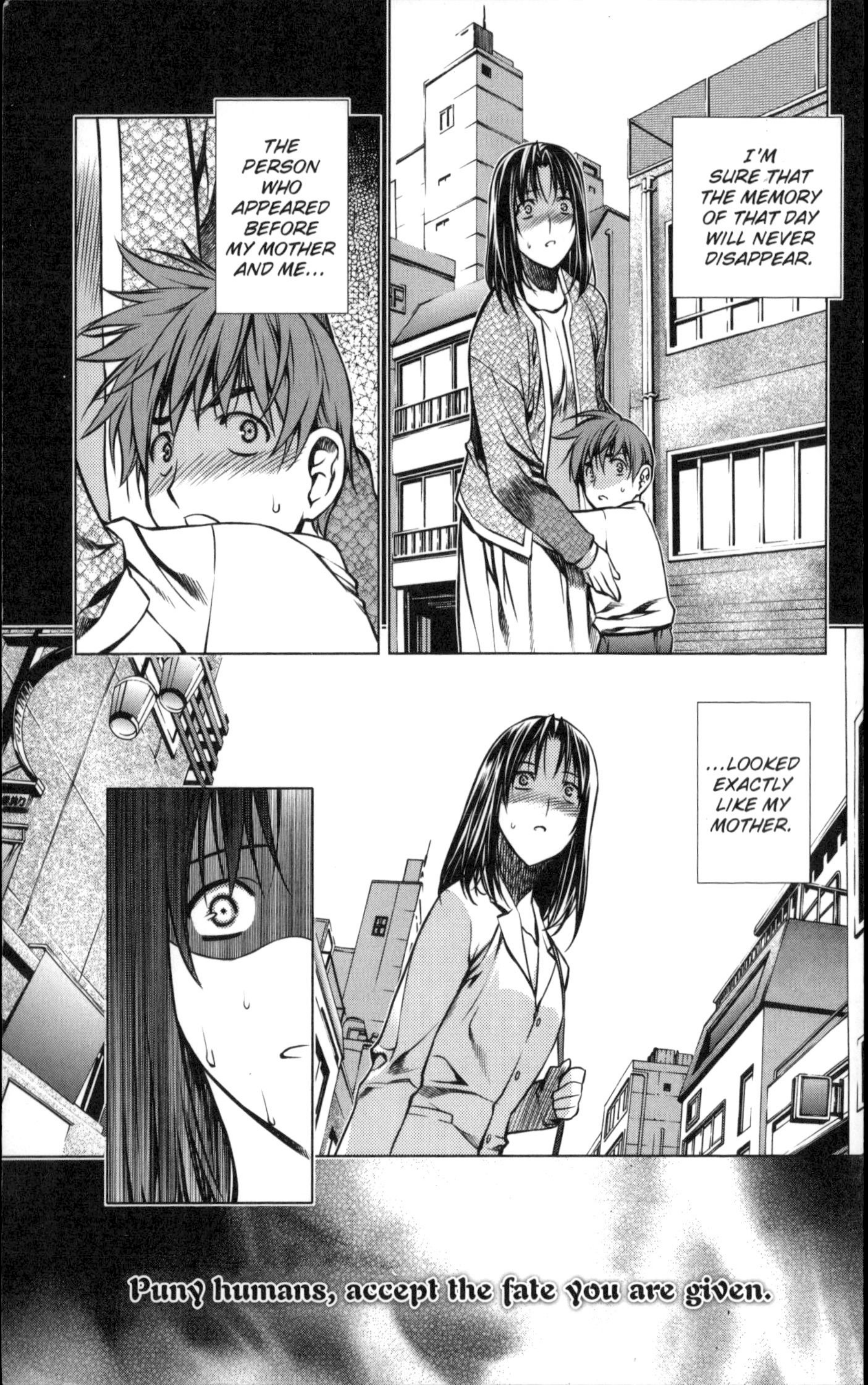
I'M SURE THAT THE MEMORY OF THAT DAY WILL NEVER DISAPPEAR.
THE PERSON WHO APPEARED BEFORE MY MOTHER AND ME...
...LOOKED EXACTLY LIKE MY MOTHER.
Puny humans, accept the fate you are given.

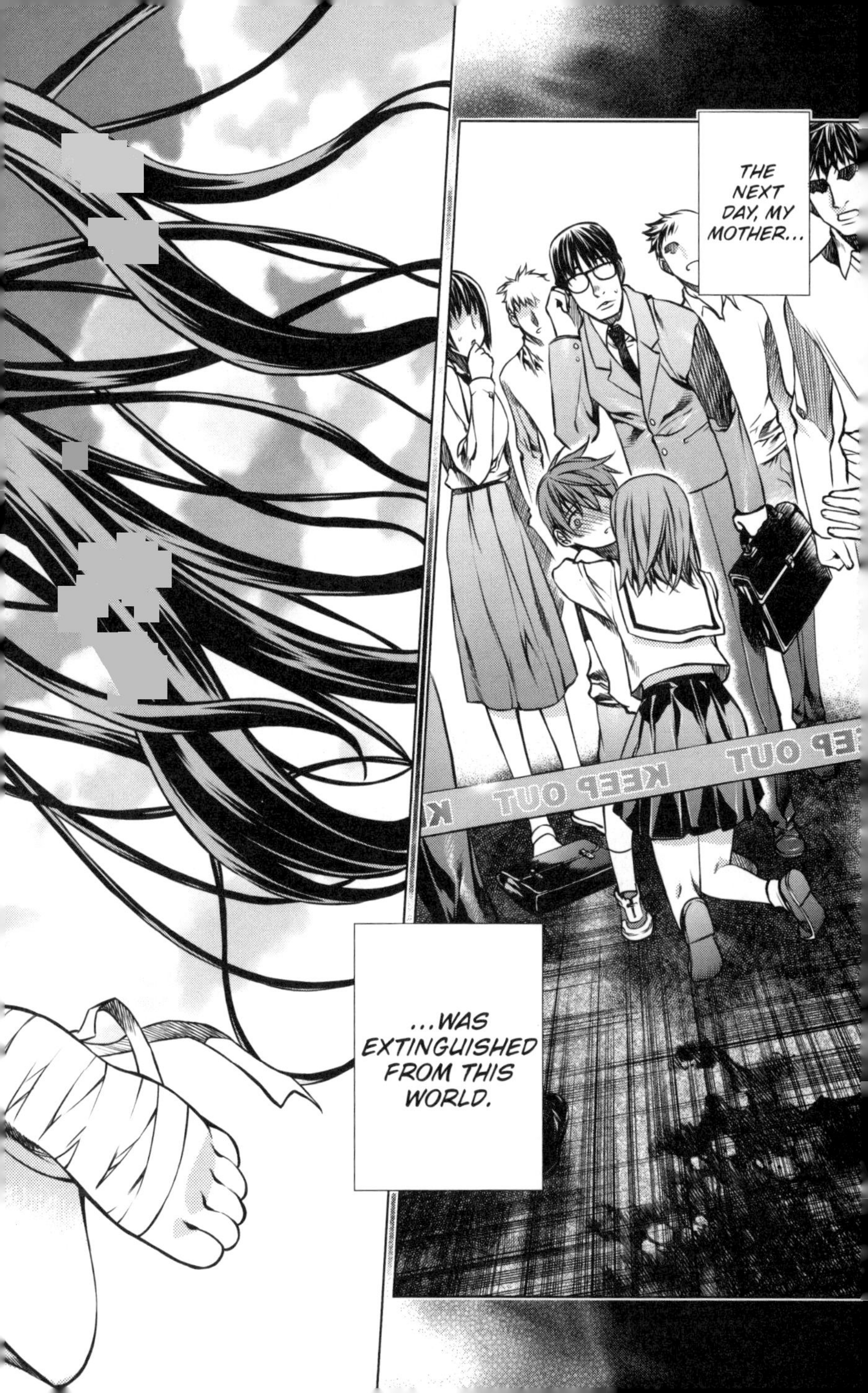
THE NEXT DAY, MY MOTHER...
KEEP OUT
KEEP OUT
...WAS EXTINGUISHED FROM THIS WORLD.

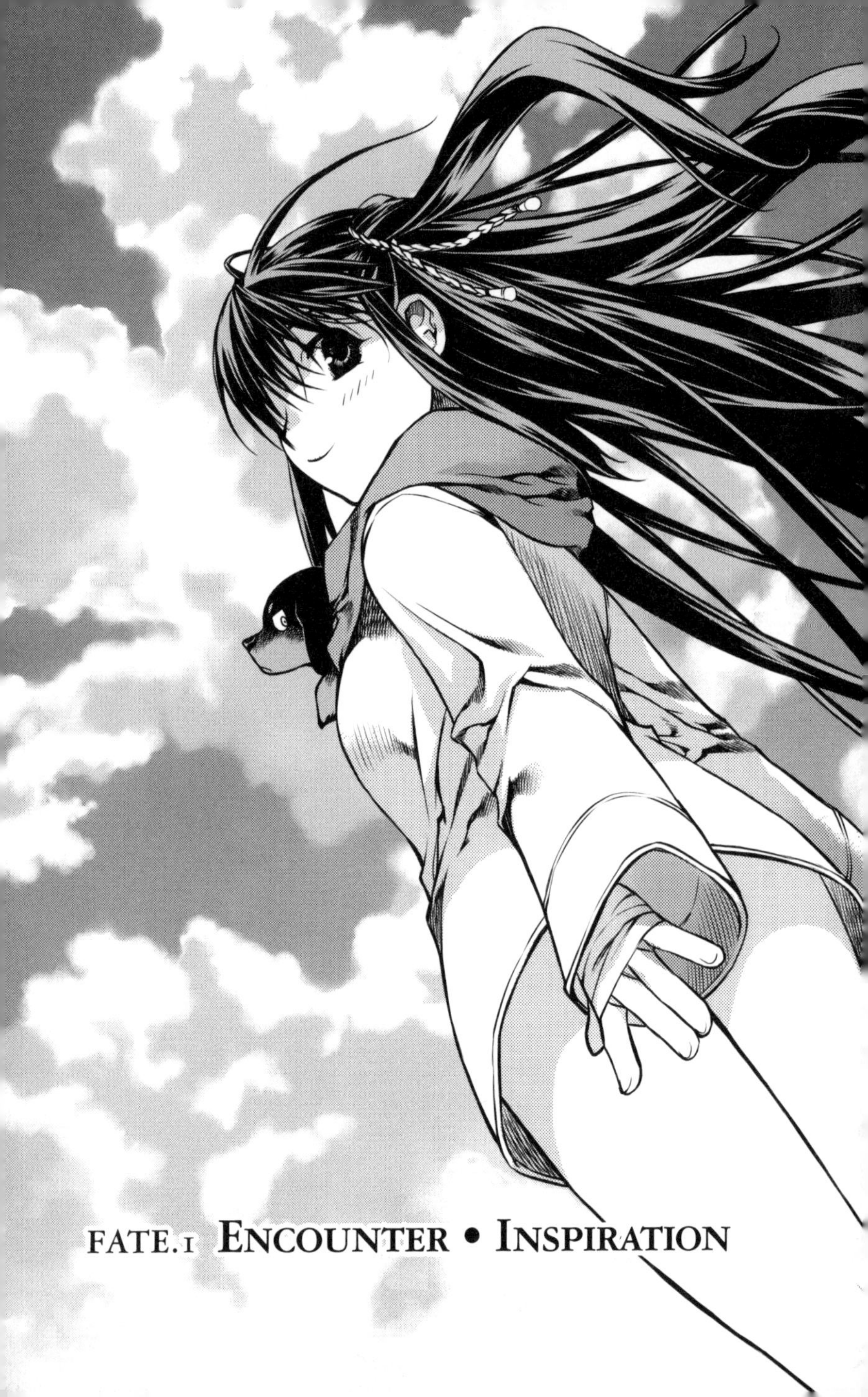

FATE.1 Encounter • Inspiration

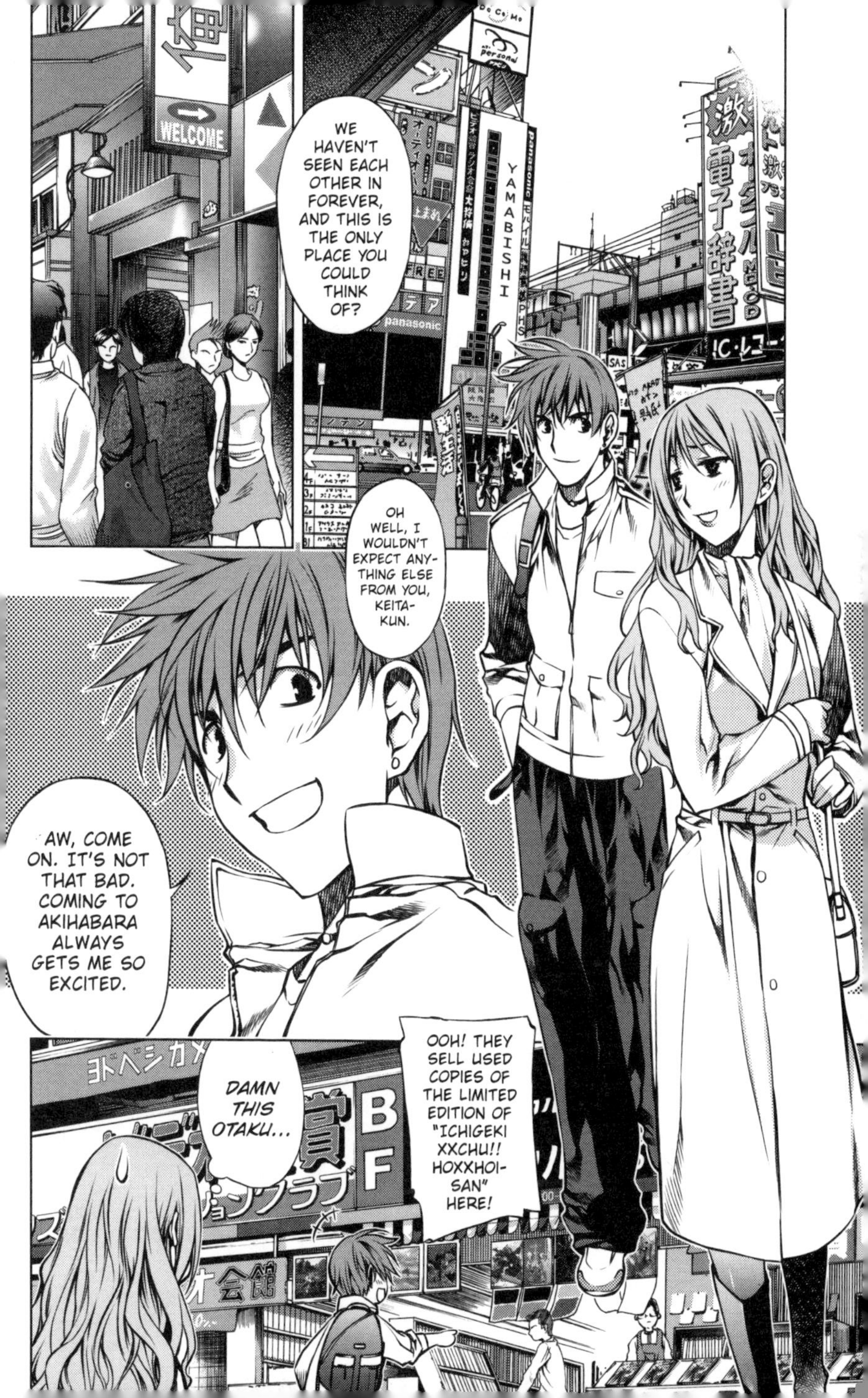
WE HAVEN'T SEEN EACH OTHER IN FOREVER, AND THIS IS THE ONLY PLACE YOU COULD THINK OF?
OH WELL, I WOULDN'T EXPECT ANYTHING ELSE FROM YOU, KEITA-KUN.
AW, COME ON. IT'S NOT THAT BAD. COMING TO AKIHABARA ALWAYS GETS ME SO EXCITED.
OOH! THEY SELL USED COPIES OF THE LIMITED EDITION OF "ICHIGEKI XXCHU!! HOXXHOI-SAN" HERE!
DAMN THIS OTAKU...
WELCOME
YAMABISHI

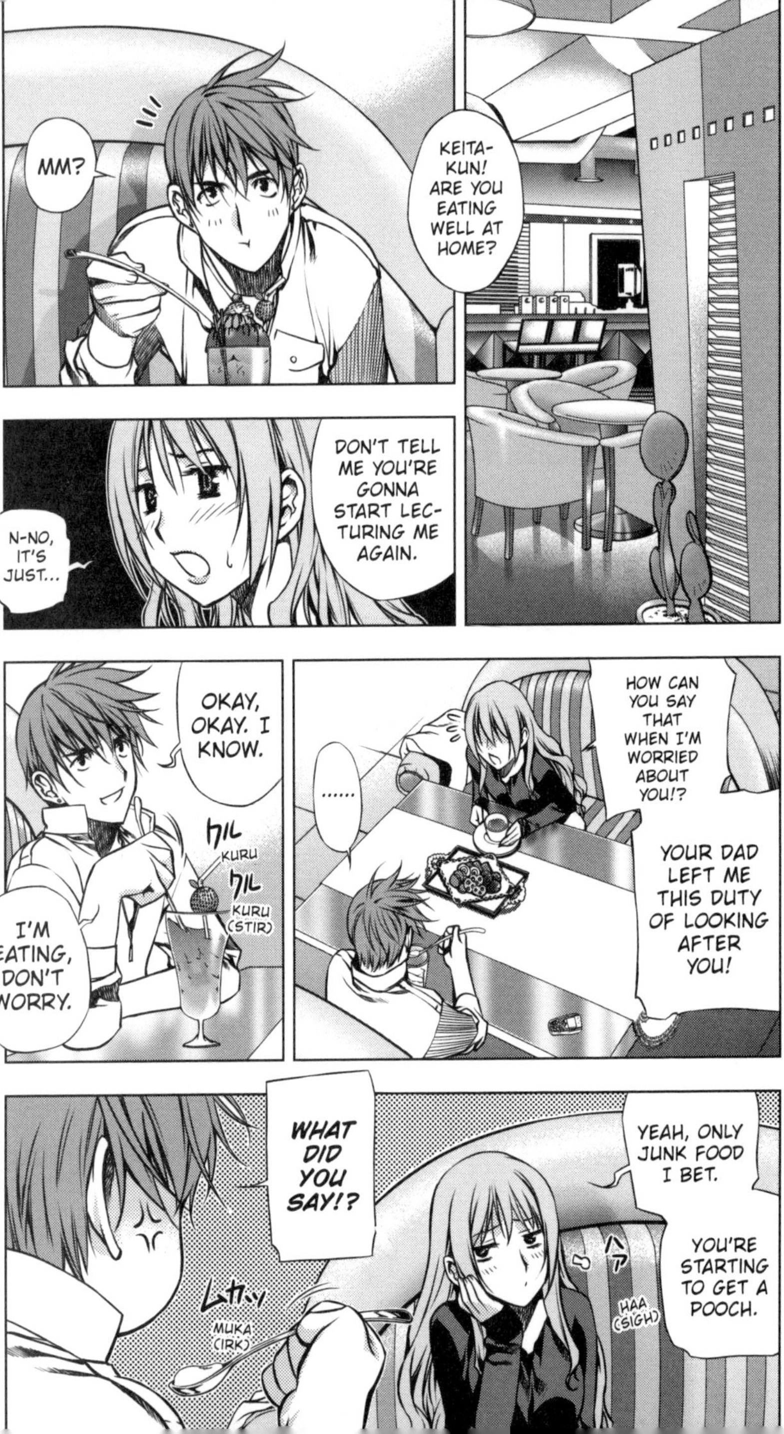
KEITA-KUN! ARE YOU EATING WELL AT HOME?
MM?
DON'T TELL ME YOU'RE GONNA START LEC-TURING ME AGAIN.
N-NO, IT'S JUST...
HOW CAN YOU SAY THAT WHEN I'M WORRIED ABOUT YOU!?
YOUR DAD LEFT ME THIS DUTY OF LOOKING AFTER YOU!
......
OKAY, OKAY. I KNOW.
クル
KURU
クル
KURU (STIR)
I'M EATING, DON'T WORRY.
YEAH, ONLY JUNK FOOD I BET.
YOU'RE STARTING TO GET A POOCH.
ハア
HAA (SIGH)
WHAT DID YOU SAY!?
ムカッ
MUKA (IRK)

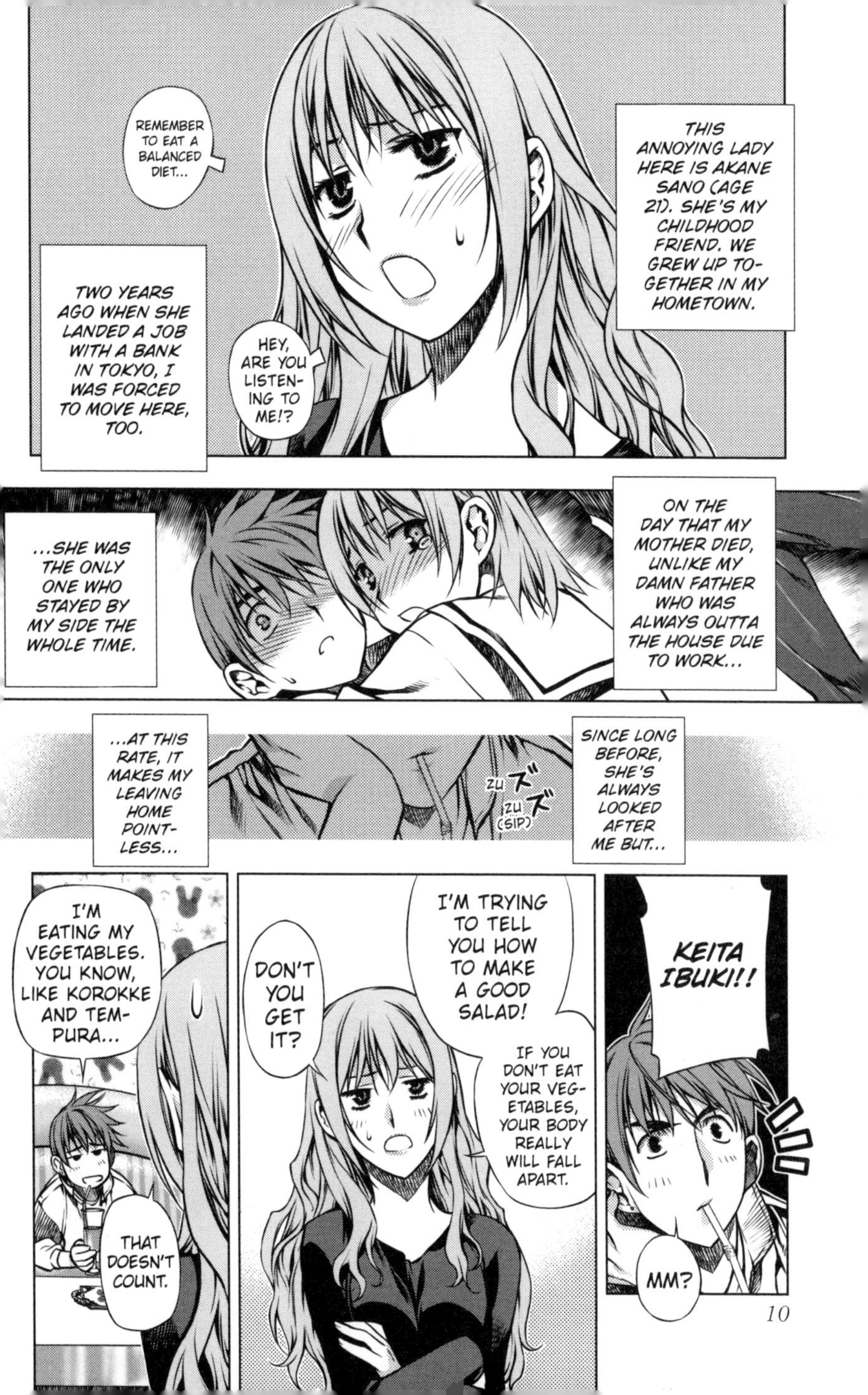
THIS ANNOYING LADY HERE IS AKANE SANO (AGE 21). SHE'S MY CHILDHOOD FRIEND. WE GREW UP TO-GETHER IN MY HOMETOWN.
REMEMBER TO EAT A BALANCED DIET...
TWO YEARS AGO WHEN SHE LANDED A JOB WITH A BANK IN TOKYO, I WAS FORCED TO MOVE HERE, TOO.
HEY, ARE YOU LISTEN-ING TO ME!?
ON THE DAY THAT MY MOTHER DIED, UNLIKE MY DAMN FATHER WHO WAS ALWAYS OUTTA THE HOUSE DUE TO WORK...
...SHE WAS THE ONLY ONE WHO STAYED BY MY SIDE THE WHOLE TIME.
SINCE LONG BEFORE, SHE'S ALWAYS LOOKED AFTER ME BUT...
ZU ズ
ZU ズ (SIP)
...AT THIS RATE, IT MAKES MY LEAVING HOME POINT-LESS...
KEITA IBUKI!!
MM?
I'M TRYING TO TELL YOU HOW TO MAKE A GOOD SALAD!
DON'T YOU GET IT?
IF YOU DON'T EAT YOUR VEG-ETABLES, YOUR BODY REALLY WILL FALL APART.
I'M EATING MY VEGETABLES. YOU KNOW, LIKE KOROKKE AND TEM-PURA...
THAT DOESN'T COUNT.

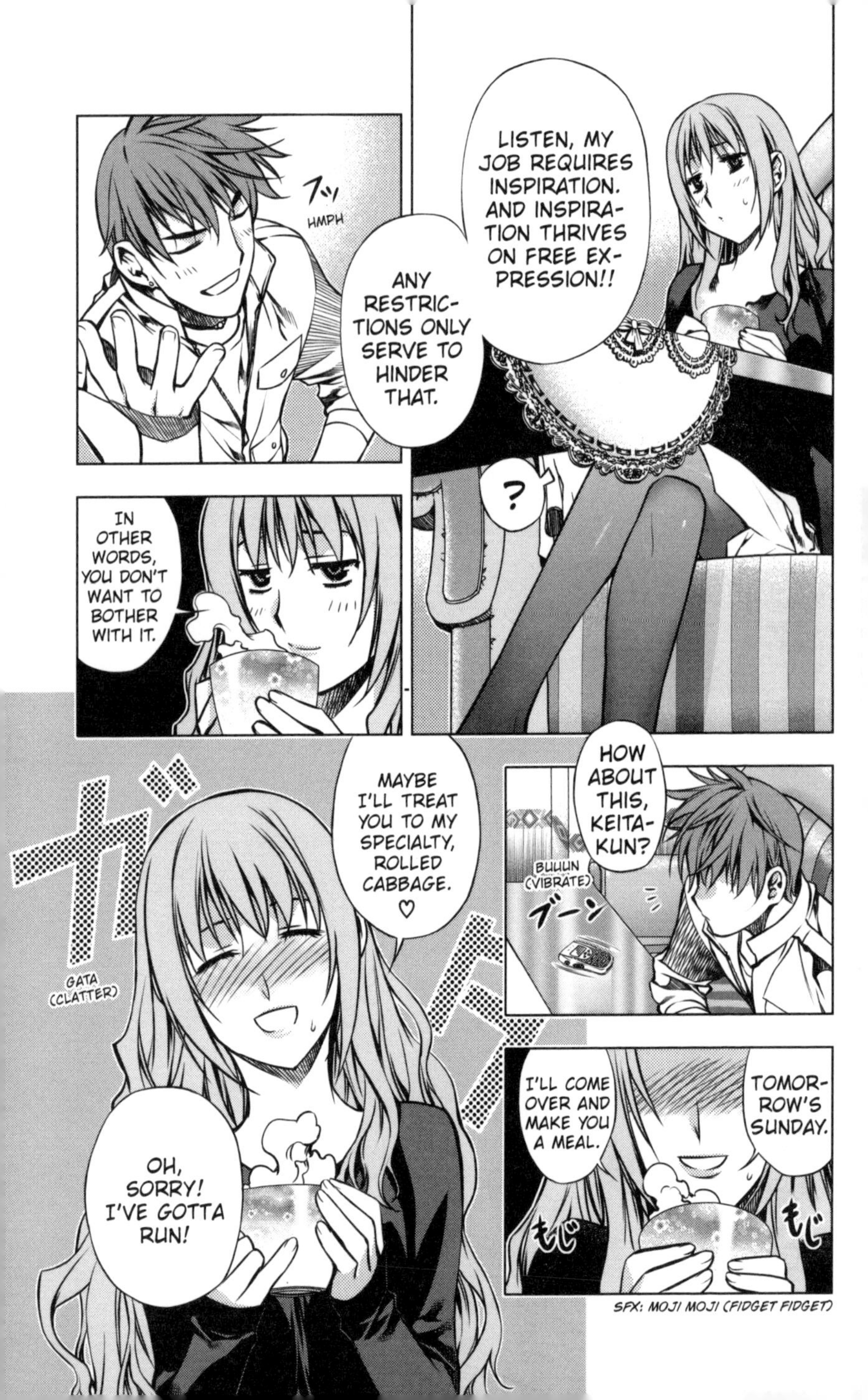
LISTEN, MY JOB REQUIRES INSPIRATION. AND INSPIRATION THRIVES ON FREE EXPRESSION!!
?
ANY RESTRICTIONS ONLY SERVE TO HINDER THAT.
ブッ
HMPH
IN OTHER WORDS, YOU DON'T WANT TO BOTHER WITH IT.
HOW ABOUT THIS, KEITA-KUN?
ブーン
BUUUN (VIBRATE)
TOMORROW'S SUNDAY.
I'LL COME OVER AND MAKE YOU A MEAL.
もじ
もじ
MAYBE I'LL TREAT YOU TO MY SPECIALTY, ROLLED CABBAGE. ♡
GATA (CLATTER)
OH, SORRY! I'VE GOTTA RUN!

SFX: MOJI MOJI (FIDGET FIDGET)

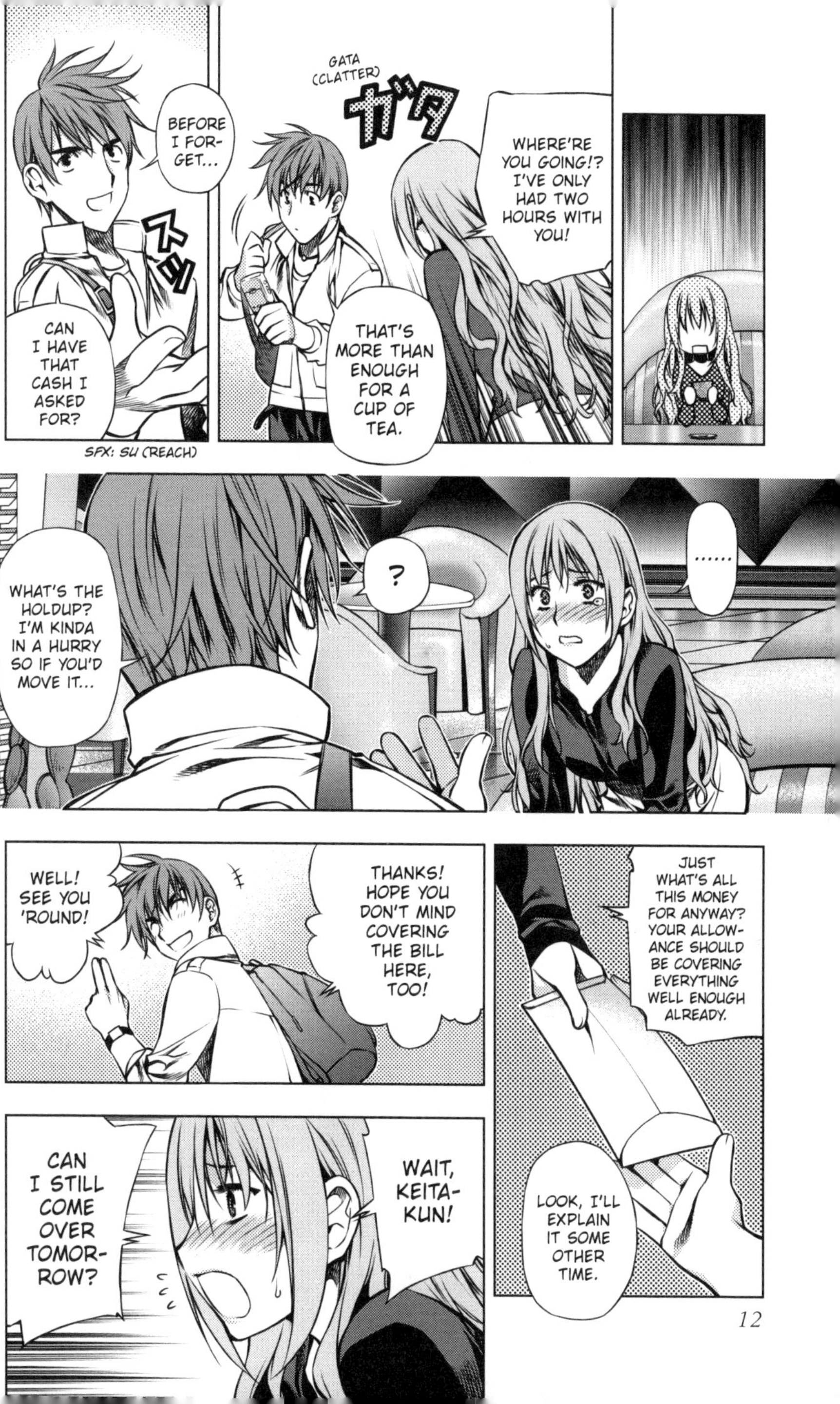
WHERE'RE YOU GOING!? I'VE ONLY HAD TWO HOURS WITH YOU!
GATA (CLATTER)
THAT'S MORE THAN ENOUGH FOR A CUP OF TEA.
BEFORE I FOR-GET...
CAN I HAVE THAT CASH I ASKED FOR?
SFX: SU (REACH)
......
?
WHAT'S THE HOLDUP? I'M KINDA IN A HURRY SO IF YOU'D MOVE IT...
JUST WHAT'S ALL THIS MONEY FOR ANYWAY? YOUR ALLOW-ANCE SHOULD BE COVERING EVERYTHING WELL ENOUGH ALREADY.
LOOK, I'LL EXPLAIN IT SOME OTHER TIME.
THANKS! HOPE YOU DON'T MIND COVERING THE BILL HERE, TOO!
WELL! SEE YOU 'ROUND!
WAIT, KEITA-KUN!
CAN I STILL COME OVER TOMOR-ROW?

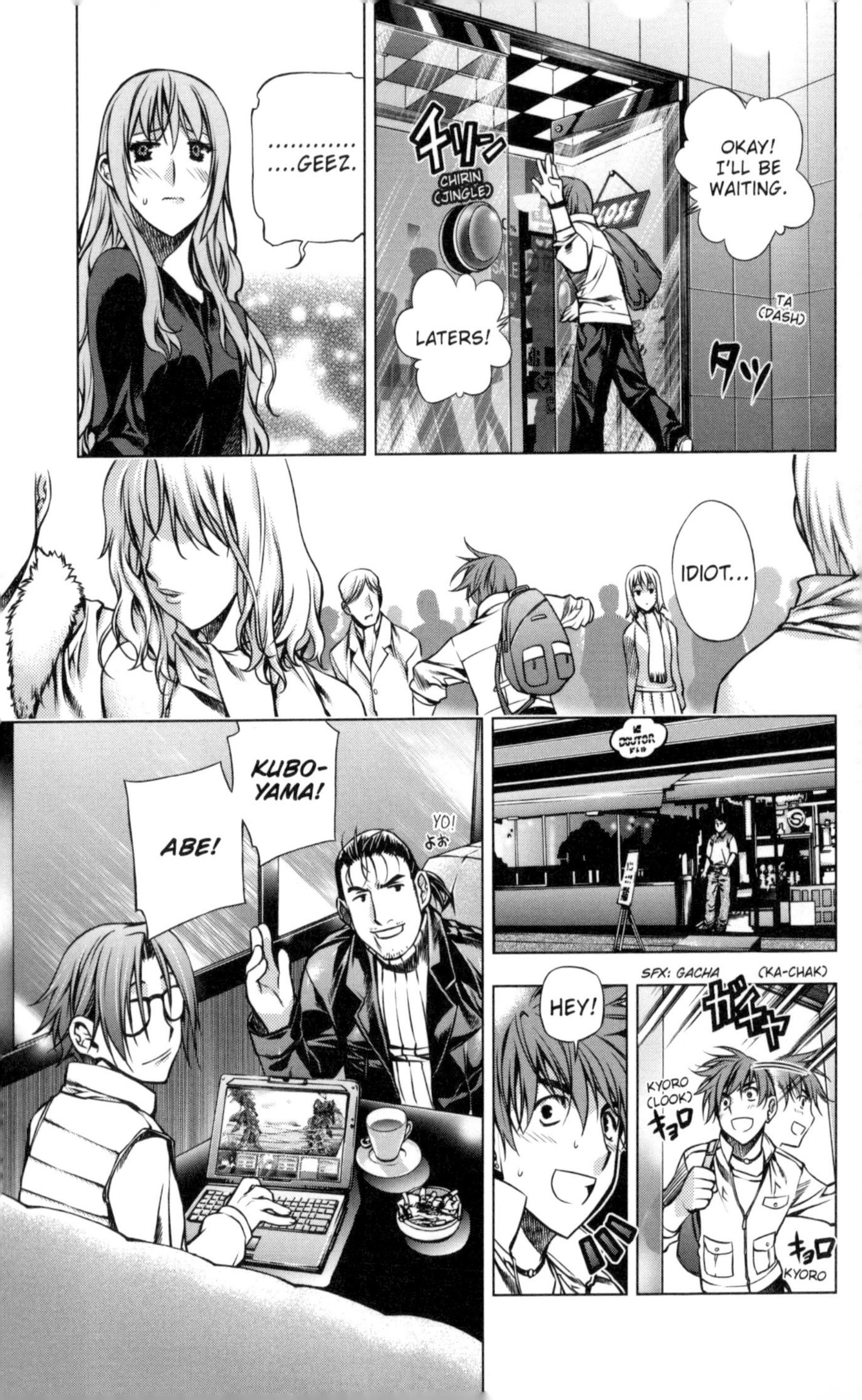
OKAY! I'LL BE WAITING.
チリーン
CHIRIN (JINGLE)
TA (DASH)
タッ
LATERS!
....
....GEEZ.
IDIOT...
DOUTOR
ドトール
SFX: GACHA (KA-CHAK)
ガチャ
KYORO (LOOK)
キョロ
キョロ
KYORO
HEY!
KUBO-YAMA!
YO!
よぉ
ABE!

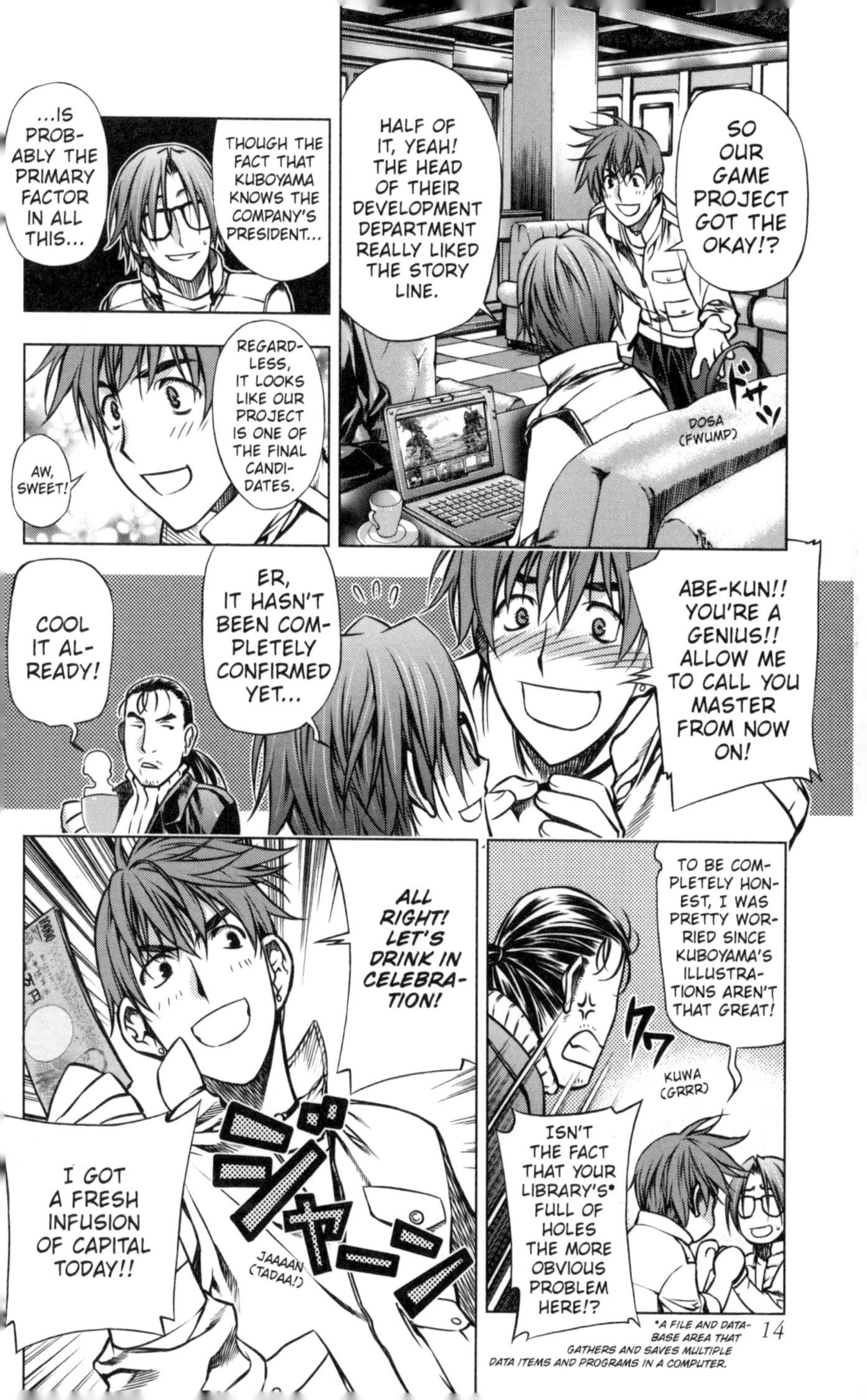
SO OUR GAME PROJECT GOT THE OKAY!?
HALF OF IT, YEAH! THE HEAD OF THEIR DEVELOPMENT DEPARTMENT REALLY LIKED THE STORY LINE.
DOSA (FWUMP)
THOUGH THE FACT THAT KUBOYAMA KNOWS THE COMPANY'S PRESIDENT...
...IS PROBABLY THE PRIMARY FACTOR IN ALL THIS...
REGARDLESS, IT LOOKS LIKE OUR PROJECT IS ONE OF THE FINAL CANDIDATES.
AW, SWEET!
ABE-KUN!! YOU'RE A GENIUS!! ALLOW ME TO CALL YOU MASTER FROM NOW ON!
ER, IT HASN'T BEEN COMPLETELY CONFIRMED YET...
COOL IT ALREADY!
TO BE COMPLETELY HONEST, I WAS PRETTY WORRIED SINCE KUBOYAMA'S ILLUSTRATIONS AREN'T THAT GREAT!
KUWA (GRRR)
ISN'T THE FACT THAT YOUR LIBRARY'S* FULL OF HOLES THE MORE OBVIOUS PROBLEM HERE!?
ALL RIGHT! LET'S DRINK IN CELEBRATION!
I GOT A FRESH INFUSION OF CAPITAL TODAY!!
JAAAAN (TADAA!)

*A FILE AND DATABASE AREA THAT GATHERS AND SAVES MULTIPLE DATA ITEMS AND PROGRAMS IN A COMPUTER.

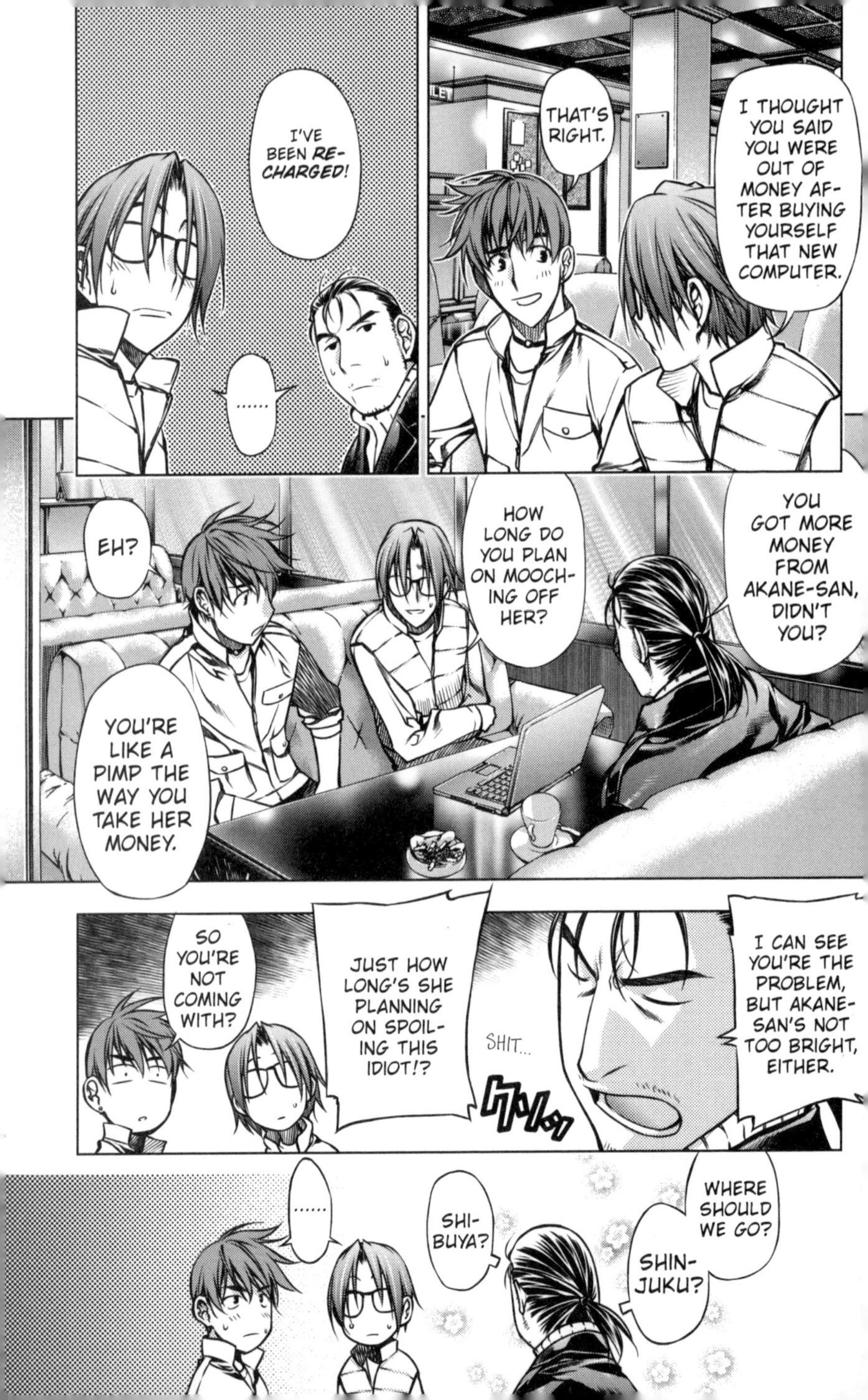
I THOUGHT YOU SAID YOU WERE OUT OF MONEY AFTER BUYING YOURSELF THAT NEW COMPUTER.
THAT'S RIGHT.
I'VE BEEN *RE-CHARGED*!
......
YOU GOT MORE MONEY FROM AKANE-SAN, DIDN'T YOU?
HOW LONG DO YOU PLAN ON MOOCHING OFF HER?
EH?
YOU'RE LIKE A PIMP THE WAY YOU TAKE HER MONEY.
I CAN SEE YOU'RE THE PROBLEM, BUT AKANE-SAN'S NOT TOO BRIGHT, EITHER.
SHIT...
JUST HOW LONG'S SHE PLANNING ON SPOILING THIS IDIOT!?
SO YOU'RE NOT COMING WITH?
WHERE SHOULD WE GO?
SHINJUKU?
SHIBUYA?
......

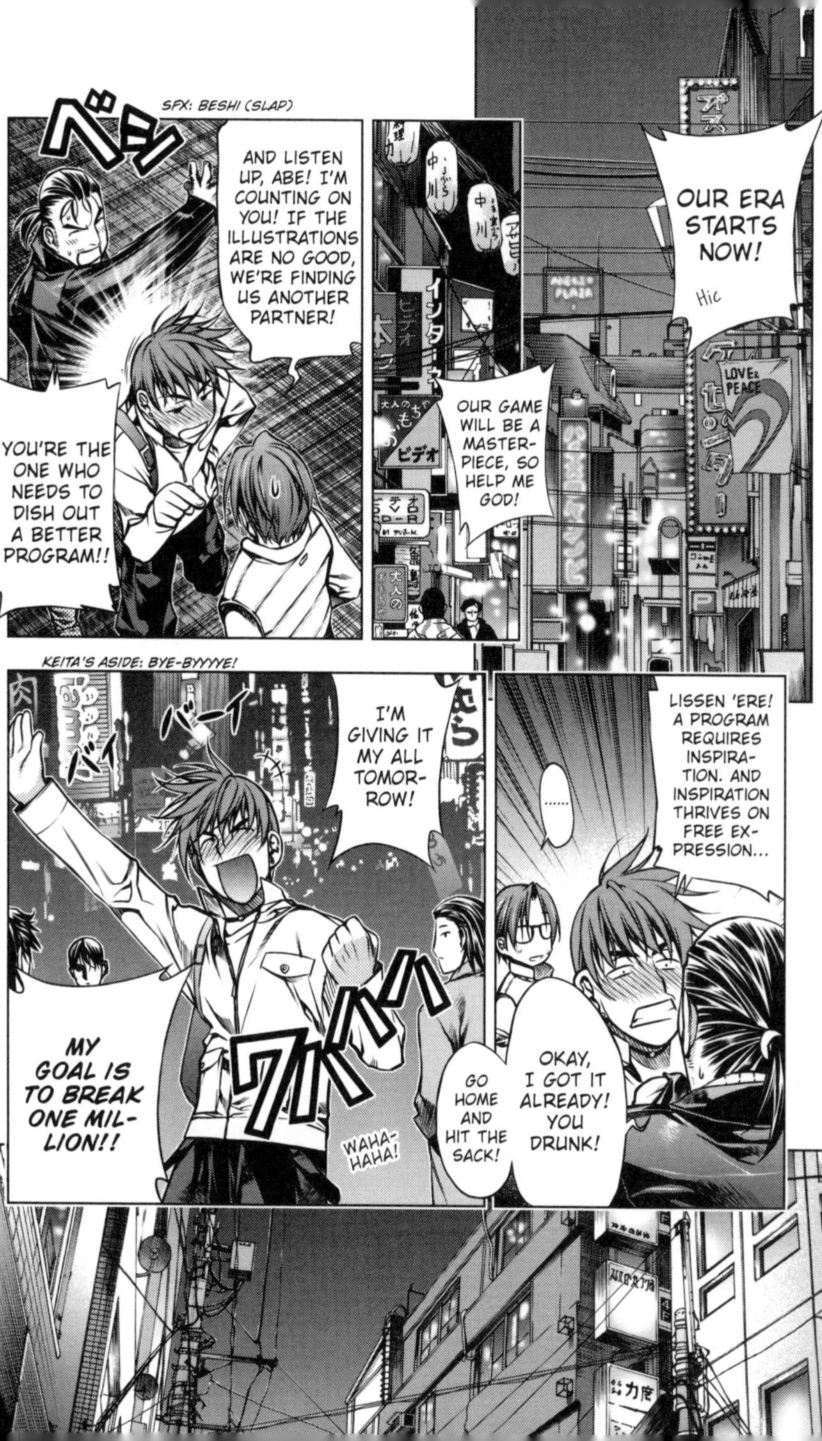
OUR ERA STARTS NOW!
Hic
OUR GAME WILL BE A MASTER-PIECE, SO HELP ME GOD!
SFX: BESHI (SLAP)
AND LISTEN UP, ABE! I'M COUNTING ON YOU! IF THE ILLUSTRATIONS ARE NO GOOD, WE'RE FINDING US ANOTHER PARTNER!
YOU'RE THE ONE WHO NEEDS TO DISH OUT A BETTER PROGRAM!!
LISSEN 'ERE! A PROGRAM REQUIRES INSPIRA-TION. AND INSPIRATION THRIVES ON FREE EX-PRESSION...
......
OKAY, I GOT IT ALREADY! YOU DRUNK!
GO HOME AND HIT THE SACK!
KEITA'S ASIDE: BYE-BYYYYE!
I'M GIVING IT MY ALL TOMOR-ROW!
MY GOAL IS TO BREAK ONE MIL-LION!!
WAHA-HAHA!

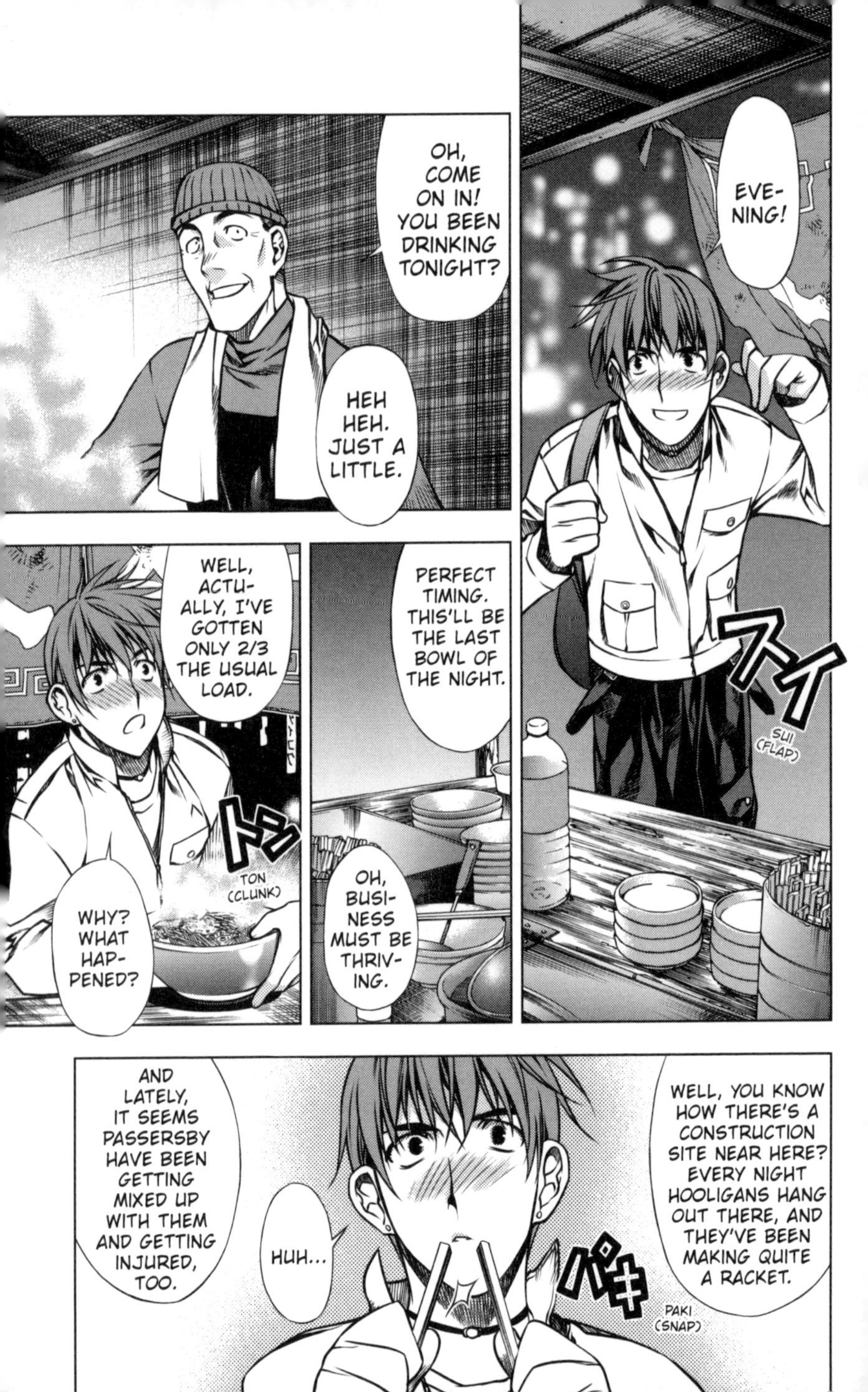
EVE-NING!
スイ
SUI (FLAP)
OH, COME ON IN! YOU BEEN DRINKING TONIGHT?
HEH HEH. JUST A LITTLE.
PERFECT TIMING. THIS'LL BE THE LAST BOWL OF THE NIGHT.
OH, BUSI-NESS MUST BE THRIV-ING.
WELL, ACTU-ALLY, I'VE GOTTEN ONLY 2/3 THE USUAL LOAD.
トン
TON (CLUNK)
WHY? WHAT HAP-PENED?
WELL, YOU KNOW HOW THERE'S A CONSTRUCTION SITE NEAR HERE? EVERY NIGHT HOOLIGANS HANG OUT THERE, AND THEY'VE BEEN MAKING QUITE A RACKET.
パキ
PAKI (SNAP)
HUH...
AND LATELY, IT SEEMS PASSERSBY HAVE BEEN GETTING MIXED UP WITH THEM AND GETTING INJURED, TOO.

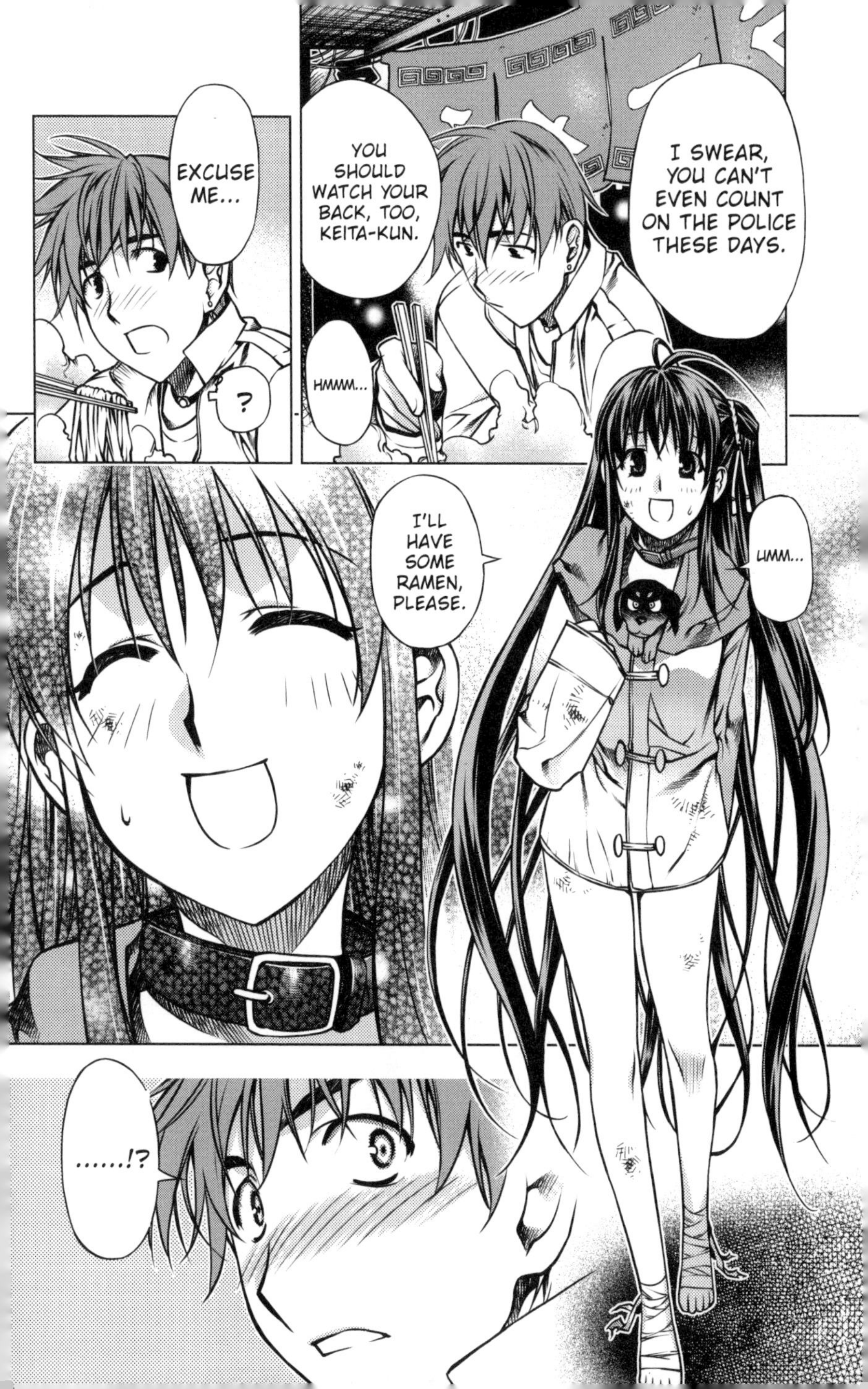
I SWEAR, YOU CAN'T EVEN COUNT ON THE POLICE THESE DAYS.
YOU SHOULD WATCH YOUR BACK, TOO, KEITA-KUN.
HMMM...
EXCUSE ME...
?
UMM...
I'LL HAVE SOME RAMEN, PLEASE.
......!?

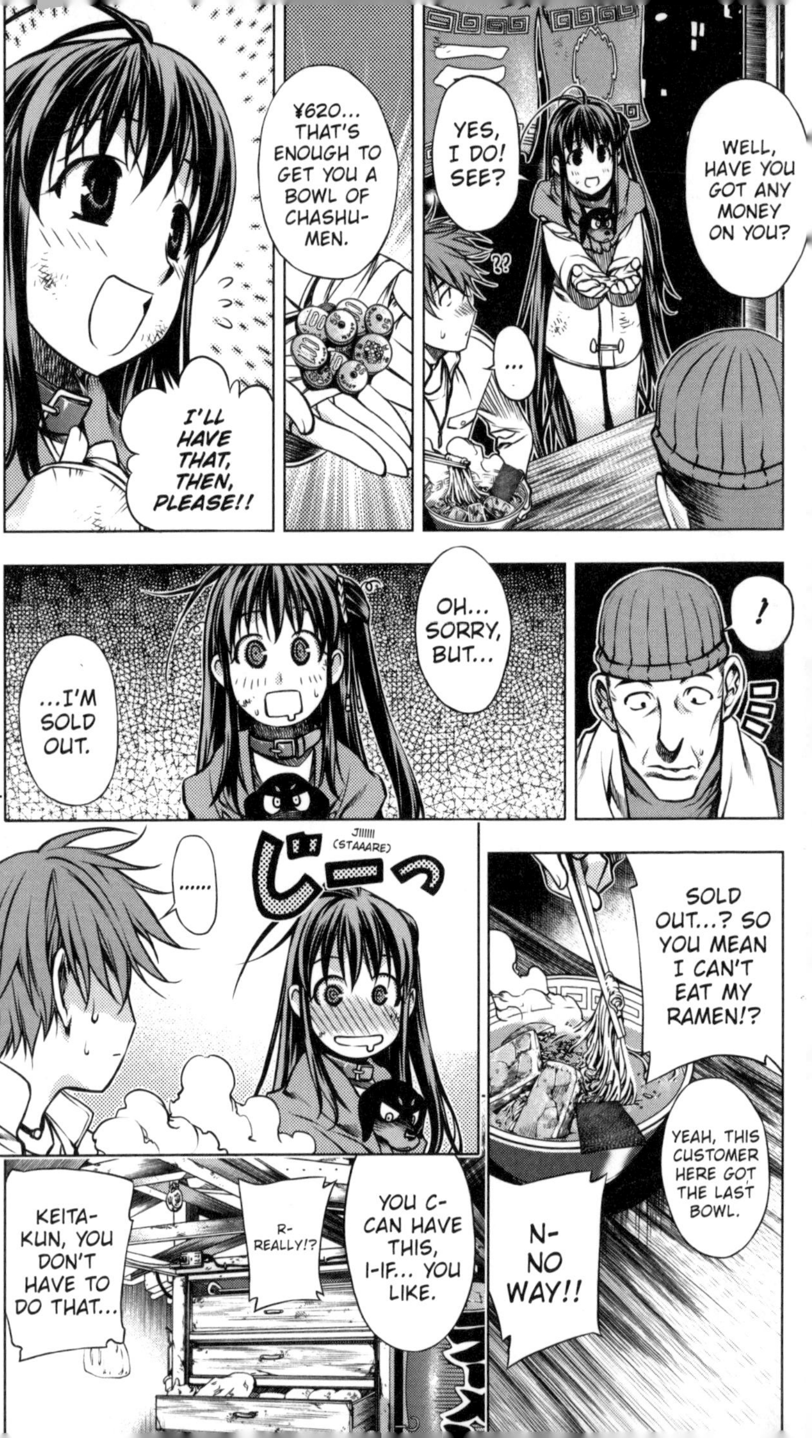
WELL, HAVE YOU GOT ANY MONEY ON YOU?
YES, I DO! SEE?
??
...
¥620... THAT'S ENOUGH TO GET YOU A BOWL OF CHASHU-MEN.
I'LL HAVE THAT, THEN, PLEASE!!
!
OH... SORRY, BUT...
...I'M SOLD OUT.
SOLD OUT...? SO YOU MEAN I CAN'T EAT MY RAMEN!?
YEAH, THIS CUSTOMER HERE GOT THE LAST BOWL.
N-NO WAY!!
......
じーっ
JIIIIII (STAAARE)
YOU C-CAN HAVE THIS, I-IF... YOU LIKE.
R-REALLY!?
KEITA-KUN, YOU DON'T HAVE TO DO THAT...

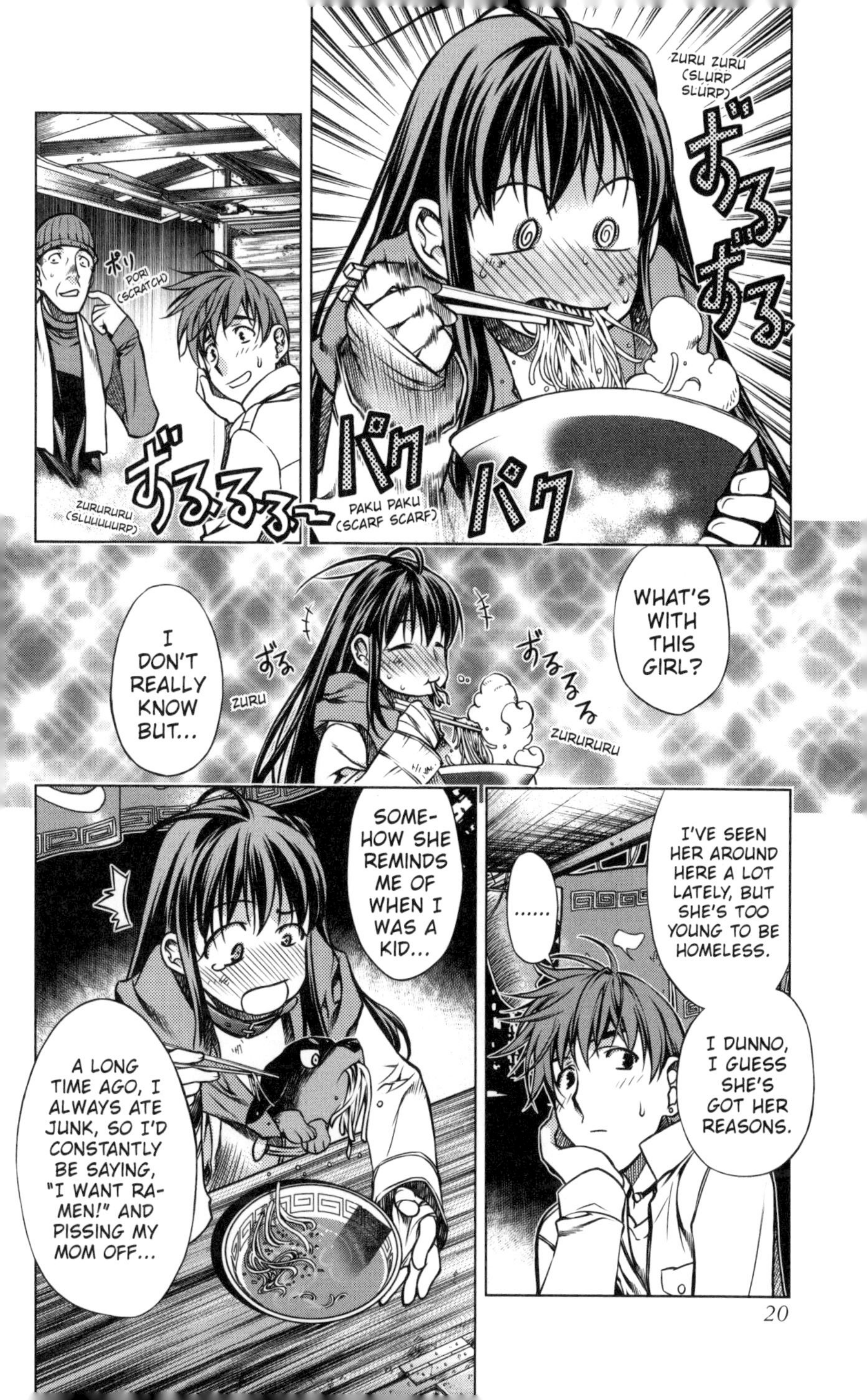
ZURU ZURU (SLURP SLURP)
ずるずる
パク
パク
PAKU PAKU (SCARF SCARF)
ポリ
PORI (SCRATCH)
ずるるる～
ZURURURU (SLUUUUURP)
WHAT'S WITH THIS GIRL?
ずるるる
ZURURURU
ずる
ZURU
I DON'T REALLY KNOW BUT...
I'VE SEEN HER AROUND HERE A LOT LATELY, BUT SHE'S TOO YOUNG TO BE HOMELESS.
......
I DUNNO, I GUESS SHE'S GOT HER REASONS.
SOME-HOW SHE REMINDS ME OF WHEN I WAS A KID...
A LONG TIME AGO, I ALWAYS ATE JUNK, SO I'D CONSTANTLY BE SAYING, "I WANT RA-MEN!" AND PISSING MY MOM OFF...

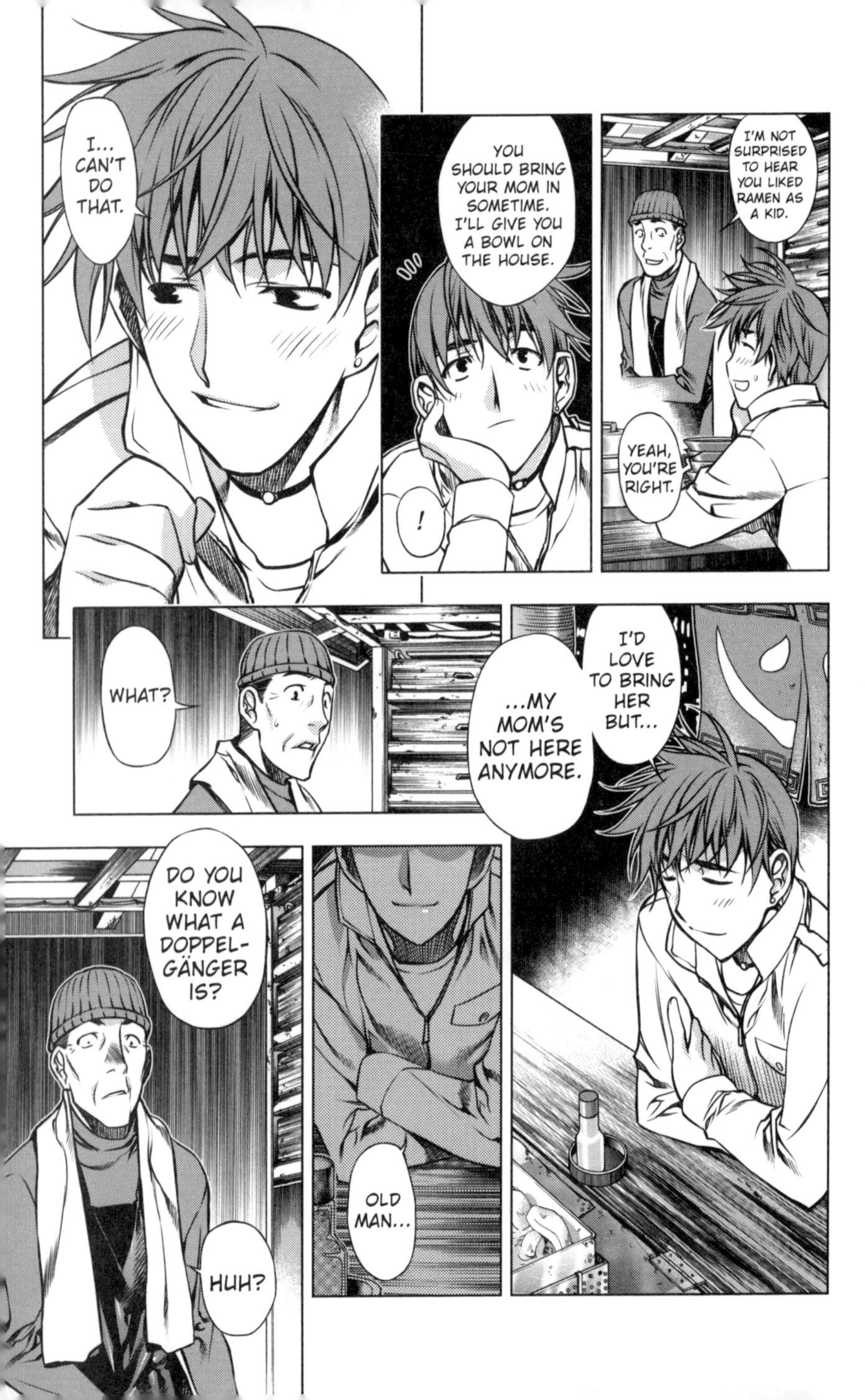
I'M NOT SURPRISED TO HEAR YOU LIKED RAMEN AS A KID.
YEAH, YOU'RE RIGHT.
YOU SHOULD BRING YOUR MOM IN SOMETIME. I'LL GIVE YOU A BOWL ON THE HOUSE.
!
I... CAN'T DO THAT.
I'D LOVE TO BRING HER BUT...
...MY MOM'S NOT HERE ANYMORE.
WHAT?
OLD MAN...
DO YOU KNOW WHAT A DOPPEL-GÄNGER IS?
HUH?

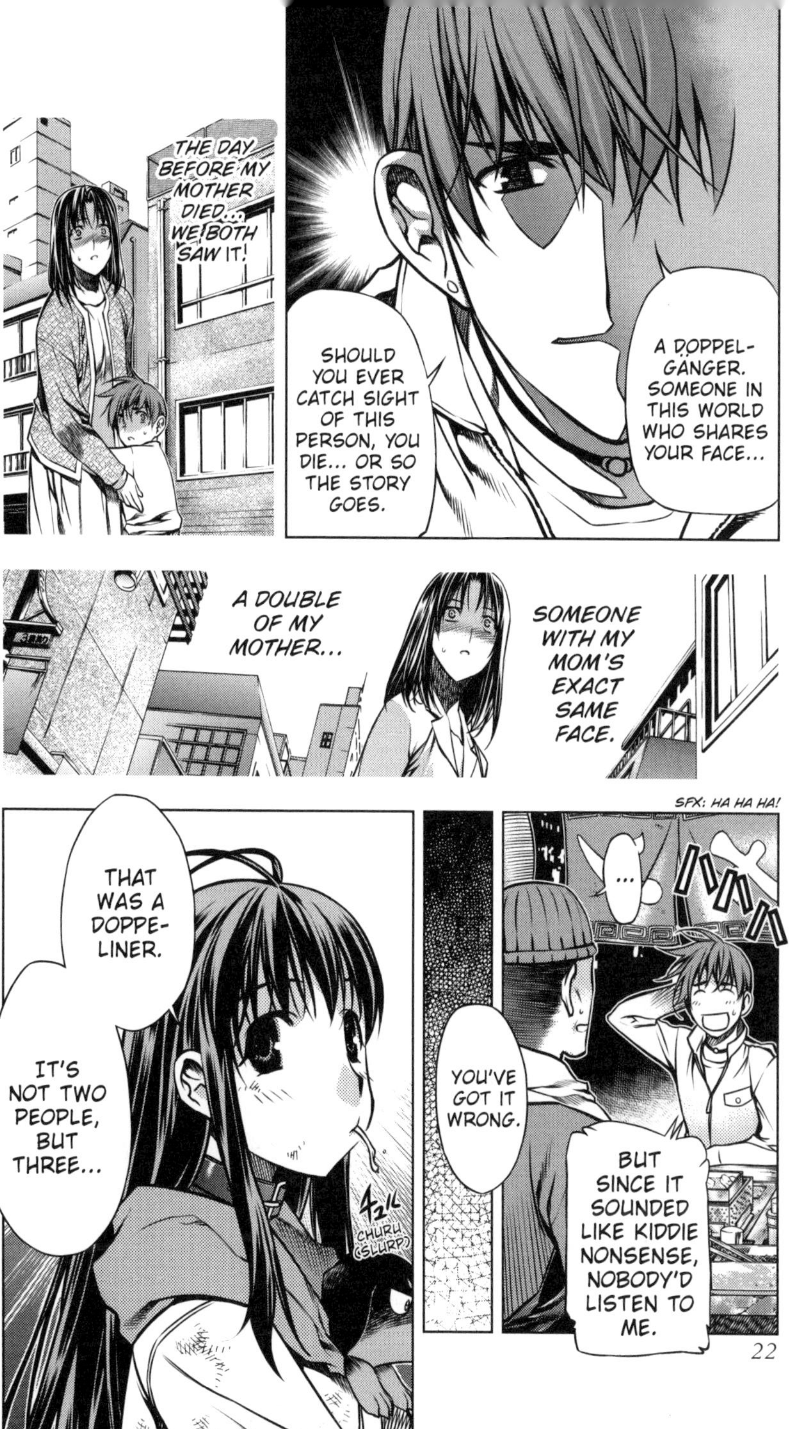
A DOPPEL-GÄNGER. SOMEONE IN THIS WORLD WHO SHARES YOUR FACE...
SHOULD YOU EVER CATCH SIGHT OF THIS PERSON, YOU DIE... OR SO THE STORY GOES.
THE DAY BEFORE MY MOTHER DIED... WE BOTH SAW IT!
SOMEONE WITH MY MOM'S EXACT SAME FACE.
A DOUBLE OF MY MOTHER...
SFX: HA HA HA!
...
YOU'VE GOT IT WRONG.
BUT SINCE IT SOUNDED LIKE KIDDIE NONSENSE, NOBODY'D LISTEN TO ME.
THAT WAS A DOPPE-LINER.
IT'S NOT TWO PEOPLE, BUT THREE...
CHURU (SLURP)

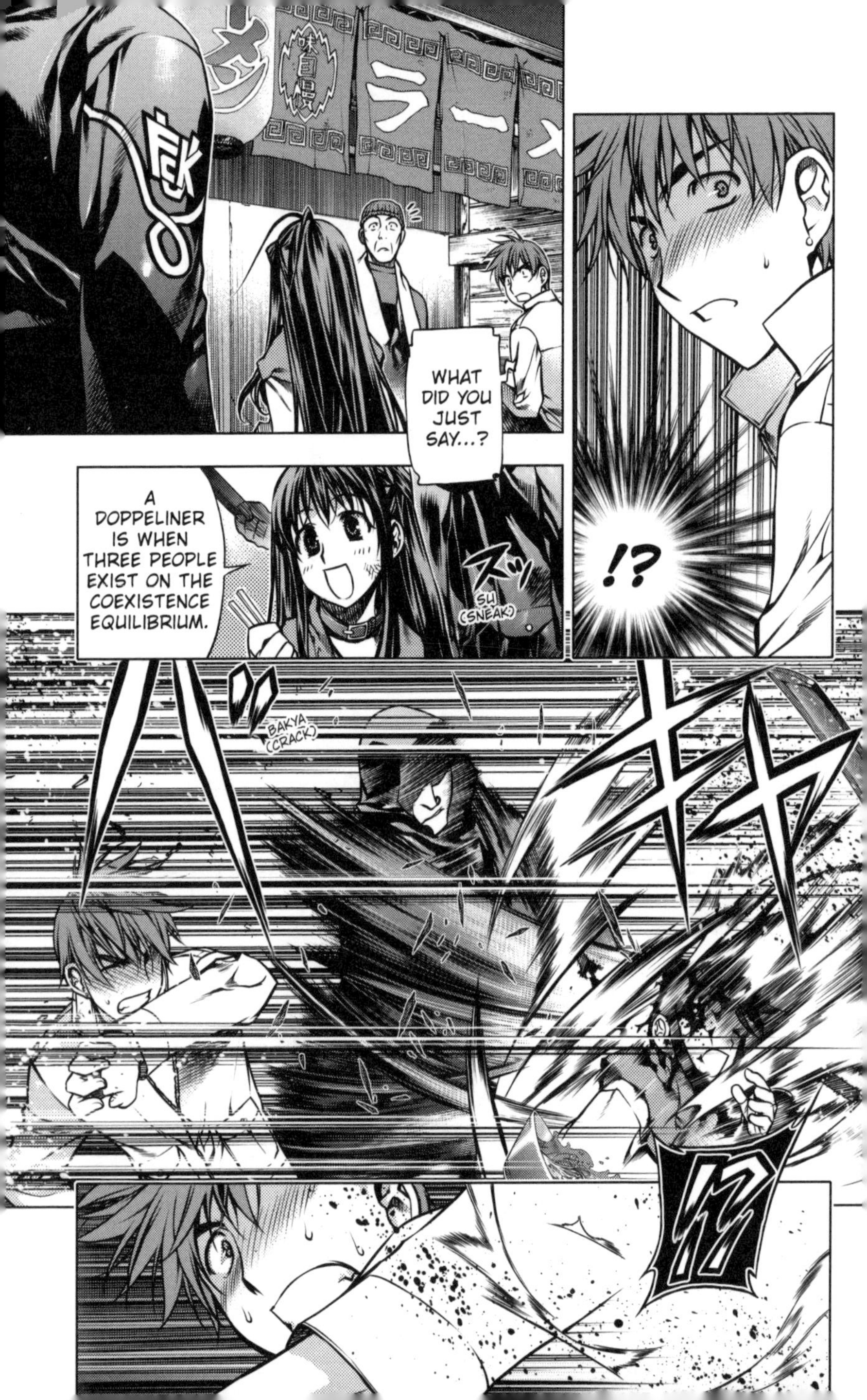
!?
WHAT DID YOU JUST SAY...?
A DOPPELINER IS WHEN THREE PEOPLE EXIST ON THE COEXISTENCE EQUILIBRIUM.
SU (SNEAK)
BAKYA (CRACK)

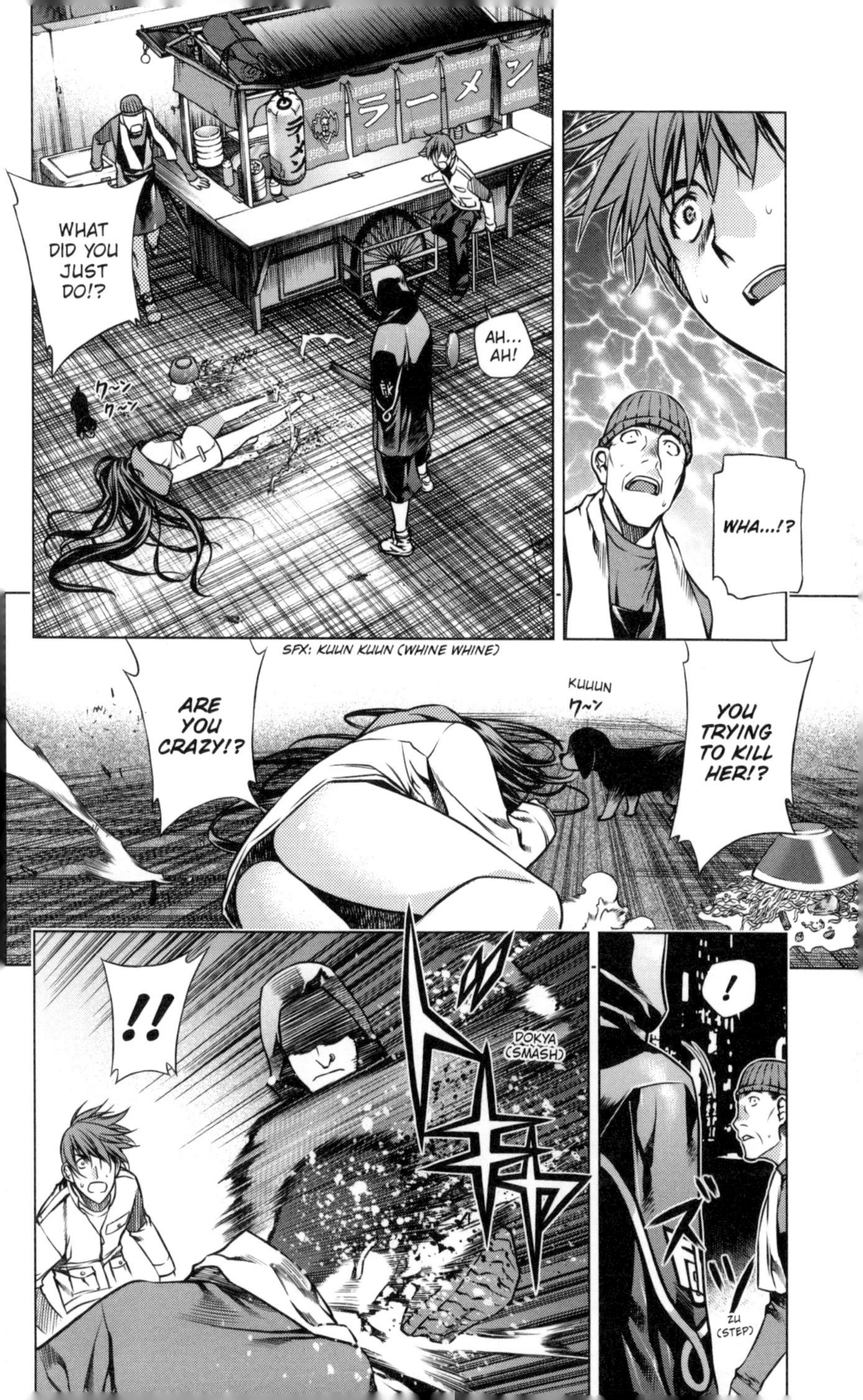
WHA...!?
ラーメン
WHAT DID YOU JUST DO!?
AH... AH!
ク~ン ク~ン
SFX: KUUN KUUN (WHINE WHINE)
YOU TRYING TO KILL HER!?
KUUUN
ク~ン
ARE YOU CRAZY!?
!
ZU (STEP)
!!
DOKYA (SMASH)

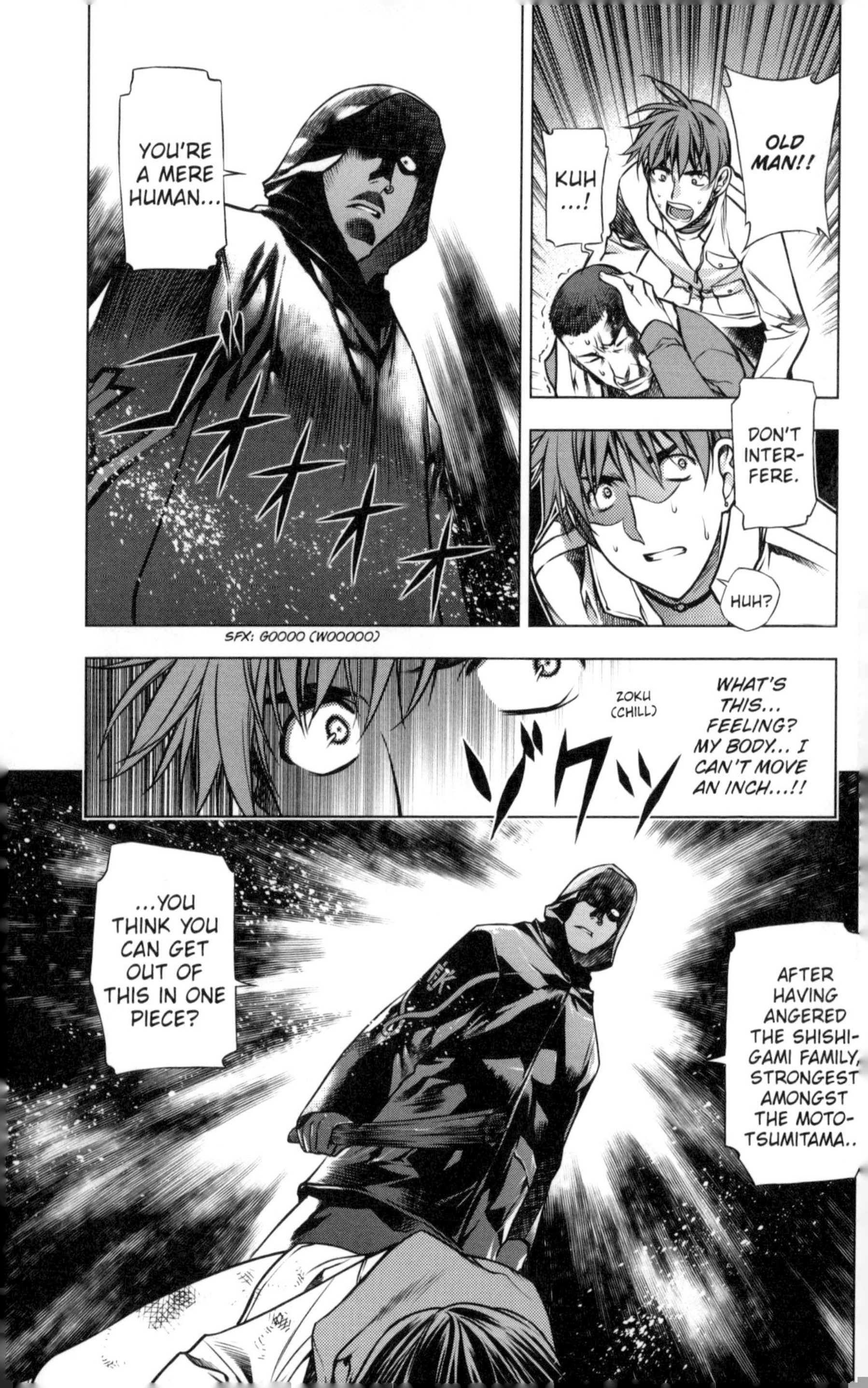
OLD MAN!!
KUH ...!
DON'T INTERFERE.
HUH?
YOU'RE A MERE HUMAN...
SFX: GOOOO (WOOOOO)
WHAT'S THIS... FEELING? MY BODY... I CAN'T MOVE AN INCH...!!
ZOKU (CHILL)
AFTER HAVING ANGERED THE SHISHIGAMI FAMILY, STRONGEST AMONGST THE MOTOTSUMITAMA..
...YOU THINK YOU CAN GET OUT OF THIS IN ONE PIECE?

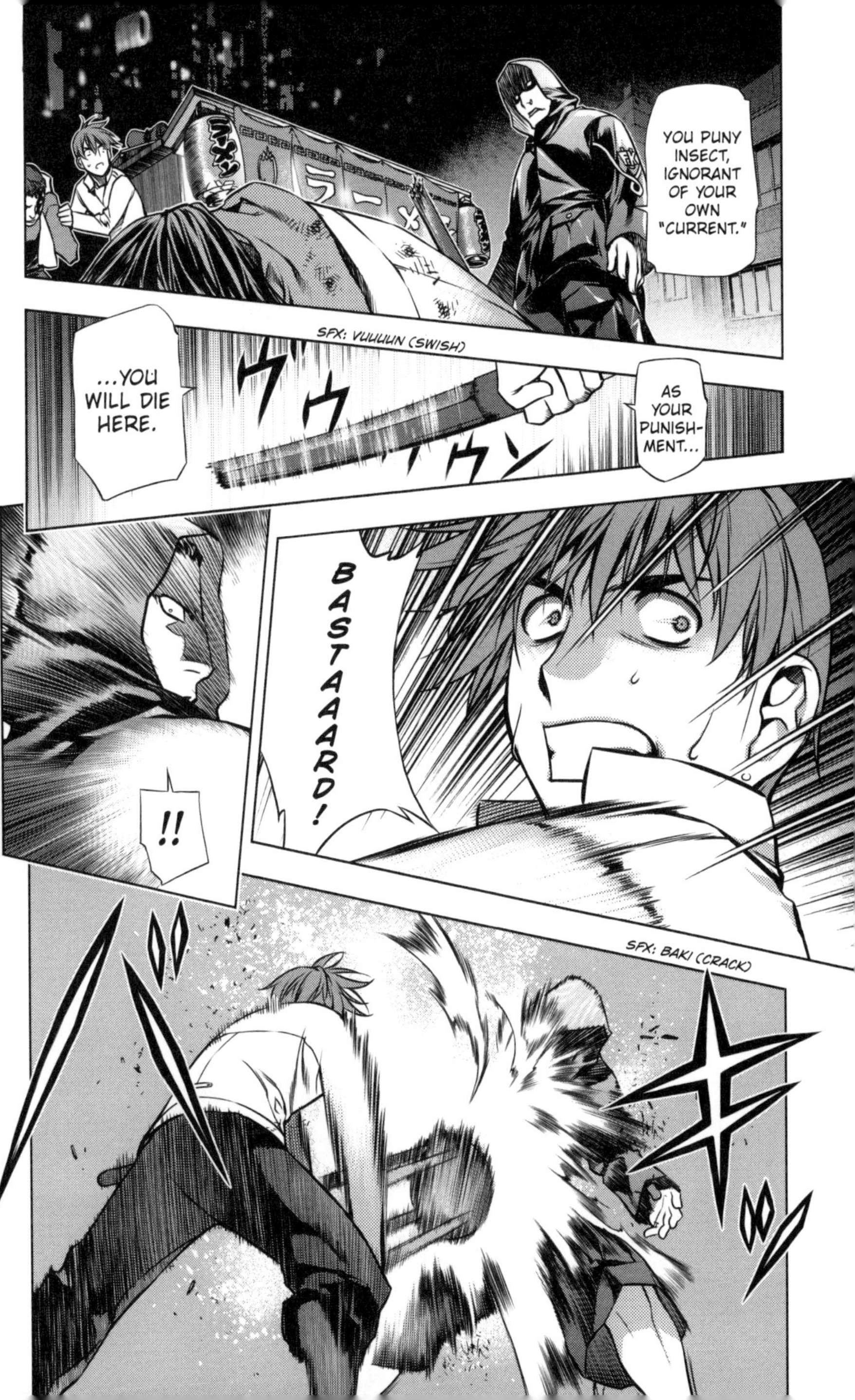
YOU PUNY INSECT, IGNORANT OF YOUR OWN "CURRENT."
SFX: VUUUUN (SWISH)
AS YOUR PUNISHMENT...
...YOU WILL DIE HERE.
BASTAAAARD!
!!
SFX: BAKI (CRACK)

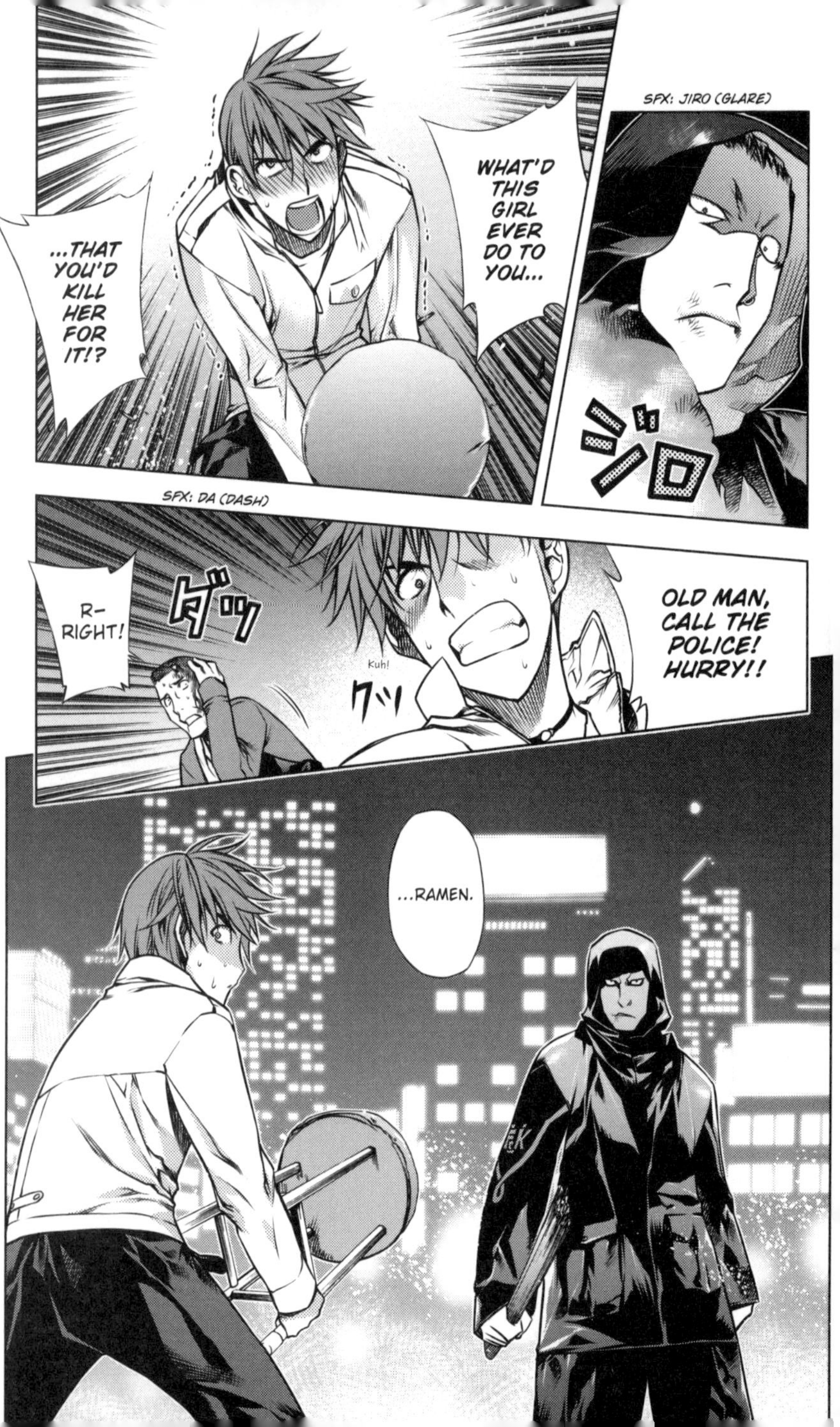
SFX: JIRO (GLARE)
ジロ
WHAT'D THIS GIRL EVER DO TO YOU...
...THAT YOU'D KILL HER FOR IT!?
SFX: DA (DASH)
OLD MAN, CALL THE POLICE! HURRY!!
Kuh!
クッ
ダッ
R-RIGHT!
...RAMEN.

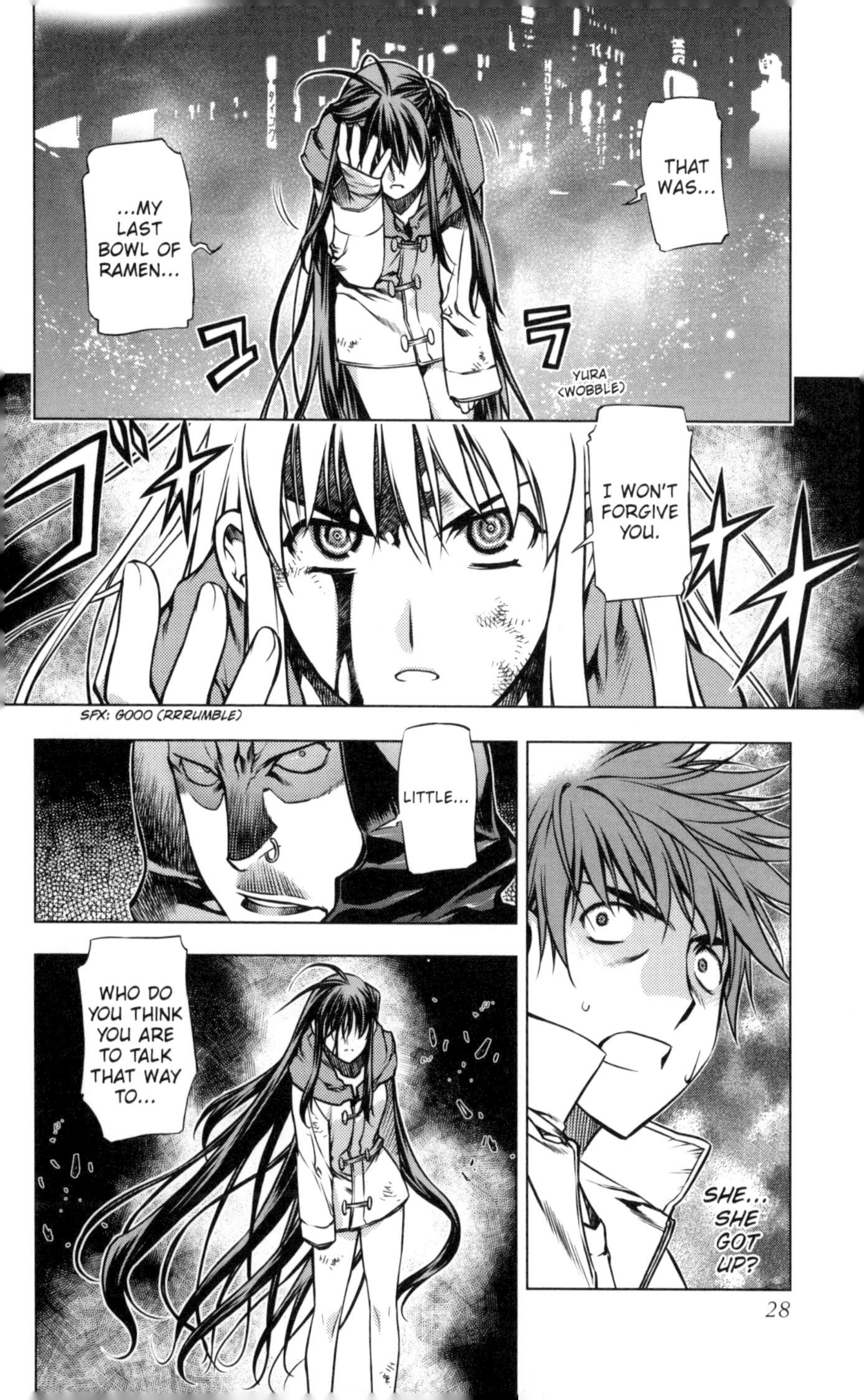
THAT WAS...
...MY LAST BOWL OF RAMEN...
ユラ
YURA (WOBBLE)
I WON'T FORGIVE YOU.
ゴッ
SFX: GOOO (RRRUMBLE)
SHE... SHE GOT UP?
LITTLE...
WHO DO YOU THINK YOU ARE TO TALK THAT WAY TO...

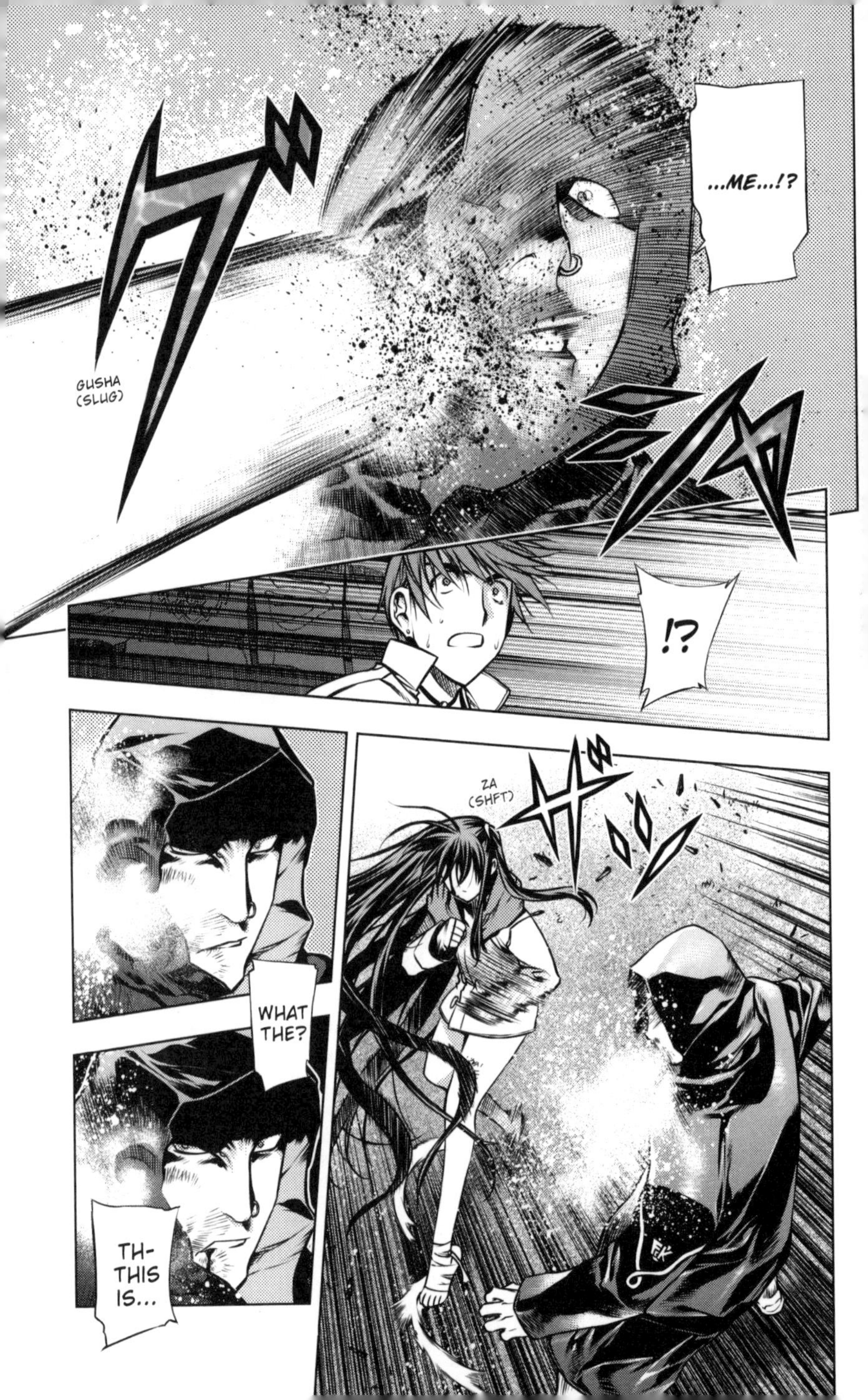
...ME...!?
GUSHA (SLUG)
!?
ZA (SHFT)
WHAT THE?
TH- THIS IS...

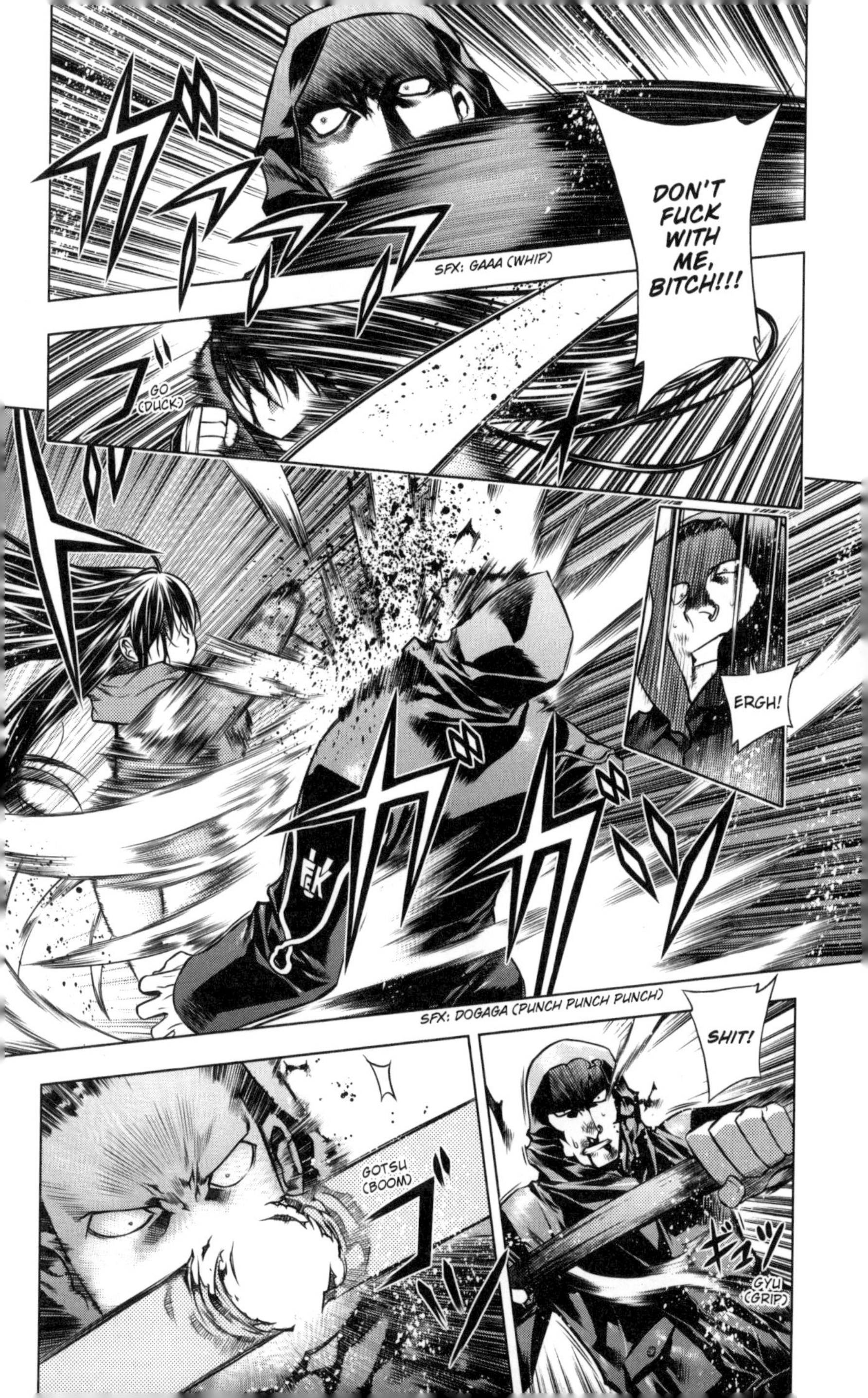
DON'T FUCK WITH ME, BITCH!!!
SFX: GAAA (WHIP)
GO (DUCK)
ERGH!
SFX: DOGAGA (PUNCH PUNCH PUNCH)
SHIT!
GYU (GRIP)
GOTSU (BOOM)

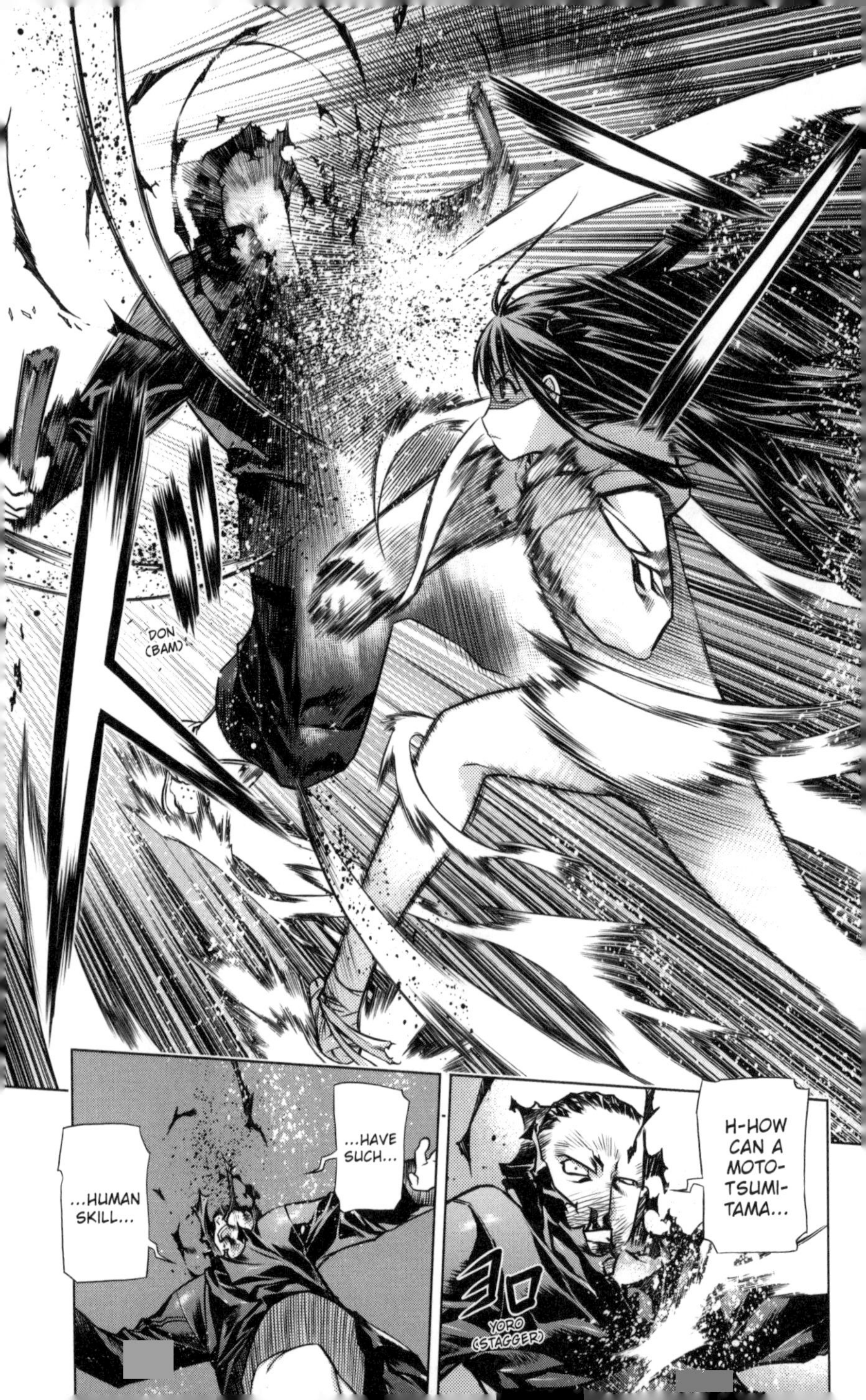
DON (BAM)
H-HOW CAN A MOTO-TSUMI-TAMA...
YORO (STAGGER)
...HAVE SUCH...
...HUMAN SKILL...

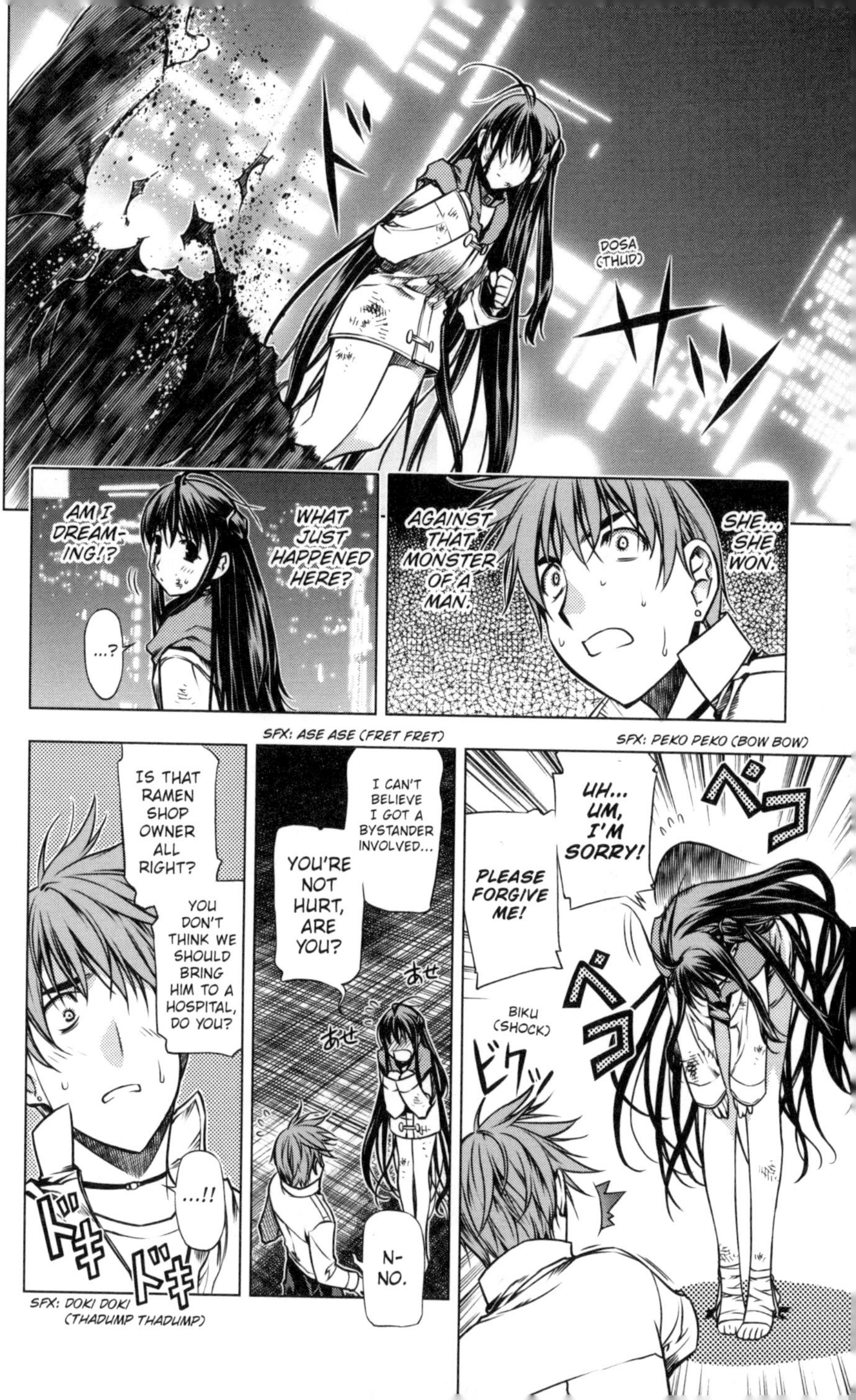
DOSA (THUD)
SHE... SHE WON.
AGAINST THAT MONSTER OF A MAN.
WHAT JUST HAPPENED HERE?
AM I DREAMING!?
...?
SFX: PEKO PEKO (BOW BOW)
UH... UM, I'M SORRY!
PLEASE FORGIVE ME!
BIKU (SHOCK)
SFX: ASE ASE (FRET FRET)
I CAN'T BELIEVE I GOT A BYSTANDER INVOLVED...
YOU'RE NOT HURT, ARE YOU?
あせ
あせ
N-NO.
IS THAT RAMEN SHOP OWNER ALL RIGHT?
YOU DON'T THINK WE SHOULD BRING HIM TO A HOSPITAL, DO YOU?
...!!
SFX: DOKI DOKI (THADUMP THADUMP)

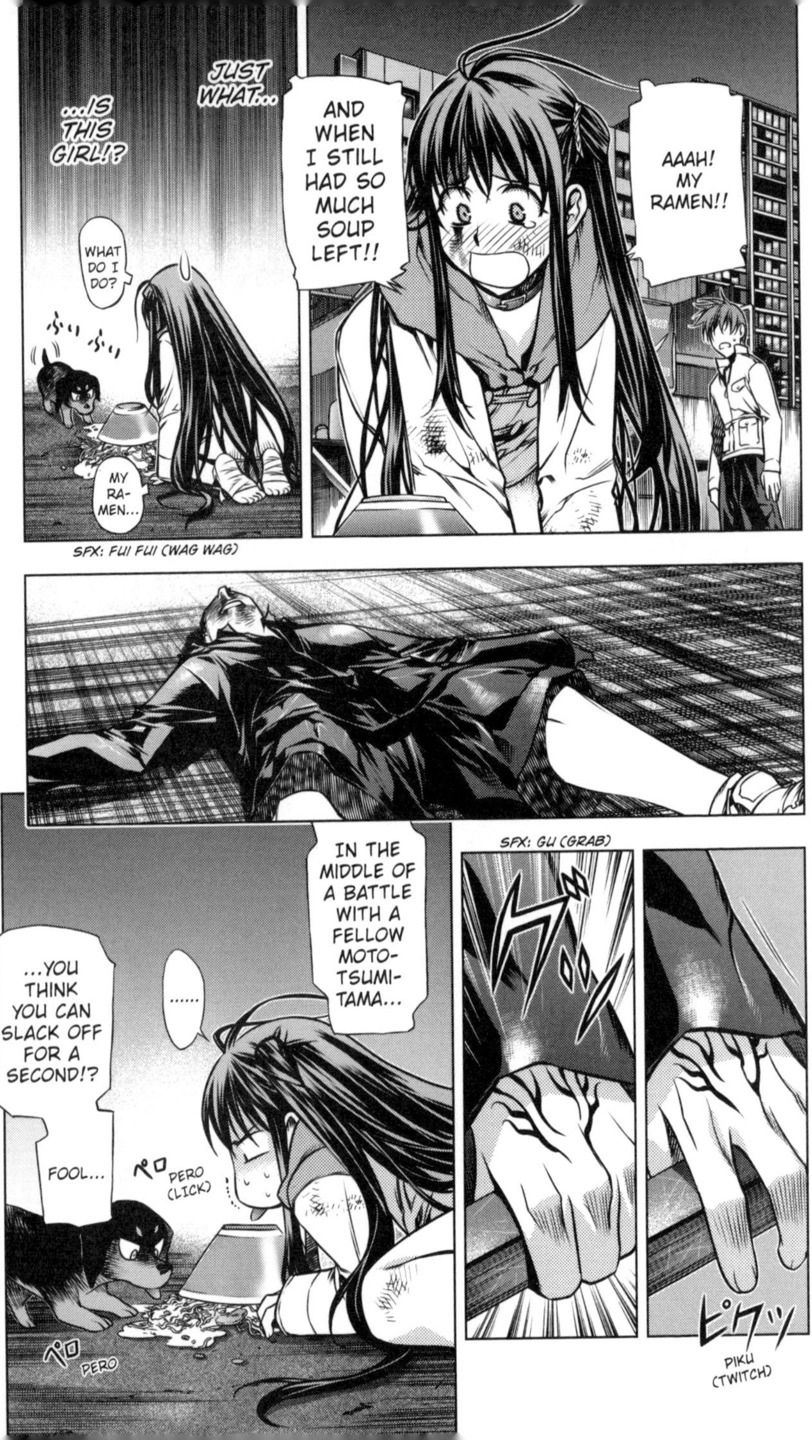
AAAH! MY RAMEN!!
AND WHEN I STILL HAD SO MUCH SOUP LEFT!!
JUST WHAT...
...IS THIS GIRL!?
WHAT DO I DO?
ふい ふい
MY RA-MEN...
SFX: FUI FUI (WAG WAG)
ピクッ
PIKU (TWITCH)
SFX: GU (GRAB)
IN THE MIDDLE OF A BATTLE WITH A FELLOW MOTO-TSUMI-TAMA...
......
...YOU THINK YOU CAN SLACK OFF FOR A SECOND!?
ペロ
PERO (LICK)
FOOL...
ペロ
PERO

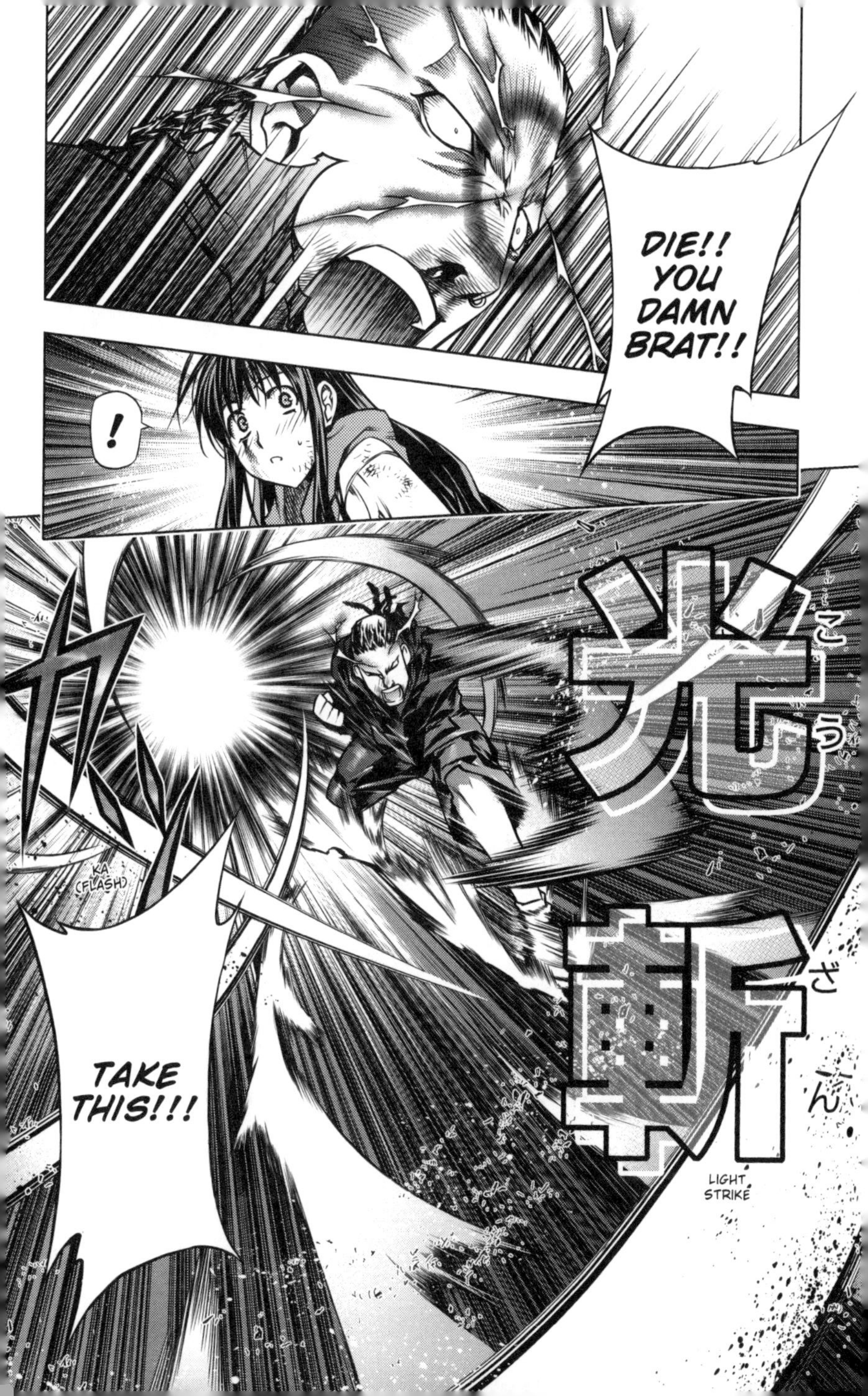

DIE!! YOU DAMN BRAT!!
!
光斬
LIGHT STRIKE
KA (FLASH)
TAKE THIS!!!

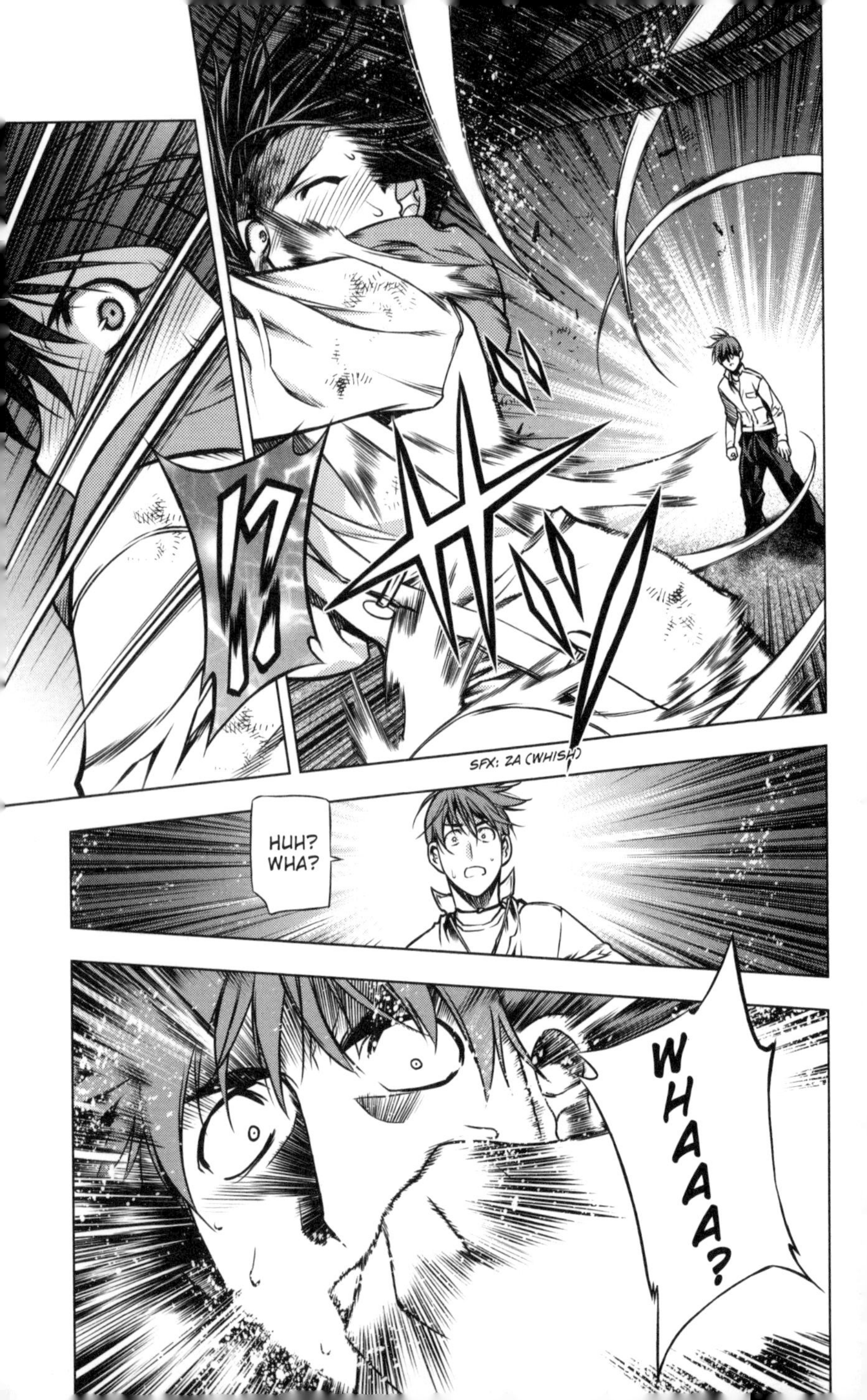
SFX: ZA (WHISH)
HUH? WHA?
WHAAA?

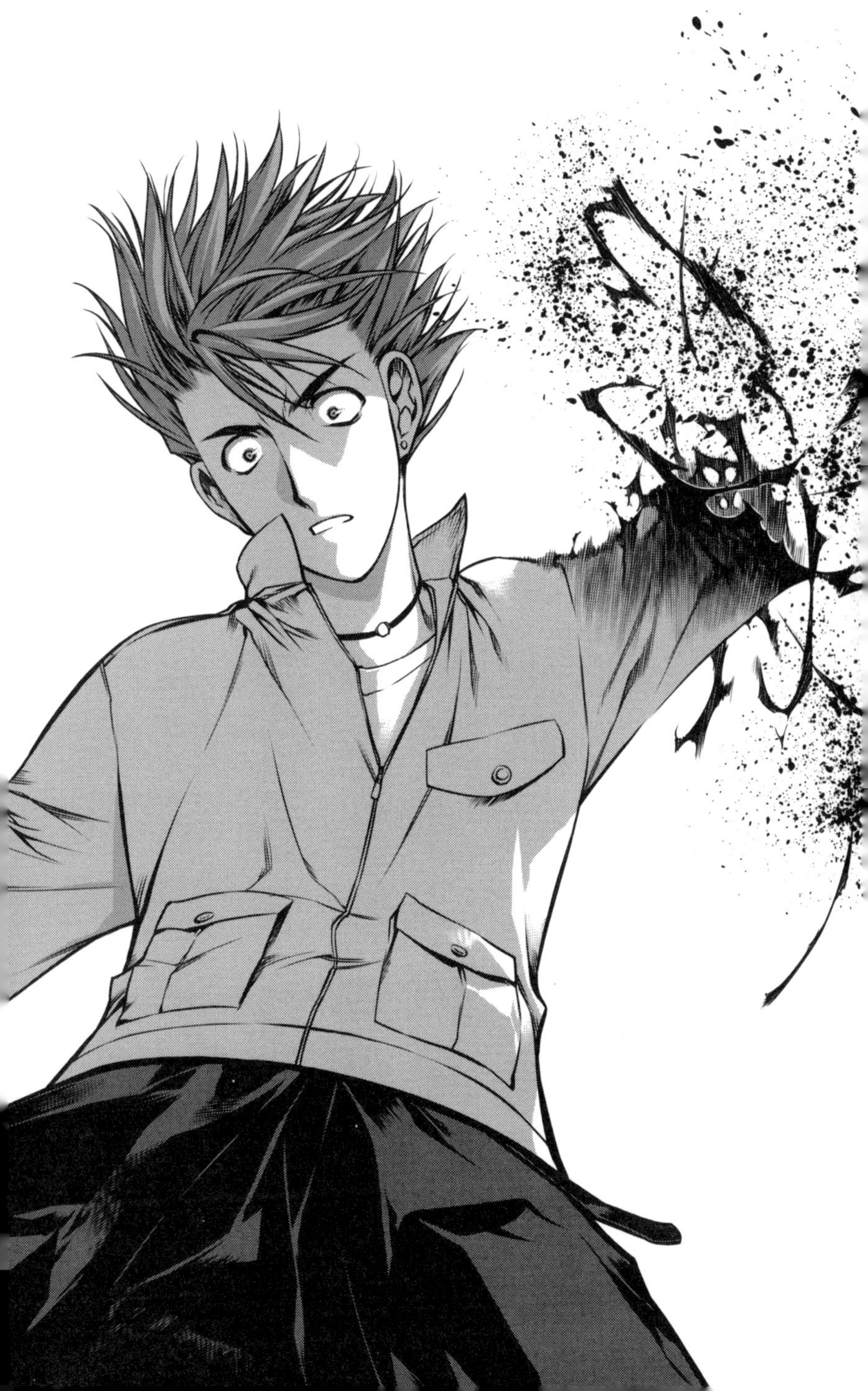

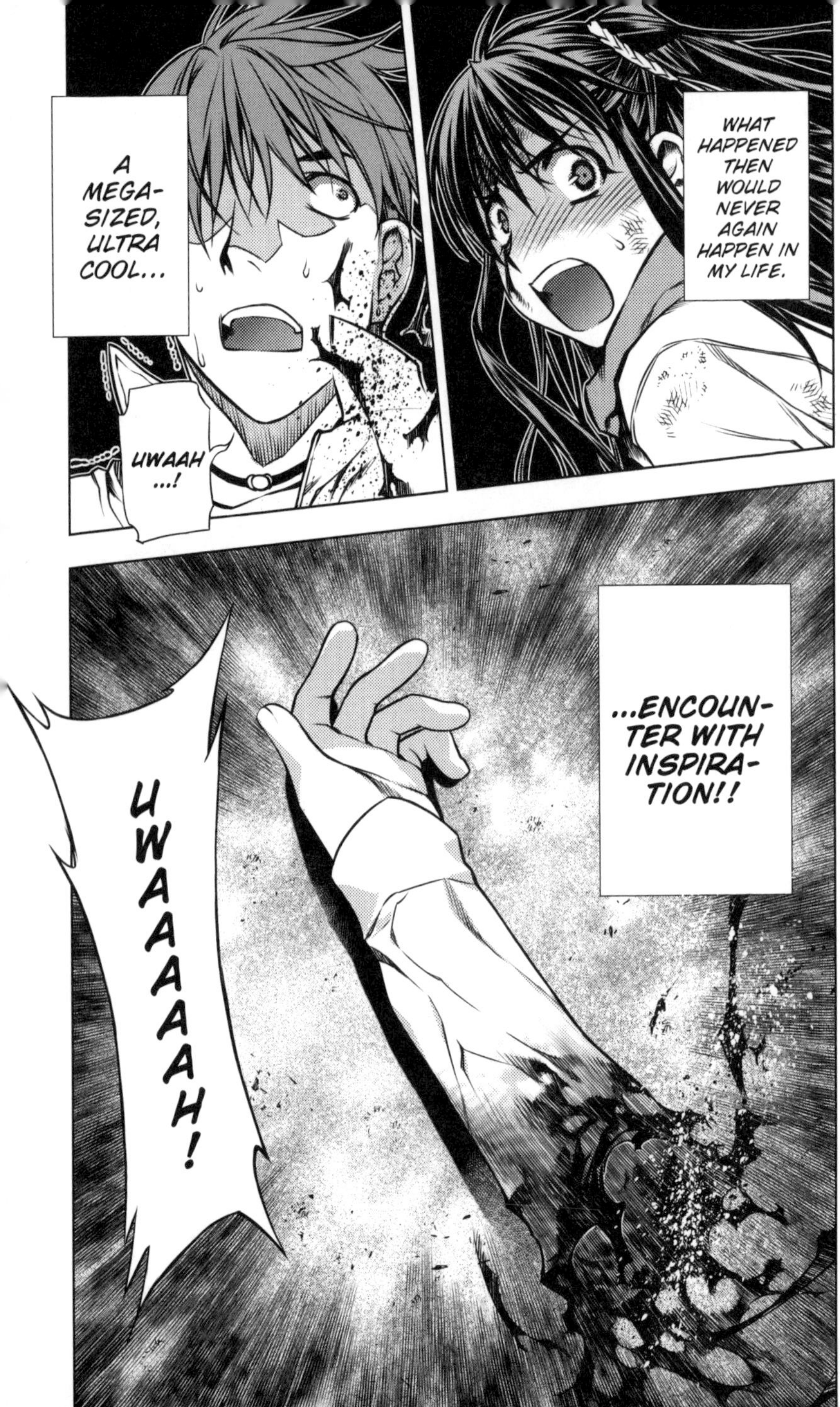
WHAT HAPPENED THEN WOULD NEVER AGAIN HAPPEN IN MY LIFE.
A MEGA-SIZED, ULTRA COOL...
UWAAH ...!
...ENCOUNTER WITH INSPIRATION!!
UWAAAAAAAH!

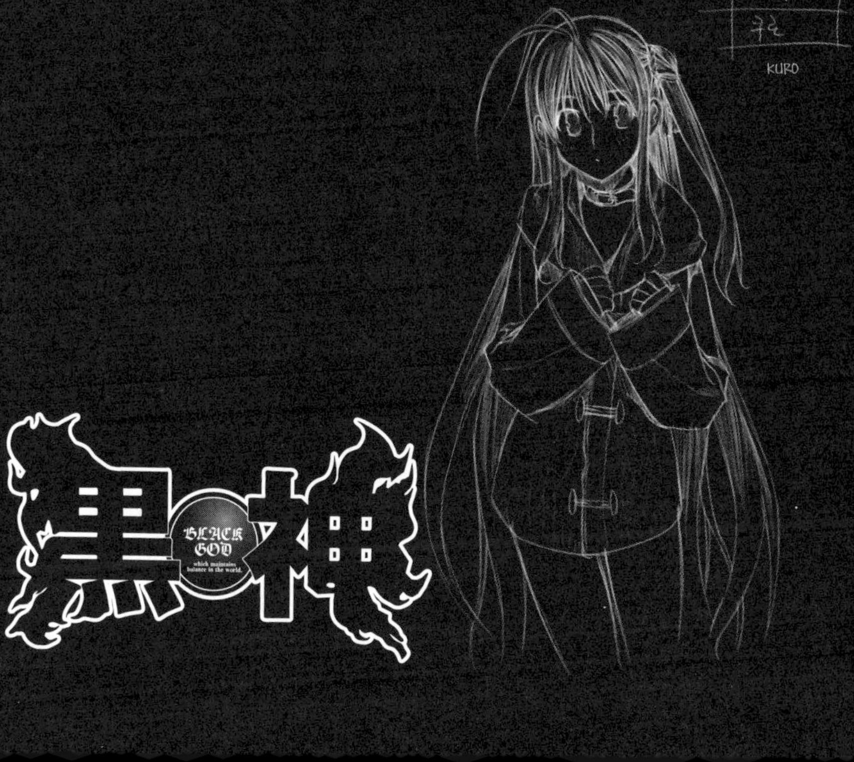
クロ
KURO
BLACK GOD
which maintains balance in the world.

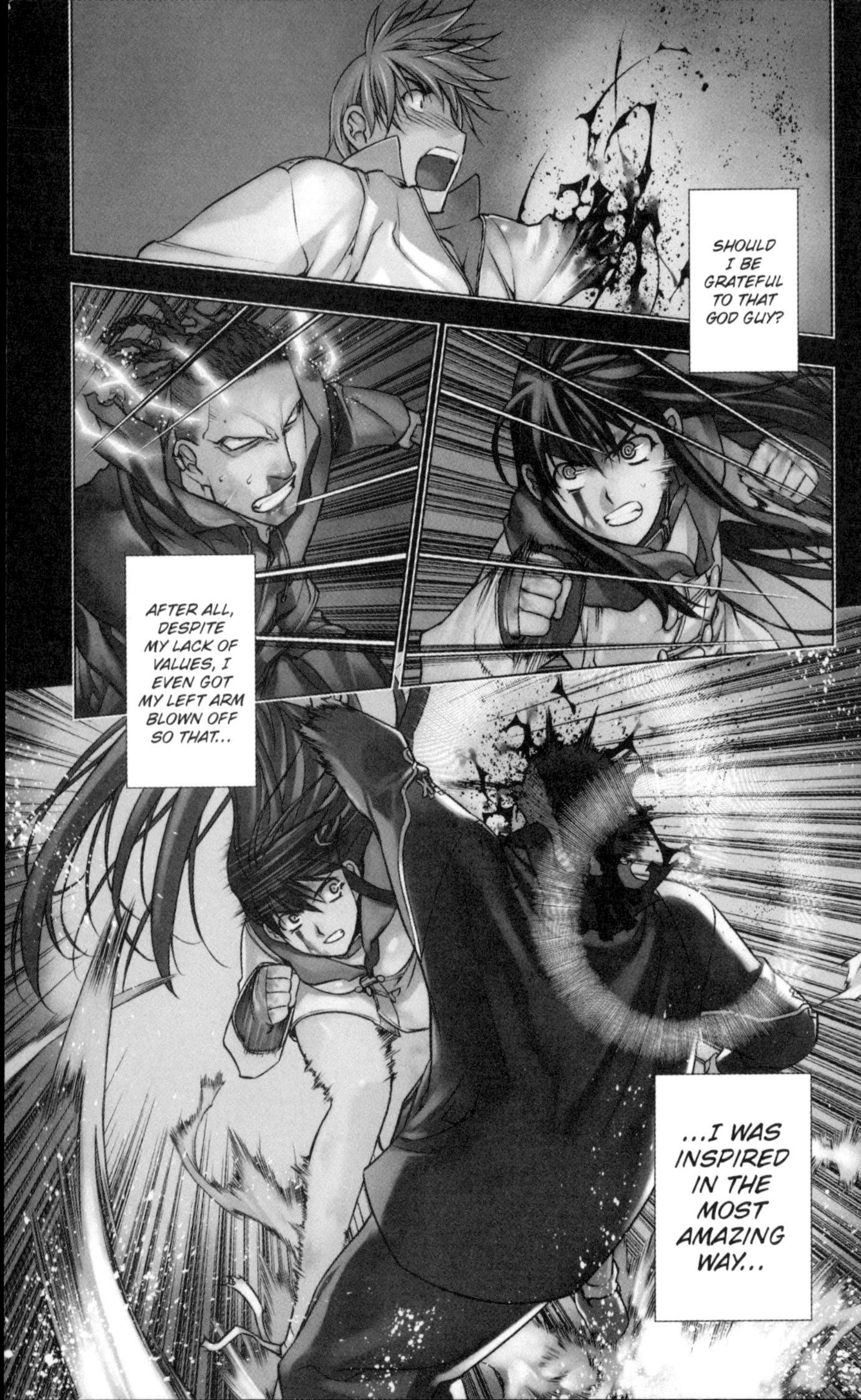
SHOULD I BE GRATEFUL TO THAT GOD GUY?
AFTER ALL, DESPITE MY LACK OF VALUES, I EVEN GOT MY LEFT ARM BLOWN OFF SO THAT...
...I WAS INSPIRED IN THE MOST AMAZING WAY...

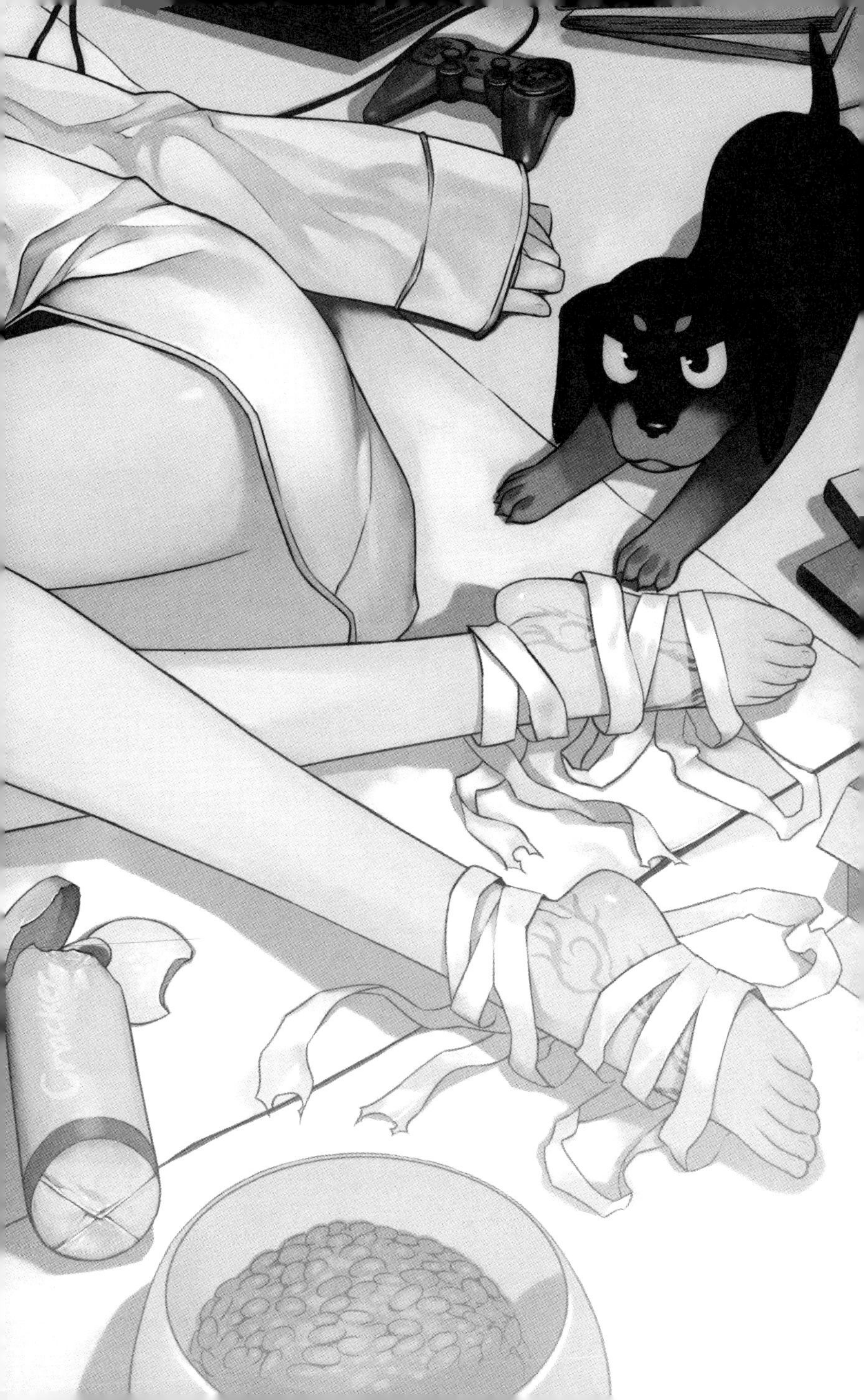

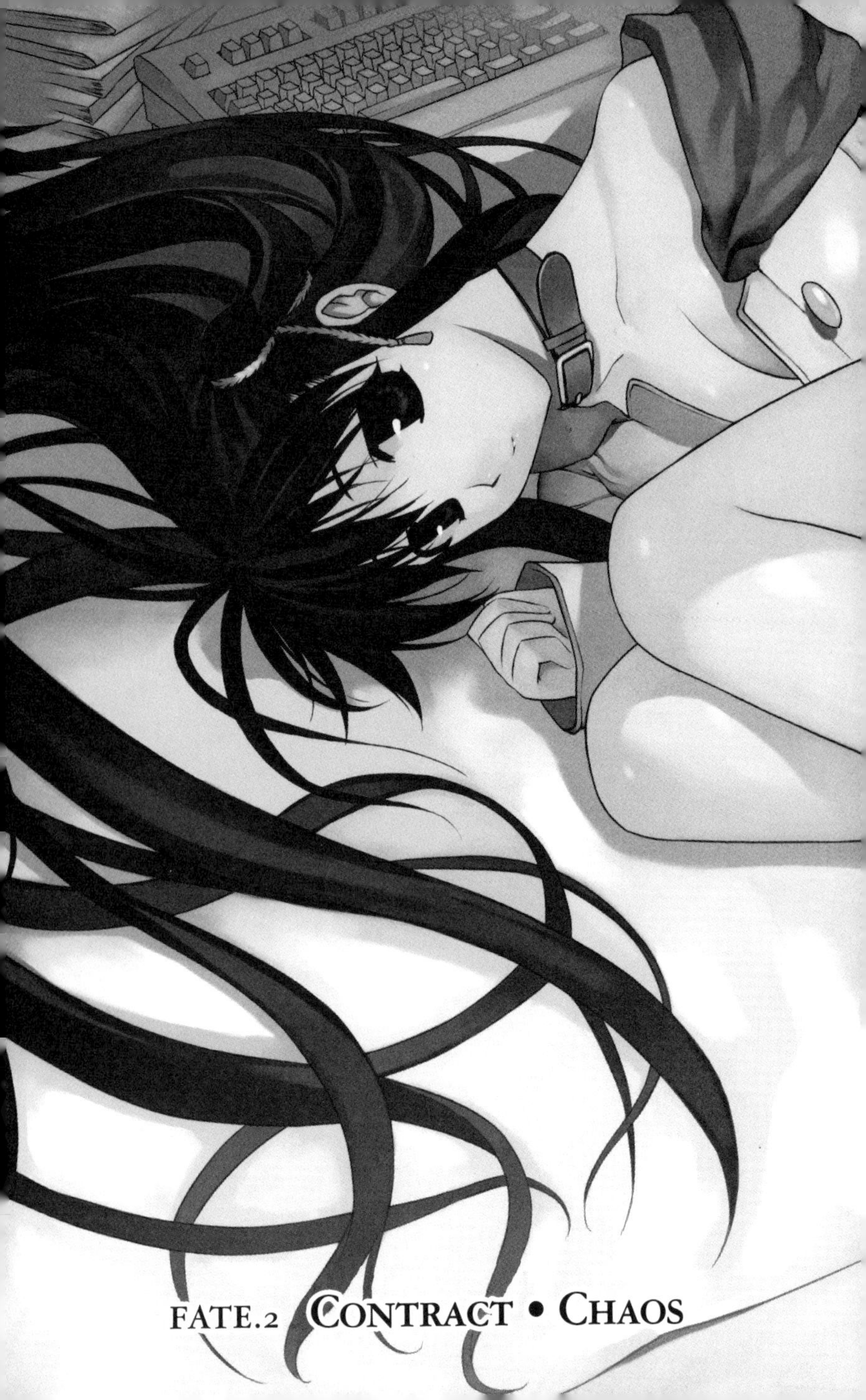

FATE.2 CONTRACT • CHAOS

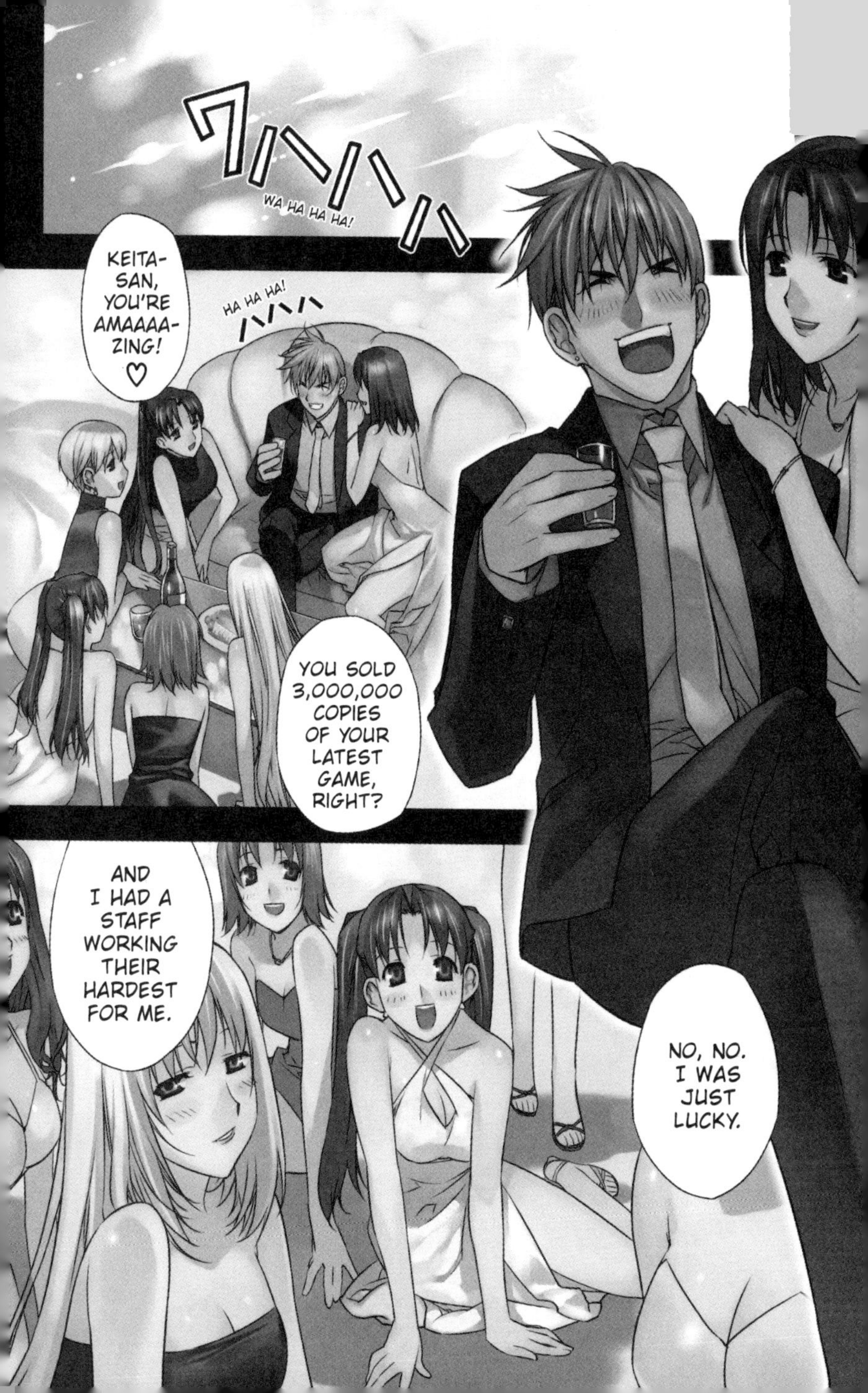
ワハハハ
WA HA HA HA!
KEITA-SAN, YOU'RE AMAAAAZING! ♡
ハハハ
HA HA HA!
YOU SOLD 3,000,000 COPIES OF YOUR LATEST GAME, RIGHT?
NO, NO. I WAS JUST LUCKY.
AND I HAD A STAFF WORKING THEIR HARDEST FOR ME.

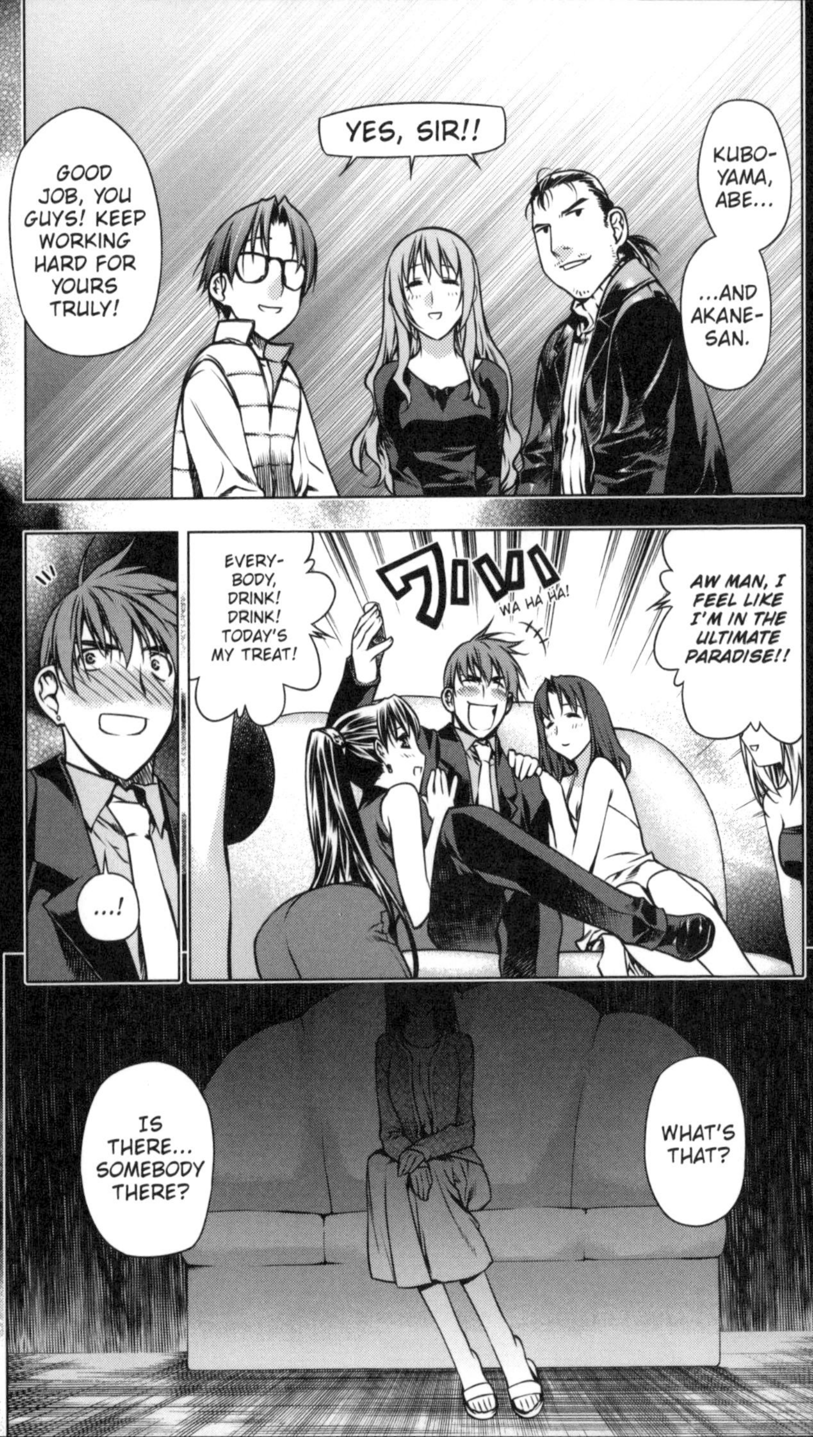
KUBO-YAMA, ABE...
...AND AKANE-SAN.
YES, SIR!!
GOOD JOB, YOU GUYS! KEEP WORKING HARD FOR YOURS TRULY!
AW MAN, I FEEL LIKE I'M IN THE ULTIMATE PARADISE!!
ワハハ
WA HA HA!
EVERY-BODY, DRINK! DRINK! TODAY'S MY TREAT!
...!
WHAT'S THAT?
IS THERE... SOMEBODY THERE?

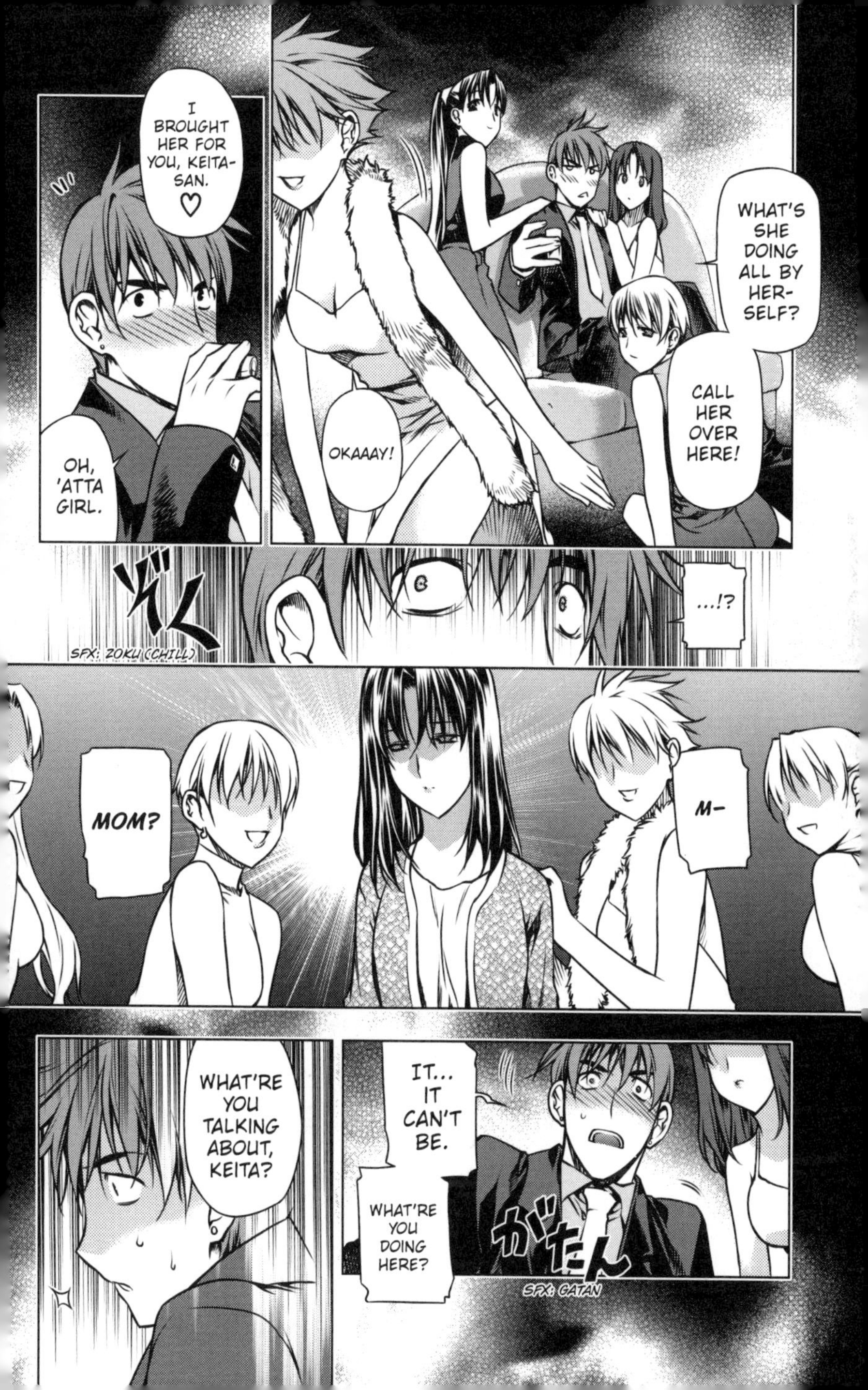
WHAT'S SHE DOING ALL BY HER-SELF?
CALL HER OVER HERE!
OKAAAY!
I BROUGHT HER FOR YOU, KEITA-SAN. ♡
OH, 'ATTA GIRL.
...!?
ぞく
SFX: ZOKU (CHILL)
M-
MOM?
IT... IT CAN'T BE.
WHAT'RE YOU DOING HERE?
がたん
SFX: GATAN
WHAT'RE YOU TALKING ABOUT, KEITA?

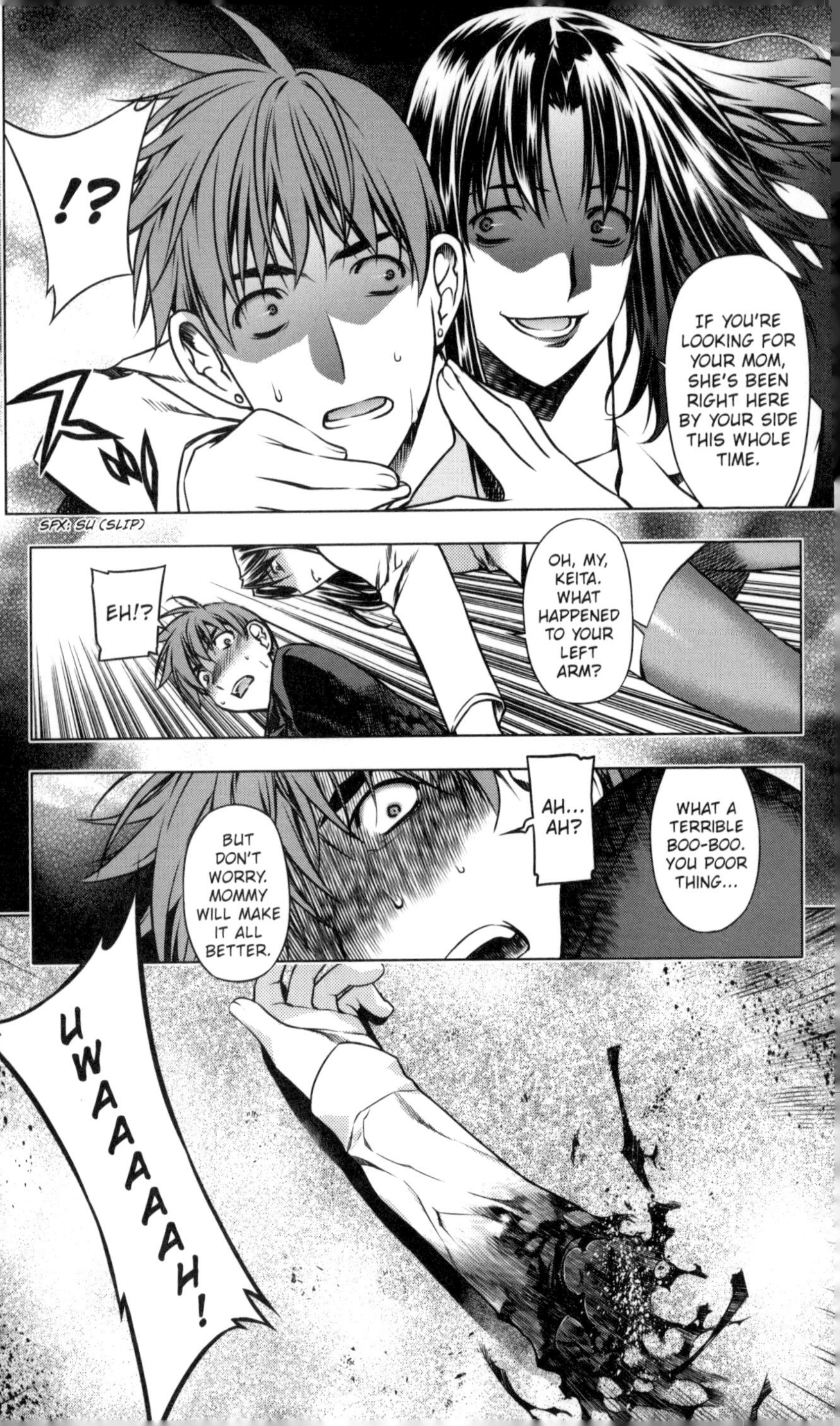
IF YOU'RE LOOKING FOR YOUR MOM, SHE'S BEEN RIGHT HERE BY YOUR SIDE THIS WHOLE TIME.
!?
SFX: SU (SLIP)
OH, MY, KEITA. WHAT HAPPENED TO YOUR LEFT ARM?
EH!?
WHAT A TERRIBLE BOO-BOO. YOU POOR THING...
AH... AH?
BUT DON'T WORRY. MOMMY WILL MAKE IT ALL BETTER.
UWAAAAAH!

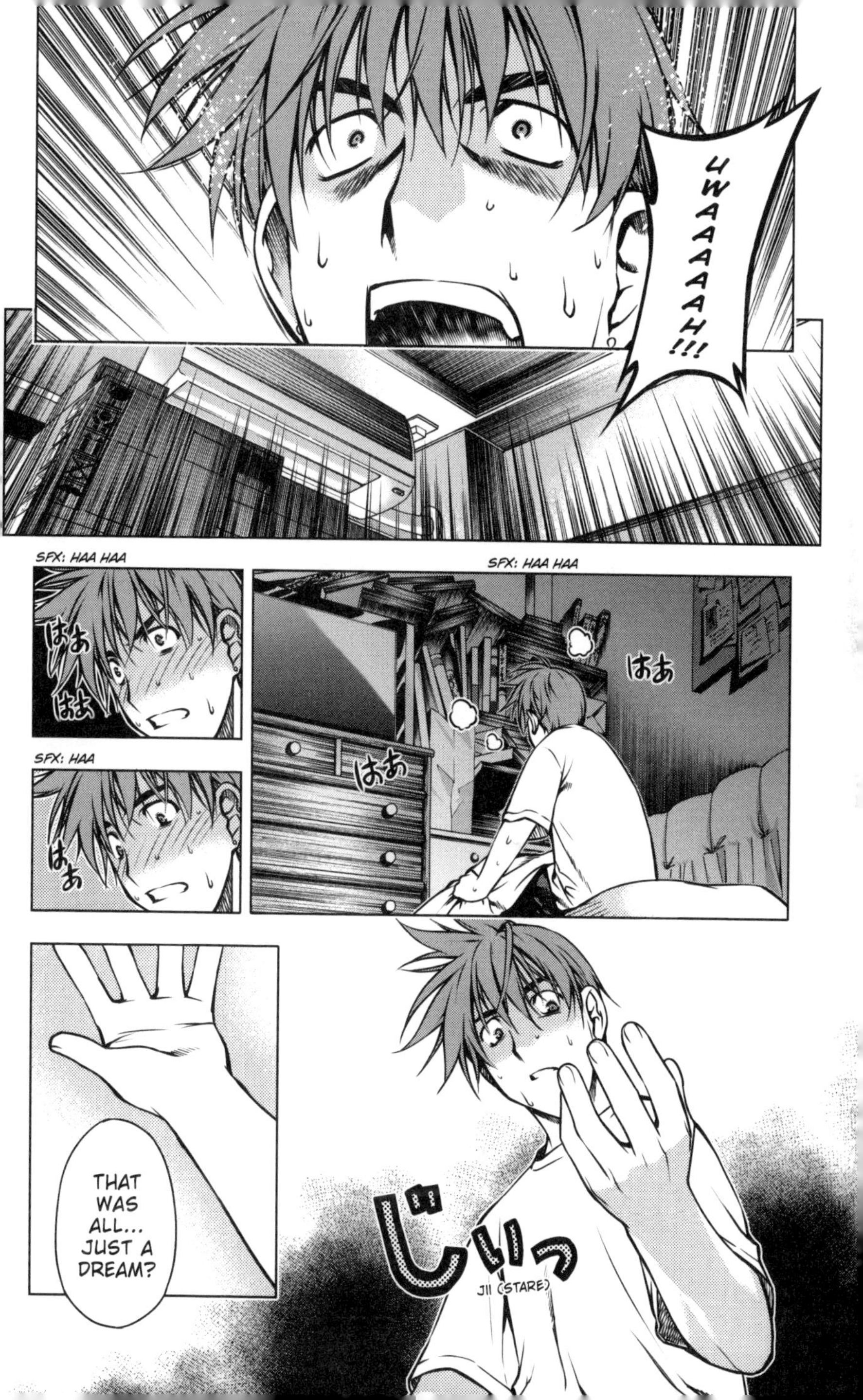
UWAAAAAAH!!!
SFX: HAA HAA
はぁ
はぁ
SFX: HAA HAA
はぁ はぁ
SFX: HAA
はぁ
じいっ
JII (STARE)
THAT WAS ALL... JUST A DREAM?

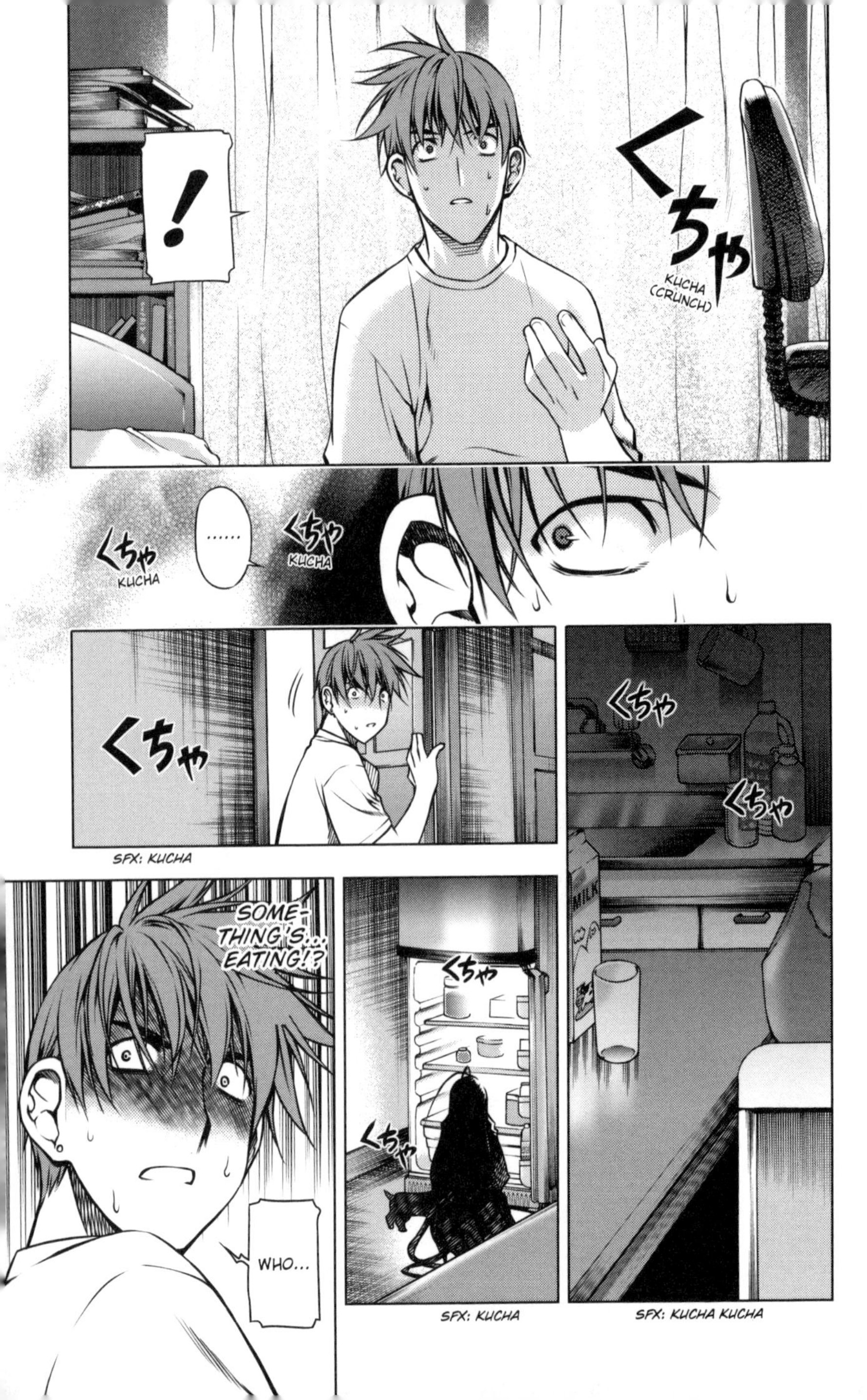
!
くちゃ
KUCHA (CRUNCH)
くちゃ
KUCHA
……
くちゃ
KUCHA
くちゃ
くちゃ
SFX: KUCHA KUCHA
くちゃ
SFX: KUCHA
くちゃ
くちゃ
SFX: KUCHA
SOMETHING'S... EATING!?
WHO...

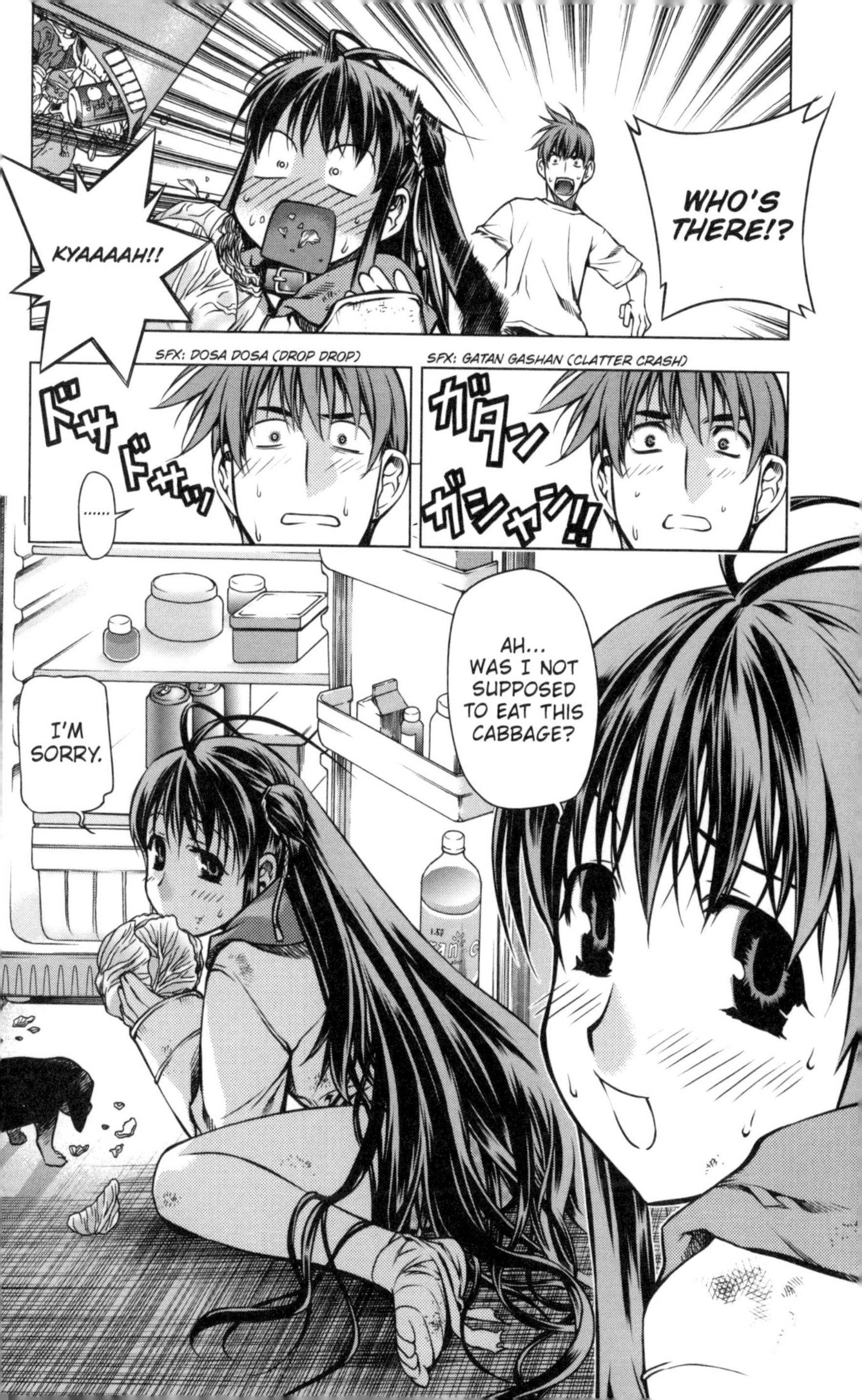
WHO'S THERE!?
KYAAAAH!!
SFX: GATAN GASHAN (CLATTER CRASH)
ガタン ガシャン!!
SFX: DOSA DOSA (DROP DROP)
ドサ ドサッ
......
AH... WAS I NOT SUPPOSED TO EAT THIS CABBAGE?
I'M SORRY.

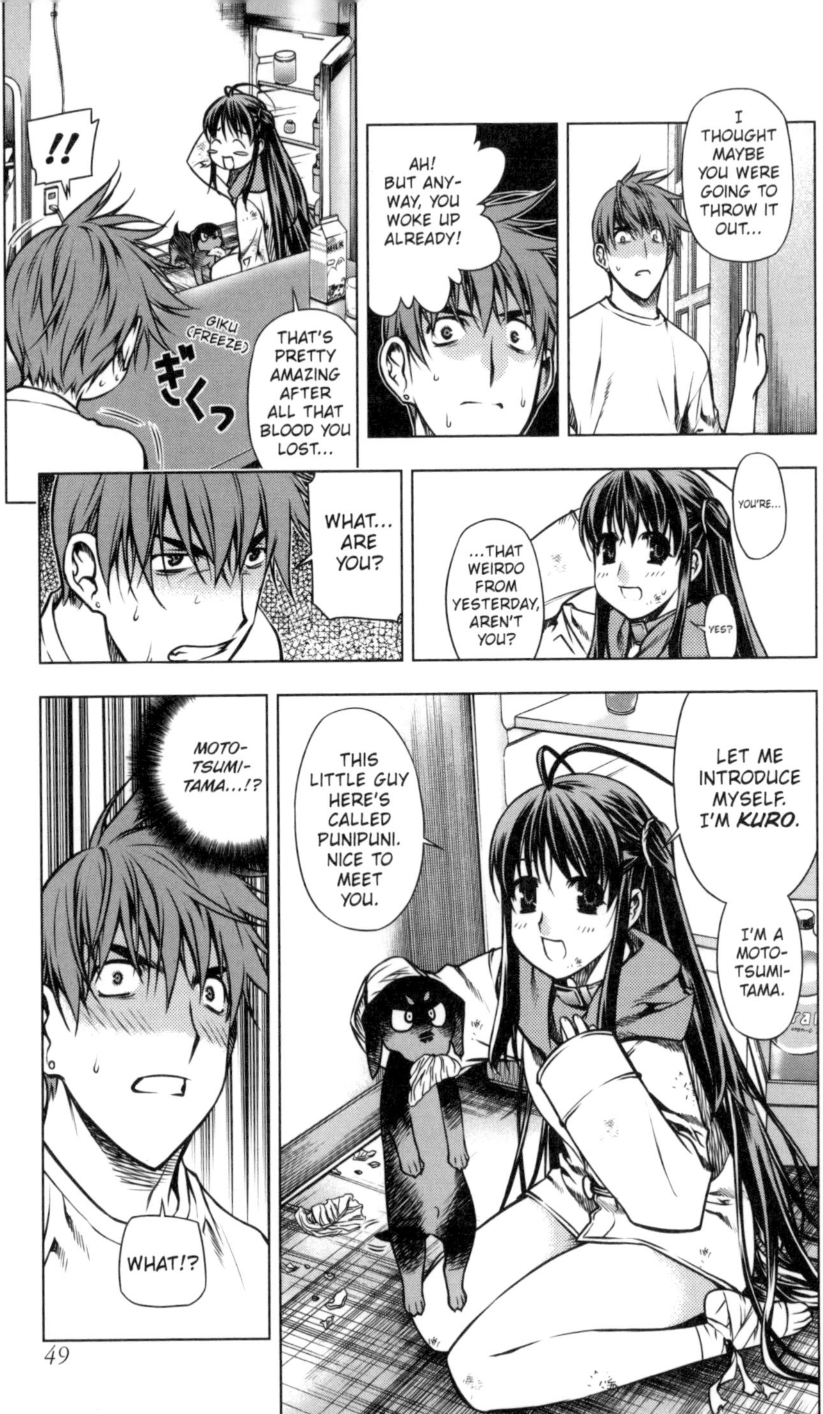
I THOUGHT MAYBE YOU WERE GOING TO THROW IT OUT...
AH! BUT ANYWAY, YOU WOKE UP ALREADY!
!!
THAT'S PRETTY AMAZING AFTER ALL THAT BLOOD YOU LOST...
GIKU (FREEZE)
ぎくっ
YOU'RE...
...THAT WEIRDO FROM YESTERDAY, AREN'T YOU?
YES?
WHAT... ARE YOU?
LET ME INTRODUCE MYSELF. I'M *KURO*.
I'M A MOTO-TSUMI-TAMA.
THIS LITTLE GUY HERE'S CALLED PUNIPUNI. NICE TO MEET YOU.
MOTO-TSUMI-TAMA...!?
WHAT!?

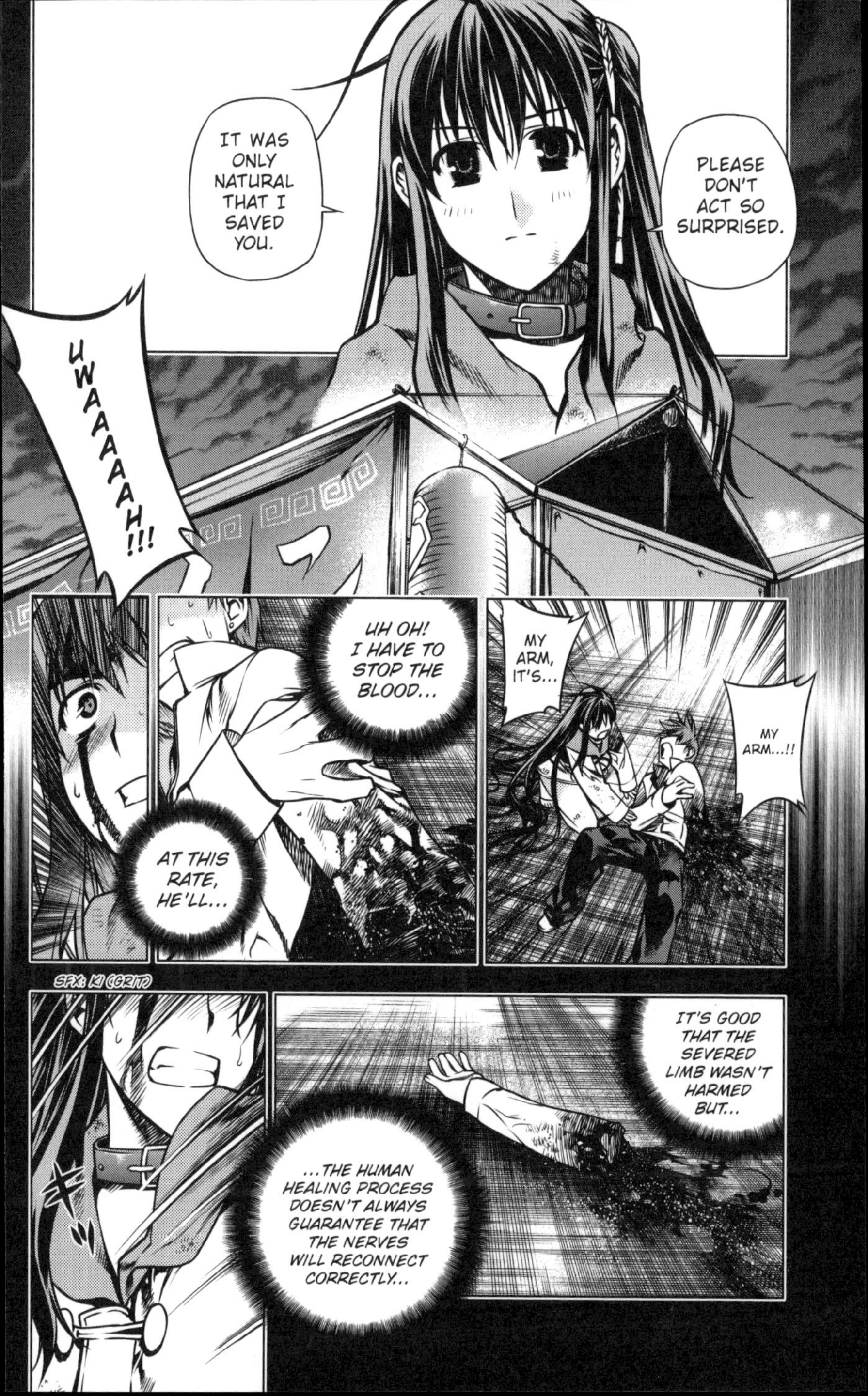
PLEASE DON'T ACT SO SURPRISED.
IT WAS ONLY NATURAL THAT I SAVED YOU.
UWAAAAAAH!!!
MY ARM, IT'S...
MY ARM...!!
UH OH! I HAVE TO STOP THE BLOOD...
AT THIS RATE, HE'LL...
SFX: KI (GRIT)
IT'S GOOD THAT THE SEVERED LIMB WASN'T HARMED BUT...
...THE HUMAN HEALING PROCESS DOESN'T ALWAYS GUARANTEE THAT THE NERVES WILL RECONNECT CORRECTLY...

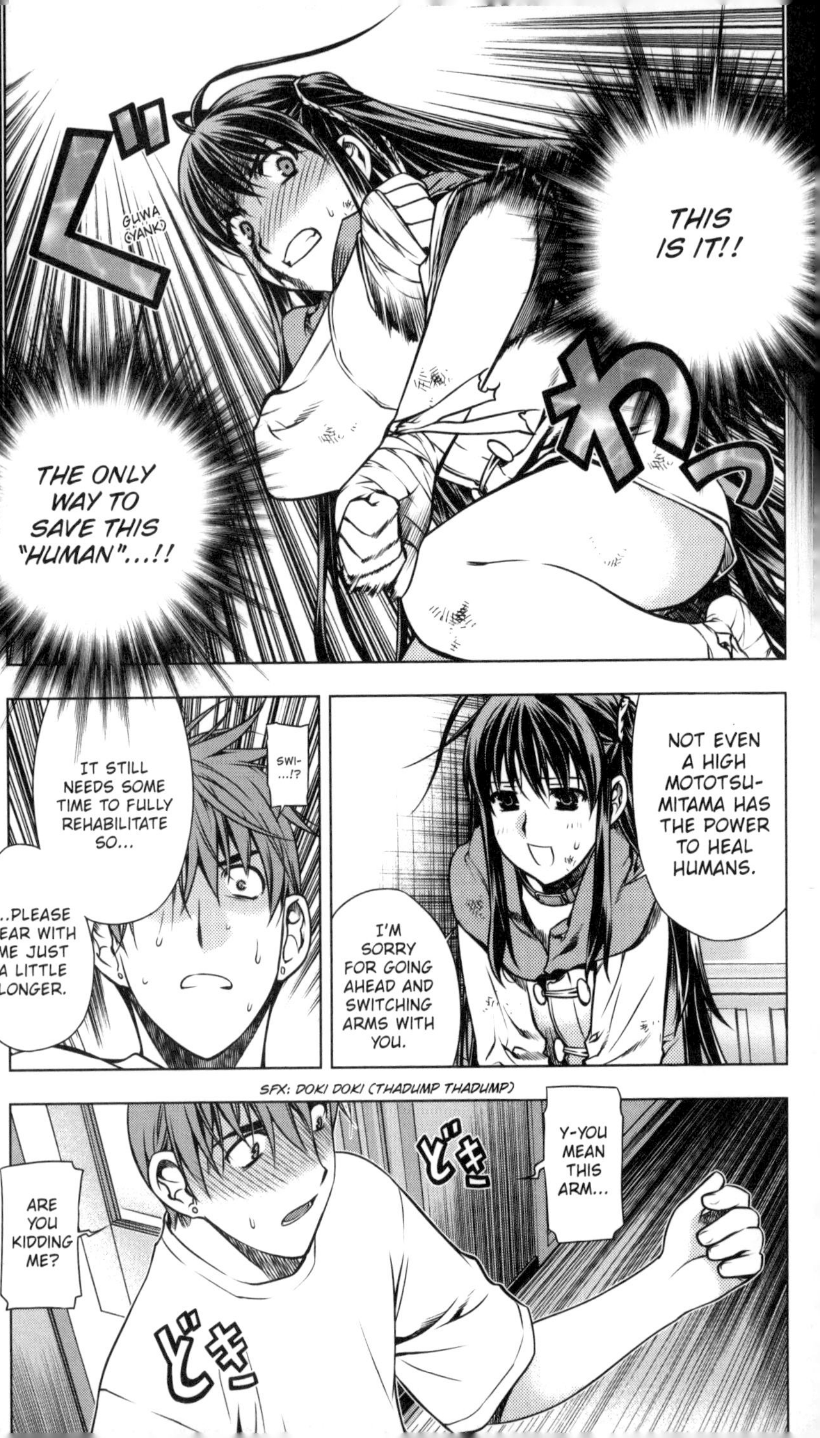
THIS IS IT!!
GUWA (YANK)
THE ONLY WAY TO SAVE THIS "HUMAN"...!!
NOT EVEN A HIGH MOTOTSU-MITAMA HAS THE POWER TO HEAL HUMANS.
I'M SORRY FOR GOING AHEAD AND SWITCHING ARMS WITH YOU.
SWI-...!?
IT STILL NEEDS SOME TIME TO FULLY REHABILITATE SO...
...PLEASE BEAR WITH ME JUST A LITTLE LONGER.
SFX: DOKI DOKI (THADUMP THADUMP)
Y-YOU MEAN THIS ARM...
ARE YOU KIDDING ME?

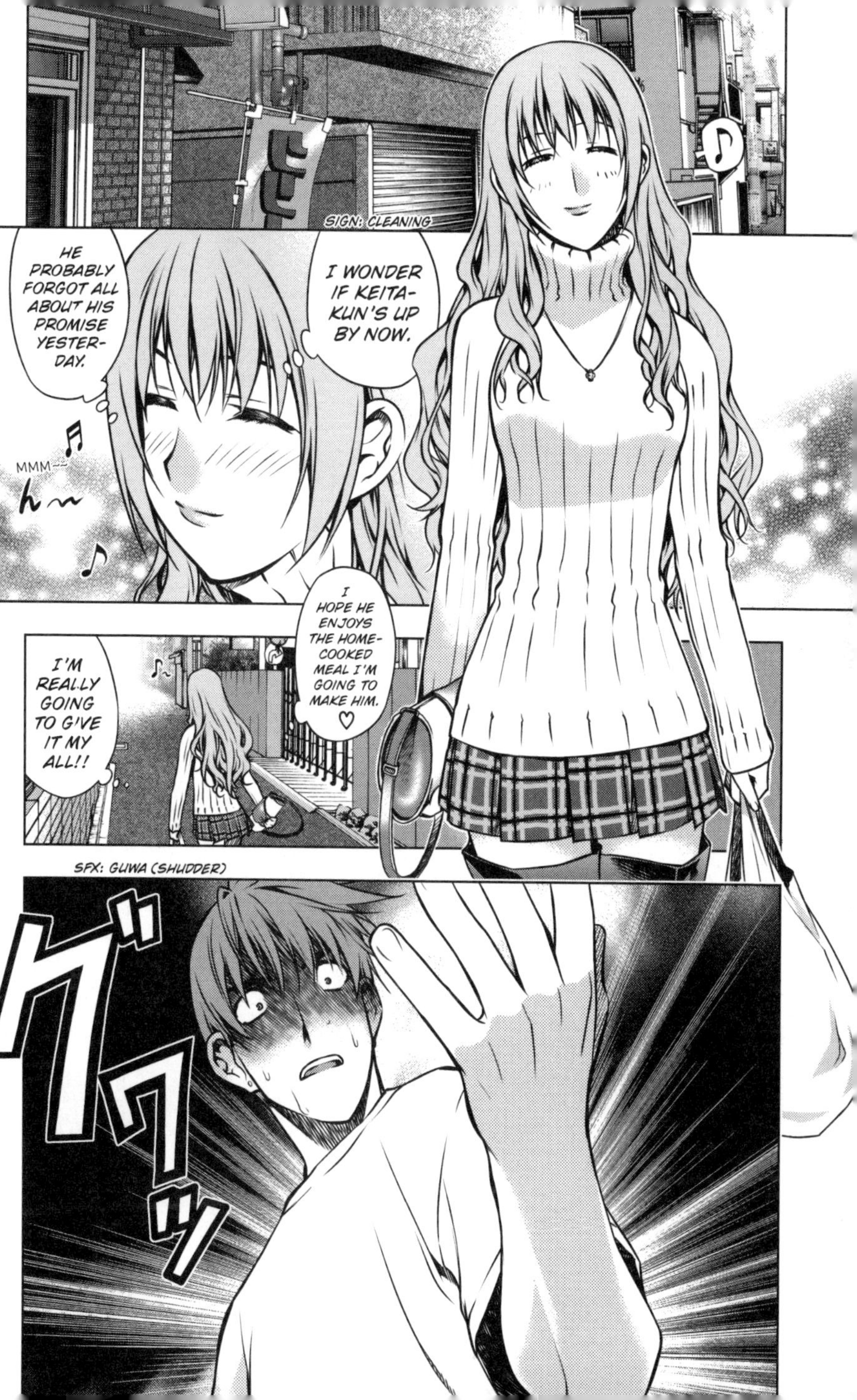
SIGN: CLEANING
I WONDER IF KEITA-KUN'S UP BY NOW.
HE PROBABLY FORGOT ALL ABOUT HIS PROMISE YESTERDAY.
MMM~~
I HOPE HE ENJOYS THE HOME-COOKED MEAL I'M GOING TO MAKE HIM. ♡
I'M REALLY GOING TO GIVE IT MY ALL!!
SFX: GUWA (SHUDDER)

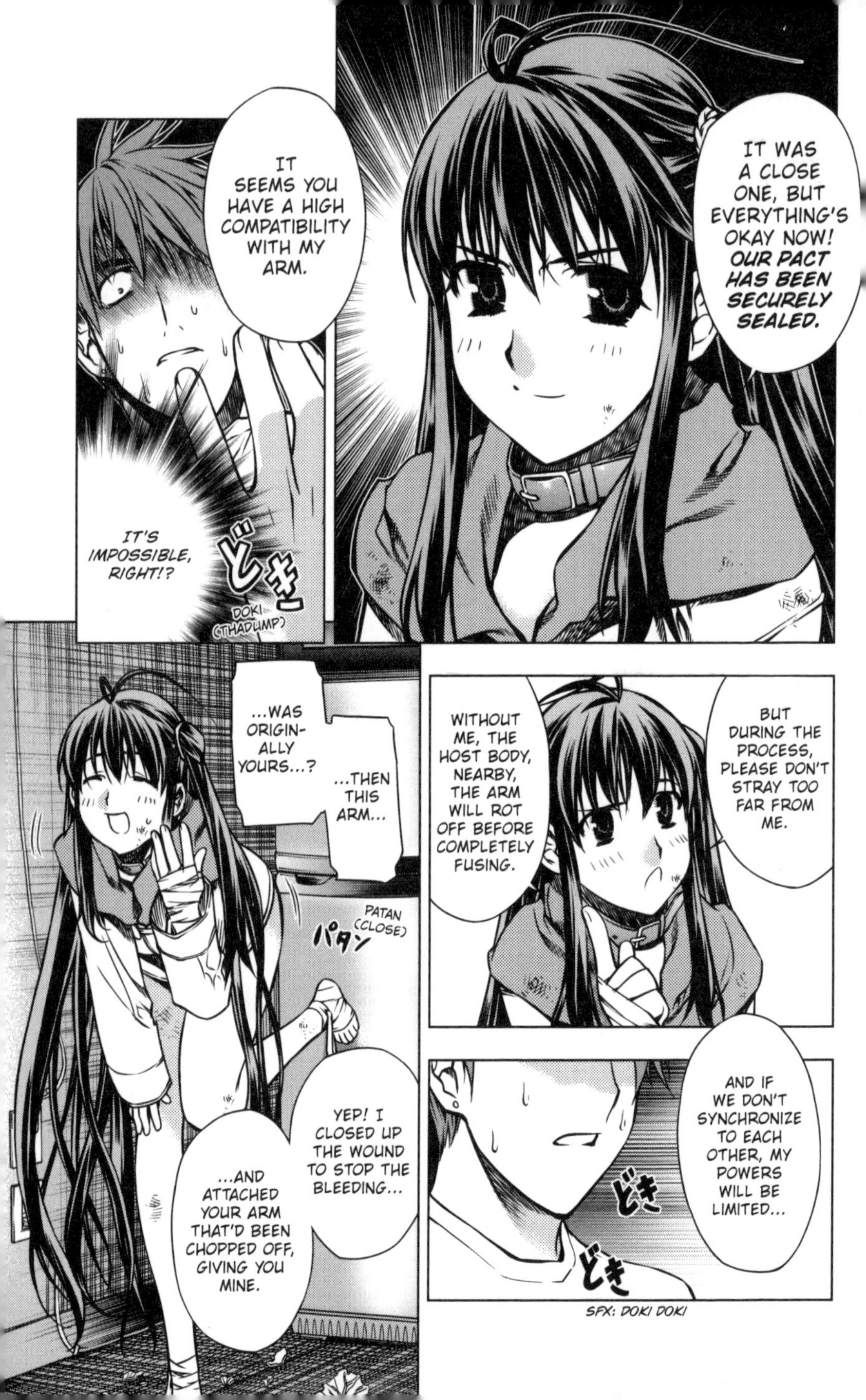
IT WAS A CLOSE ONE, BUT EVERYTHING'S OKAY NOW! **OUR PACT HAS BEEN SECURELY SEALED.**
IT SEEMS YOU HAVE A HIGH COMPATIBILITY WITH MY ARM.
IT'S IMPOSSIBLE, RIGHT!?
どき
DOKI (THADUMP)
BUT DURING THE PROCESS, PLEASE DON'T STRAY TOO FAR FROM ME.
WITHOUT ME, THE HOST BODY, NEARBY, THE ARM WILL ROT OFF BEFORE COMPLETELY FUSING.
AND IF WE DON'T SYNCHRONIZE TO EACH OTHER, MY POWERS WILL BE LIMITED...
どき
どき
SFX: DOKI DOKI
...THEN THIS ARM...
...WAS ORIGIN-ALLY YOURS...?
PATAN (CLOSE)
パタン
YEP! I CLOSED UP THE WOUND TO STOP THE BLEEDING...
...AND ATTACHED YOUR ARM THAT'D BEEN CHOPPED OFF, GIVING YOU MINE.

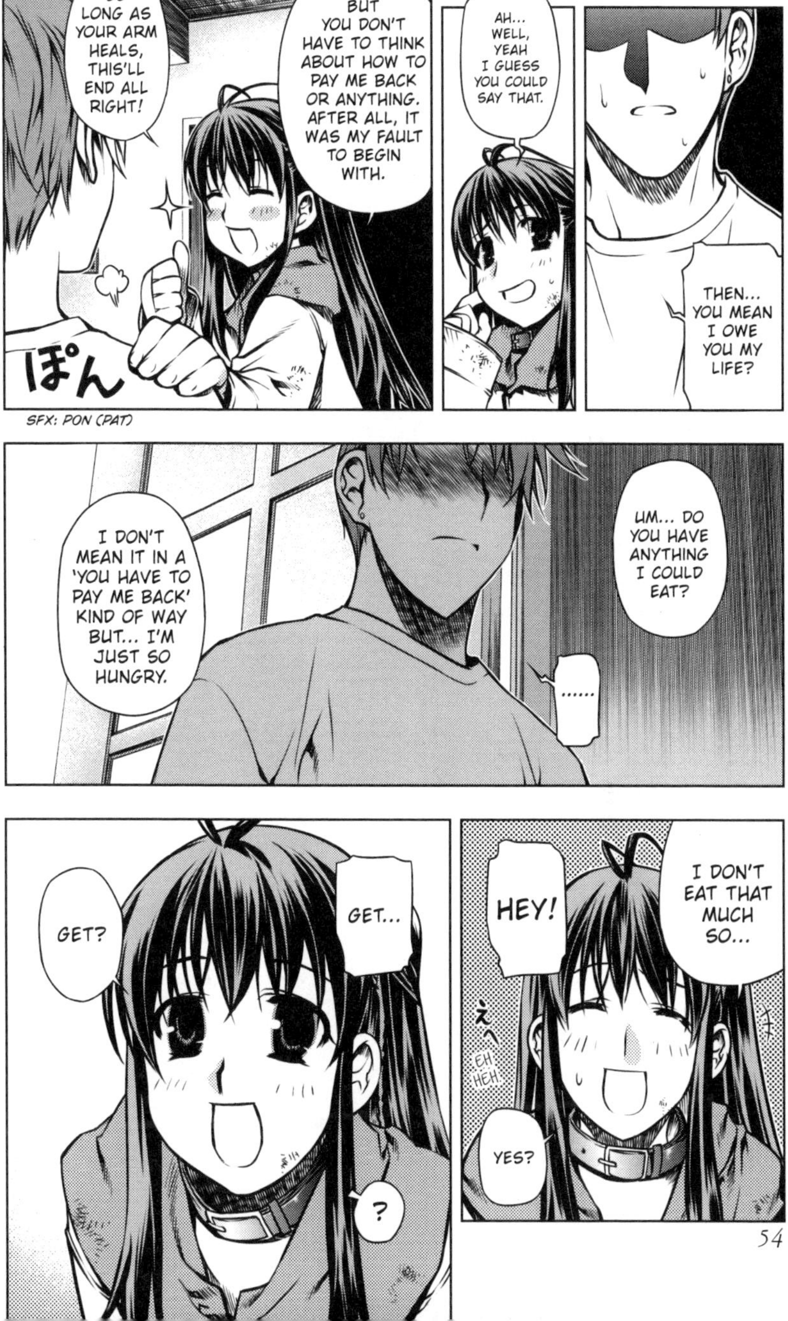
THEN... YOU MEAN I OWE YOU MY LIFE?
AH... WELL, YEAH I GUESS YOU COULD SAY THAT.
BUT YOU DON'T HAVE TO THINK ABOUT HOW TO PAY ME BACK OR ANYTHING. AFTER ALL, IT WAS MY FAULT TO BEGIN WITH.
SO LONG AS YOUR ARM HEALS, THIS'LL END ALL RIGHT!
ぽん
SFX: PON (PAT)
UM... DO YOU HAVE ANYTHING I COULD EAT?
......
I DON'T MEAN IT IN A 'YOU HAVE TO PAY ME BACK' KIND OF WAY BUT... I'M JUST SO HUNGRY.
I DON'T EAT THAT MUCH SO...
HEY!
えへ
EH HEH
YES?
GET...
GET?
?

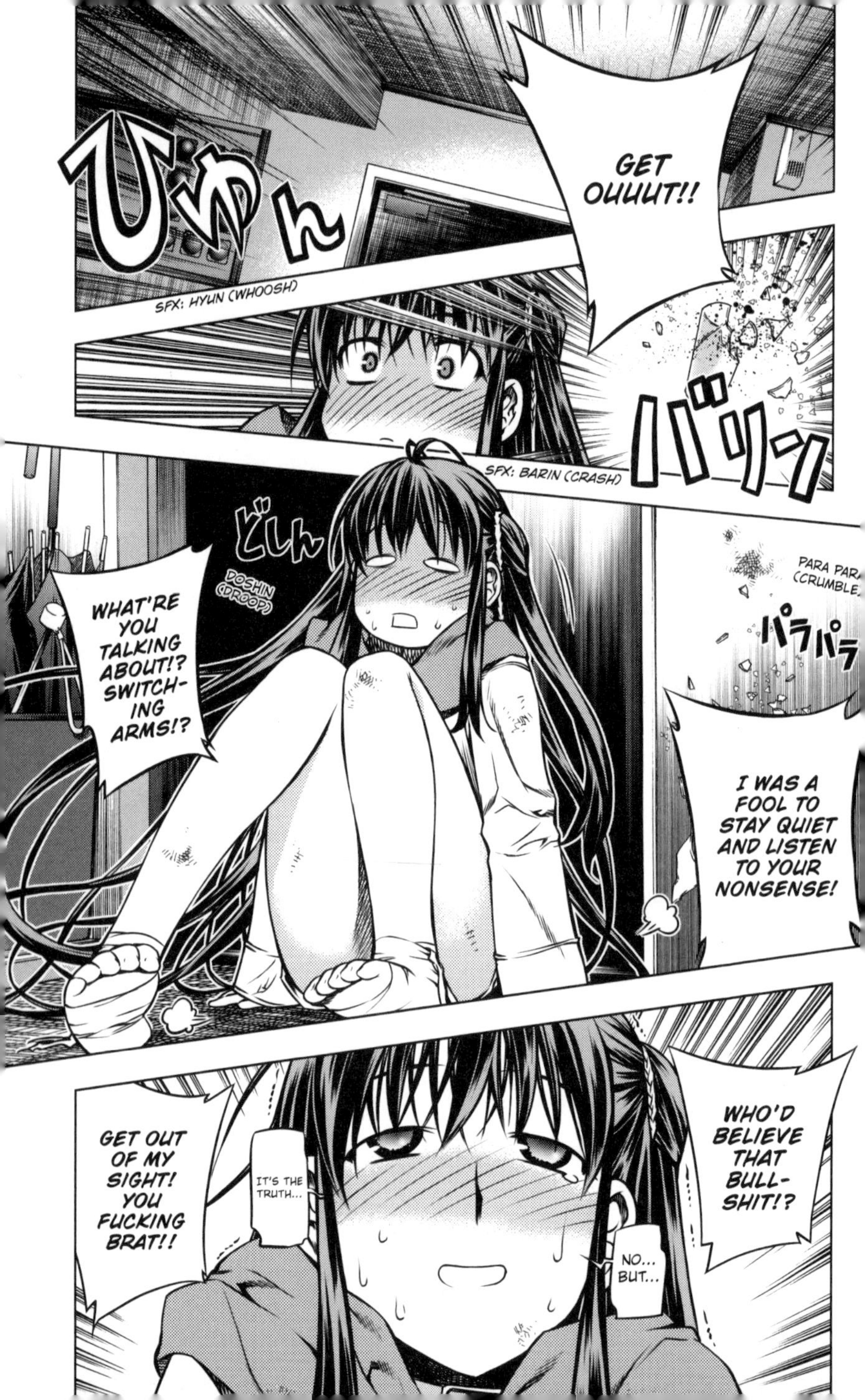
GET OUUUT!!
ひゅん
SFX: HYUN (WHOOSH)
バリーン
SFX: BARIN (CRASH)
パラパラ
PARA PARA (CRUMBLE)
どしん
DOSHIN (DROOP)
WHAT'RE YOU TALKING ABOUT!? SWITCHING ARMS!?
I WAS A FOOL TO STAY QUIET AND LISTEN TO YOUR NONSENSE!
WHO'D BELIEVE THAT BULL-SHIT!?
NO... BUT...
IT'S THE TRUTH...
GET OUT OF MY SIGHT! YOU FUCKING BRAT!!

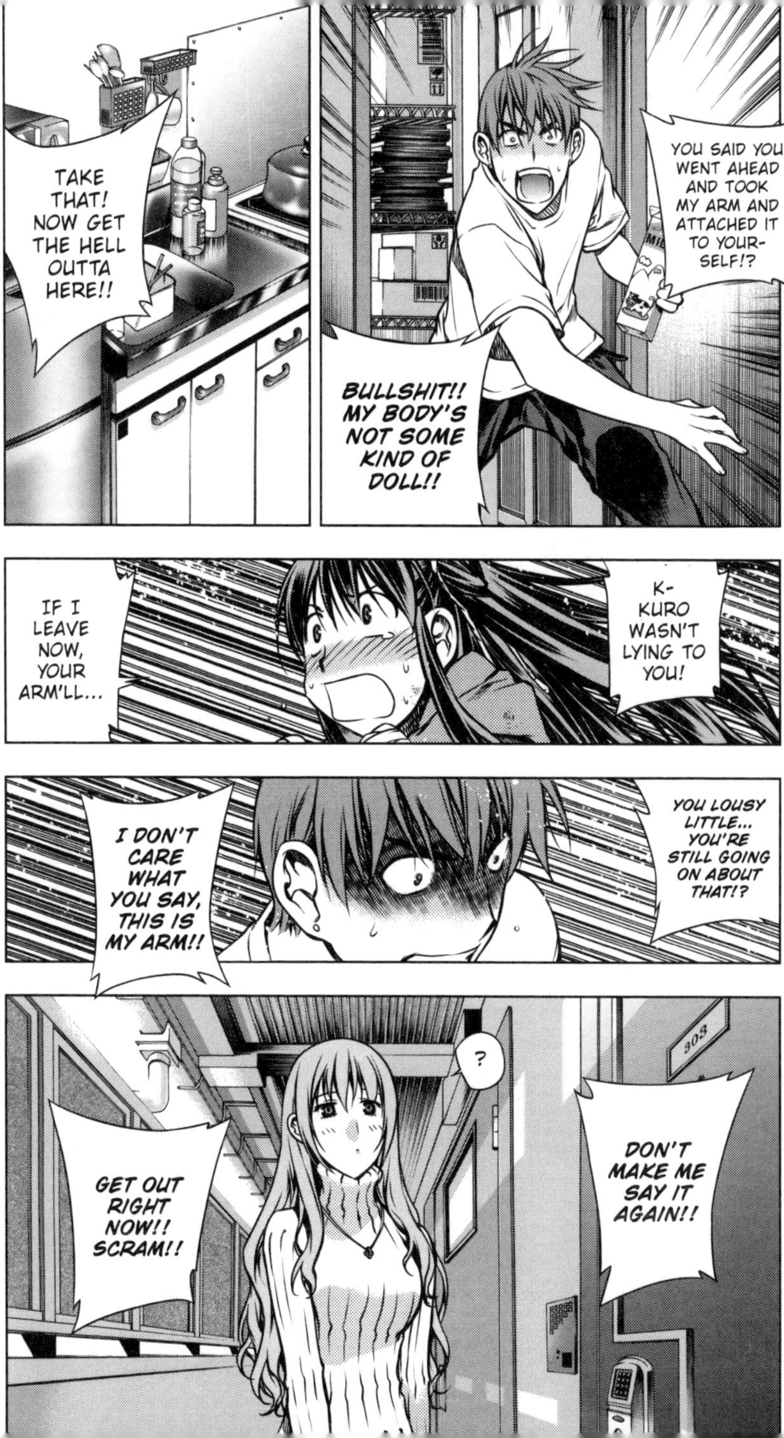
YOU SAID YOU WENT AHEAD AND TOOK MY ARM AND ATTACHED IT TO YOUR-SELF!?
BULLSHIT!! MY BODY'S NOT SOME KIND OF DOLL!!
TAKE THAT! NOW GET THE HELL OUTTA HERE!!
K-KURO WASN'T LYING TO YOU!
IF I LEAVE NOW, YOUR ARM'LL...
YOU LOUSY LITTLE... YOU'RE STILL GOING ON ABOUT THAT!?
I DON'T CARE WHAT YOU SAY, THIS IS MY ARM!!
303
?
DON'T MAKE ME SAY IT AGAIN!!
GET OUT RIGHT NOW!! SCRAM!!

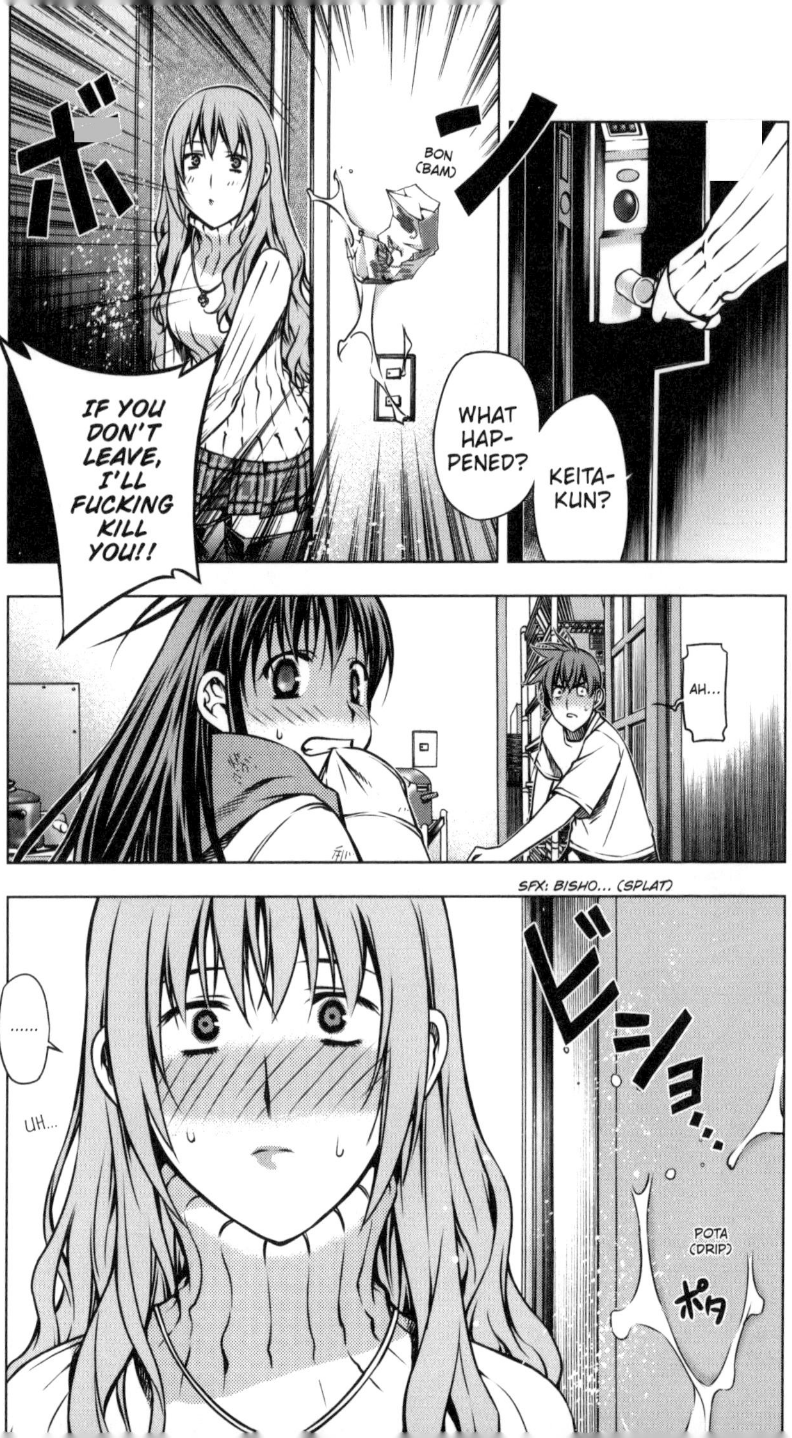
KEITA-KUN?
WHAT HAP-PENED?
BON (BAM)
IF YOU DON'T LEAVE, I'LL FUCKING KILL YOU!!
AH...
SFX: BISHO... (SPLAT)
POTA (DRIP)
......
UH...

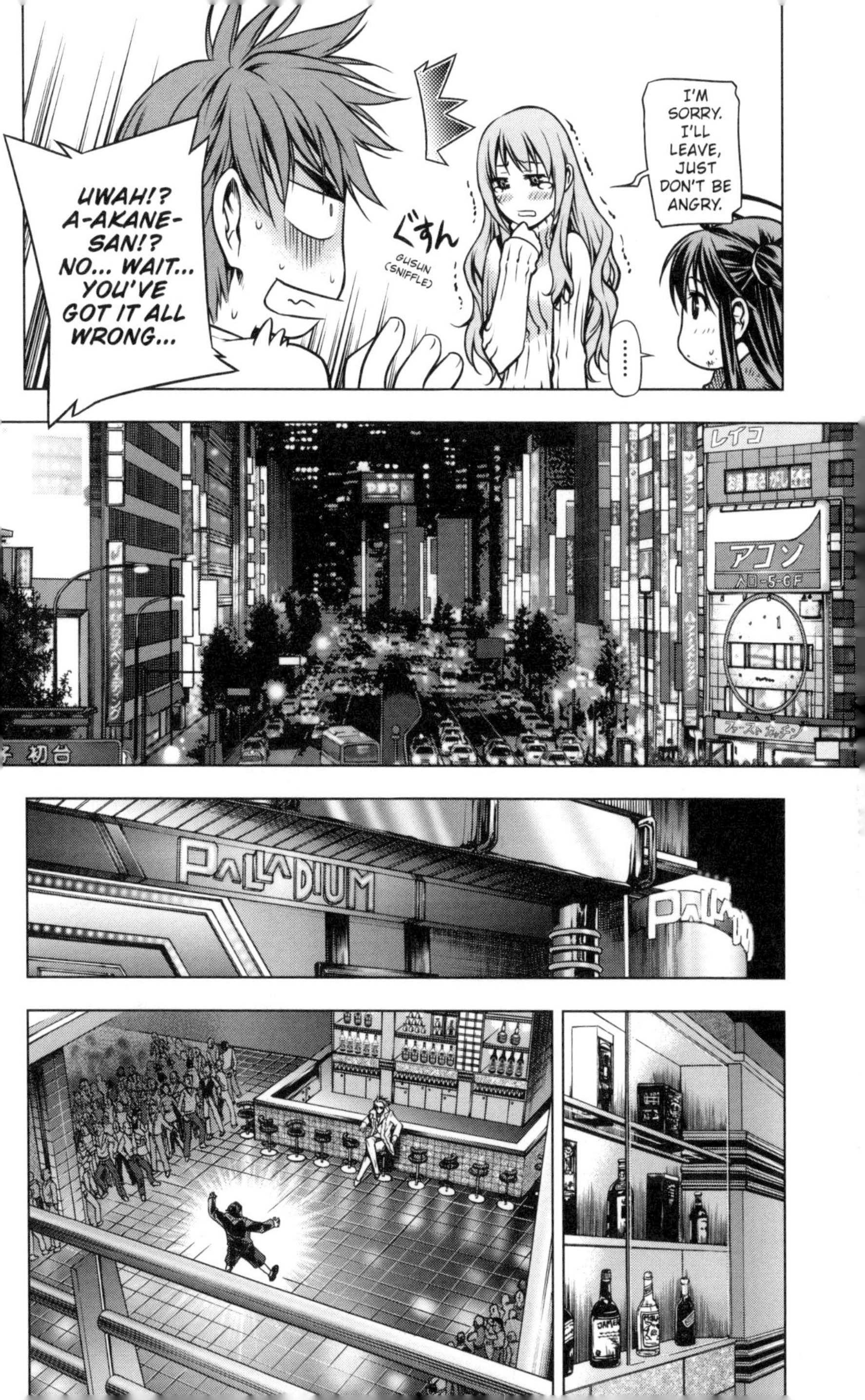
I'M SORRY. I'LL LEAVE, JUST DON'T BE ANGRY.
......
ぐすん
GUSUN (SNIFFLE)
UWAH!? A-AKANE-SAN!? NO... WAIT... YOU'VE GOT IT ALL WRONG...
レイコ
アコン
ファースト キッチン
初台
PALLADIUM

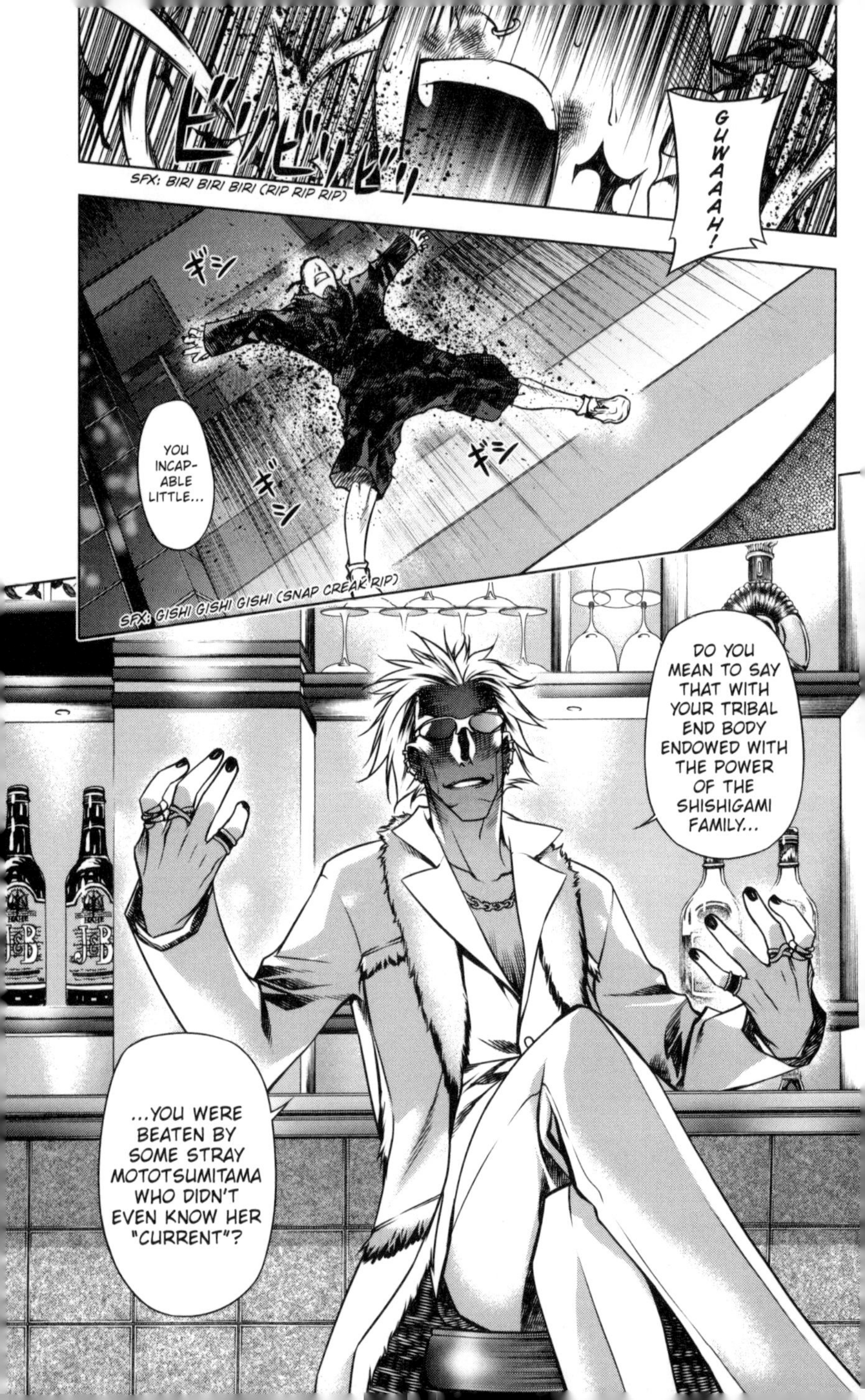
GUWAAAAH!
SFX: BIRI BIRI BIRI (RIP RIP RIP)
YOU INCAPABLE LITTLE...
SFX: GISHI GISHI GISHI (SNAP CREAK RIP)
DO YOU MEAN TO SAY THAT WITH YOUR TRIBAL END BODY ENDOWED WITH THE POWER OF THE SHISHIGAMI FAMILY...
...YOU WERE BEATEN BY SOME STRAY MOTOTSUMITAMA WHO DIDN'T EVEN KNOW HER "CURRENT"?

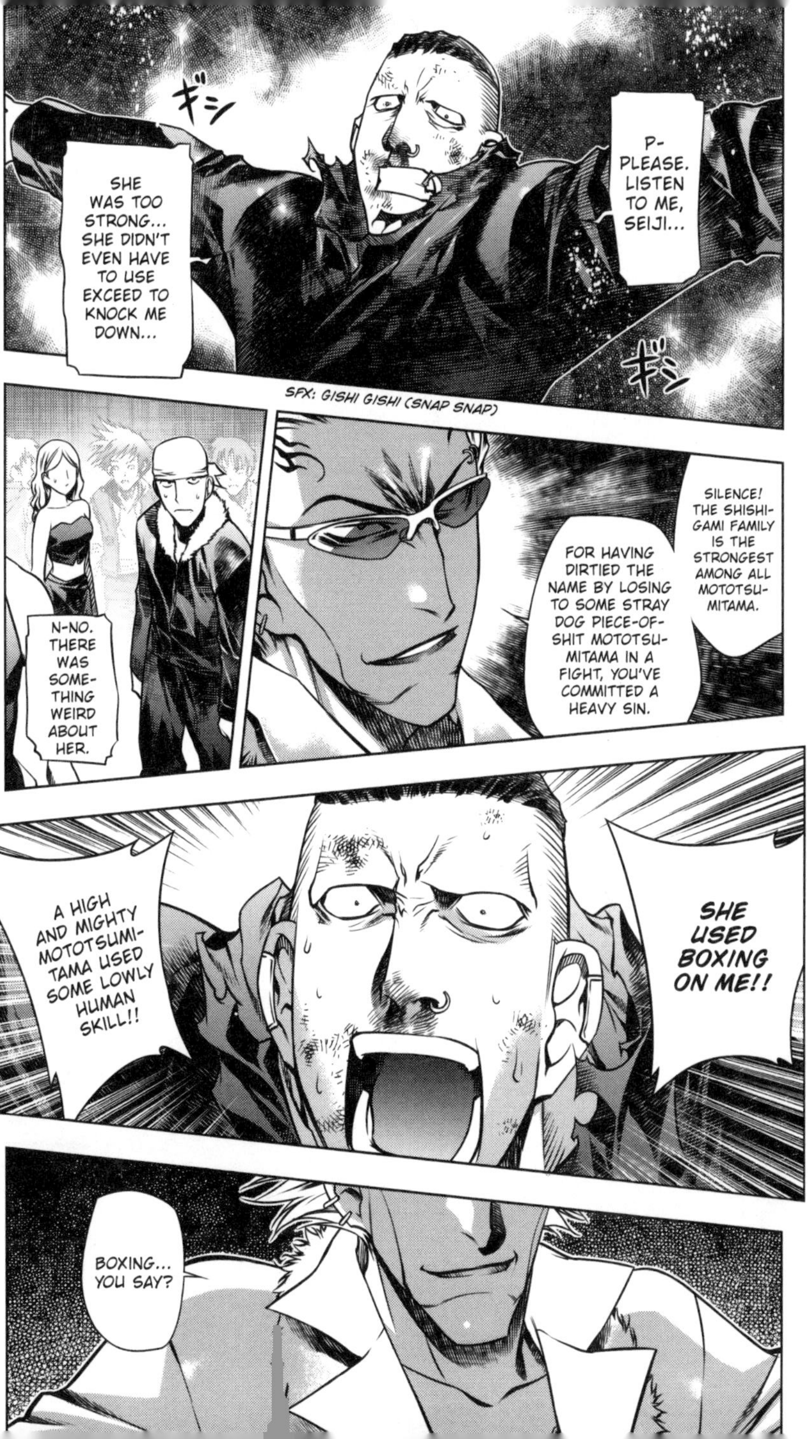

ギシ
P-PLEASE. LISTEN TO ME, SEIJI...
SHE WAS TOO STRONG... SHE DIDN'T EVEN HAVE TO USE EXCEED TO KNOCK ME DOWN...
ギシ
SFX: GISHI GISHI (SNAP SNAP)
SILENCE! THE SHISHIGAMI FAMILY IS THE STRONGEST AMONG ALL MOTOTSUMITAMA.
FOR HAVING DIRTIED THE NAME BY LOSING TO SOME STRAY DOG PIECE-OF-SHIT MOTOTSUMITAMA IN A FIGHT, YOU'VE COMMITTED A HEAVY SIN.
N-NO. THERE WAS SOMETHING WEIRD ABOUT HER.
SHE USED BOXING ON ME!!
A HIGH AND MIGHTY MOTOTSUMITAMA USED SOME LOWLY HUMAN SKILL!!
BOXING... YOU SAY?

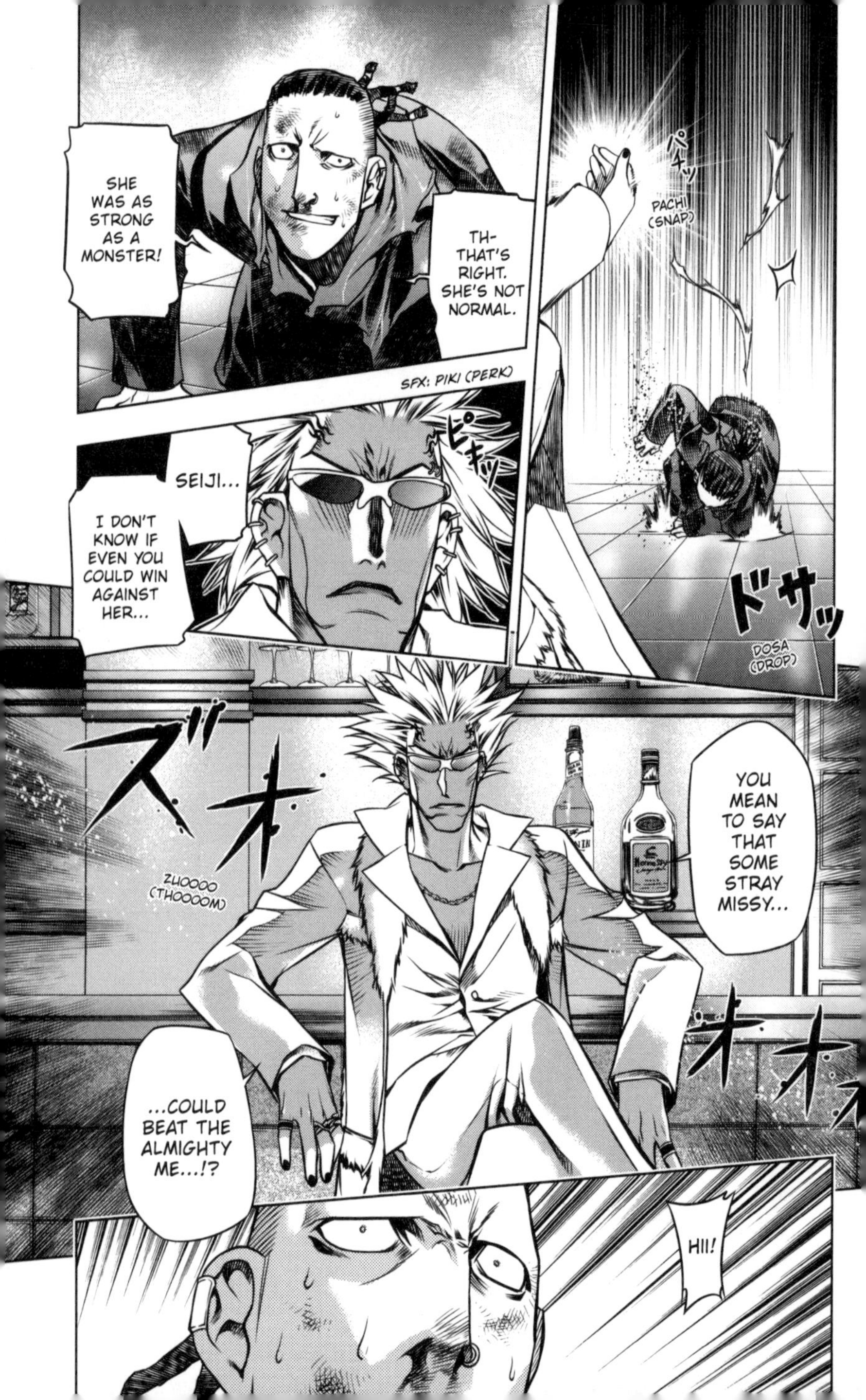
パキッ
PACHI (SNAP)
ドサッ
DOSA (DROP)
TH- THAT'S RIGHT. SHE'S NOT NORMAL.
SHE WAS AS STRONG AS A MONSTER!
SFX: PIKI (PERK)
ピキッ
SEIJI...
I DON'T KNOW IF EVEN YOU COULD WIN AGAINST HER...
YOU MEAN TO SAY THAT SOME STRAY MISSY...
ズオ
ZHOOOO (THOOOOM)
オオ
...COULD BEAT THE ALMIGHTY ME...!?
HII!

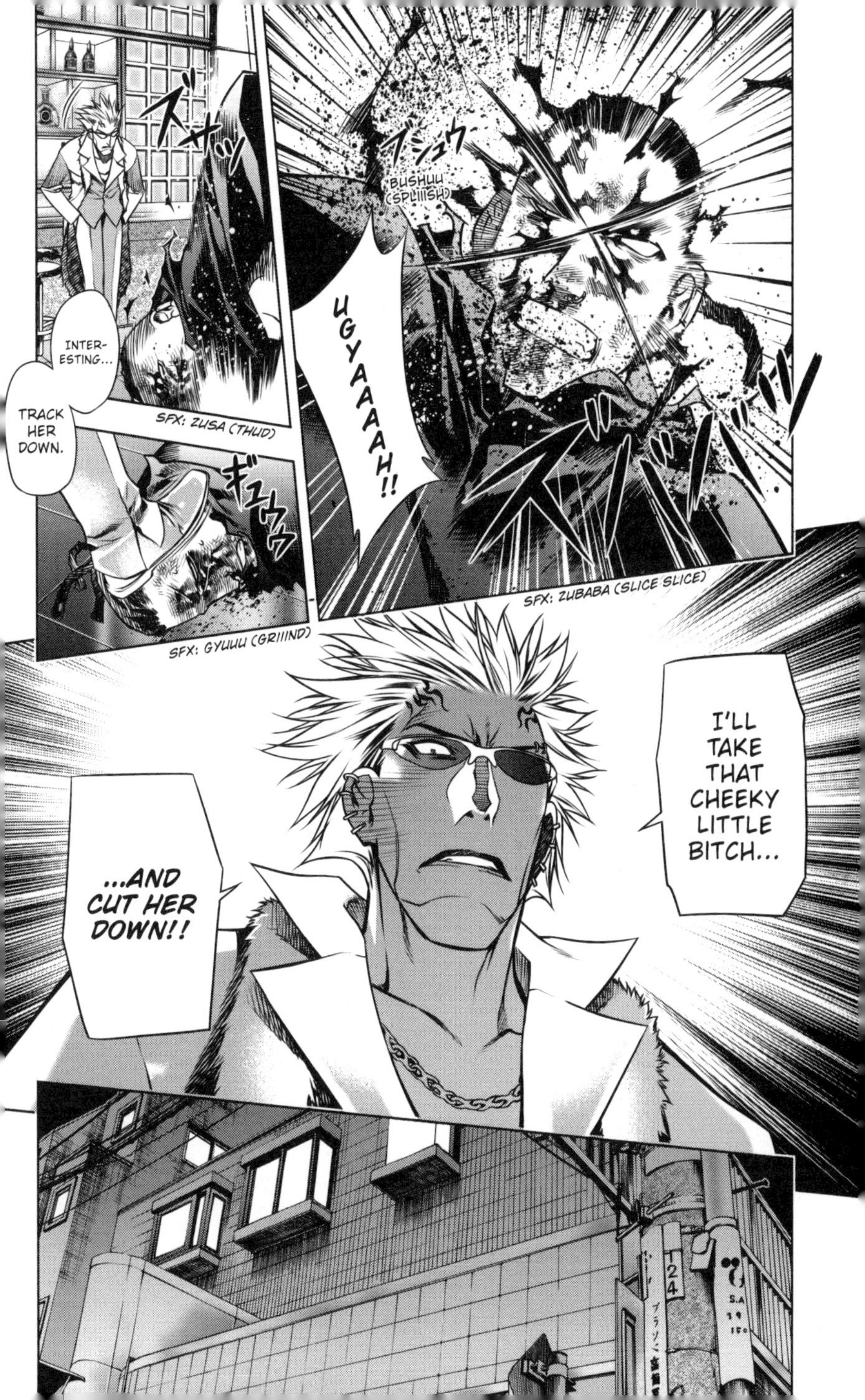
BUSHUU (SPLIIISH)
UGYAAAAAH!!
SFX: ZUBABA (SLICE SLICE)
SFX: ZUSA (THUD)
INTER-ESTING...
TRACK HER DOWN.
SFX: GYUUU (GRIIIND)
I'LL TAKE THAT CHEEKY LITTLE BITCH...
...AND CUT HER DOWN!!
124

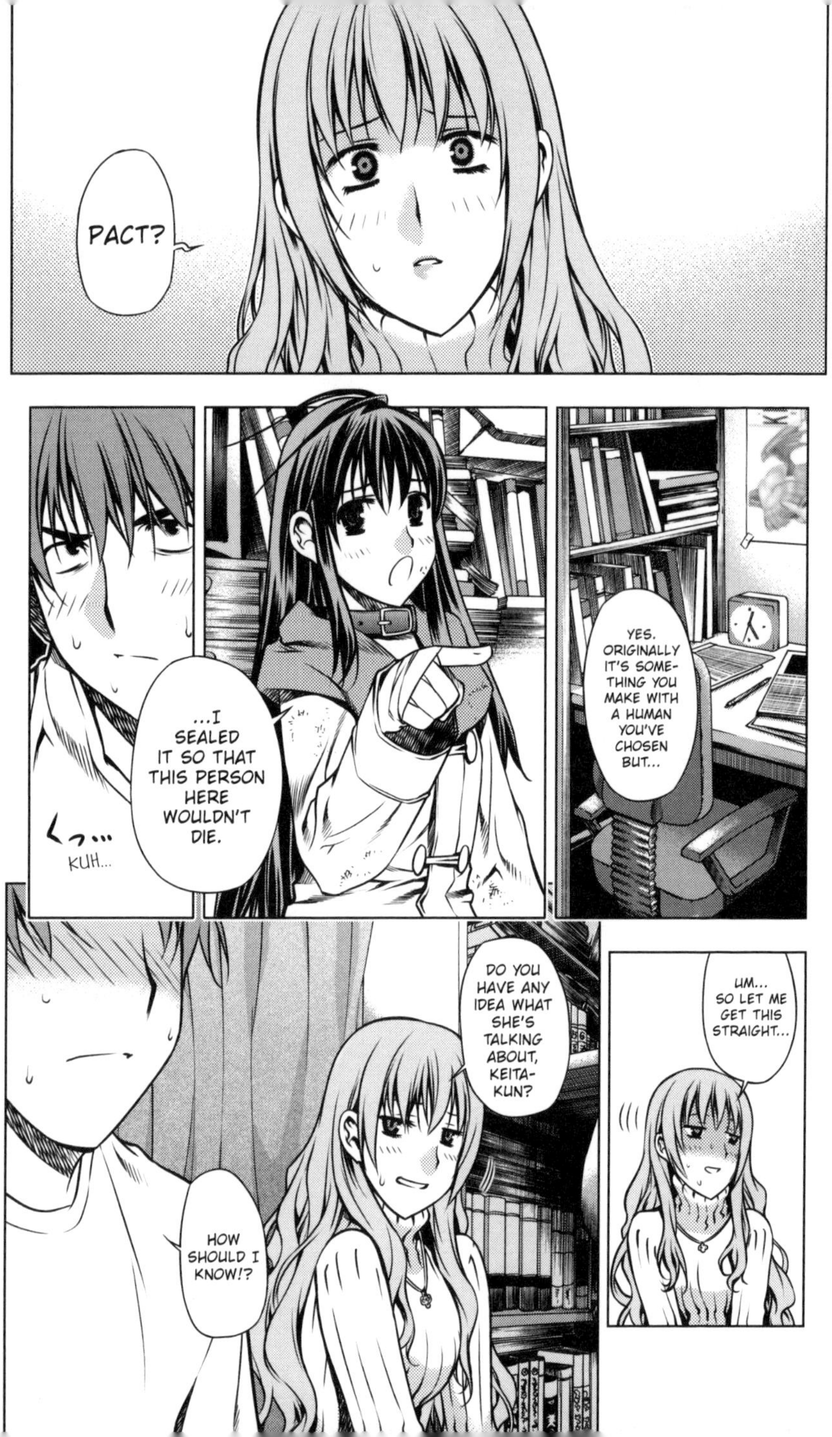
PACT?
YES. ORIGINALLY IT'S SOME-THING YOU MAKE WITH A HUMAN YOU'VE CHOSEN BUT...
...I SEALED IT SO THAT THIS PERSON HERE WOULDN'T DIE.
くっ…
KUH...
UM... SO LET ME GET THIS STRAIGHT...
DO YOU HAVE ANY IDEA WHAT SHE'S TALKING ABOUT, KEITA-KUN?
HOW SHOULD I KNOW!?

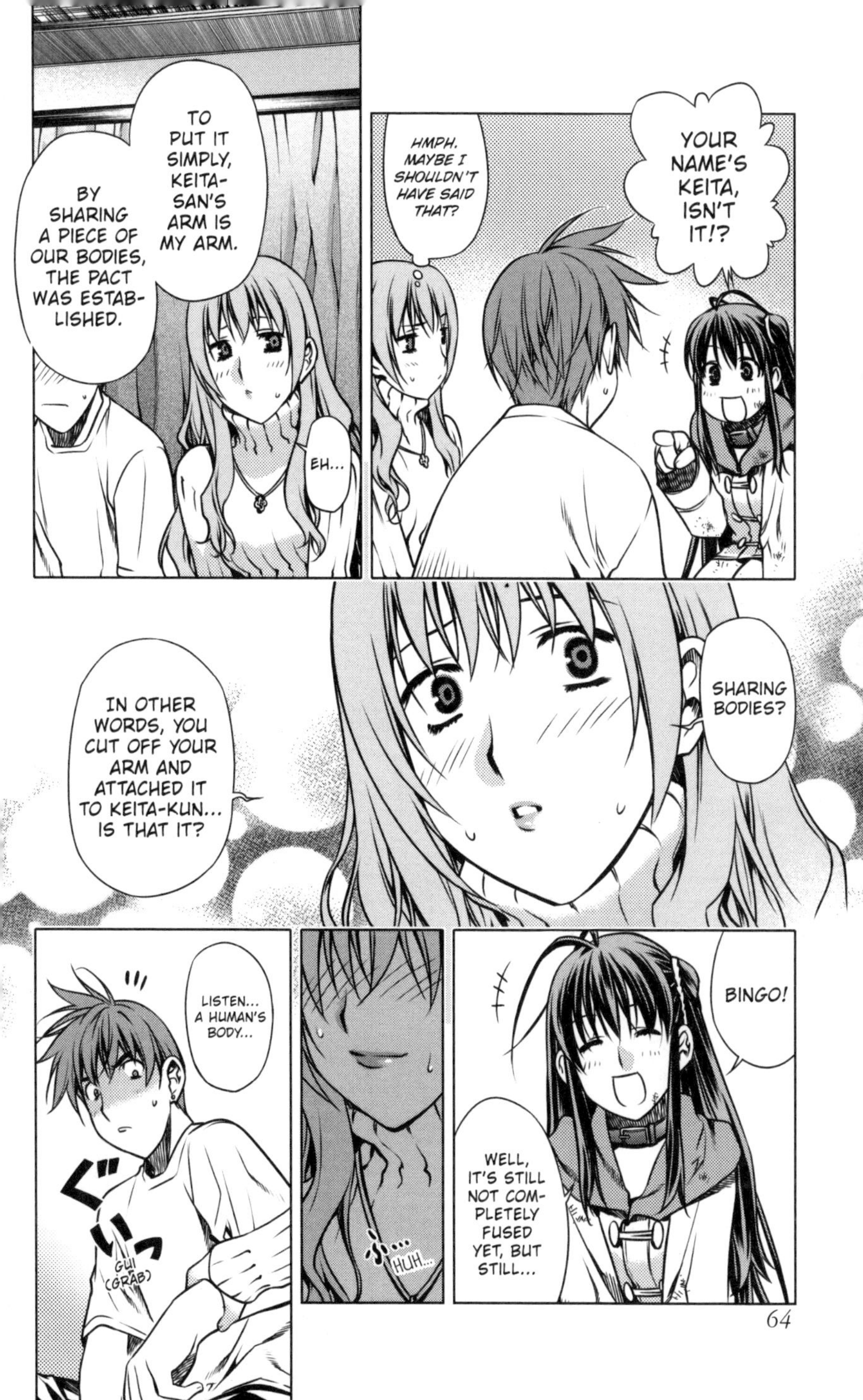
YOUR NAME'S KEITA, ISN'T IT!?
HMPH. MAYBE I SHOULDN'T HAVE SAID THAT?
TO PUT IT SIMPLY, KEITA-SAN'S ARM IS MY ARM.
BY SHARING A PIECE OF OUR BODIES, THE PACT WAS ESTAB-LISHED.
EH...
SHARING BODIES?
IN OTHER WORDS, YOU CUT OFF YOUR ARM AND ATTACHED IT TO KEITA-KUN... IS THAT IT?
BINGO!
WELL, IT'S STILL NOT COM-PLETELY FUSED YET, BUT STILL...
ふ... HUH...
LISTEN... A HUMAN'S BODY...
ぐいっ
GUI (GRAB)

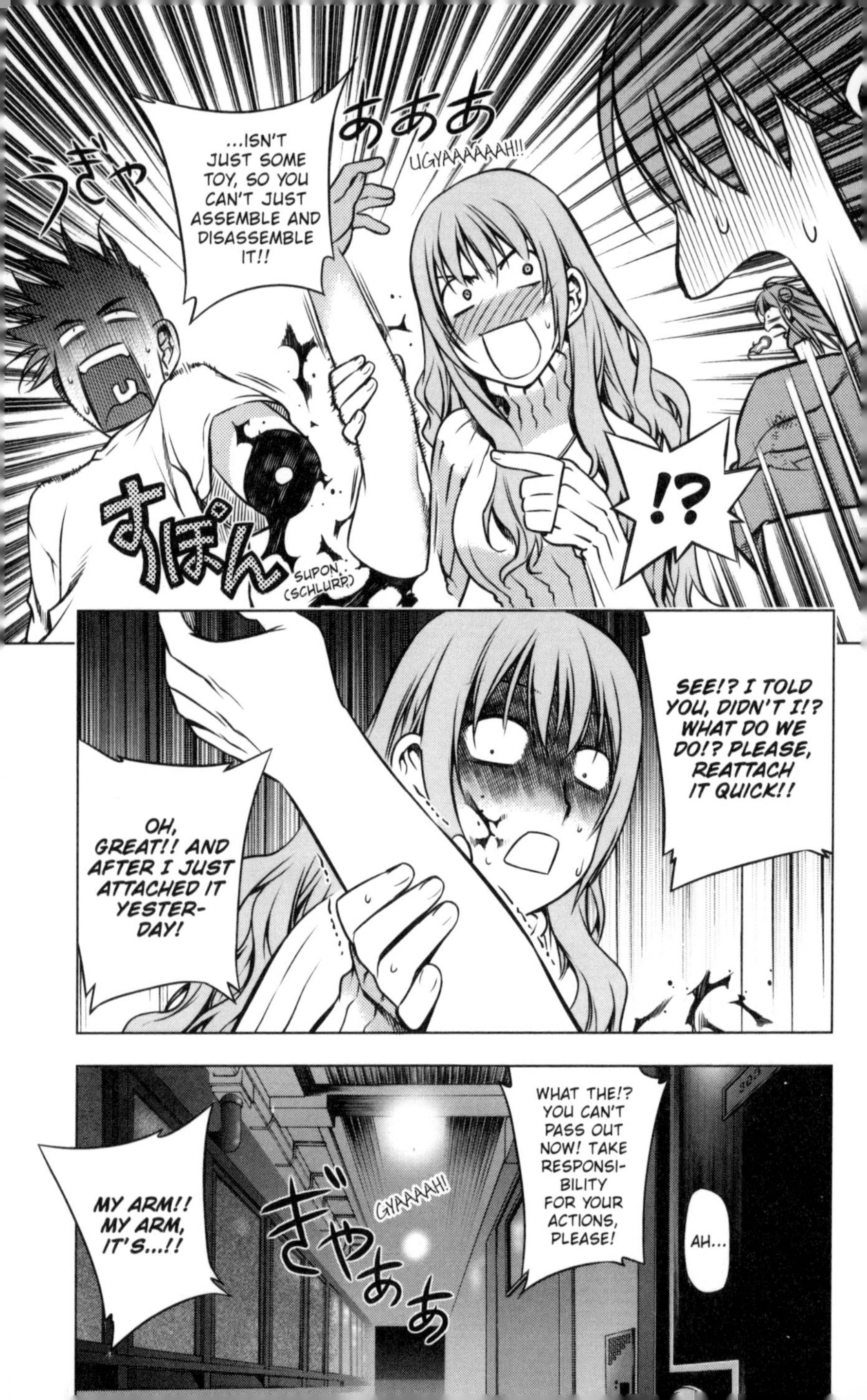
...ISN'T JUST SOME TOY, SO YOU CAN'T JUST ASSEMBLE AND DISASSEMBLE IT!!
うぎゃあああ
UGYAAAAAAH!!
!?
すぽん
SUPON (SCHLURP)
SEE!? I TOLD YOU, DIDN'T I!? WHAT DO WE DO!? PLEASE, REATTACH IT QUICK!!
OH, GREAT!! AND AFTER I JUST ATTACHED IT YESTER-DAY!
AH...
WHAT THE!? YOU CAN'T PASS OUT NOW! TAKE RESPONSI-BILITY FOR YOUR ACTIONS, PLEASE!
ぎゃあああ
GYAAAAH!
MY ARM!! MY ARM, IT'S...!!

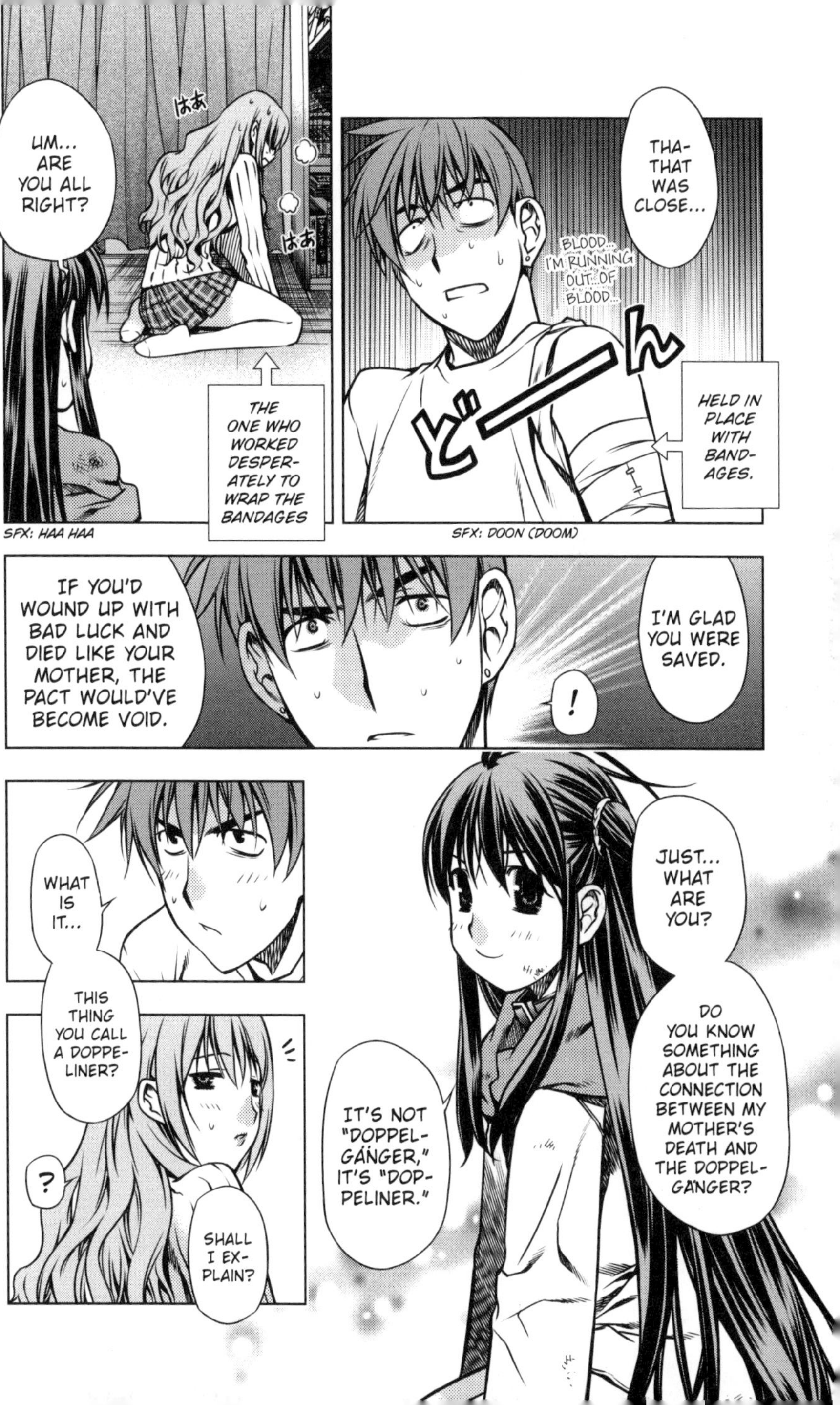
THA-THAT WAS CLOSE...
BLOOD... I'M RUNNING OUT OF BLOOD...
どーーん
HELD IN PLACE WITH BANDAGES.
SFX: DOON (DOOM)
はあ
UM... ARE YOU ALL RIGHT?
はあ
THE ONE WHO WORKED DESPERATELY TO WRAP THE BANDAGES
SFX: HAA HAA
I'M GLAD YOU WERE SAVED.
!
IF YOU'D WOUND UP WITH BAD LUCK AND DIED LIKE YOUR MOTHER, THE PACT WOULD'VE BECOME VOID.
JUST... WHAT ARE YOU?
DO YOU KNOW SOMETHING ABOUT THE CONNECTION BETWEEN MY MOTHER'S DEATH AND THE DOPPELGÄNGER?
IT'S NOT "DOPPELGÄNGER," IT'S "DOPPELINER."
WHAT IS IT...
THIS THING YOU CALL A DOPPELINER?
?
SHALL I EXPLAIN?

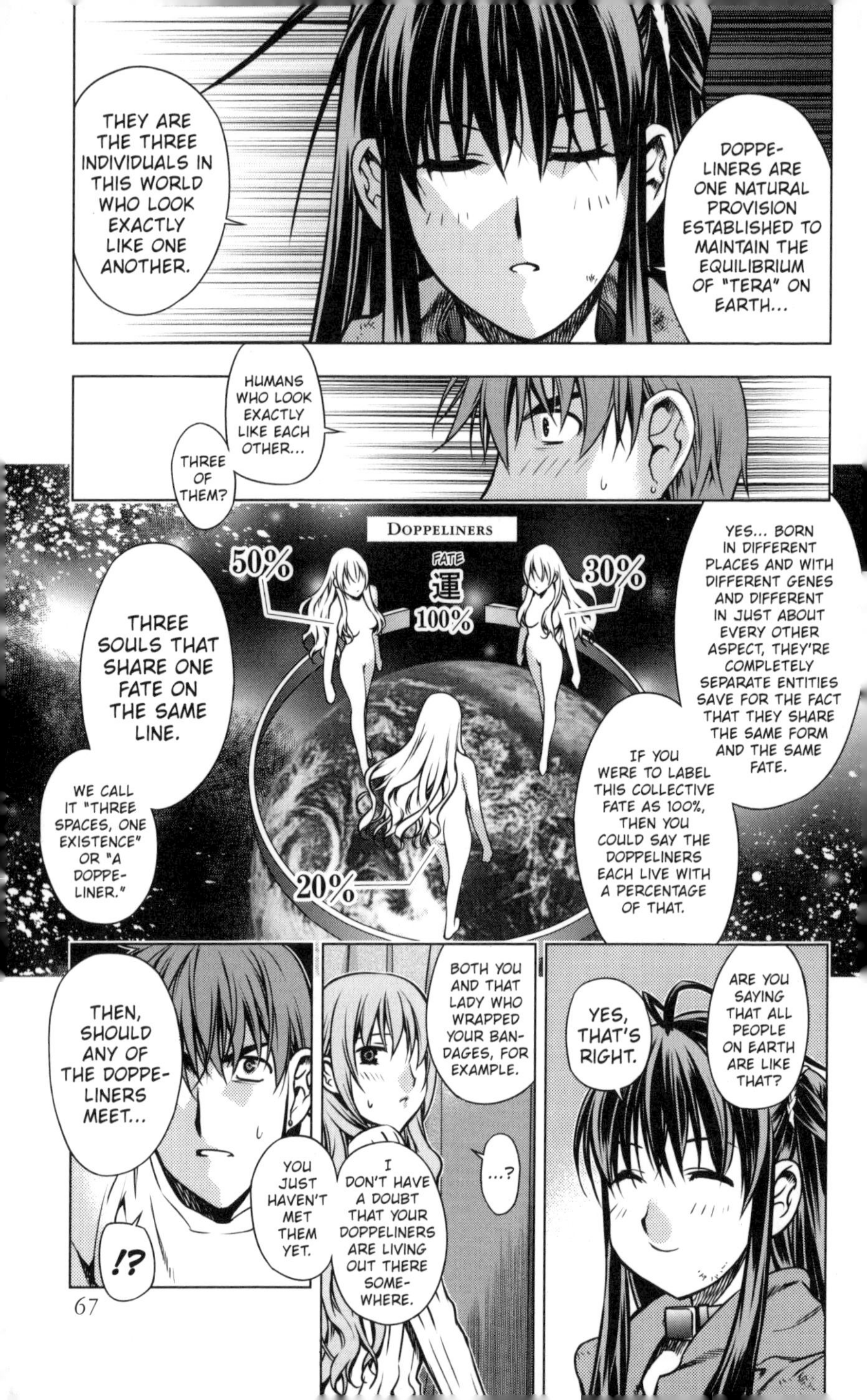
DOPPE-LINERS ARE ONE NATURAL PROVISION ESTABLISHED TO MAINTAIN THE EQUILIBRIUM OF "TERA" ON EARTH...
THEY ARE THE THREE INDIVIDUALS IN THIS WORLD WHO LOOK EXACTLY LIKE ONE ANOTHER.
HUMANS WHO LOOK EXACTLY LIKE EACH OTHER...
THREE OF THEM?
DOPPELINERS
50%
FATE
運
100%
30%
20%
YES... BORN IN DIFFERENT PLACES AND WITH DIFFERENT GENES AND DIFFERENT IN JUST ABOUT EVERY OTHER ASPECT, THEY'RE COMPLETELY SEPARATE ENTITIES SAVE FOR THE FACT THAT THEY SHARE THE SAME FORM AND THE SAME FATE.
IF YOU WERE TO LABEL THIS COLLECTIVE FATE AS 100%, THEN YOU COULD SAY THE DOPPELINERS EACH LIVE WITH A PERCENTAGE OF THAT.
THREE SOULS THAT SHARE ONE FATE ON THE SAME LINE.
WE CALL IT "THREE SPACES, ONE EXISTENCE" OR "A DOPPE-LINER."
ARE YOU SAYING THAT ALL PEOPLE ON EARTH ARE LIKE THAT?
YES, THAT'S RIGHT.
BOTH YOU AND THAT LADY WHO WRAPPED YOUR BAN-DAGES, FOR EXAMPLE.
...?
I DON'T HAVE A DOUBT THAT YOUR DOPPELINERS ARE LIVING OUT THERE SOME-WHERE.
YOU JUST HAVEN'T MET THEM YET.
THEN, SHOULD ANY OF THE DOPPE-LINERS MEET...
!?

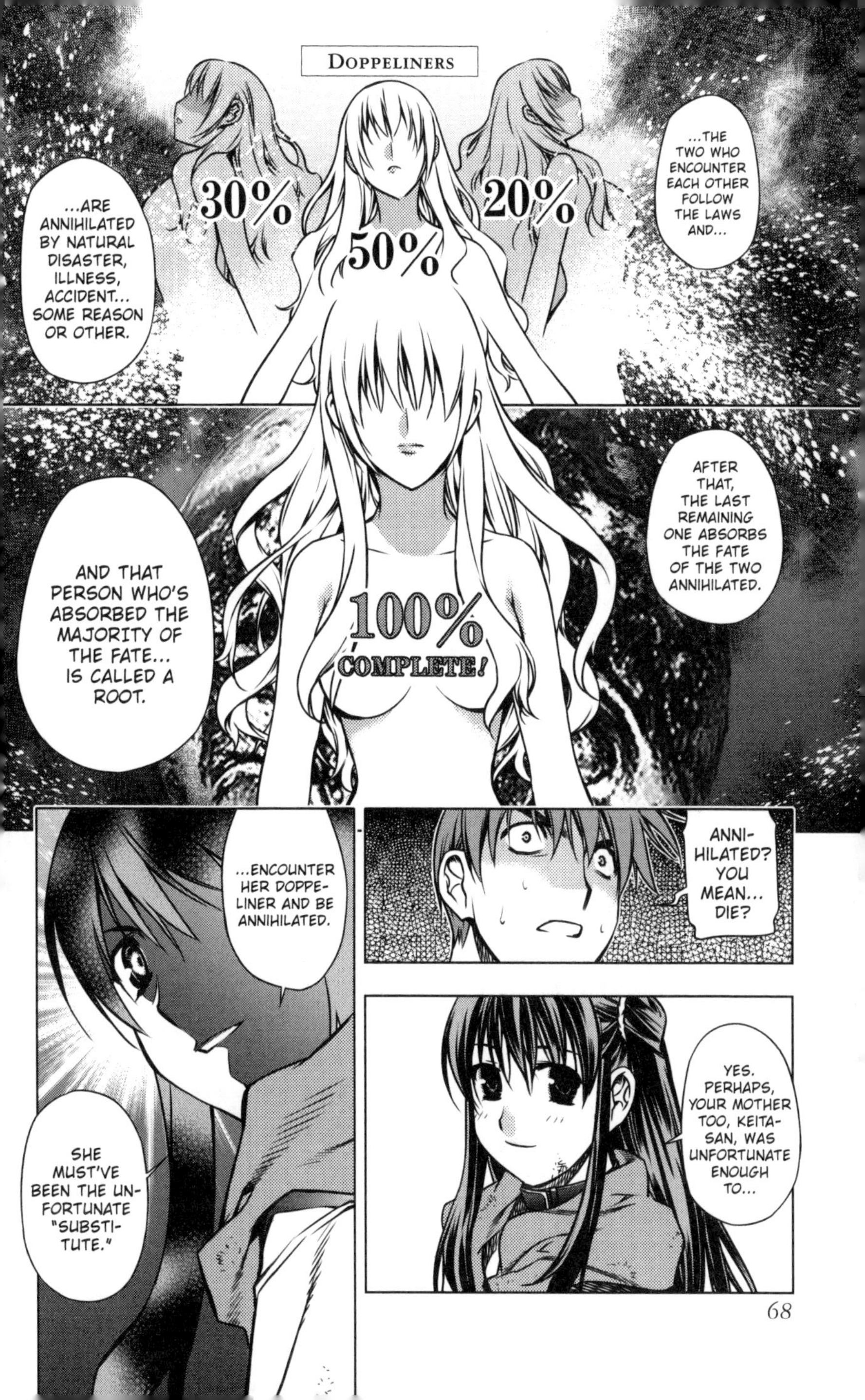
DOPPELINERS
...THE TWO WHO ENCOUNTER EACH OTHER FOLLOW THE LAWS AND...
20%
50%
30%
...ARE ANNIHILATED BY NATURAL DISASTER, ILLNESS, ACCIDENT... SOME REASON OR OTHER.
AFTER THAT, THE LAST REMAINING ONE ABSORBS THE FATE OF THE TWO ANNIHILATED.
100% COMPLETE!
AND THAT PERSON WHO'S ABSORBED THE MAJORITY OF THE FATE... IS CALLED A ROOT.
ANNI-HILATED? YOU MEAN... DIE?
YES. PERHAPS, YOUR MOTHER TOO, KEITA-SAN, WAS UNFORTUNATE ENOUGH TO...
...ENCOUNTER HER DOPPE-LINER AND BE ANNIHILATED.
SHE MUST'VE BEEN THE UN-FORTUNATE "SUBSTI-TUTE."

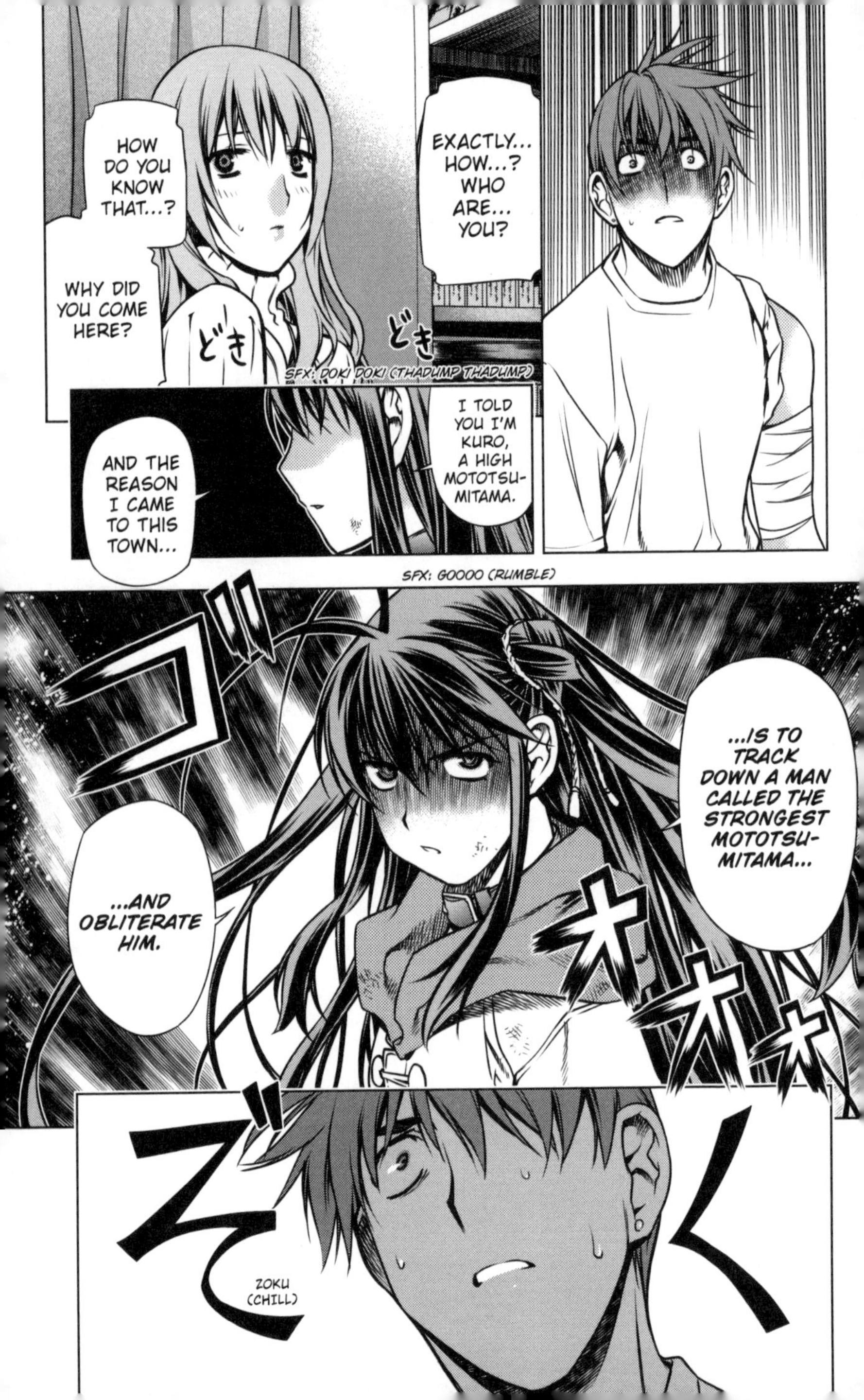
EXACTLY... HOW...? WHO ARE... YOU?
HOW DO YOU KNOW THAT...?
WHY DID YOU COME HERE?
どき
どき
SFX: DOKI DOKI (THADUMP THADUMP)
I TOLD YOU I'M KURO, A HIGH MOTOTSU-MITAMA.
AND THE REASON I CAME TO THIS TOWN...
SFX: GOOOO (RUMBLE)
...IS TO TRACK DOWN A MAN CALLED THE STRONGEST MOTOTSU-MITAMA...
...AND OBLITERATE HIM.
ZOKU (CHILL)

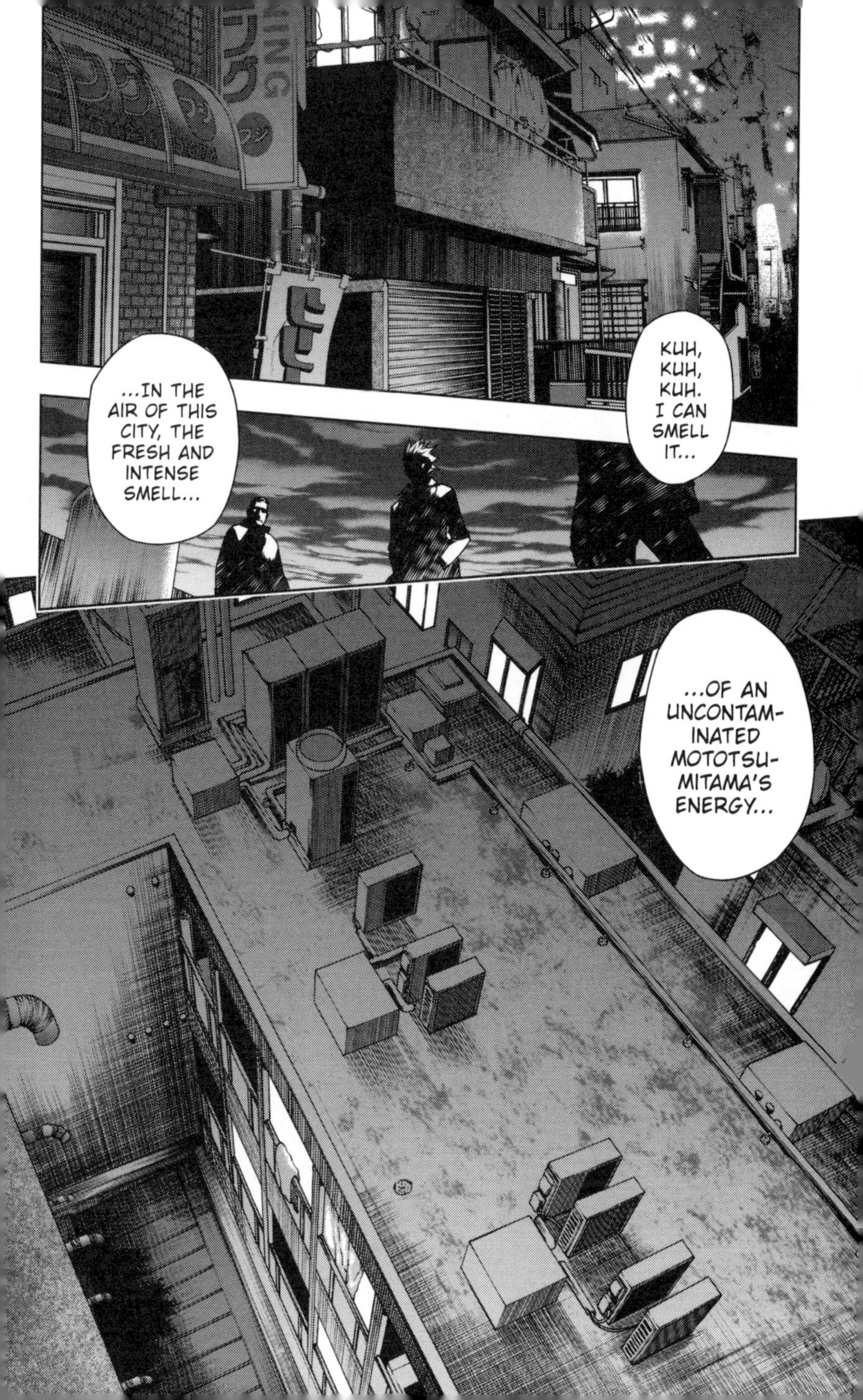
KUH, KUH, KUH. I CAN SMELL IT...
...IN THE AIR OF THIS CITY, THE FRESH AND INTENSE SMELL...
...OF AN UNCONTAMINATED MOTOTSUMITAMA'S ENERGY...

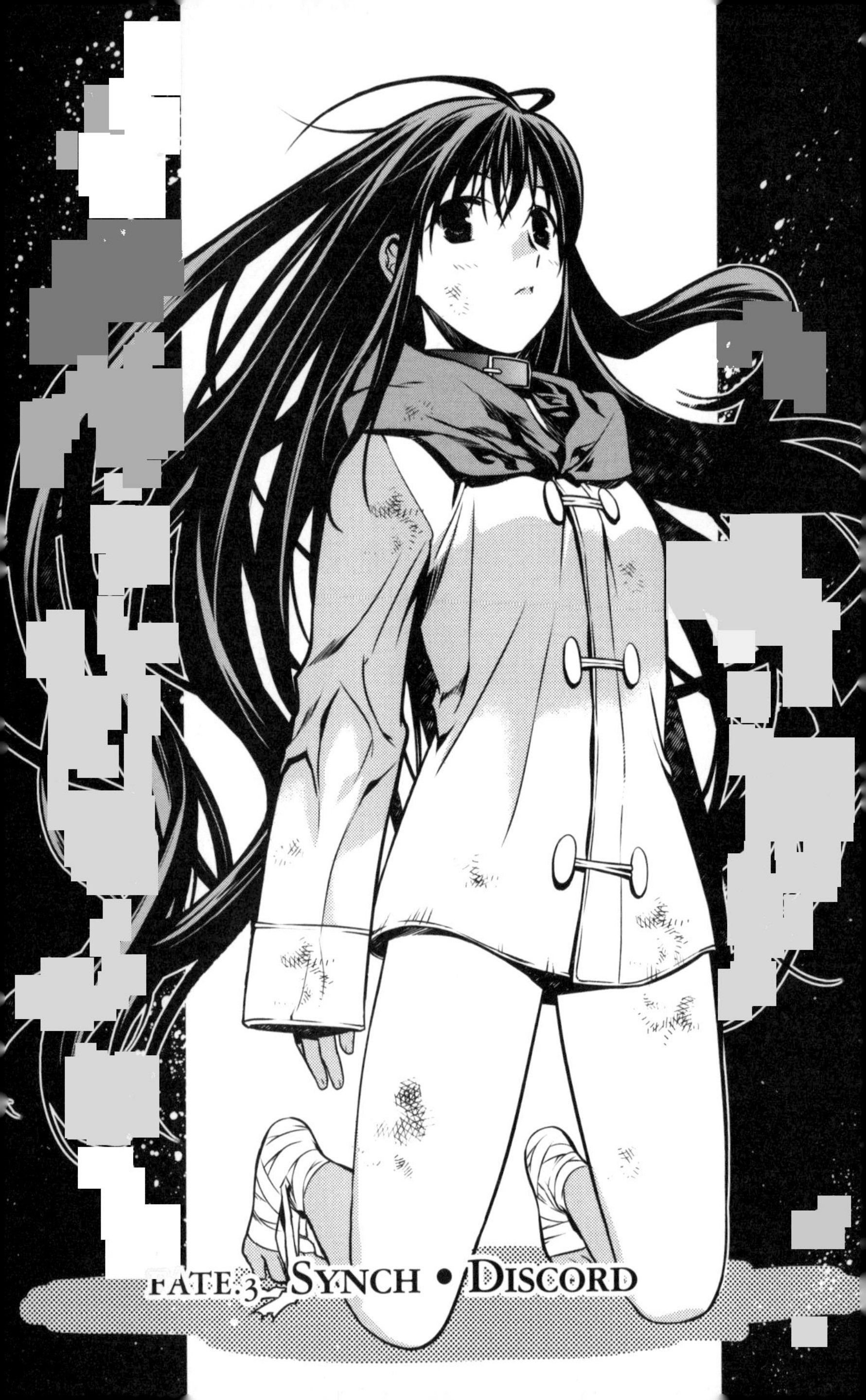
FATE.3 SYNCH • DISCORD

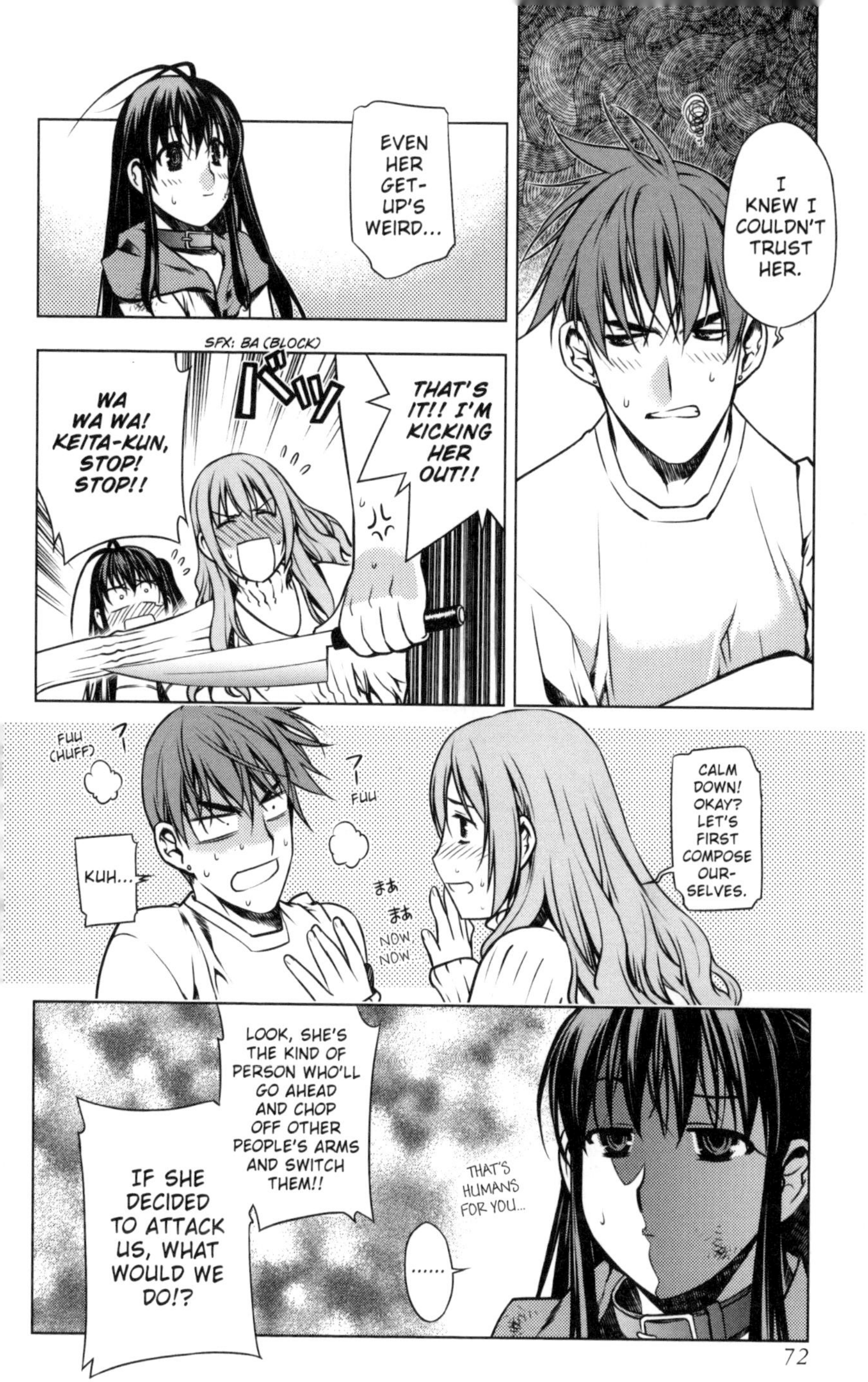
I KNEW I COULDN'T TRUST HER.
EVEN HER GET-UP'S WEIRD...
THAT'S IT!! I'M KICKING HER OUT!!
SFX: BA (BLOCK)
WA WA WA! KEITA-KUN, STOP! STOP!!
CALM DOWN! OKAY? LET'S FIRST COMPOSE OURSELVES.
まあ まあ
NOW NOW
FUU
KUH...
FUU (CHUFF)
THAT'S HUMANS FOR YOU...
......
LOOK, SHE'S THE KIND OF PERSON WHO'LL GO AHEAD AND CHOP OFF OTHER PEOPLE'S ARMS AND SWITCH THEM!!
IF SHE DECIDED TO ATTACK US, WHAT WOULD WE DO!?

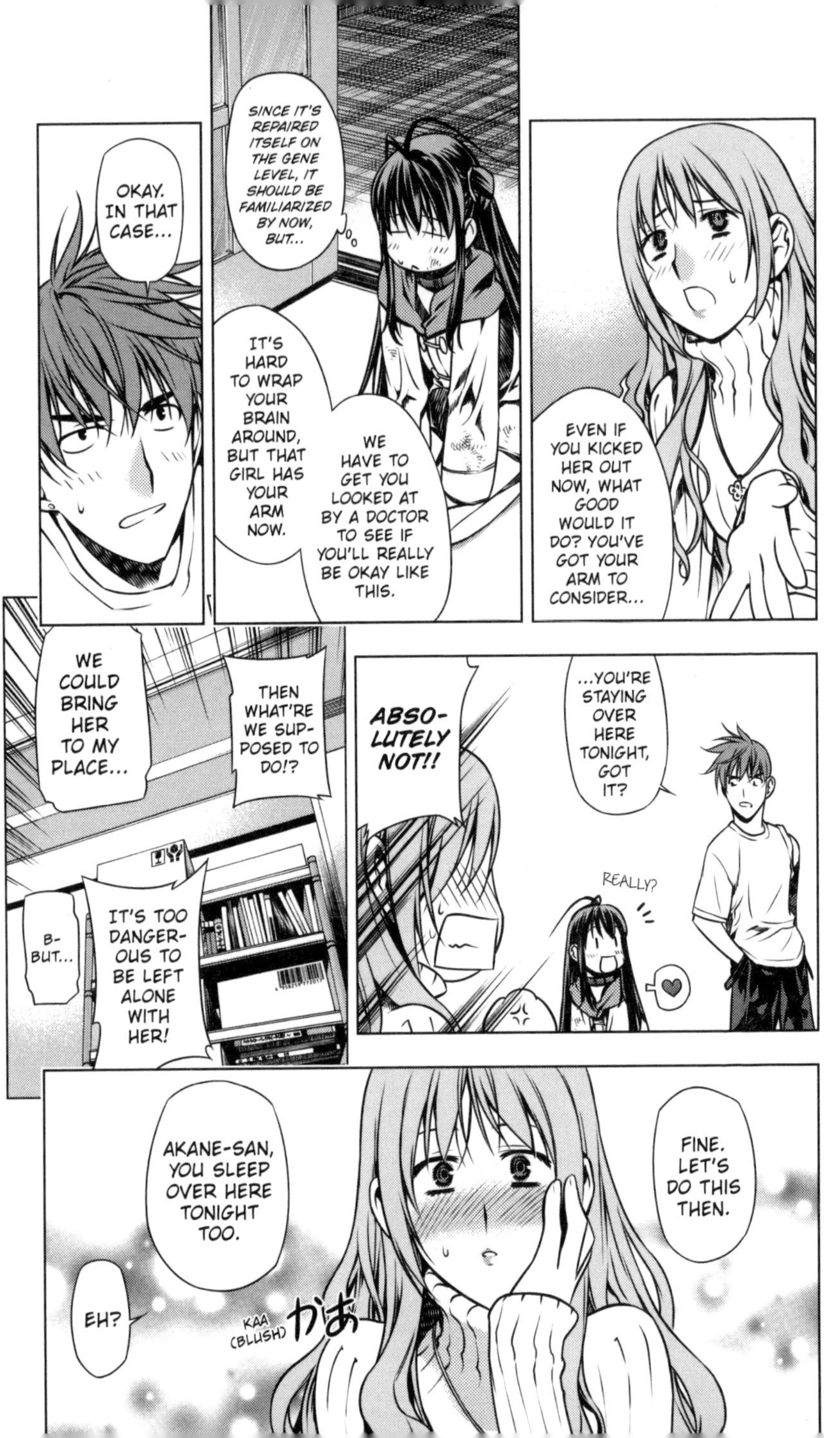
EVEN IF YOU KICKED HER OUT NOW, WHAT GOOD WOULD IT DO? YOU'VE GOT YOUR ARM TO CONSIDER...
SINCE IT'S REPAIRED ITSELF ON THE GENE LEVEL, IT SHOULD BE FAMILIARIZED BY NOW, BUT...
IT'S HARD TO WRAP YOUR BRAIN AROUND, BUT THAT GIRL HAS YOUR ARM NOW.
WE HAVE TO GET YOU LOOKED AT BY A DOCTOR TO SEE IF YOU'LL REALLY BE OKAY LIKE THIS.
OKAY. IN THAT CASE...
...YOU'RE STAYING OVER HERE TONIGHT, GOT IT?
ABSO-LUTELY NOT!!
REALLY?
THEN WHAT'RE WE SUP-POSED TO DO!?
WE COULD BRING HER TO MY PLACE...
IT'S TOO DANGER-OUS TO BE LEFT ALONE WITH HER!
B-BUT...
FINE. LET'S DO THIS THEN.
AKANE-SAN, YOU SLEEP OVER HERE TONIGHT TOO.
KAA (BLUSH) かあ
EH?

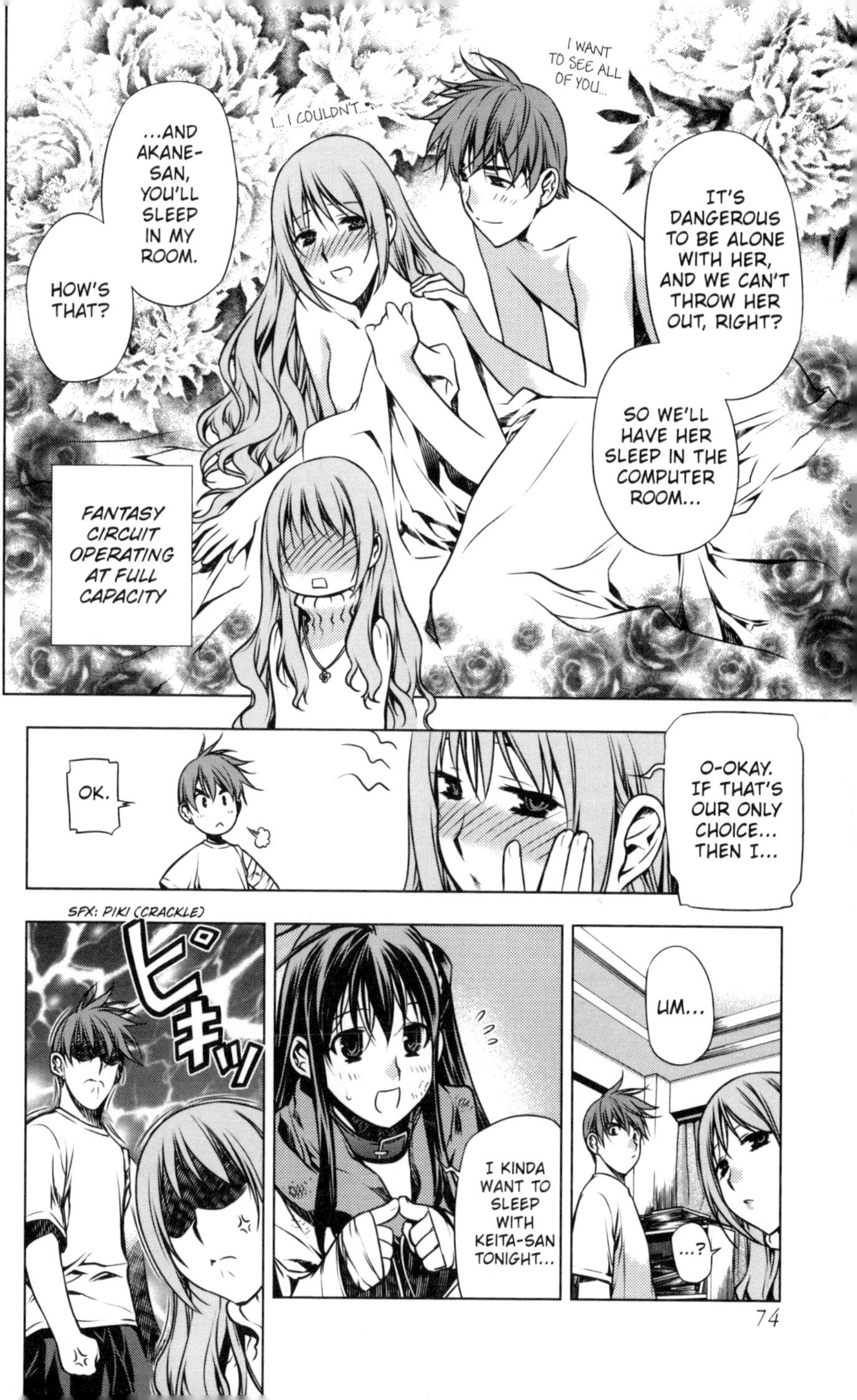
I WANT TO SEE ALL OF YOU...
IT'S DANGEROUS TO BE ALONE WITH HER, AND WE CAN'T THROW HER OUT, RIGHT?
SO WE'LL HAVE HER SLEEP IN THE COMPUTER ROOM...
I... I COULDN'T...
...AND AKANE-SAN, YOU'LL SLEEP IN MY ROOM.
HOW'S THAT?
FANTASY CIRCUIT OPERATING AT FULL CAPACITY
O-OKAY. IF THAT'S OUR ONLY CHOICE... THEN I...
OK.
UM...
...?
I KINDA WANT TO SLEEP WITH KEITA-SAN TONIGHT...
SFX: PIKI (CRACKLE)
ピキッ

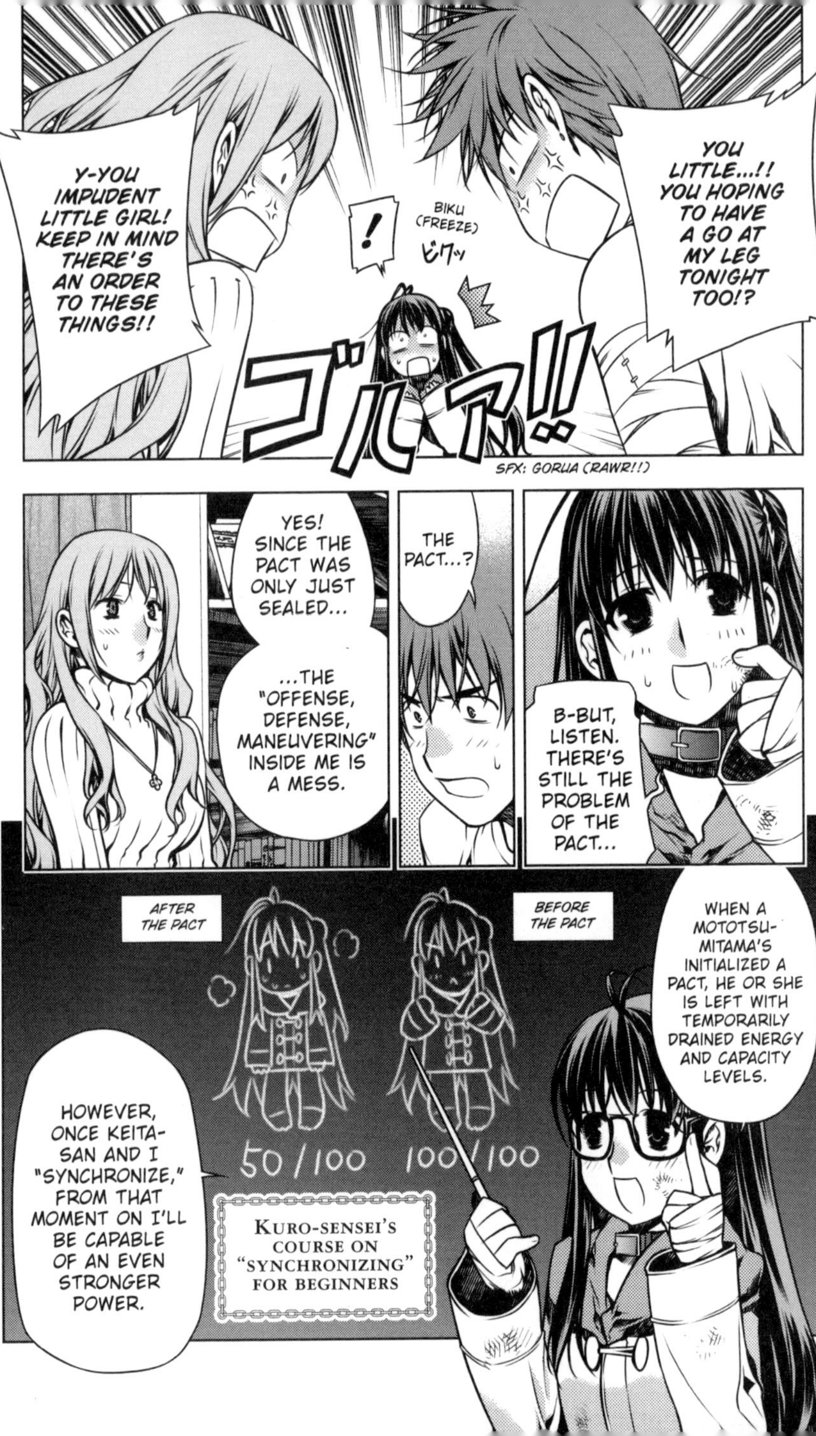
YOU LITTLE...!! YOU HOPING TO HAVE A GO AT MY LEG TONIGHT TOO!?
!
BIKU (FREEZE)
ビクッ
Y-YOU IMPUDENT LITTLE GIRL! KEEP IN MIND THERE'S AN ORDER TO THESE THINGS!!
ゴルア!!
SFX: GORUA (RAWR!!)
B-BUT, LISTEN. THERE'S STILL THE PROBLEM OF THE PACT...
THE PACT...?
YES! SINCE THE PACT WAS ONLY JUST SEALED...
...THE "OFFENSE, DEFENSE, MANEUVERING" INSIDE ME IS A MESS.
WHEN A MOTOTSU-MITAMA'S INITIALIZED A PACT, HE OR SHE IS LEFT WITH TEMPORARILY DRAINED ENERGY AND CAPACITY LEVELS.
BEFORE THE PACT
AFTER THE PACT
100/100
50/100
HOWEVER, ONCE KEITA-SAN AND I "SYNCHRONIZE," FROM THAT MOMENT ON I'LL BE CAPABLE OF AN EVEN STRONGER POWER.
KURO-SENSEI'S COURSE ON "SYNCHRONIZING" FOR BEGINNERS

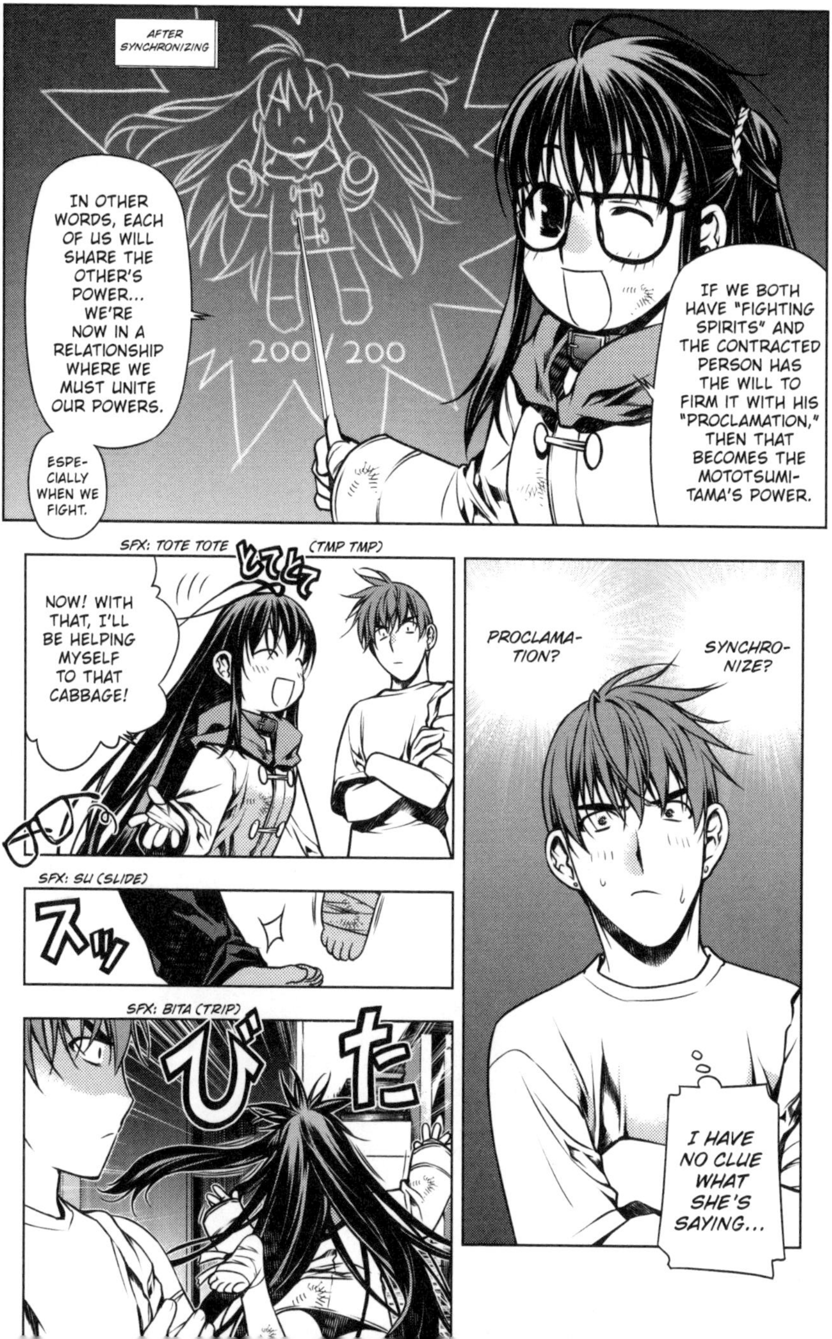
AFTER SYNCHRONIZING
IF WE BOTH HAVE "FIGHTING SPIRITS" AND THE CONTRACTED PERSON HAS THE WILL TO FIRM IT WITH HIS "PROCLAMATION," THEN THAT BECOMES THE MOTOTSUMI-TAMA'S POWER.
200/200
IN OTHER WORDS, EACH OF US WILL SHARE THE OTHER'S POWER... WE'RE NOW IN A RELATIONSHIP WHERE WE MUST UNITE OUR POWERS.
ESPE-CIALLY WHEN WE FIGHT.
SYNCHRO-NIZE?
PROCLAMA-TION?
I HAVE NO CLUE WHAT SHE'S SAYING...
SFX: TOTE TOTE (TMP TMP)
とてとて
NOW! WITH THAT, I'LL BE HELPING MYSELF TO THAT CABBAGE!
SFX: SU (SLIDE)
スッ
SFX: BITA (TRIP)
びた!

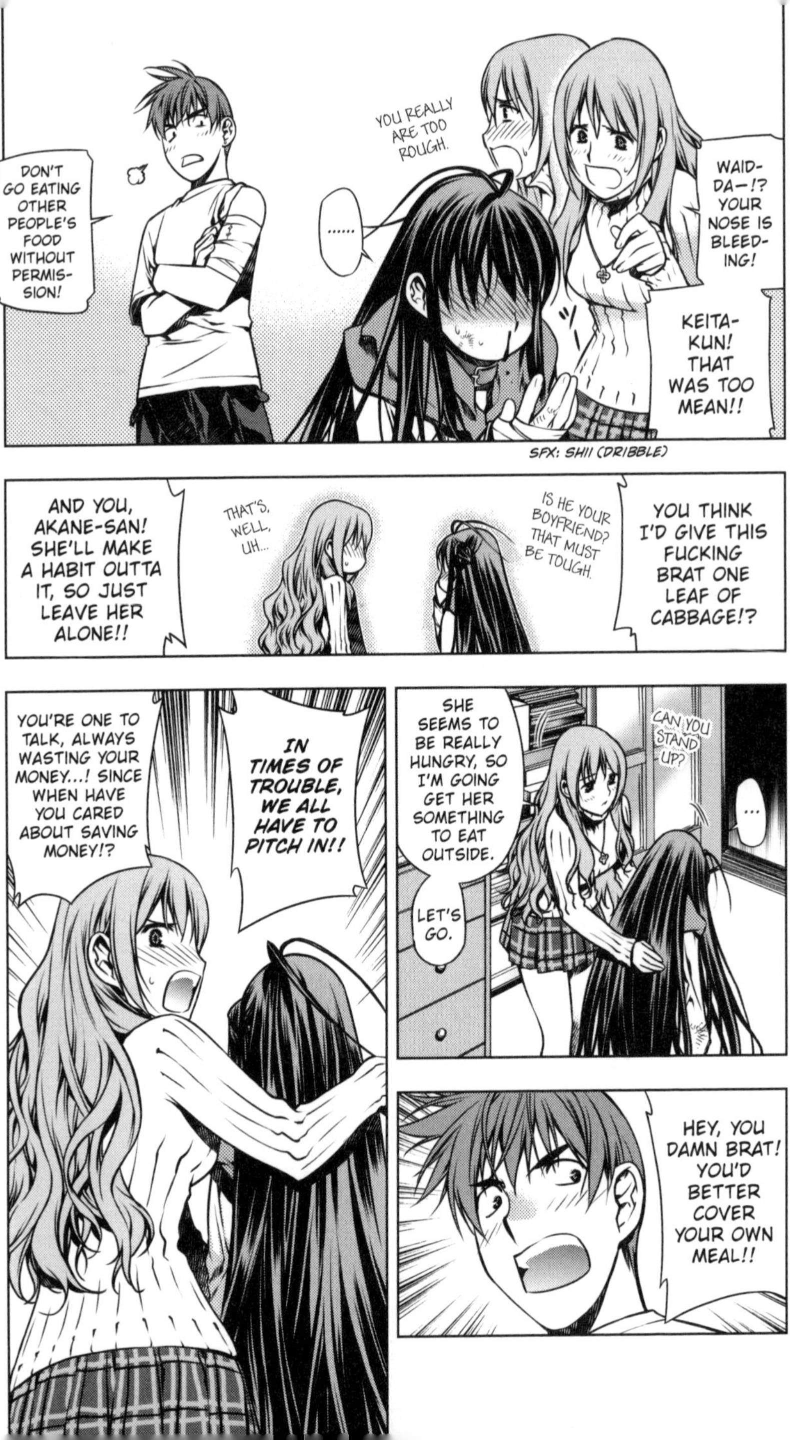
WAID-DA—!? YOUR NOSE IS BLEEDING!
YOU REALLY ARE TOO ROUGH.
KEITA-KUN! THAT WAS TOO MEAN!!
......
DON'T GO EATING OTHER PEOPLE'S FOOD WITHOUT PERMISSION!
SFX: SHII (DRIBBLE)
YOU THINK I'D GIVE THIS FUCKING BRAT ONE LEAF OF CABBAGE!?
IS HE YOUR BOYFRIEND? THAT MUST BE TOUGH.
THAT'S, WELL, UH...
AND YOU, AKANE-SAN! SHE'LL MAKE A HABIT OUTTA IT, SO JUST LEAVE HER ALONE!!
SHE SEEMS TO BE REALLY HUNGRY, SO I'M GOING GET HER SOMETHING TO EAT OUTSIDE.
CAN YOU STAND UP?
...
LET'S GO.
HEY, YOU DAMN BRAT! YOU'D BETTER COVER YOUR OWN MEAL!!
IN TIMES OF TROUBLE, WE ALL HAVE TO PITCH IN!!
YOU'RE ONE TO TALK, ALWAYS WASTING YOUR MONEY...! SINCE WHEN HAVE YOU CARED ABOUT SAVING MONEY!?

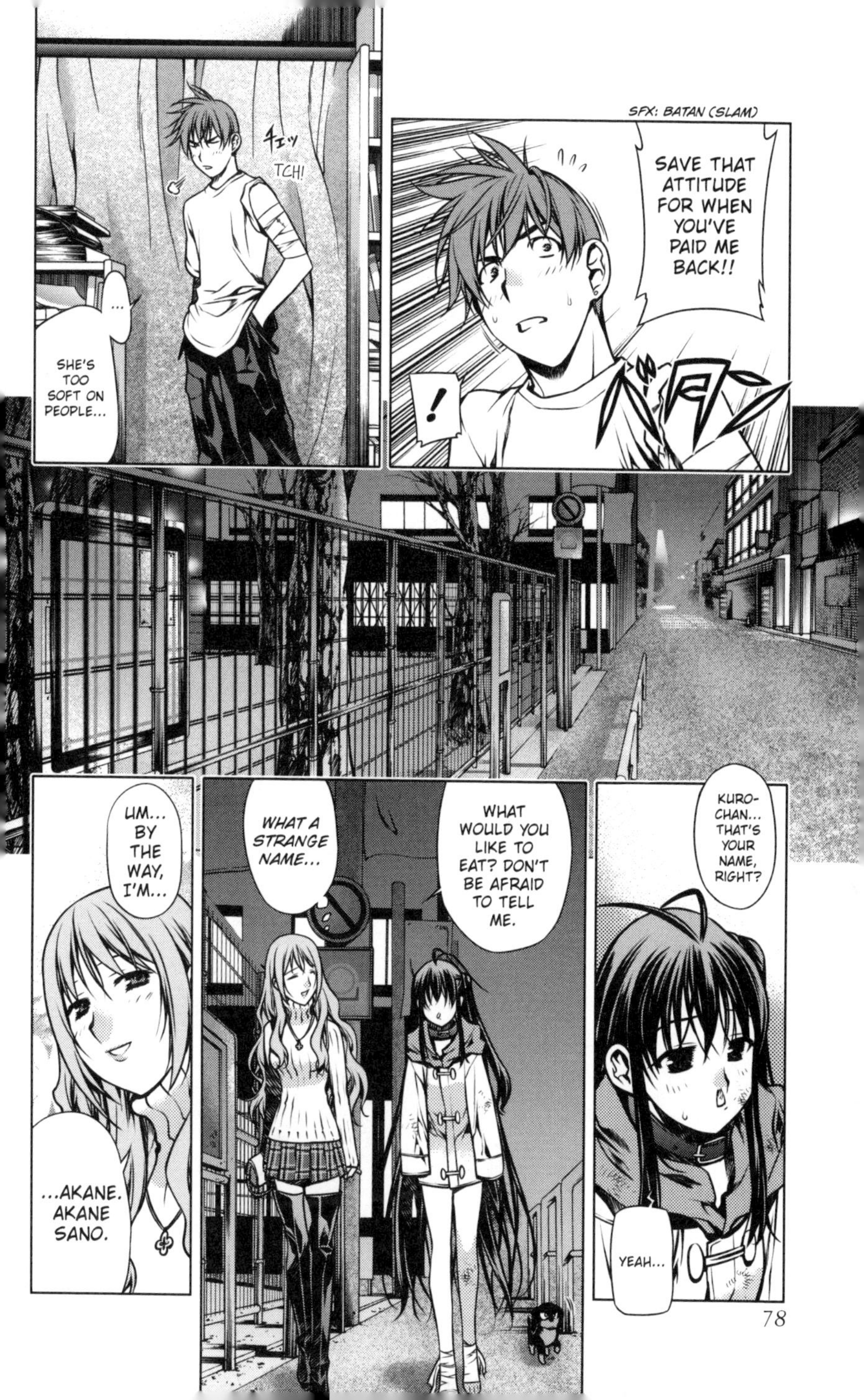
SFX: BATAN (SLAM)
SAVE THAT ATTITUDE FOR WHEN YOU'VE PAID ME BACK!!
!
チェッ
TCH!
...
SHE'S TOO SOFT ON PEOPLE...
KURO-CHAN... THAT'S YOUR NAME, RIGHT?
YEAH...
WHAT WOULD YOU LIKE TO EAT? DON'T BE AFRAID TO TELL ME.
WHAT A STRANGE NAME...
UM... BY THE WAY, I'M...
...AKANE. AKANE SANO.

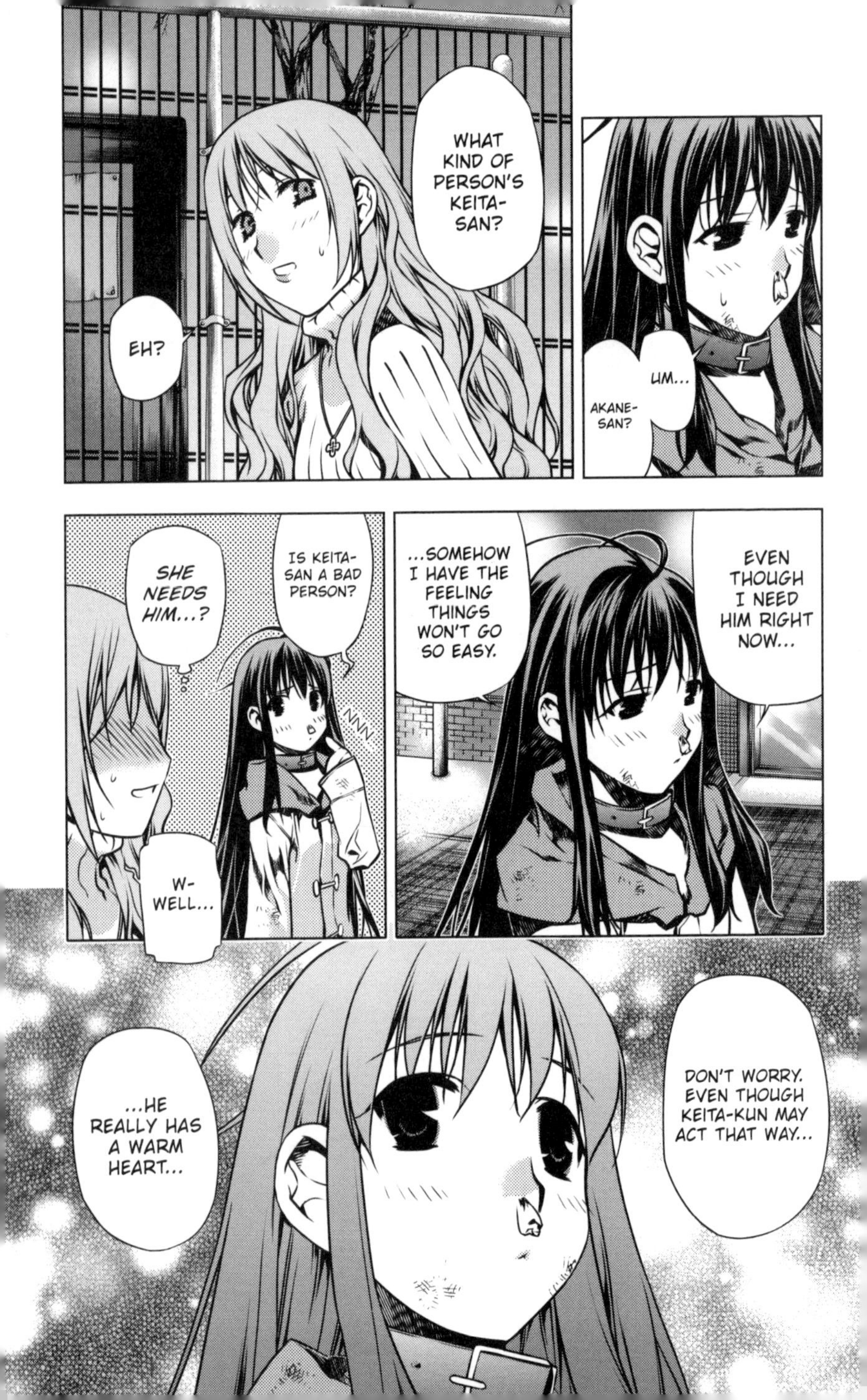
UM...
AKANE-SAN?
WHAT KIND OF PERSON'S KEITA-SAN?
EH?
EVEN THOUGH I NEED HIM RIGHT NOW...
...SOMEHOW I HAVE THE FEELING THINGS WON'T GO SO EASY.
IS KEITA-SAN A BAD PERSON?
SHE NEEDS HIM...?
NNN
W-WELL...
DON'T WORRY. EVEN THOUGH KEITA-KUN MAY ACT THAT WAY...
...HE REALLY HAS A WARM HEART...

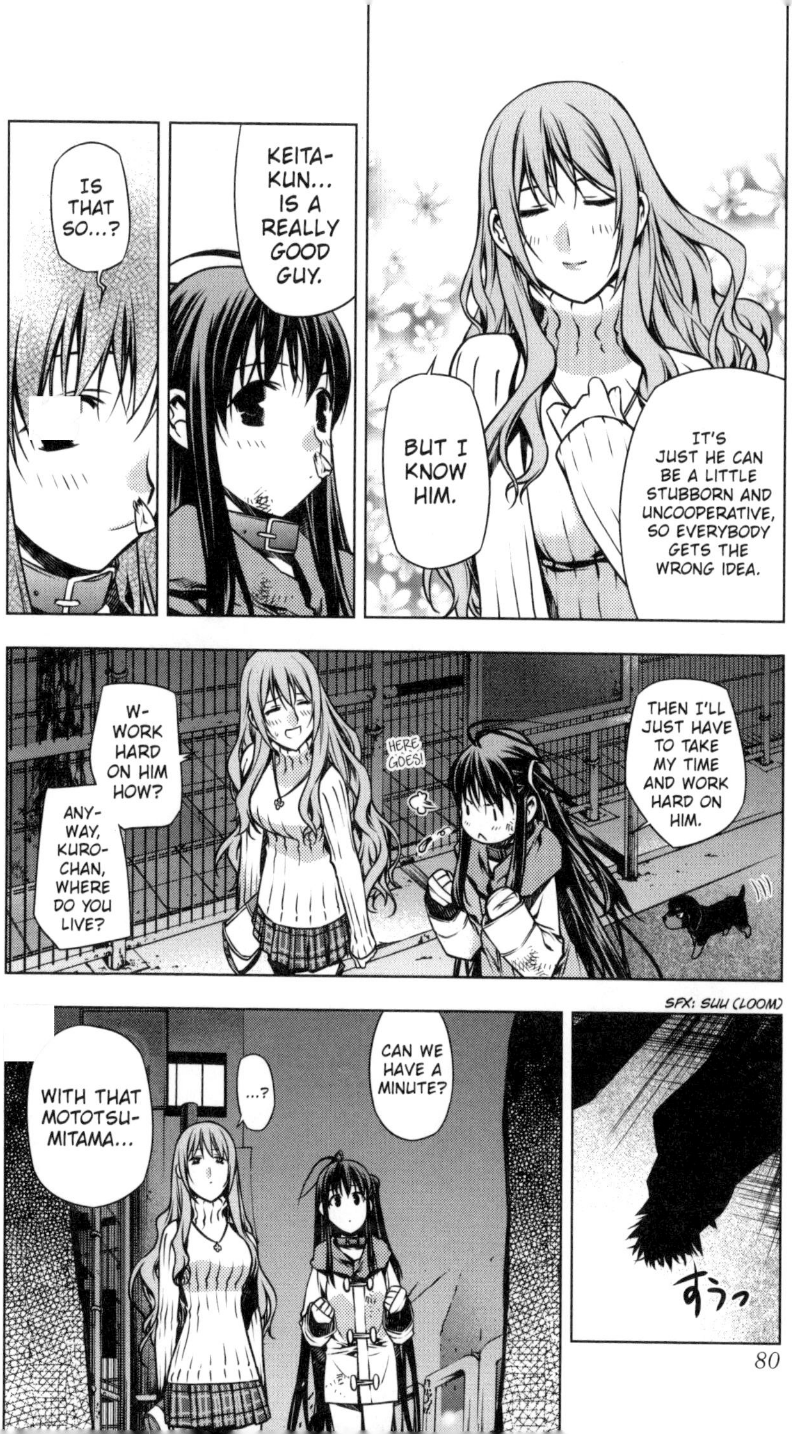
IT'S JUST HE CAN BE A LITTLE STUBBORN AND UNCOOPERATIVE, SO EVERYBODY GETS THE WRONG IDEA.
BUT I KNOW HIM.
KEITA-KUN... IS A REALLY GOOD GUY.
IS THAT SO...?
THEN I'LL JUST HAVE TO TAKE MY TIME AND WORK HARD ON HIM.
HERE GOES!
W-WORK HARD ON HIM HOW?
ANYWAY, KURO-CHAN, WHERE DO YOU LIVE?
SFX: SUU (LOOM)
すうっ
CAN WE HAVE A MINUTE?
...?
WITH THAT MOTOTSUMITAMA...

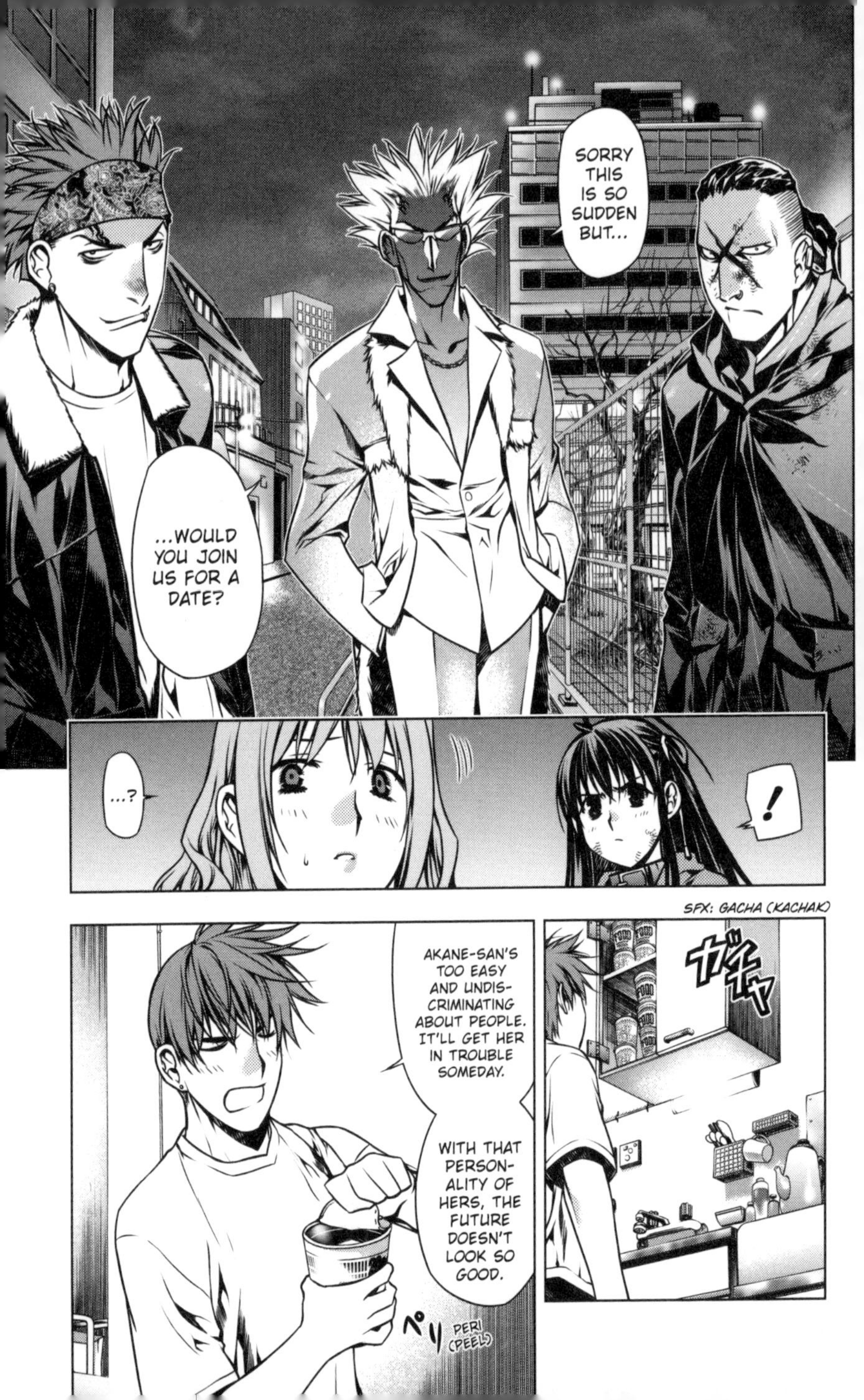
SORRY THIS IS SO SUDDEN BUT...
...WOULD YOU JOIN US FOR A DATE?
!
...?
SFX: GACHA (KACHAK)
ガチャ
AKANE-SAN'S TOO EASY AND UNDIS-CRIMINATING ABOUT PEOPLE. IT'LL GET HER IN TROUBLE SOMEDAY.
WITH THAT PERSON-ALITY OF HERS, THE FUTURE DOESN'T LOOK SO GOOD.
ペリ
PERI (PEEL)

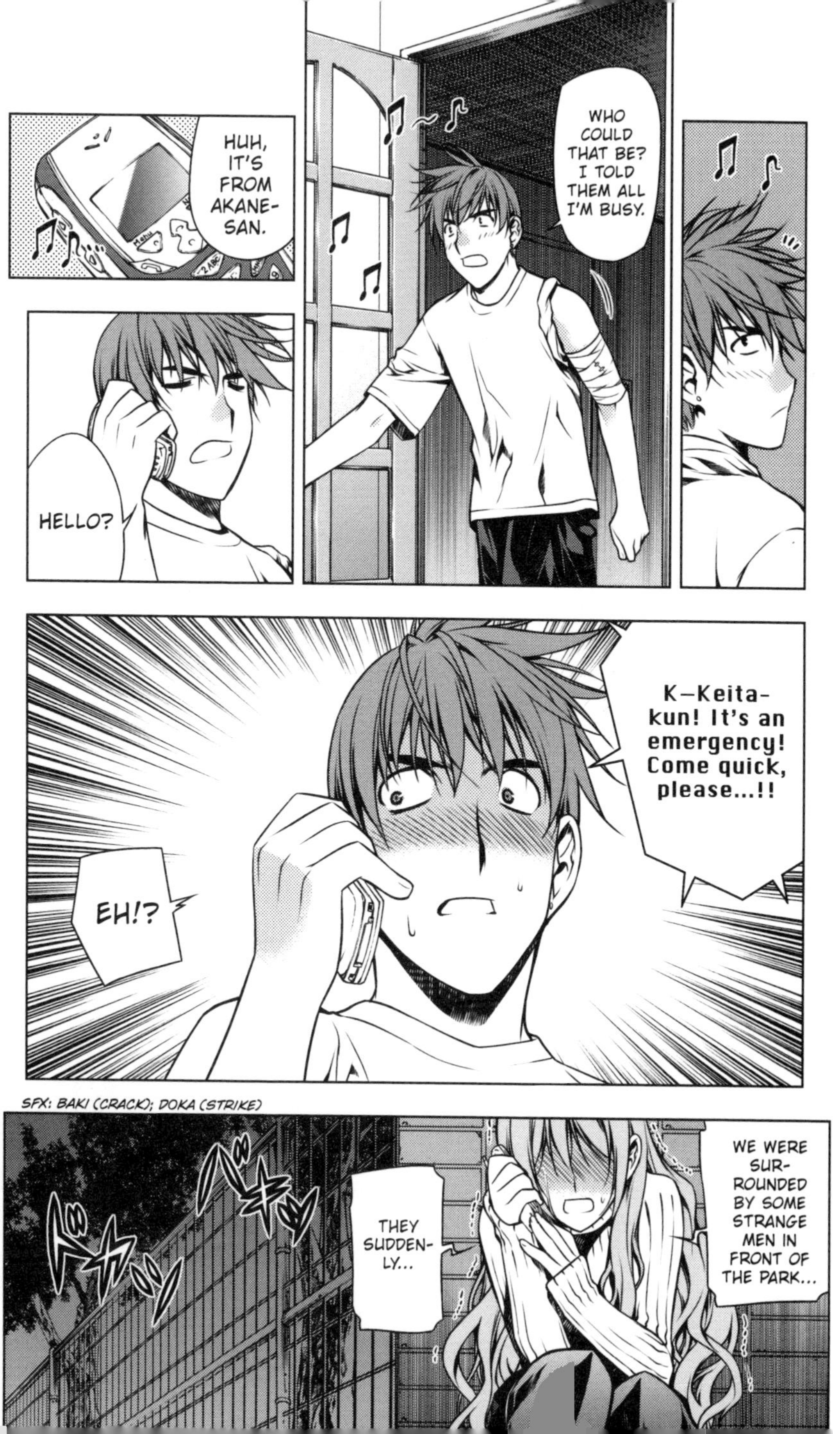
WHO COULD THAT BE? I TOLD THEM ALL I'M BUSY.
HUH, IT'S FROM AKANE-SAN.
HELLO?
K—Keita-kun! It's an emergency! Come quick, please...!!
EH!?
SFX: BAKI (CRACK); DOKA (STRIKE)
WE WERE SUR-ROUNDED BY SOME STRANGE MEN IN FRONT OF THE PARK...
THEY SUDDEN-LY...

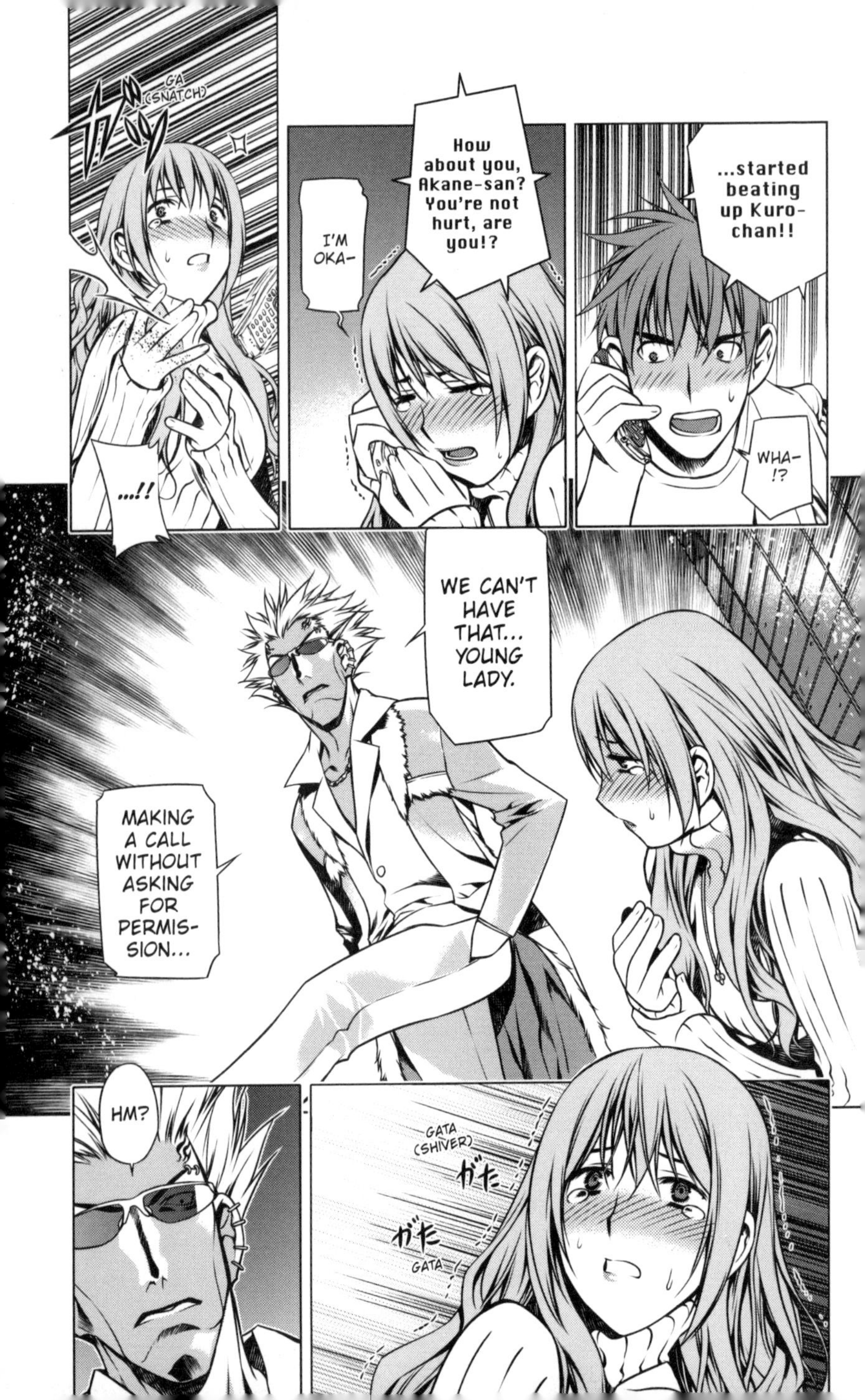
...started beating up Kuro-chan!!
WHA-!?
How about you, Akane-san? You're not hurt, are you!?
I'M OKA-
GA (SNATCH)
...!!
WE CAN'T HAVE THAT... YOUNG LADY.
MAKING A CALL WITHOUT ASKING FOR PERMIS-SION...
GATA (SHIVER)
GATA
HM?

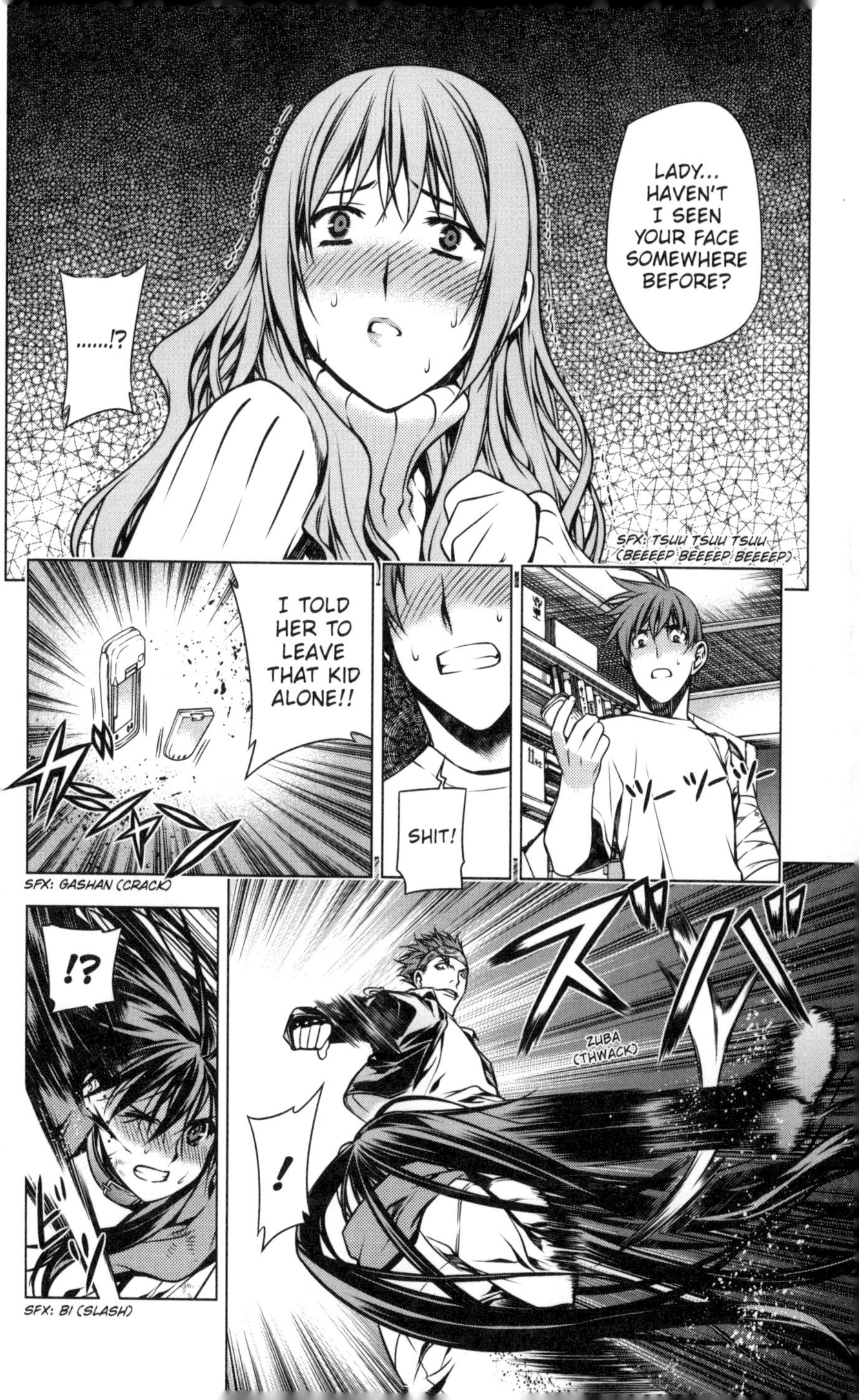
LADY... HAVEN'T I SEEN YOUR FACE SOMEWHERE BEFORE?
......!?
SFX: TSUU TSUU TSUU (BEEEEP BEEEEP BEEEEP)
SHIT!
I TOLD HER TO LEAVE THAT KID ALONE!!
SFX: GASHAN (CRACK)
ZUBA (THWACK)
!
!?
SFX: BI (SLASH)

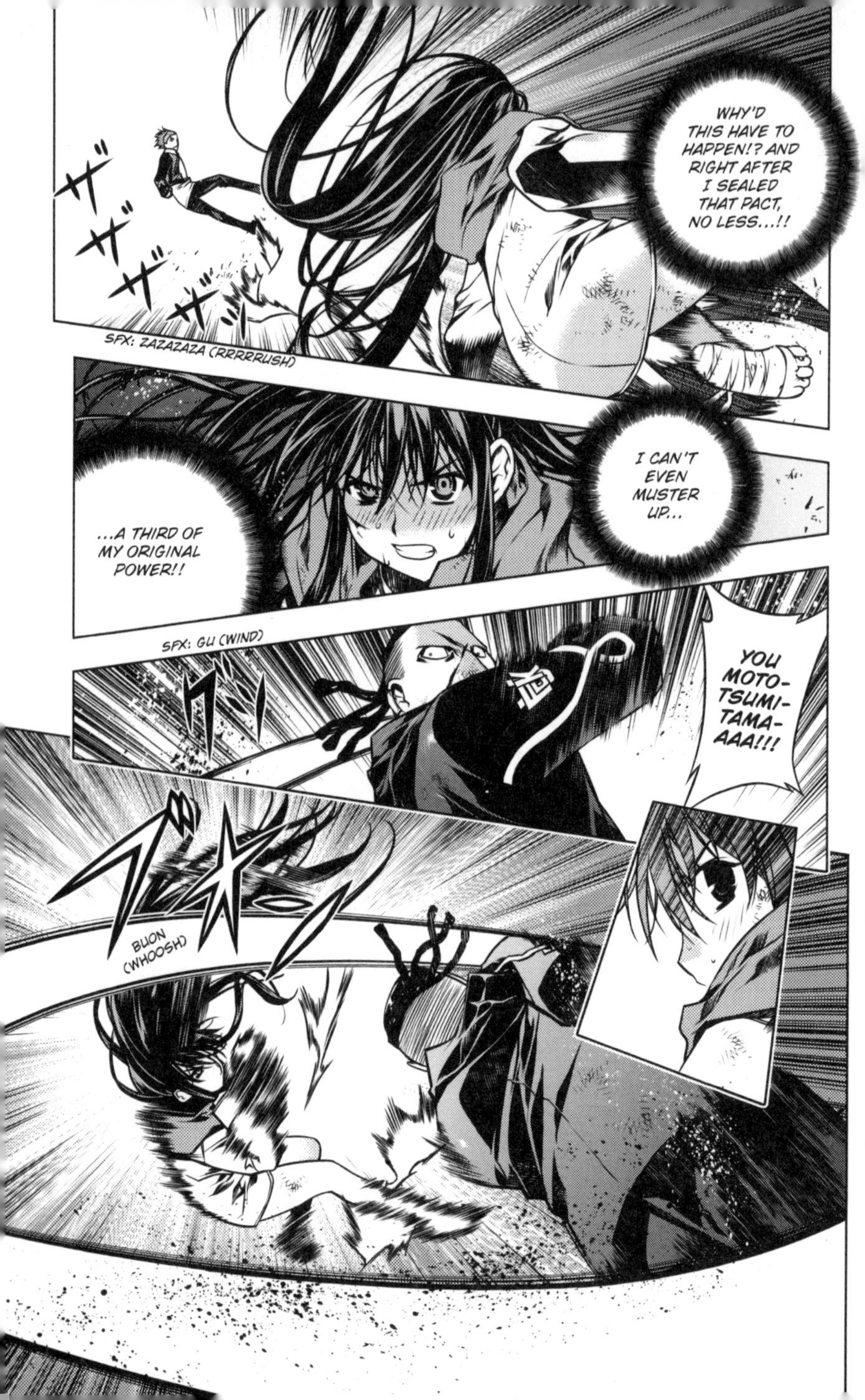
WHY'D THIS HAVE TO HAPPEN!? AND RIGHT AFTER I SEALED THAT PACT, NO LESS...!!
SFX: ZAZAZAZA (RRRRRUSH)
I CAN'T EVEN MUSTER UP...
...A THIRD OF MY ORIGINAL POWER!!
YOU MOTO-TSUMI-TAMA-AAA!!!
SFX: GU (WIND)
BUON (WHOOSH)

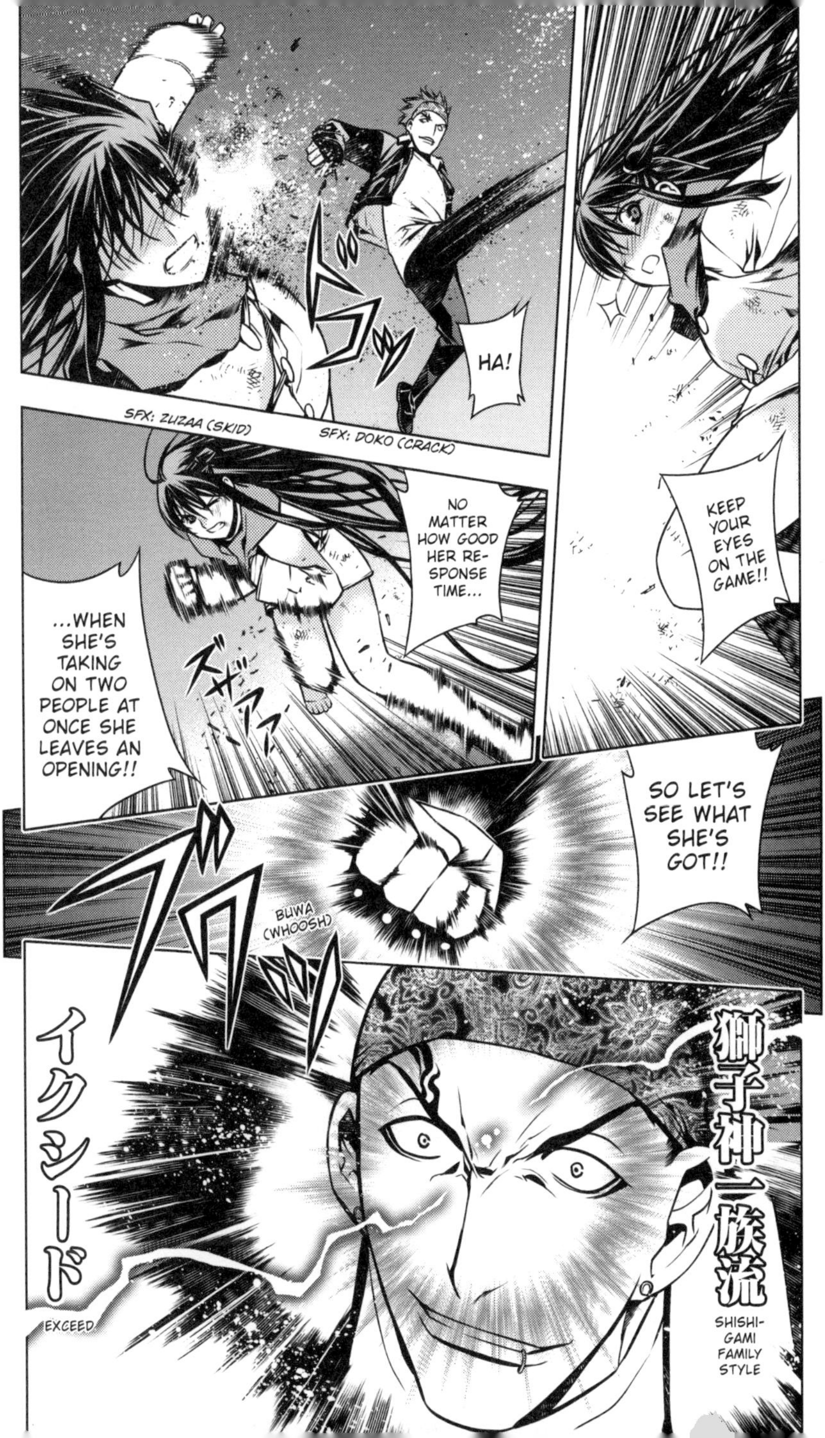
KEEP YOUR EYES ON THE GAME!!
HA!
SFX: DOKO (CRACK)
SFX: ZUZAA (SKID)
NO MATTER HOW GOOD HER RE-SPONSE TIME...
...WHEN SHE'S TAKING ON TWO PEOPLE AT ONCE SHE LEAVES AN OPENING!!
SO LET'S SEE WHAT SHE'S GOT!!
BUWA (WHOOSH)
獅子神一族流
SHISHI-GAMI FAMILY STYLE
イクシード
EXCEED

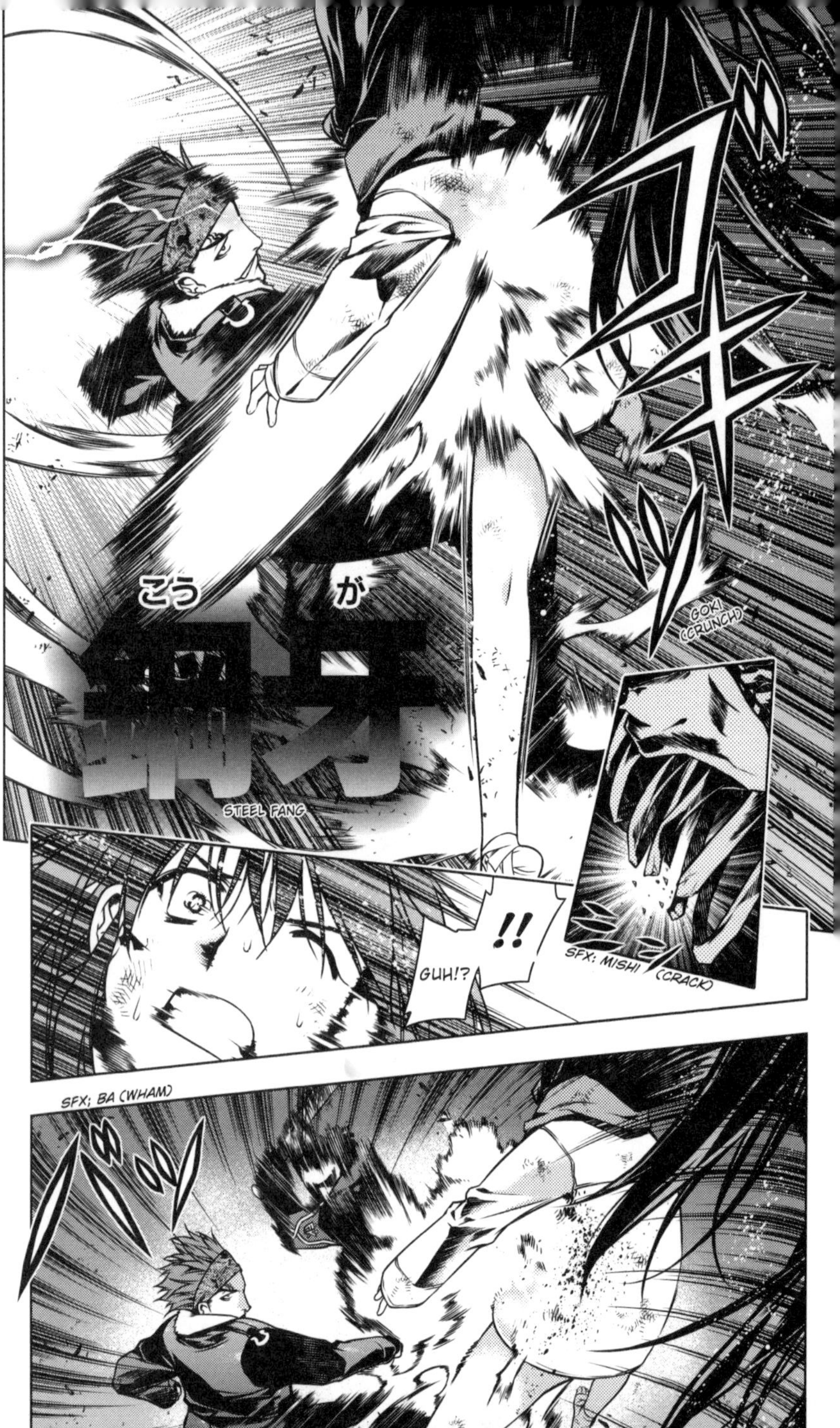
GOKI (CRUNCH)
こう が
鋼牙
STEEL FANG
SFX: MISHI (CRACK)
!!
GUH!?
SFX; BA (WHAM)

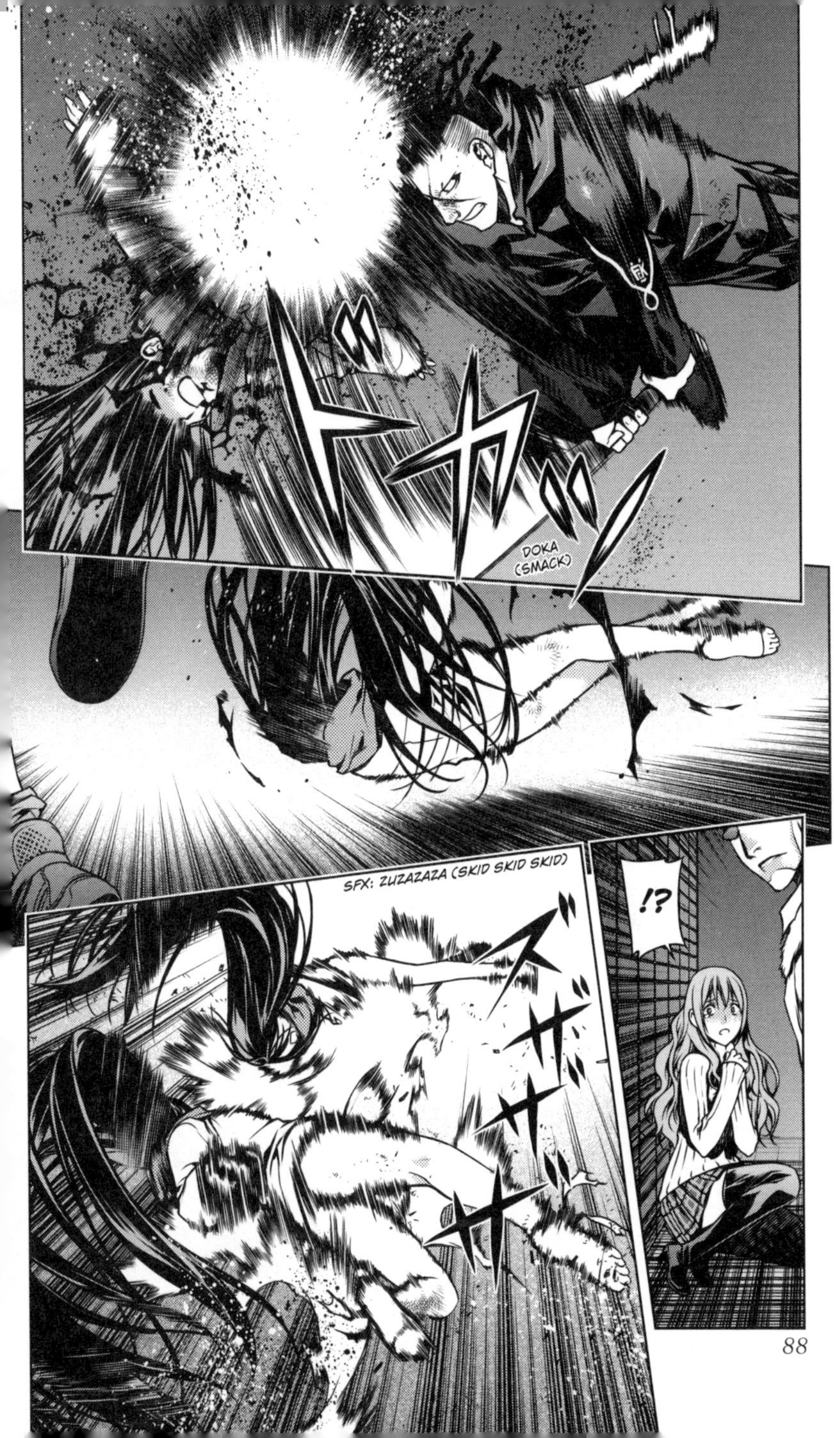
DOKA (SMACK)
SFX: ZUZAZAZA (SKID SKID SKID)
!?

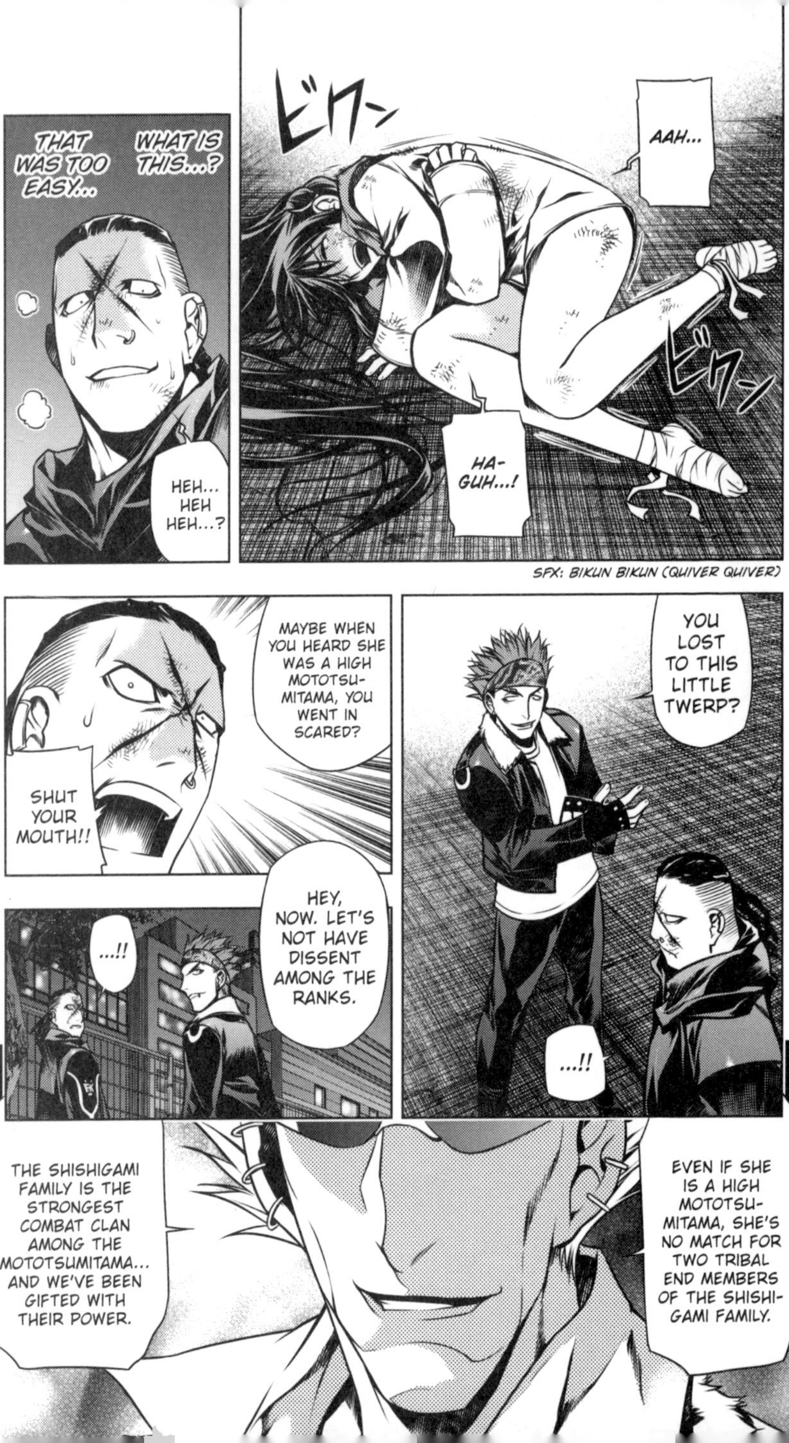
AAH...
HA-GUH...!
SFX: BIKUN BIKUN (QUIVER QUIVER)
WHAT IS THIS...?
THAT WAS TOO EASY...
HEH... HEH HEH...?
YOU LOST TO THIS LITTLE TWERP?
...!!
MAYBE WHEN YOU HEARD SHE WAS A HIGH MOTOTSUMITAMA, YOU WENT IN SCARED?
SHUT YOUR MOUTH!!
HEY, NOW. LET'S NOT HAVE DISSENT AMONG THE RANKS.
...!!
EVEN IF SHE IS A HIGH MOTOTSUMITAMA, SHE'S NO MATCH FOR TWO TRIBAL END MEMBERS OF THE SHISHIGAMI FAMILY.
THE SHISHIGAMI FAMILY IS THE STRONGEST COMBAT CLAN AMONG THE MOTOTSUMITAMA... AND WE'VE BEEN GIFTED WITH THEIR POWER.

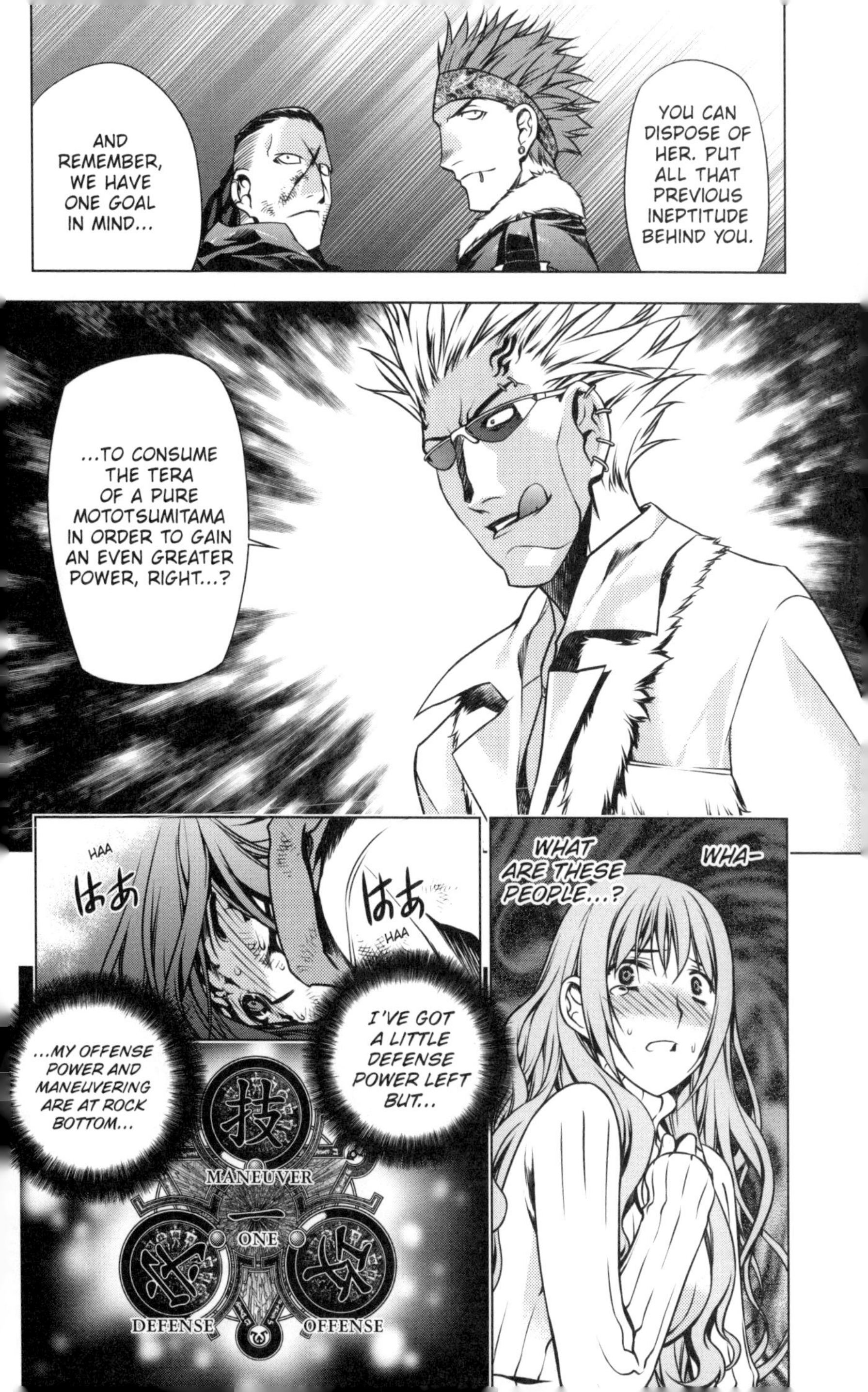
YOU CAN DISPOSE OF HER. PUT ALL THAT PREVIOUS INEPTITUDE BEHIND YOU.
AND REMEMBER, WE HAVE ONE GOAL IN MIND...
...TO CONSUME THE TERA OF A PURE MOTOTSUMITAMA IN ORDER TO GAIN AN EVEN GREATER POWER, RIGHT...?
WHA-
WHAT ARE THESE PEOPLE...?
はあ
HAA
はあ
HAA
I'VE GOT A LITTLE DEFENSE POWER LEFT BUT...
...MY OFFENSE POWER AND MANEUVERING ARE AT ROCK BOTTOM...
技
MANEUVER
ONE
DEFENSE
OFFENSE

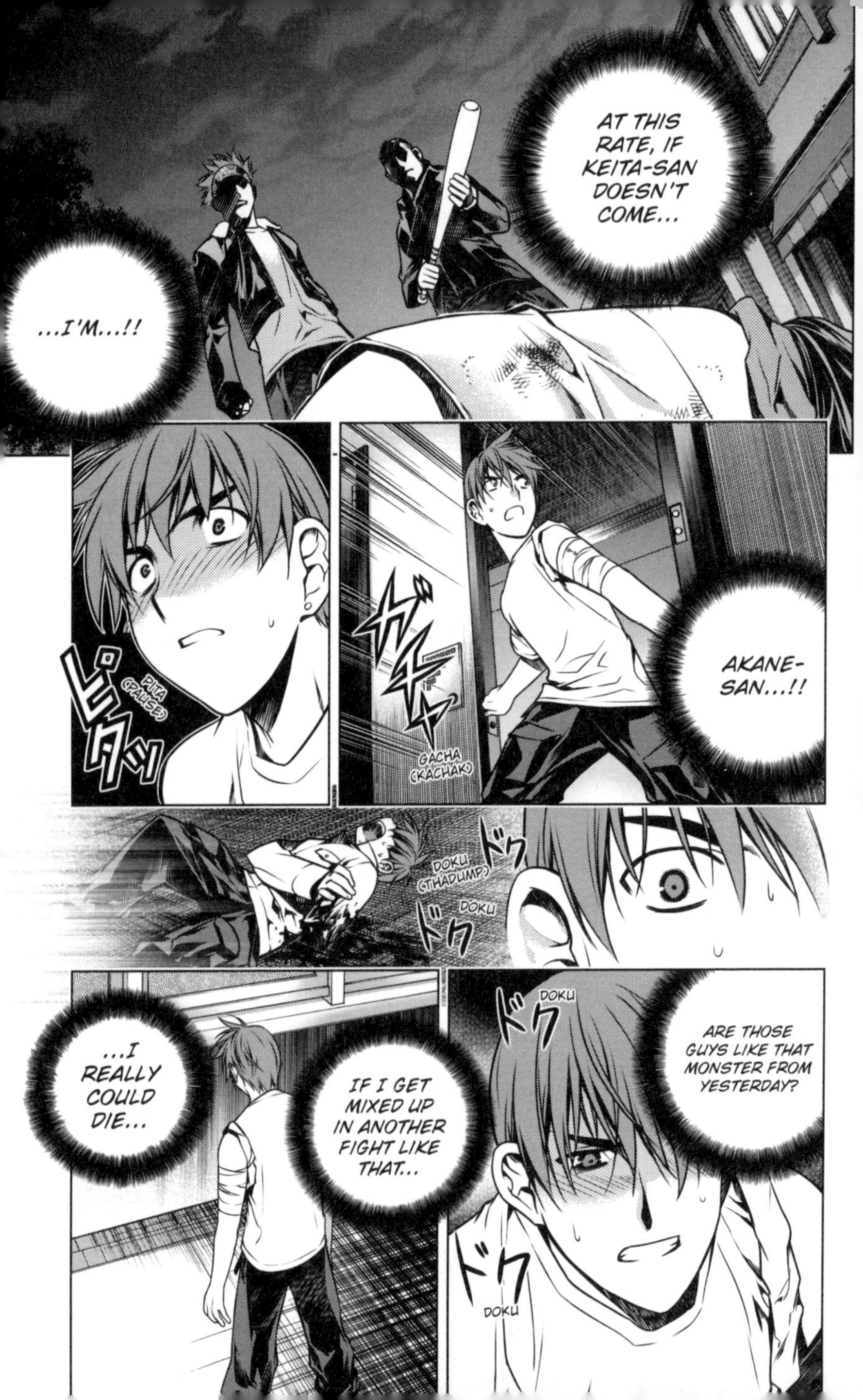
AT THIS RATE, IF KEITA-SAN DOESN'T COME...
...I'M...!!
AKANE-SAN...!!
GACHA (KACHAK)
PITA (PAUSE)
DOKU (THADUMP)
DOKU
ARE THOSE GUYS LIKE THAT MONSTER FROM YESTERDAY?
DOKU
DOKU
IF I GET MIXED UP IN ANOTHER FIGHT LIKE THAT...
...I REALLY COULD DIE...

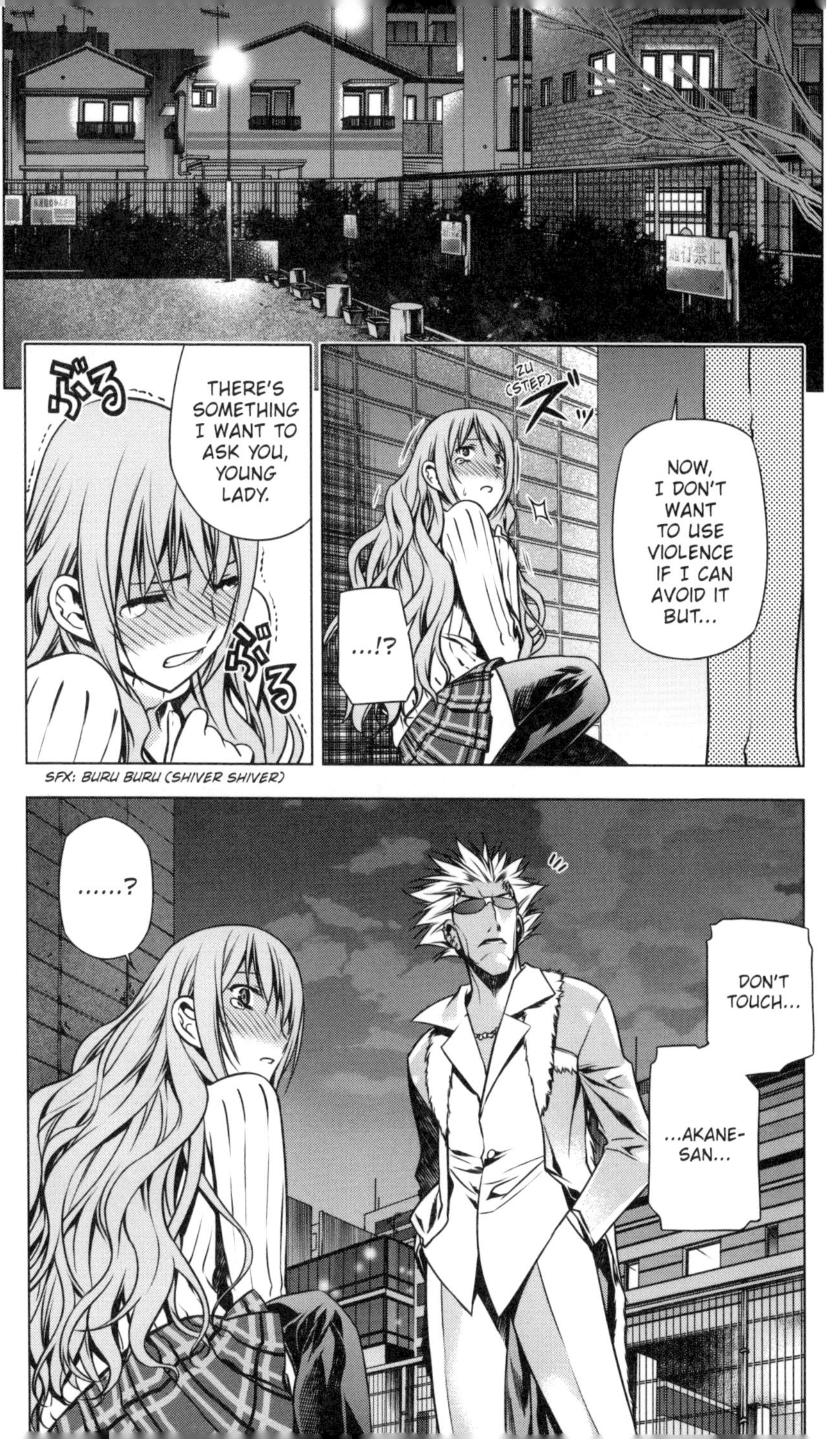
NOW, I DON'T WANT TO USE VIOLENCE IF I CAN AVOID IT BUT...
ZU (STEP)
ズッ
...!?
THERE'S SOMETHING I WANT TO ASK YOU, YOUNG LADY.
ぶる
ぶる
SFX: BURU BURU (SHIVER SHIVER)
DON'T TOUCH...
...AKANE-SAN...
......?

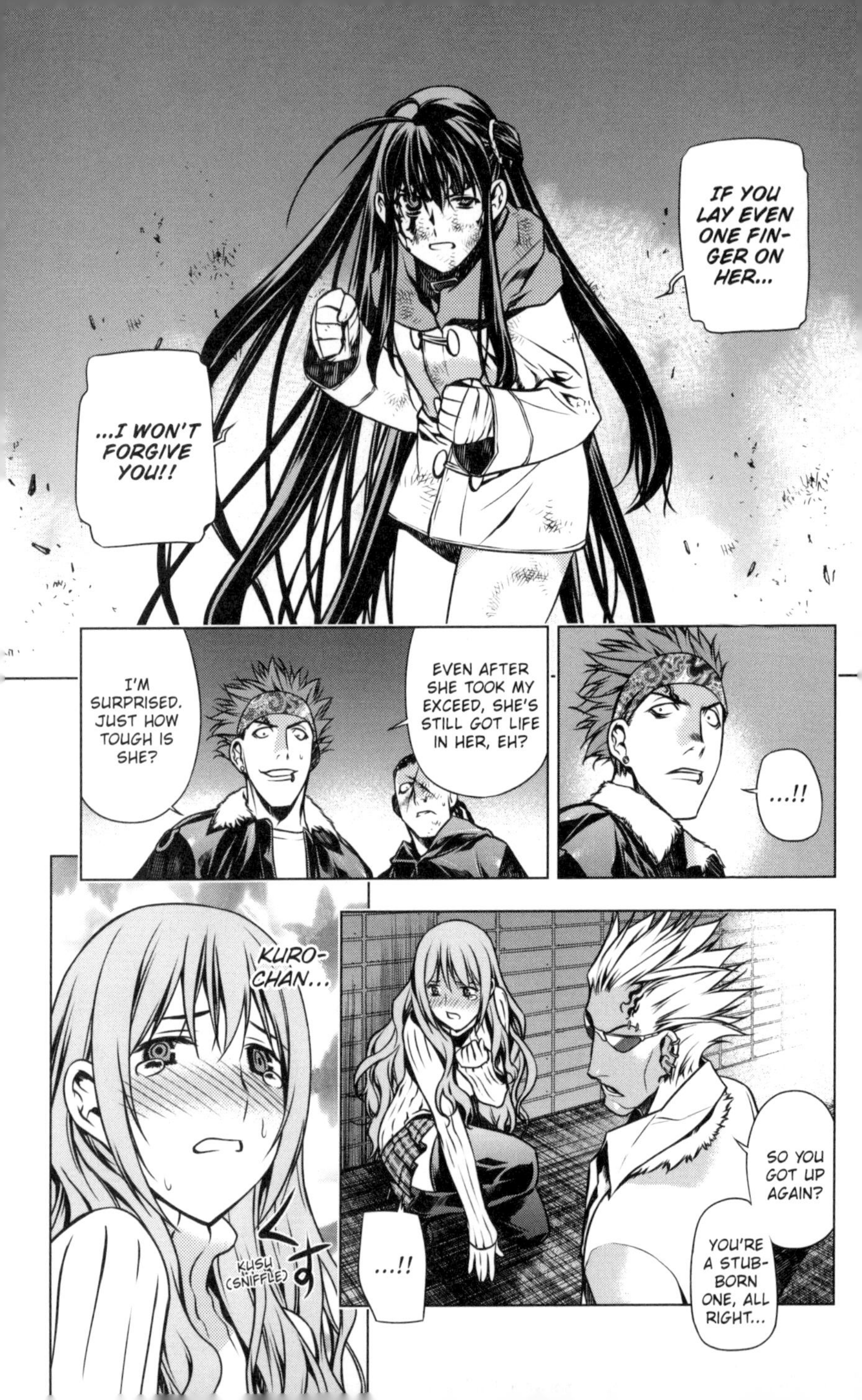

IF YOU LAY EVEN ONE FINGER ON HER...
...I WON'T FORGIVE YOU!!
...!!
EVEN AFTER SHE TOOK MY EXCEED, SHE'S STILL GOT LIFE IN HER, EH?
I'M SURPRISED. JUST HOW TOUGH IS SHE?
SO YOU GOT UP AGAIN?
YOU'RE A STUBBORN ONE, ALL RIGHT...
...!!
KURO-CHAN...
す
KUSU (SNIFFLE)

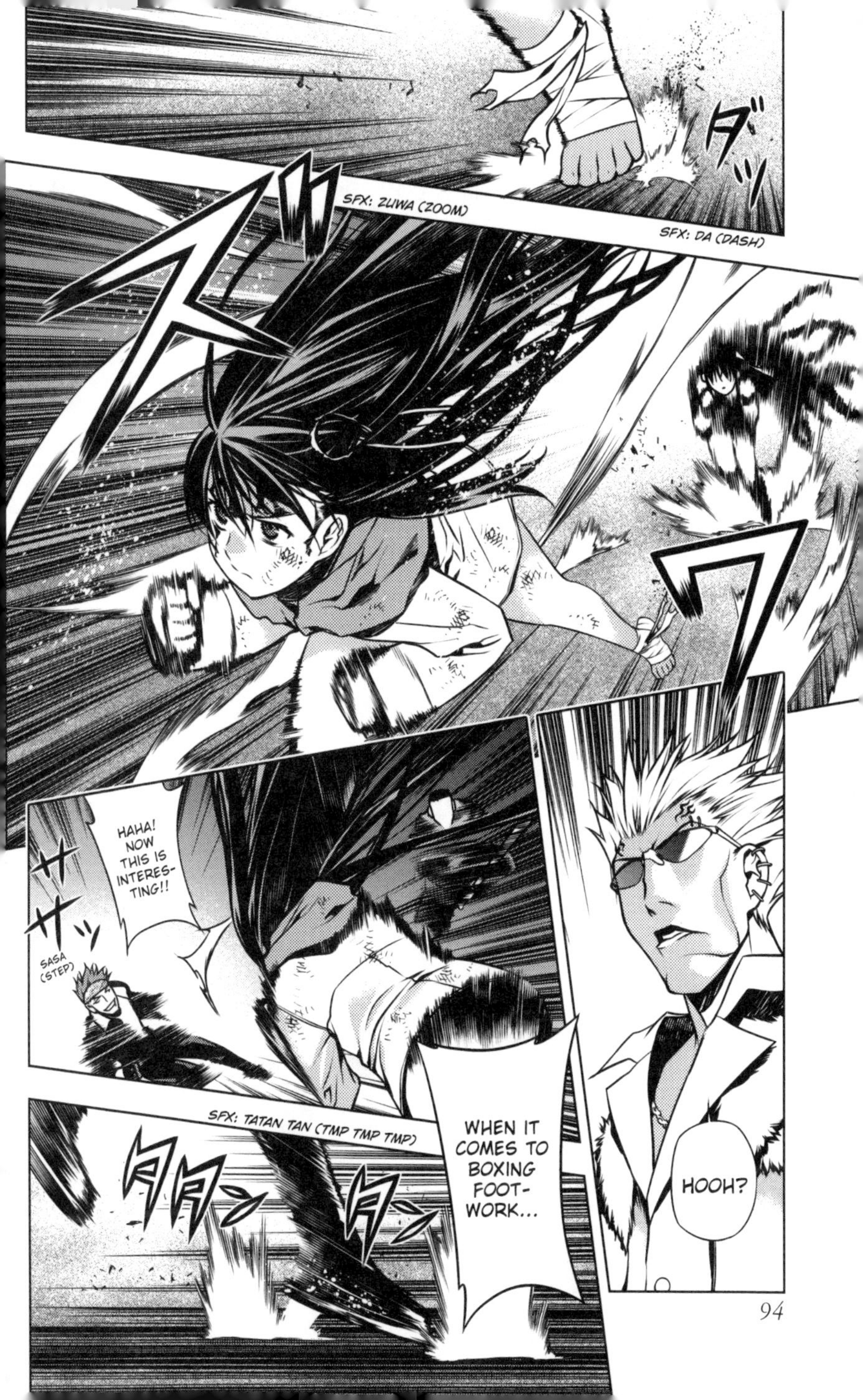
SFX: DA (DASH)
SFX: ZUWA (ZOOM)
HOOH?
HAHA! NOW THIS IS INTERESTING!!
SASA (STEP)
WHEN IT COMES TO BOXING FOOT-WORK...
SFX: TATAN TAN (TMP TMP TMP)

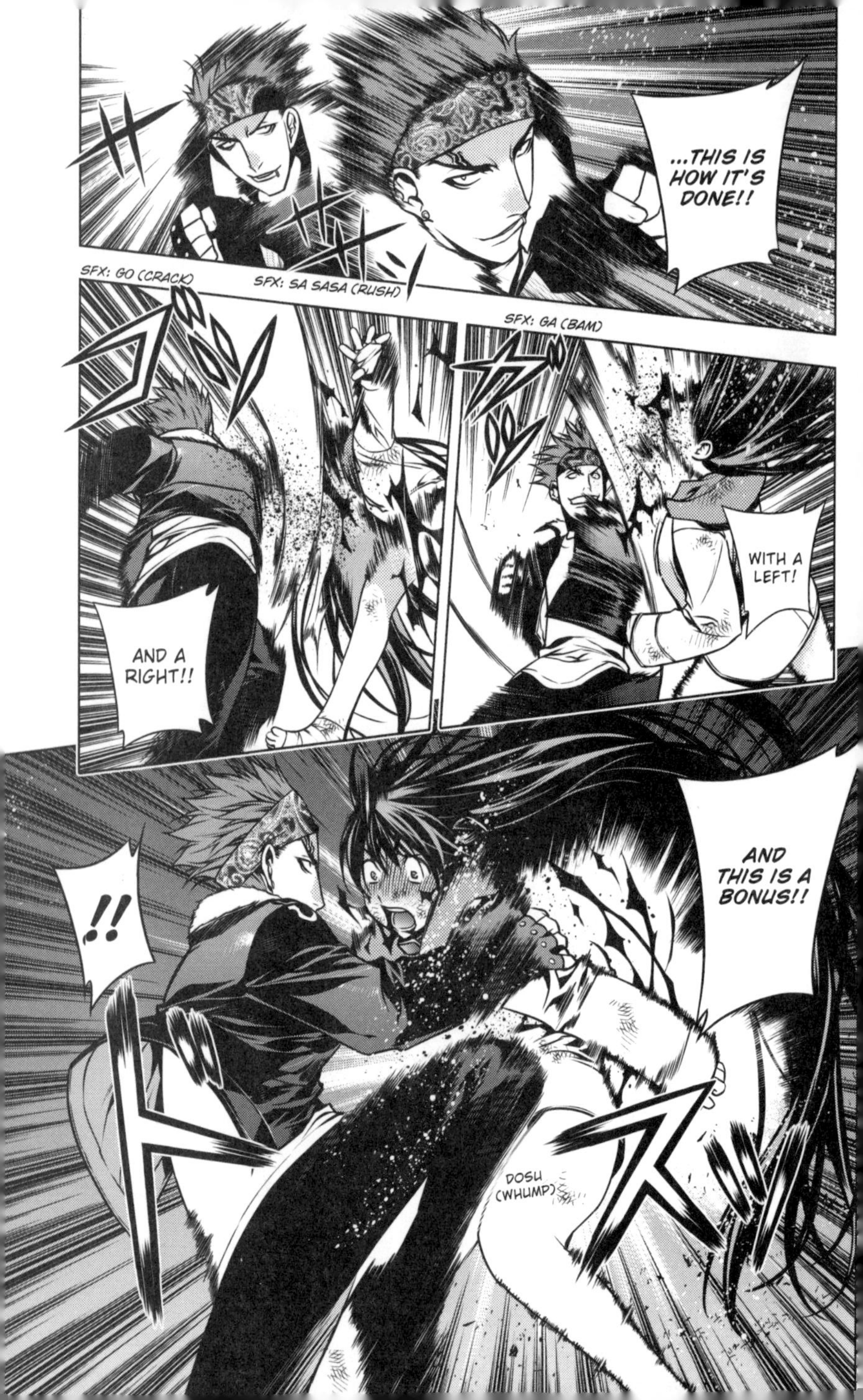
...THIS IS HOW IT'S DONE!!
SFX: SA SASA (RUSH)
SFX: GA (BAM)
WITH A LEFT!
SFX: GO (CRACK)
AND A RIGHT!!
AND THIS IS A BONUS!!
!!
DOSU (WHUMP)

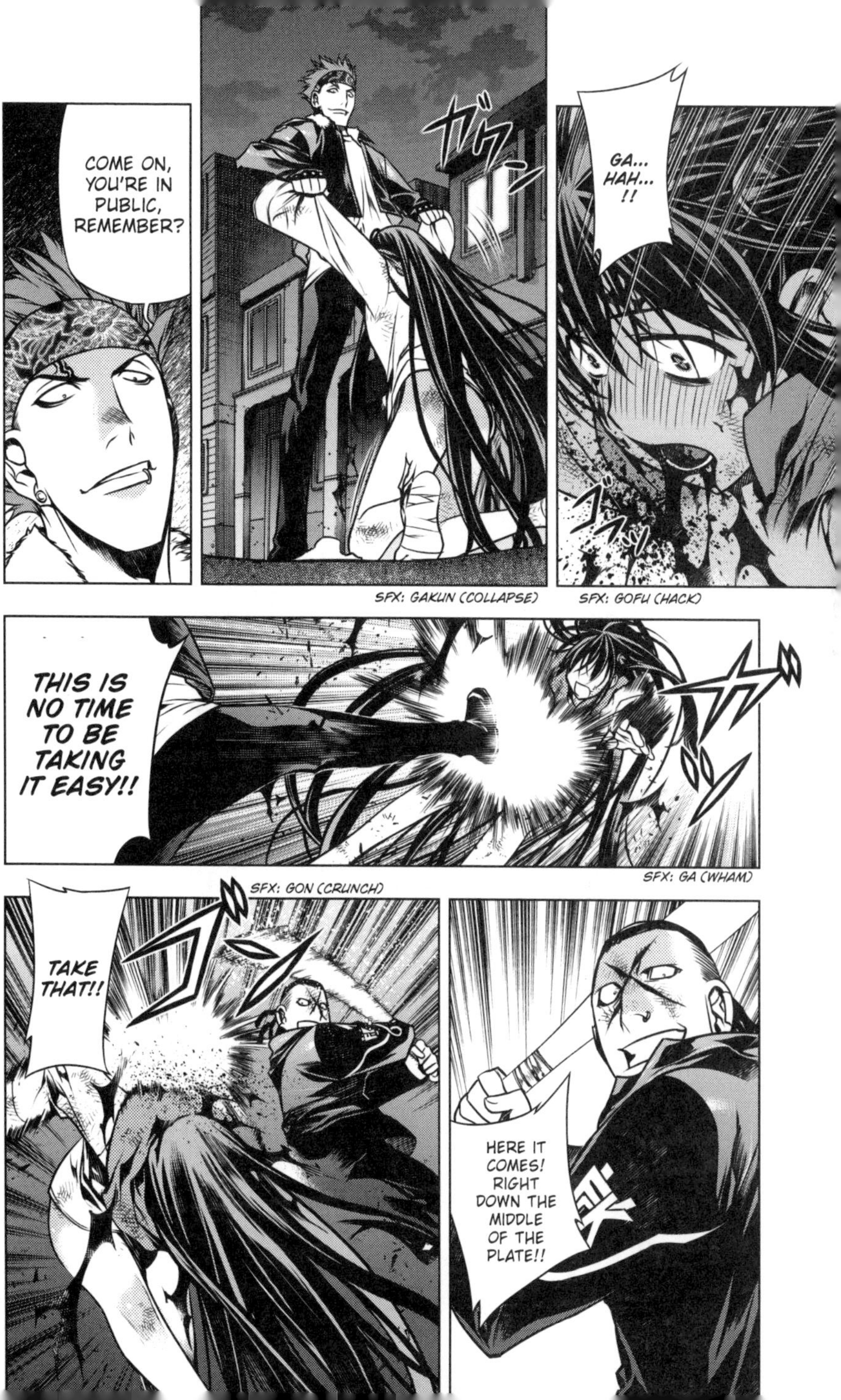
GA... HAH... !!
SFX: GOFU (HACK)
SFX: GAKUN (COLLAPSE)
COME ON, YOU'RE IN PUBLIC, REMEMBER?
THIS IS NO TIME TO BE TAKING IT EASY!!
SFX: GA (WHAM)
HERE IT COMES! RIGHT DOWN THE MIDDLE OF THE PLATE!!
SFX: GON (CRUNCH)
TAKE THAT!!

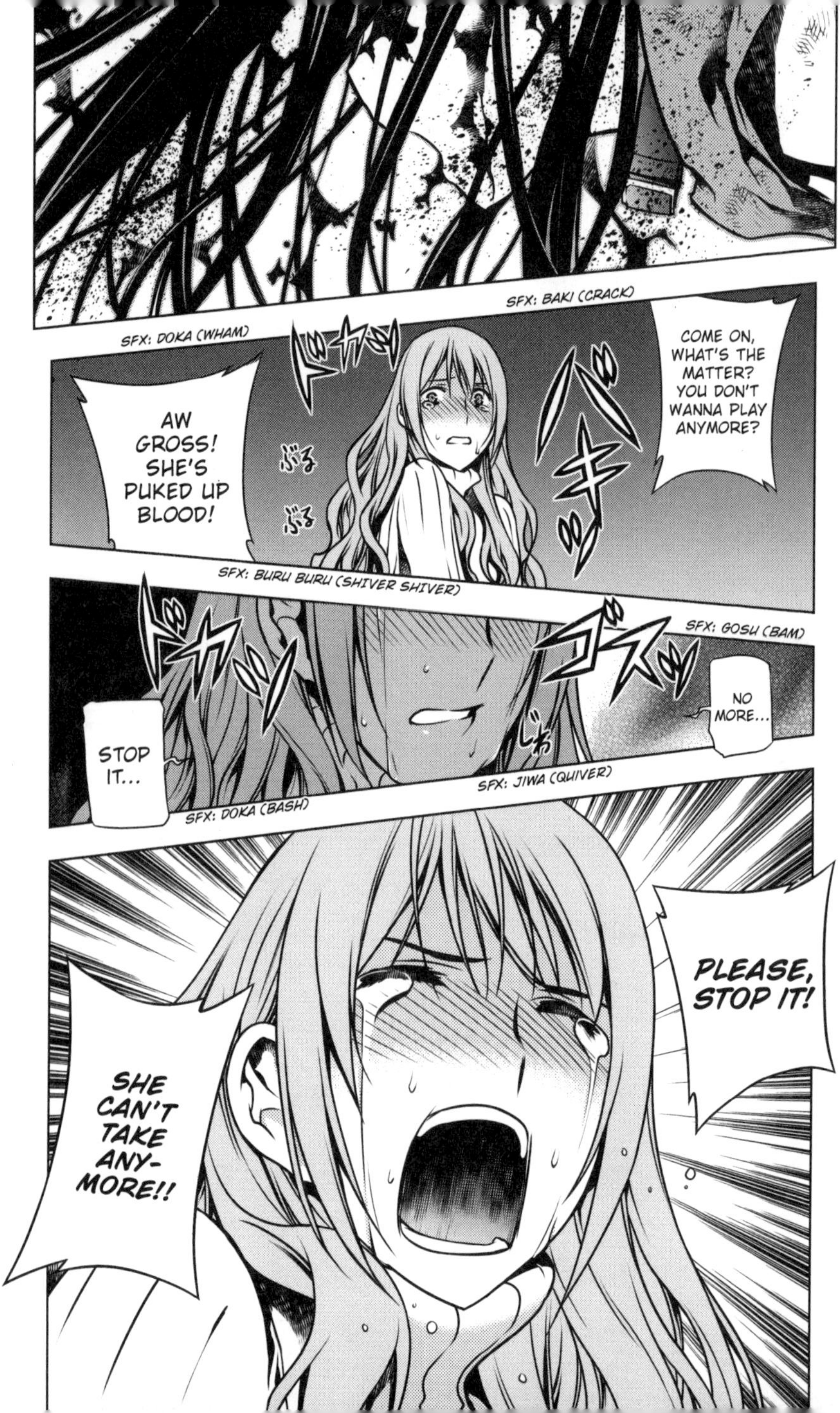
COME ON, WHAT'S THE MATTER? YOU DON'T WANNA PLAY ANYMORE?
バキッ
SFX: BAKI (CRACK)
ドカッ
SFX: DOKA (WHAM)
AW GROSS! SHE'S PUKED UP BLOOD!
ぶる ぶる
SFX: BURU BURU (SHIVER SHIVER)
ゴスッ
SFX: GOSU (BAM)
NO MORE...
じわ
SFX: JIWA (QUIVER)
ドカッ
STOP IT...
SFX: DOKA (BASH)
PLEASE, STOP IT!
SHE CAN'T TAKE ANY-MORE!!

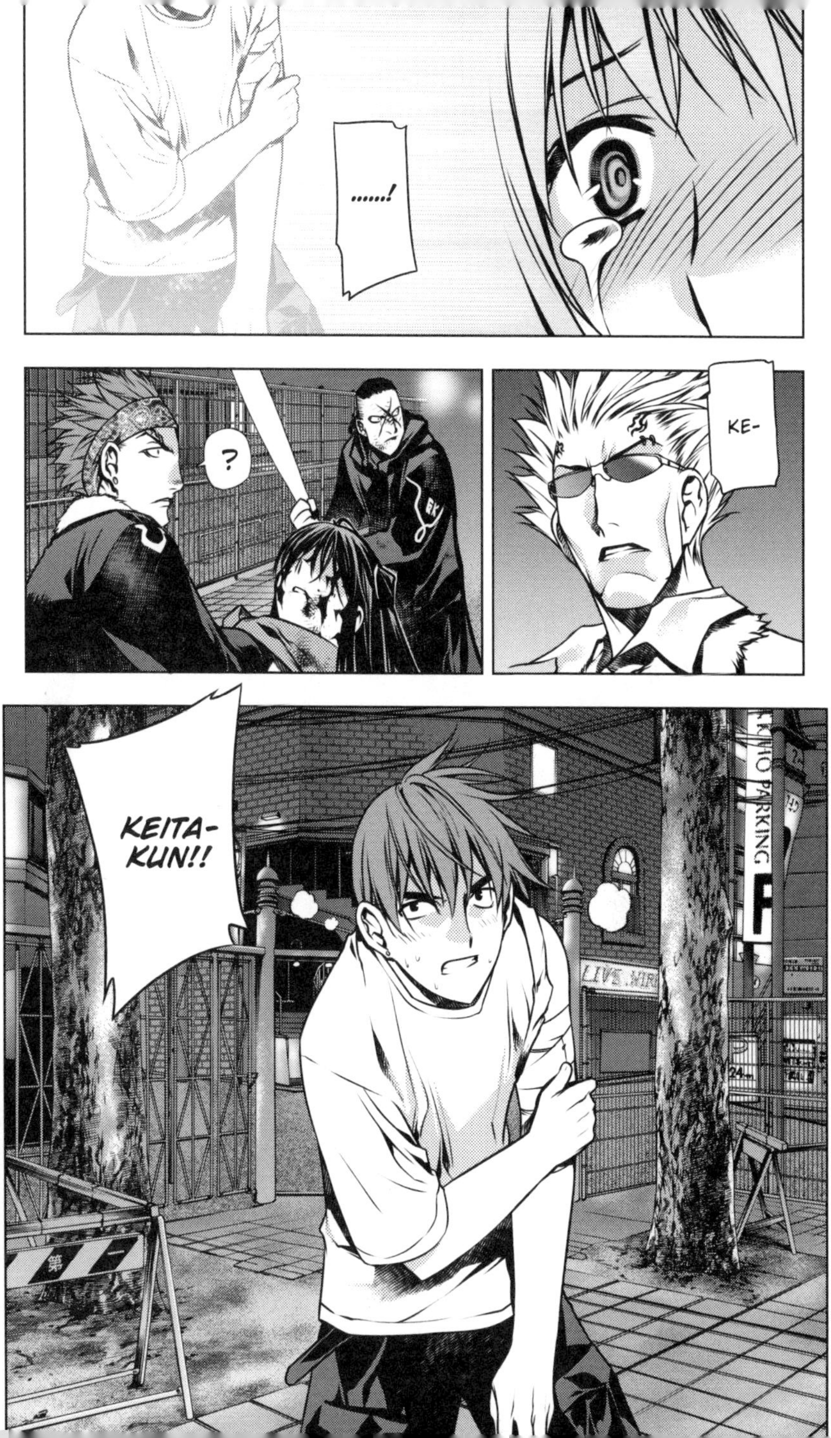
......!
KE-
?
KEITA-KUN!!

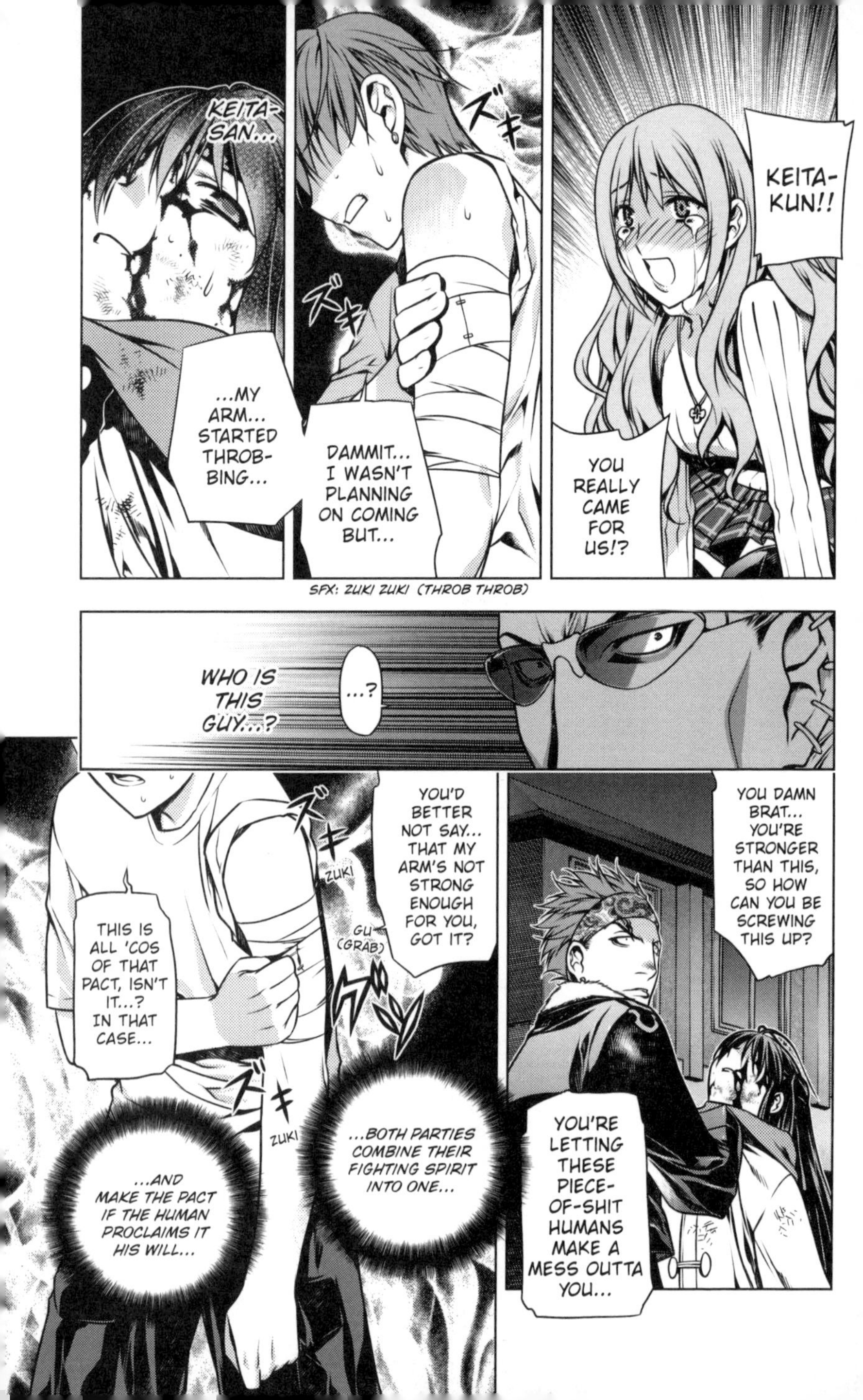
KEITA-KUN!!
YOU REALLY CAME FOR US!?
DAMMIT... I WASN'T PLANNING ON COMING BUT...
KEITA-SAN...
...MY ARM... STARTED THROBBING...
SFX: ZUKI ZUKI (THROB THROB)
...?
WHO IS THIS GUY...?
YOU DAMN BRAT... YOU'RE STRONGER THAN THIS, SO HOW CAN YOU BE SCREWING THIS UP?
YOU'RE LETTING THESE PIECE-OF-SHIT HUMANS MAKE A MESS OUTTA YOU...
YOU'D BETTER NOT SAY... THAT MY ARM'S NOT STRONG ENOUGH FOR YOU, GOT IT?
ZUKI
GU (GRAB)
THIS IS ALL 'COS OF THAT PACT, ISN'T IT...? IN THAT CASE...
...BOTH PARTIES COMBINE THEIR FIGHTING SPIRIT INTO ONE...
ZUKI
...AND MAKE THE PACT IF THE HUMAN PROCLAIMS IT HIS WILL...

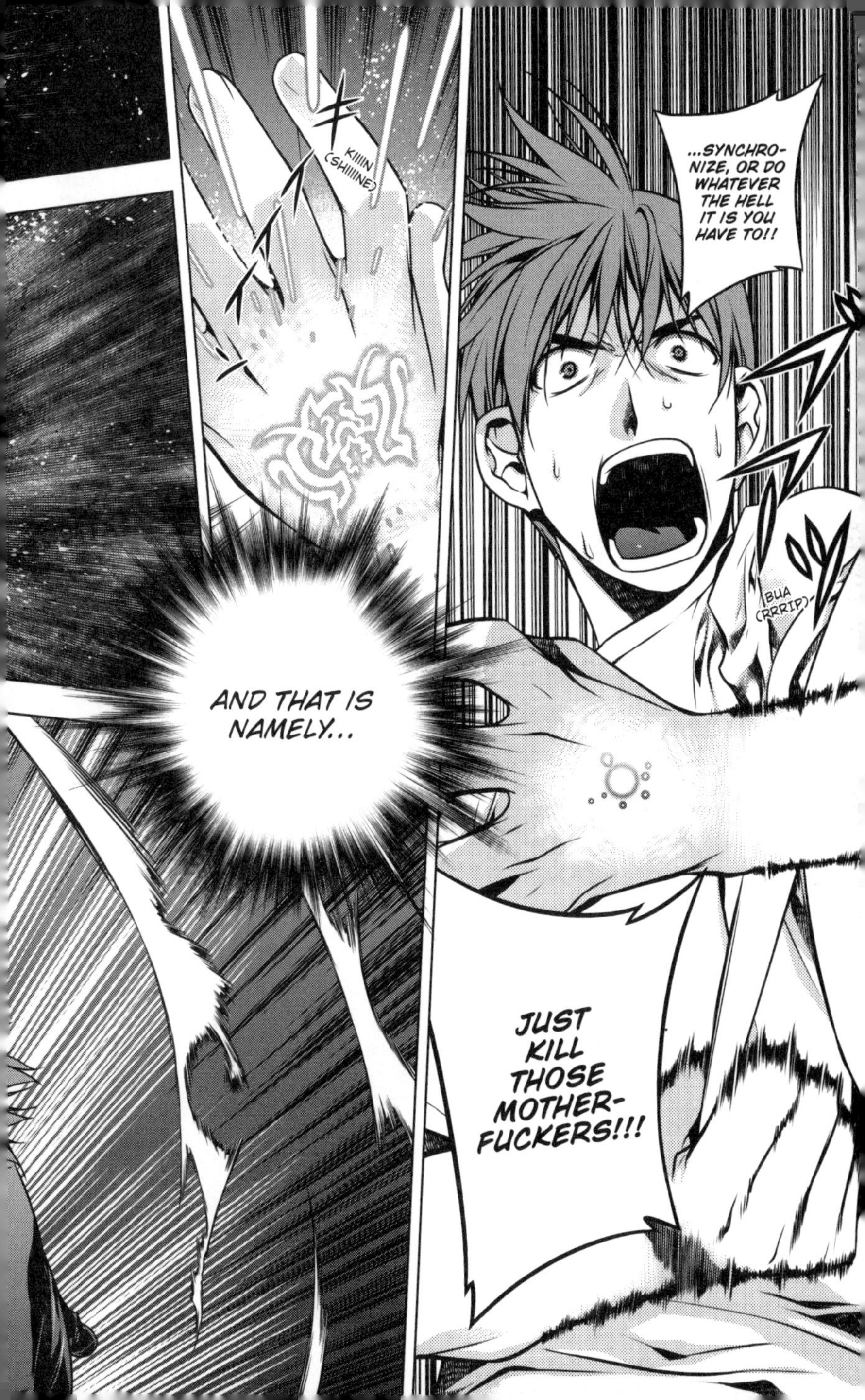
...SYNCHRONIZE, OR DO WHATEVER THE HELL IT IS YOU HAVE TO!!
BUA (RRRIP)
KIIIN (SHIIINE)
AND THAT IS NAMELY...
JUST KILL THOSE MOTHER-FUCKERS!!!

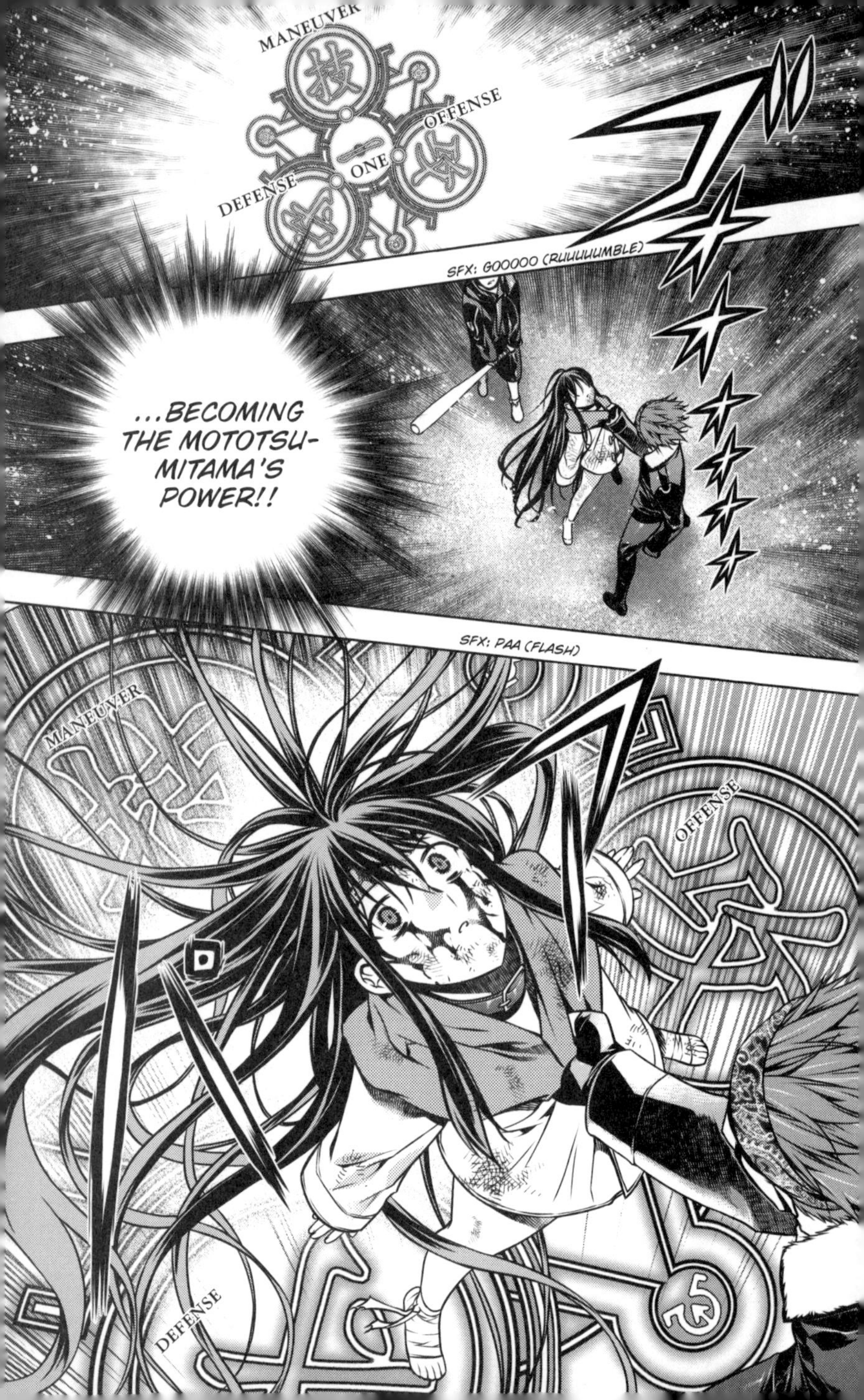
MANEUVER
OFFENSE
ONE
DEFENSE
SFX: GOOOOO (RUUUUUMBLE)
...BECOMING THE MOTOTSU-MITAMA'S POWER!!
SFX: PAA (FLASH)
OFFENSE
MANEUVER
DEFENSE

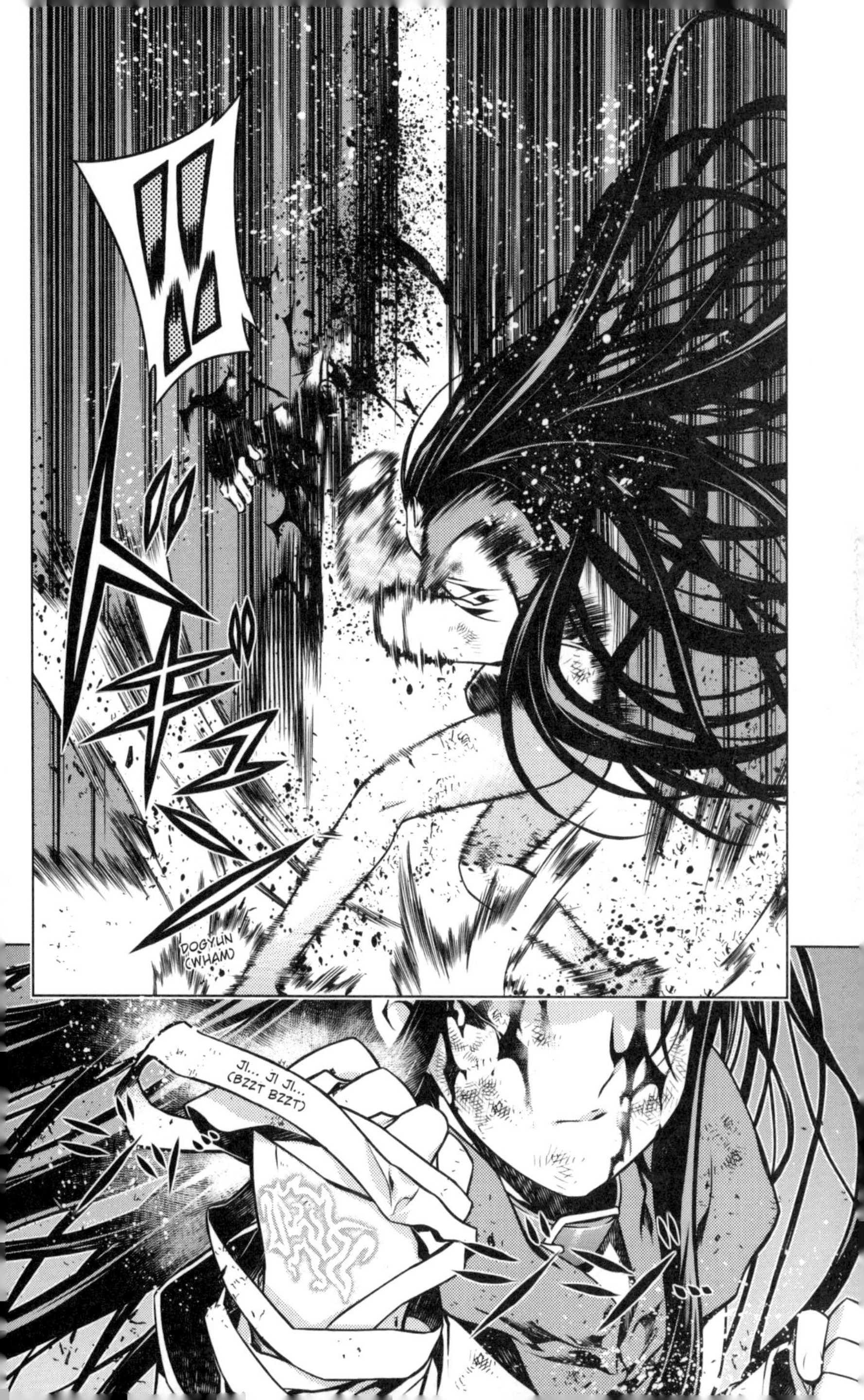
DOGYUN
(WHAM)
JI... JI JI...
(BZZT BZZT)

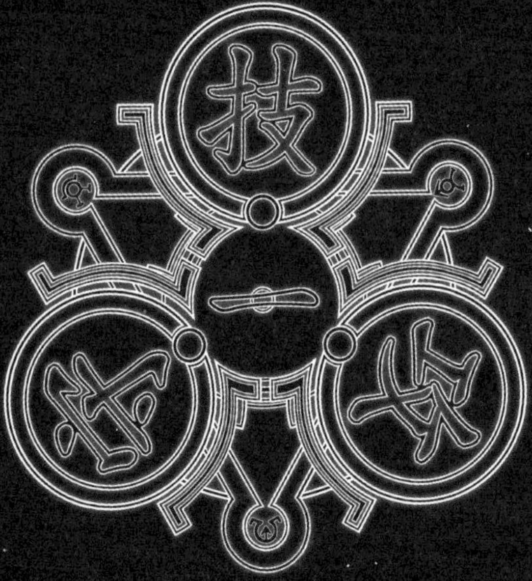
技
一

黒神

BLACK GOD

which maintains balance in the world.

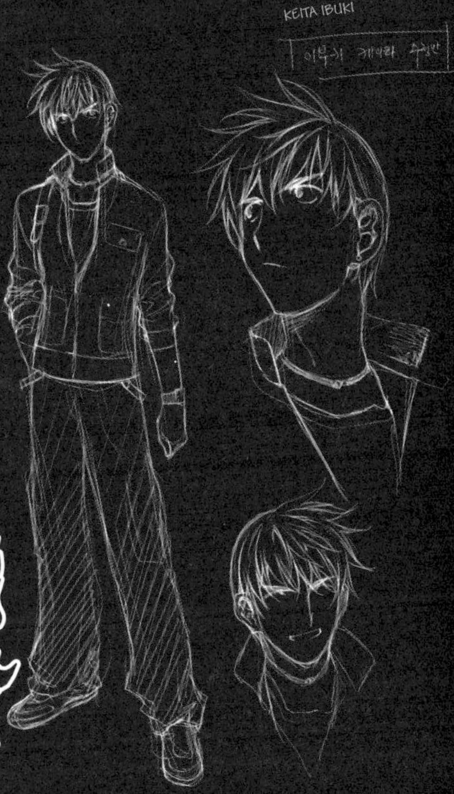
KEITA IBUKI
이부키 케이타 수정안

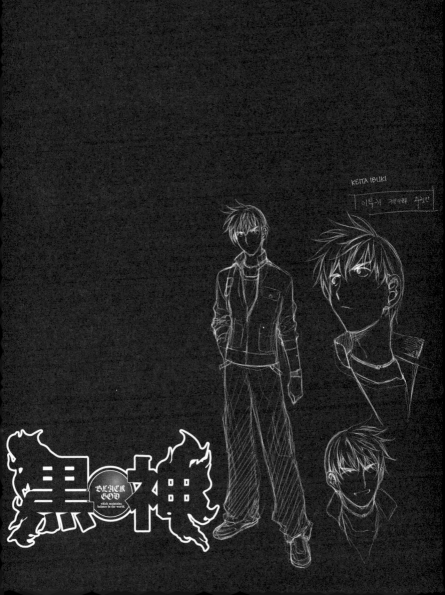

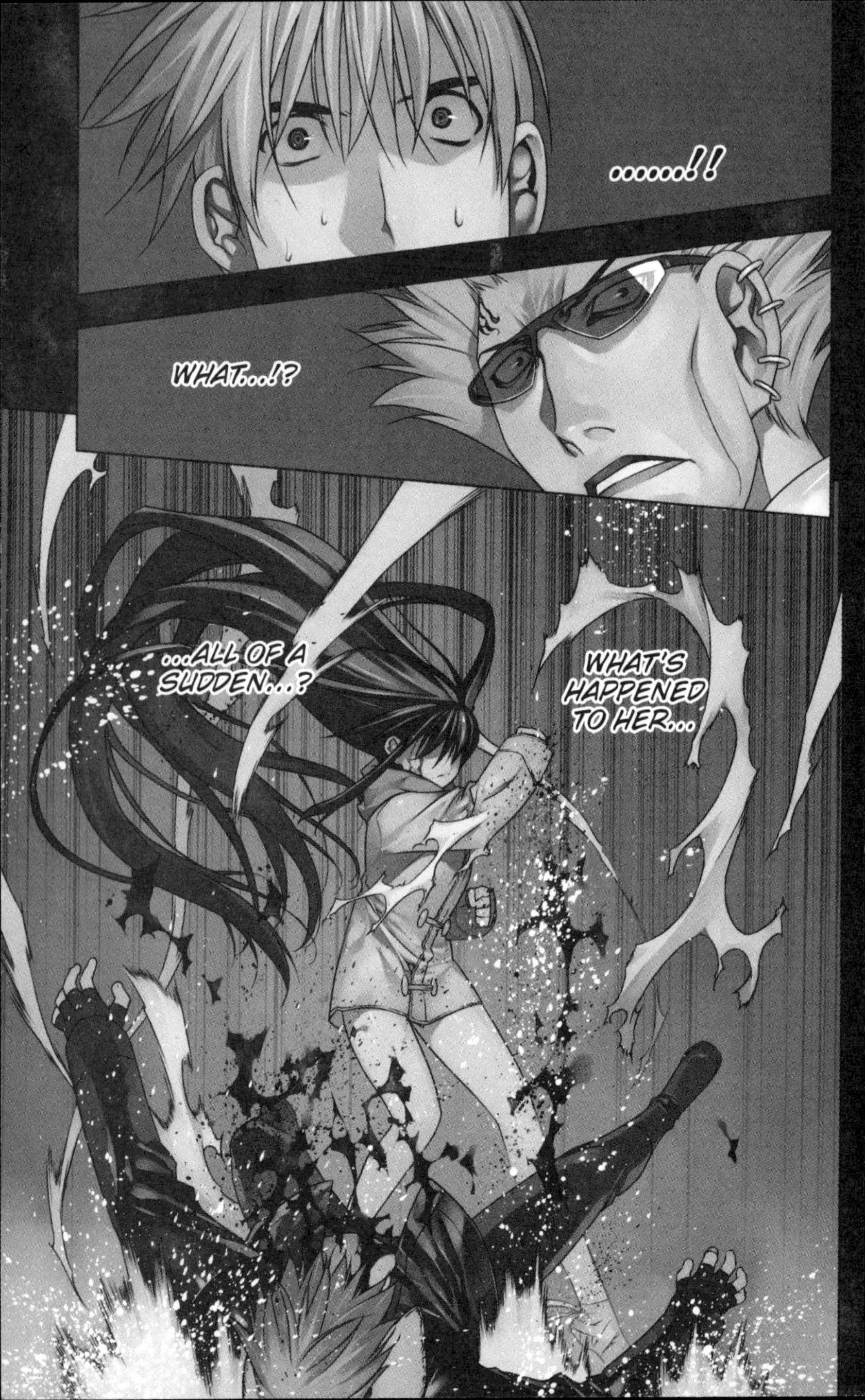
......!!
WHAT...!?
WHAT'S HAPPENED TO HER...
...ALL OF A SUDDEN...?

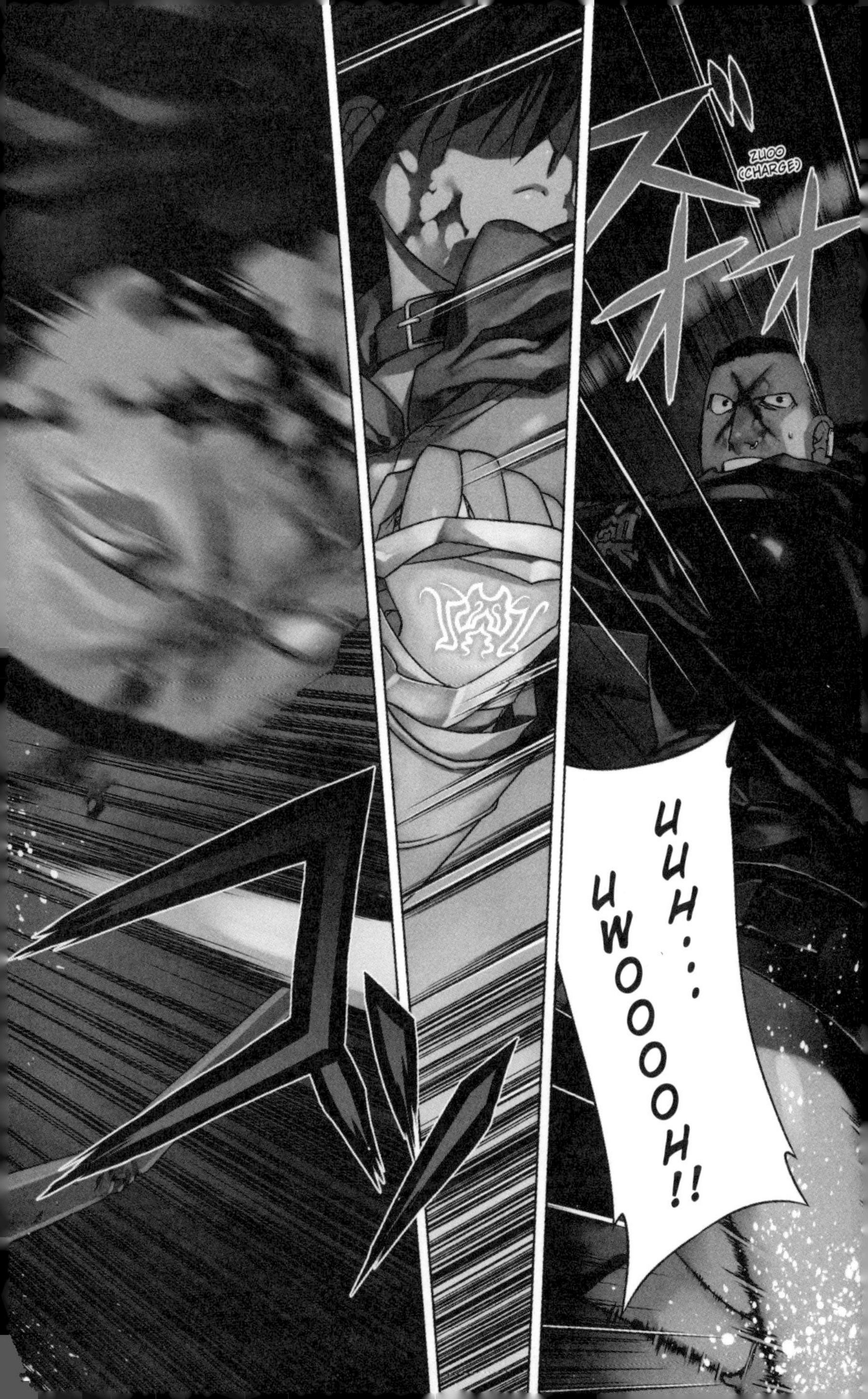
ZUOO (CHARGE)
UUH... UWOOOOOH!!

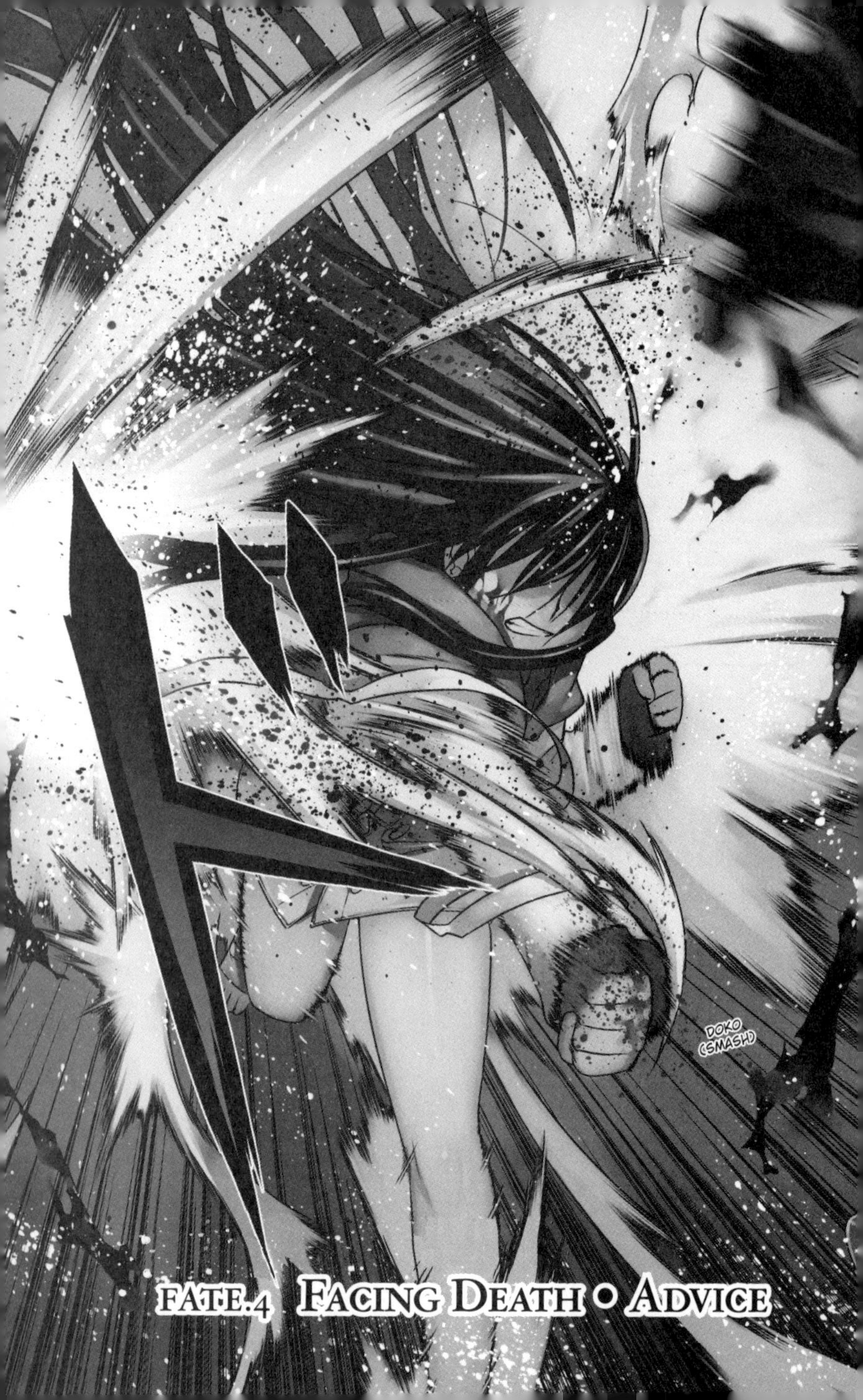
DOKO (SMASH)

FATE.4 Facing Death • Advice

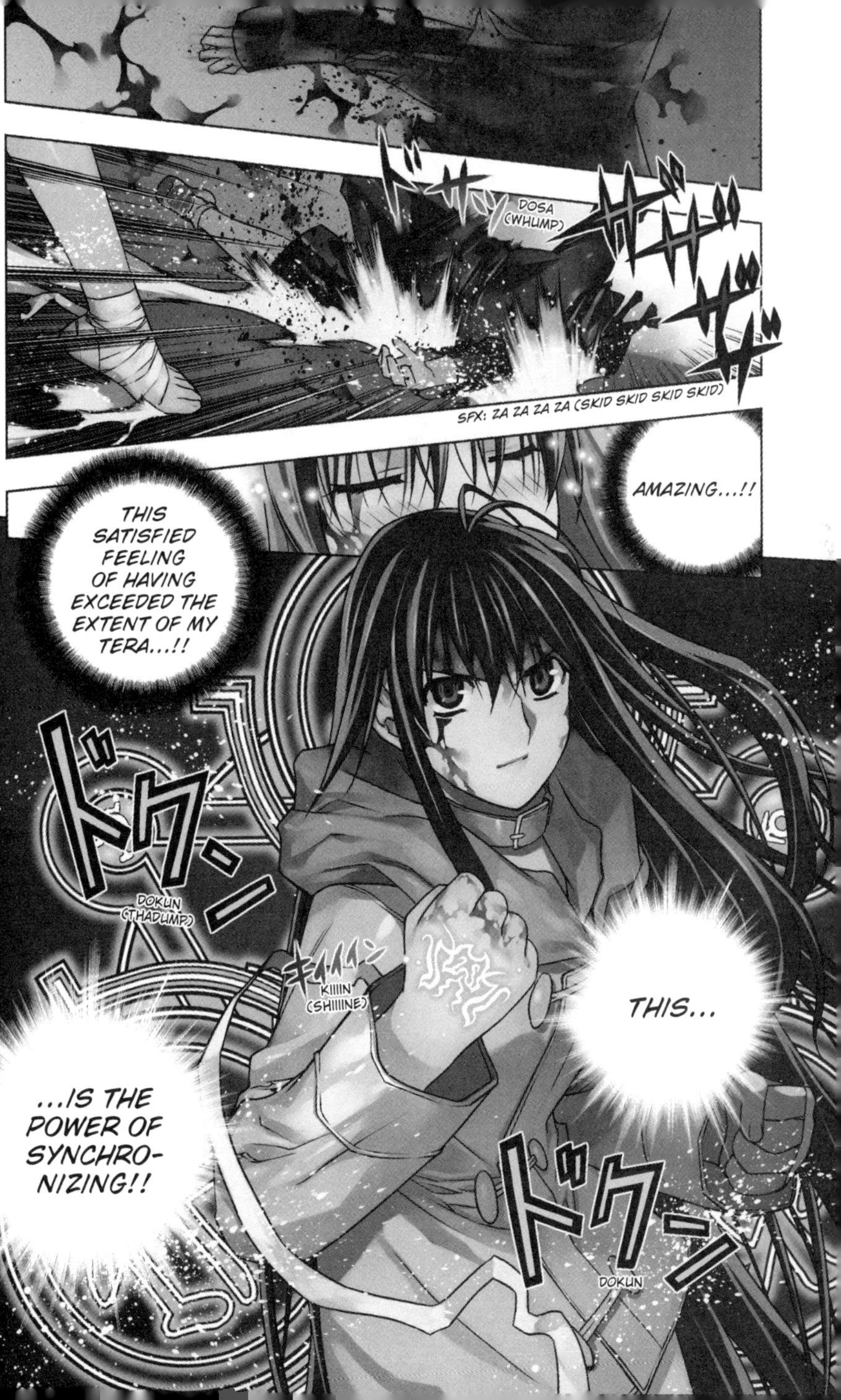
DOSA (WHUMP)
SFX: ZA ZA ZA ZA (SKID SKID SKID SKID)
AMAZING...!!
THIS SATISFIED FEELING OF HAVING EXCEEDED THE EXTENT OF MY TERA...!!
KIIIN (SHIIINE)
THIS...
DOKUN (THADUMP)
...IS THE POWER OF SYNCHRO-NIZING!!
DOKUN

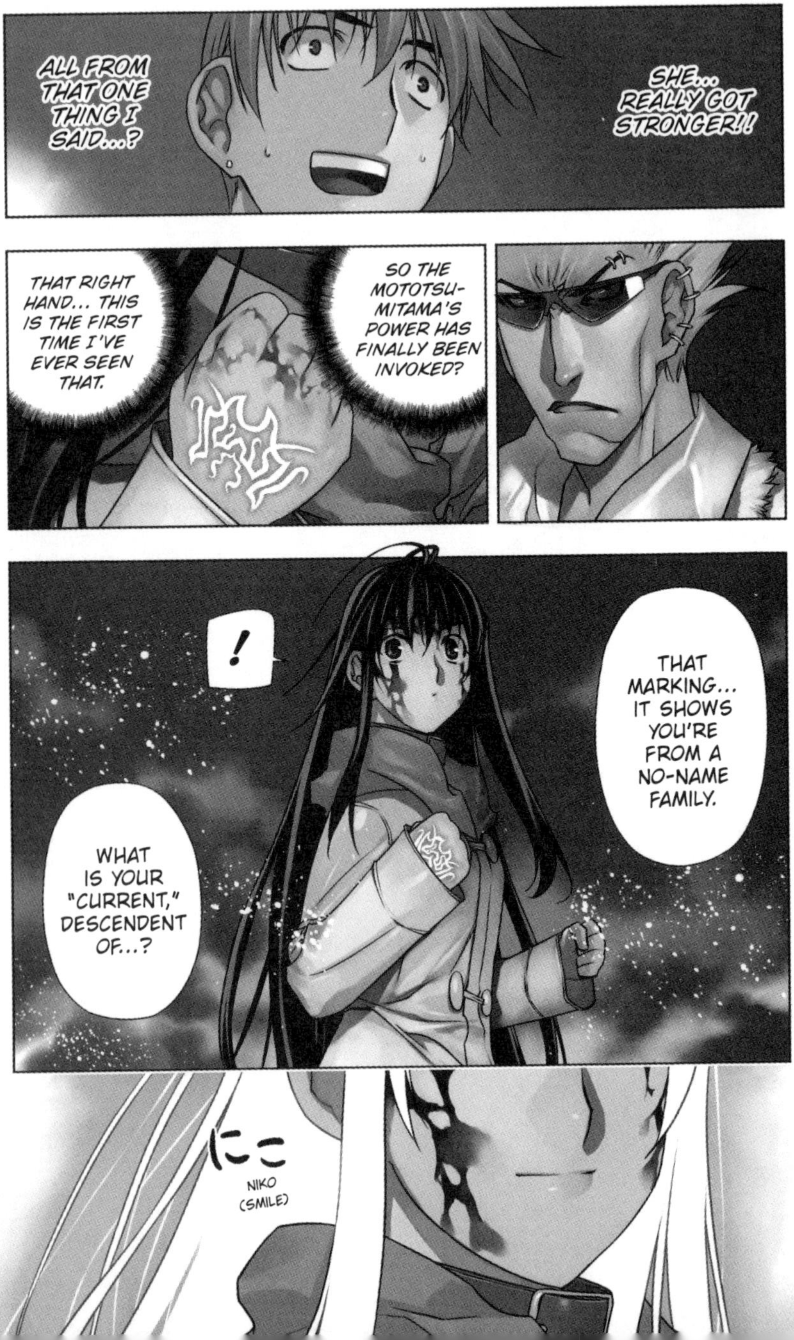
SHE... REALLY GOT STRONGER!!
ALL FROM THAT ONE THING I SAID...?
SO THE MOTOTSU-MITAMA'S POWER HAS FINALLY BEEN INVOKED?
THAT RIGHT HAND... THIS IS THE FIRST TIME I'VE EVER SEEN THAT.
THAT MARKING... IT SHOWS YOU'RE FROM A NO-NAME FAMILY.
!
WHAT IS YOUR "CURRENT," DESCENDENT OF...?
にこ
NIKO (SMILE)

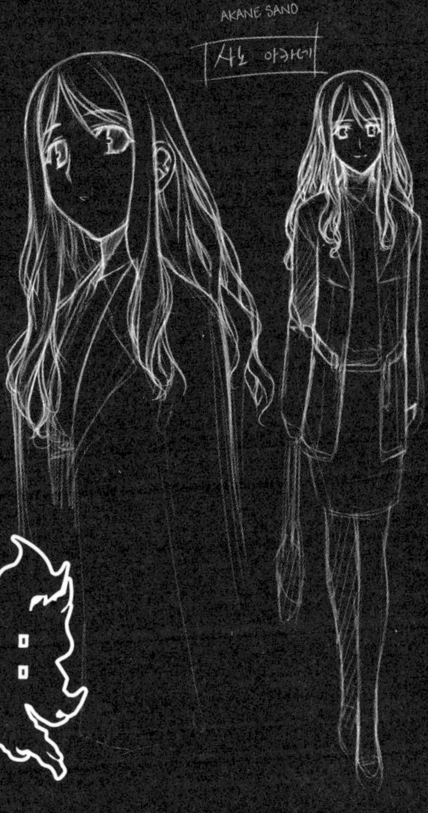
AKANE SANO
사노 아카네

BLACK GOD
which maintains balance in the world.

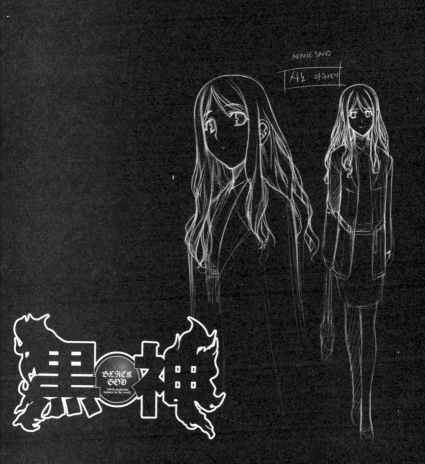

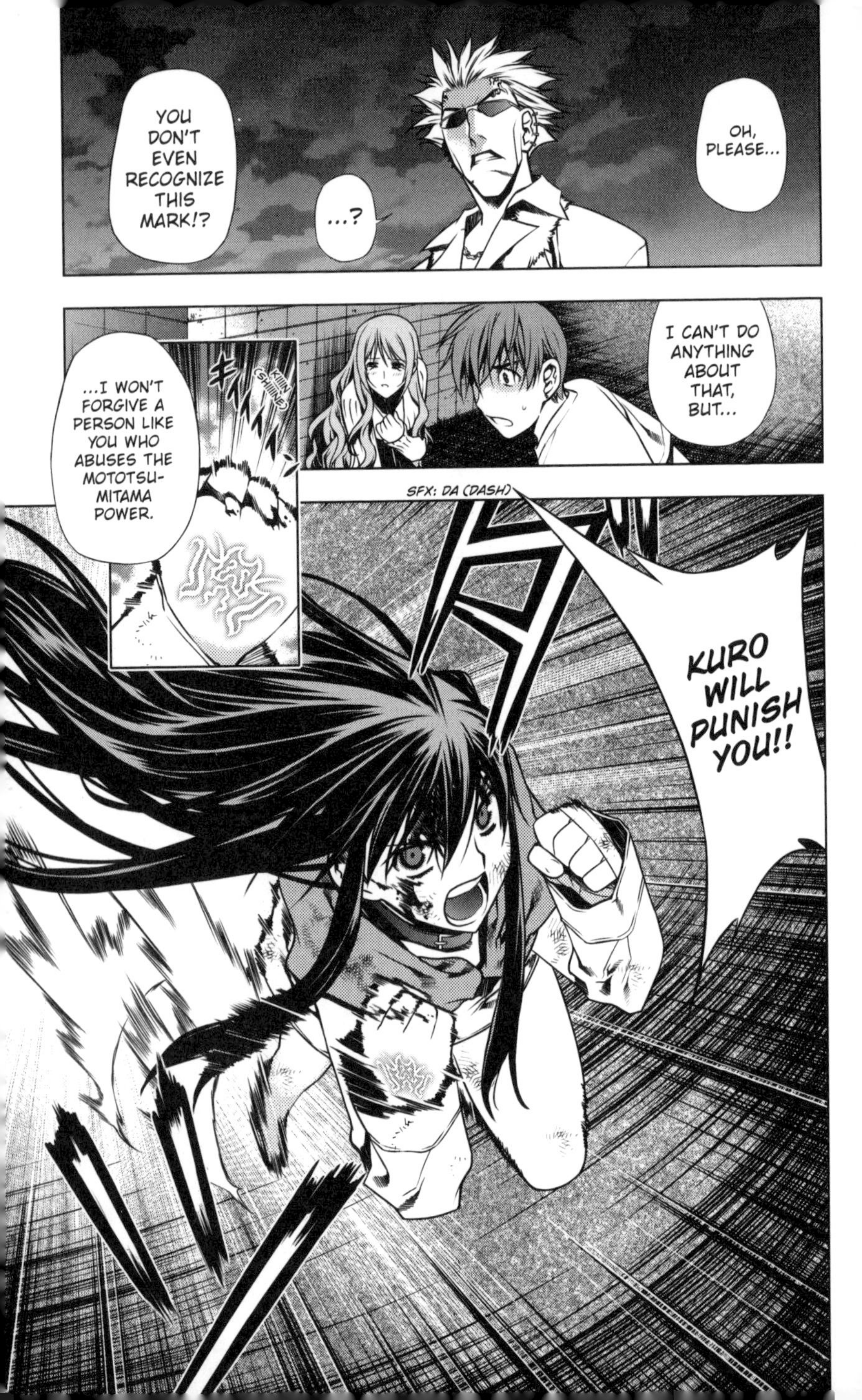
OH, PLEASE...
...?
YOU DON'T EVEN RECOGNIZE THIS MARK!?
I CAN'T DO ANYTHING ABOUT THAT, BUT...
KIIIN (SHIIINE)
...I WON'T FORGIVE A PERSON LIKE YOU WHO ABUSES THE MOTOTSU-MITAMA POWER.
SFX: DA (DASH)
KURO WILL PUNISH YOU!!

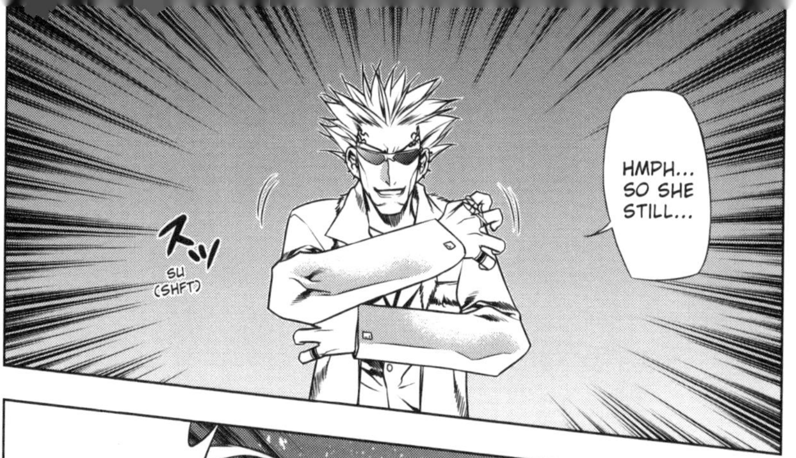
HMPH... SO SHE STILL...
スッ
SU (SHFT)
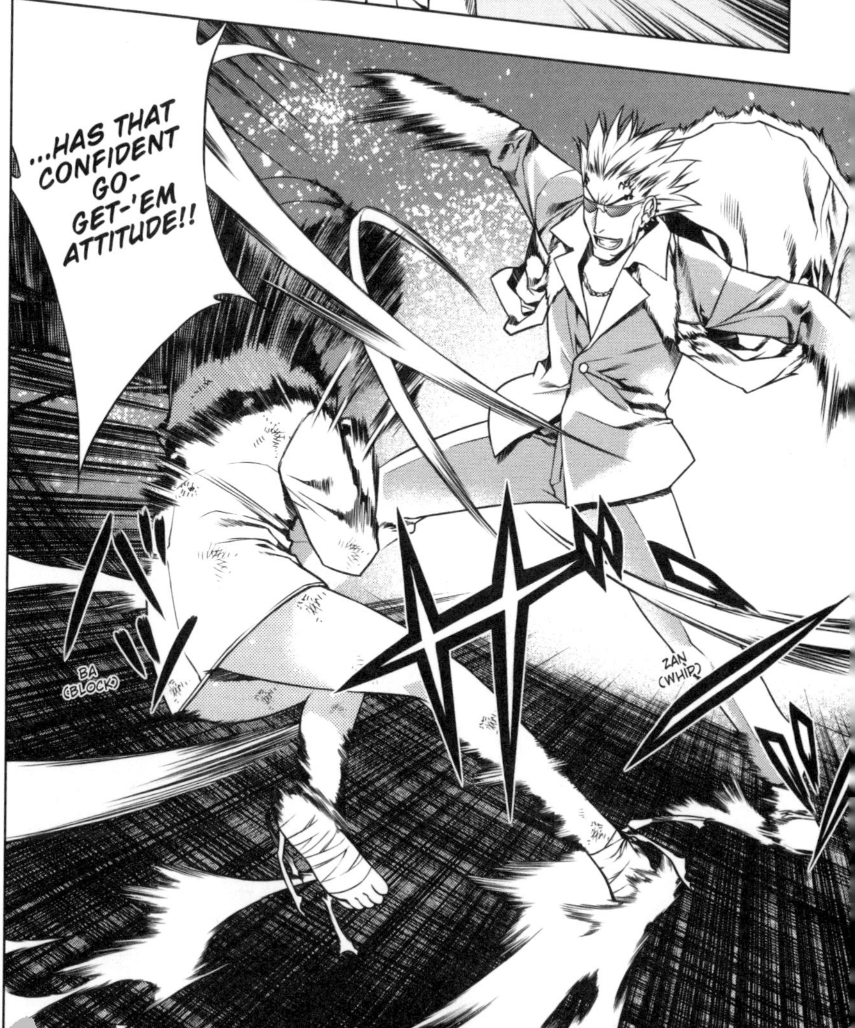
...HAS THAT CONFIDENT GO-GET-'EM ATTITUDE!!
ZAN (WHIP)
BA (BLOCK)

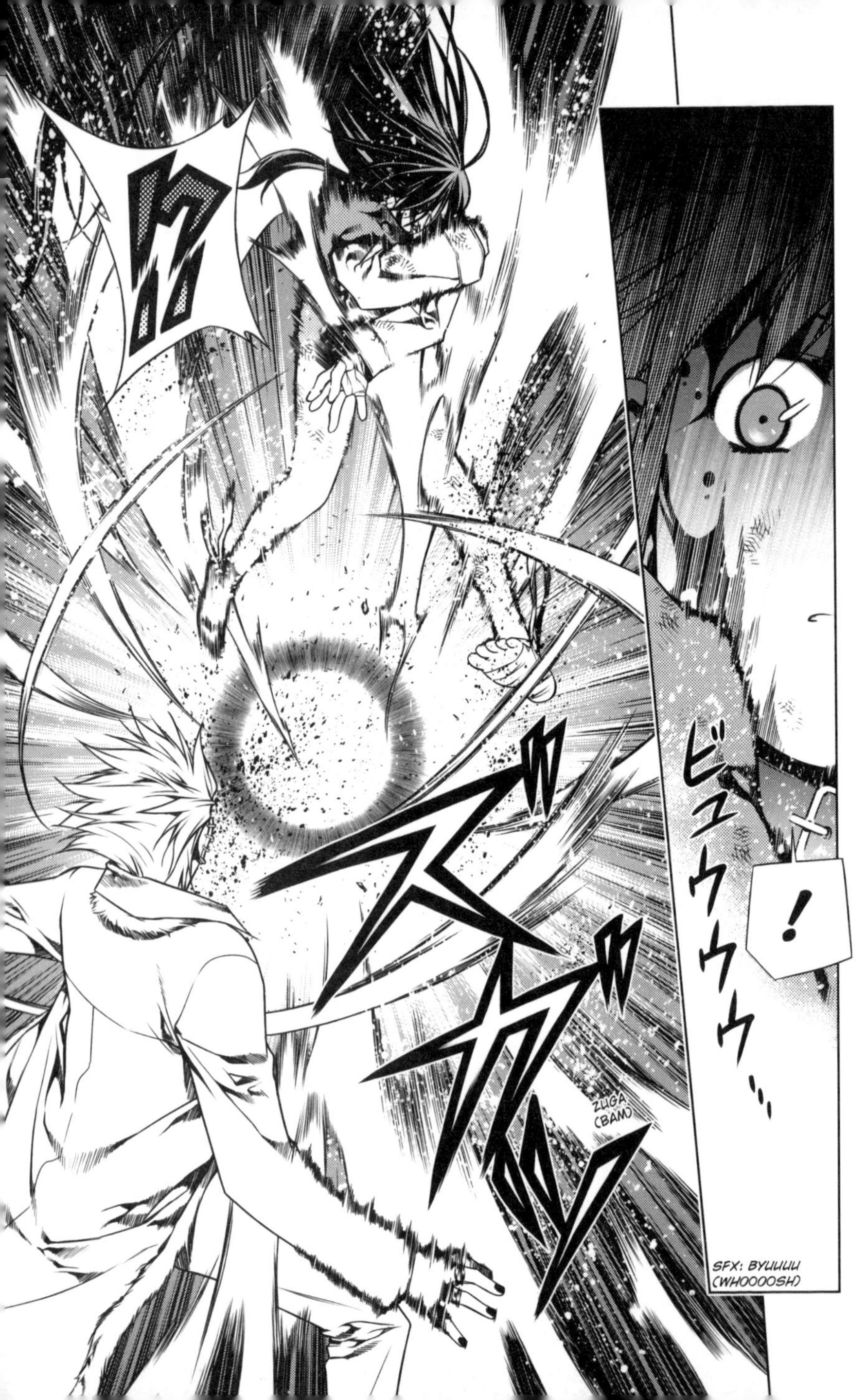
!
ビュウウウ…
SFX: BYUUUU (WHOOOOSH)
ZUGA (BAM)

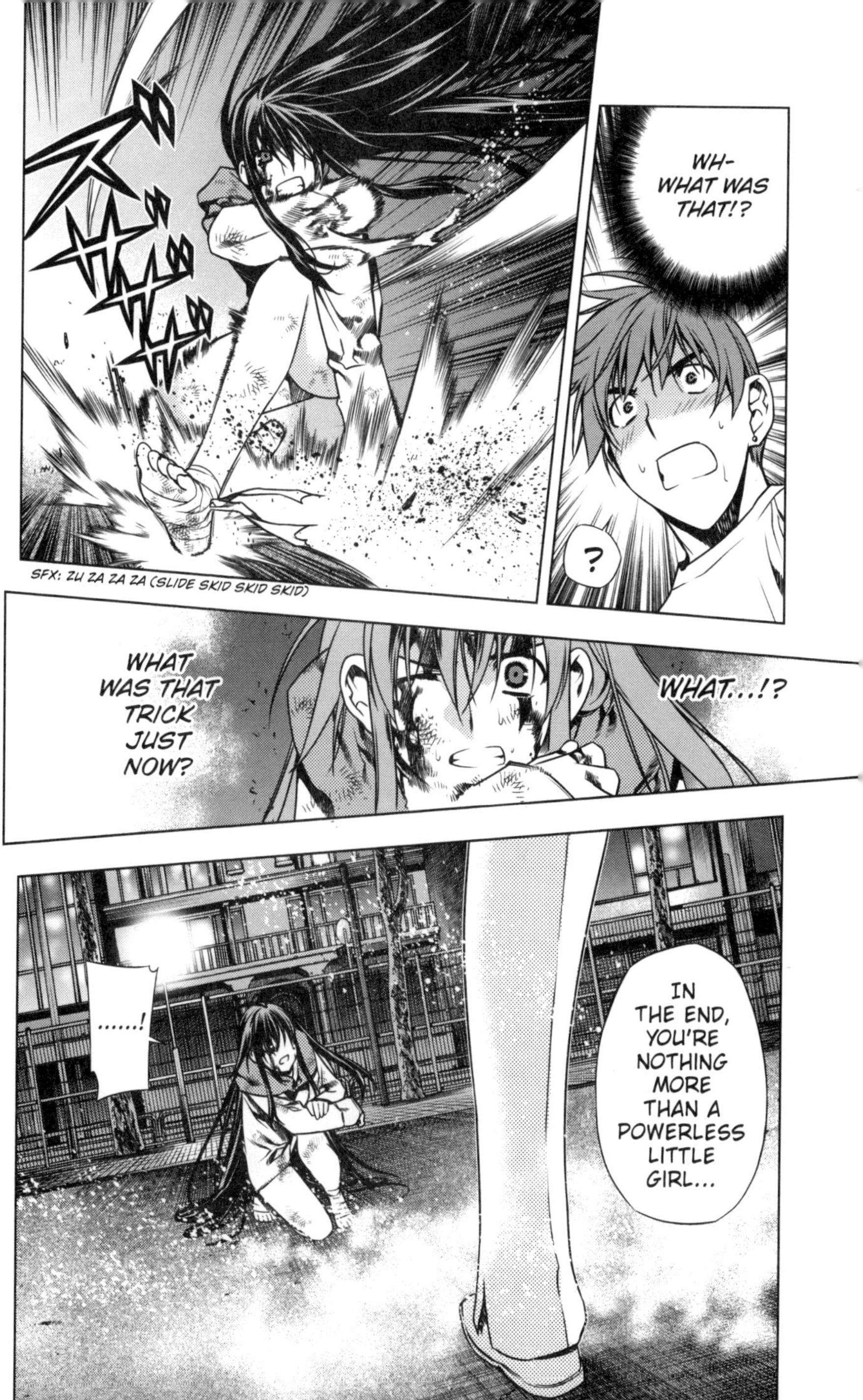
WH- WHAT WAS THAT!?
?
SFX: ZU ZA ZA ZA (SLIDE SKID SKID SKID)
WHAT...!?
WHAT WAS THAT TRICK JUST NOW?
IN THE END, YOU'RE NOTHING MORE THAN A POWERLESS LITTLE GIRL...
......!

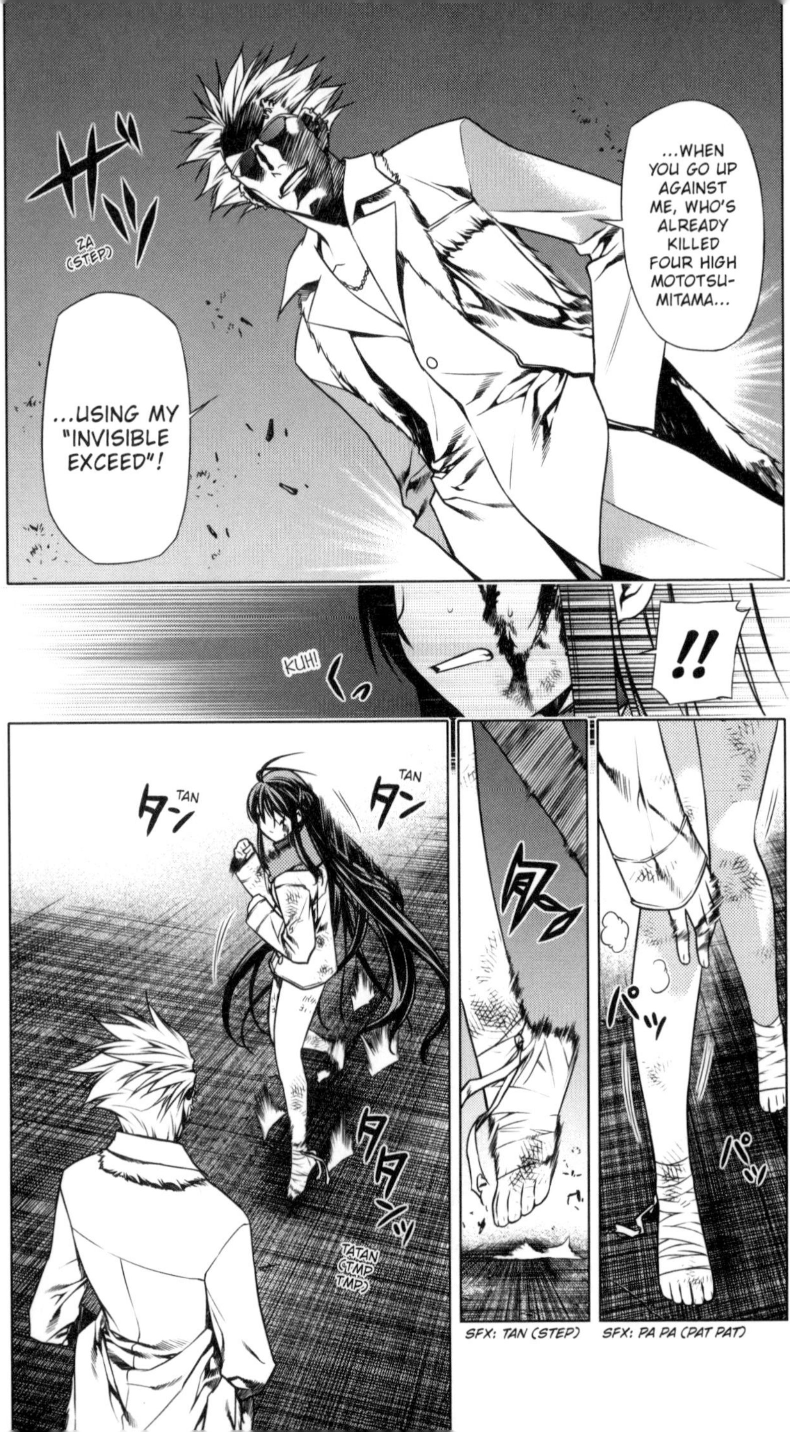
...WHEN YOU GO UP AGAINST ME, WHO'S ALREADY KILLED FOUR HIGH MOTOTSU-MITAMA...
ZA (STEP)
...USING MY "INVISIBLE EXCEED"!
!!
KUH!
TAN
TAN
TATAN (TMP TMP)
SFX: TAN (STEP) SFX: PA PA (PAT PAT)

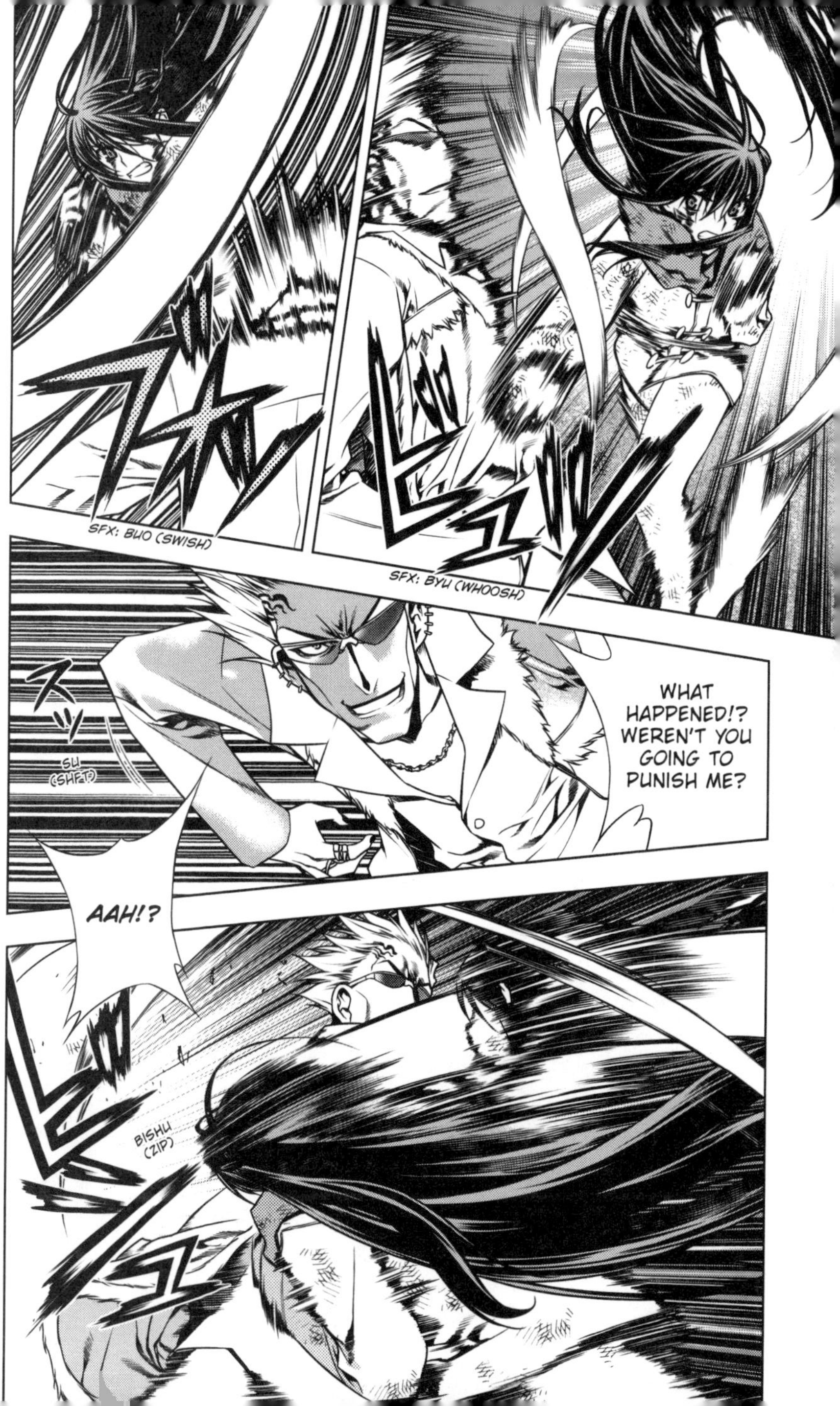
SFX: BYU (WHOOSH)
SFX: BUO (SWISH)
WHAT HAPPENED!? WEREN'T YOU GOING TO PUNISH ME?
SU (SHFT)
AAH!?
BISHU (ZIP)

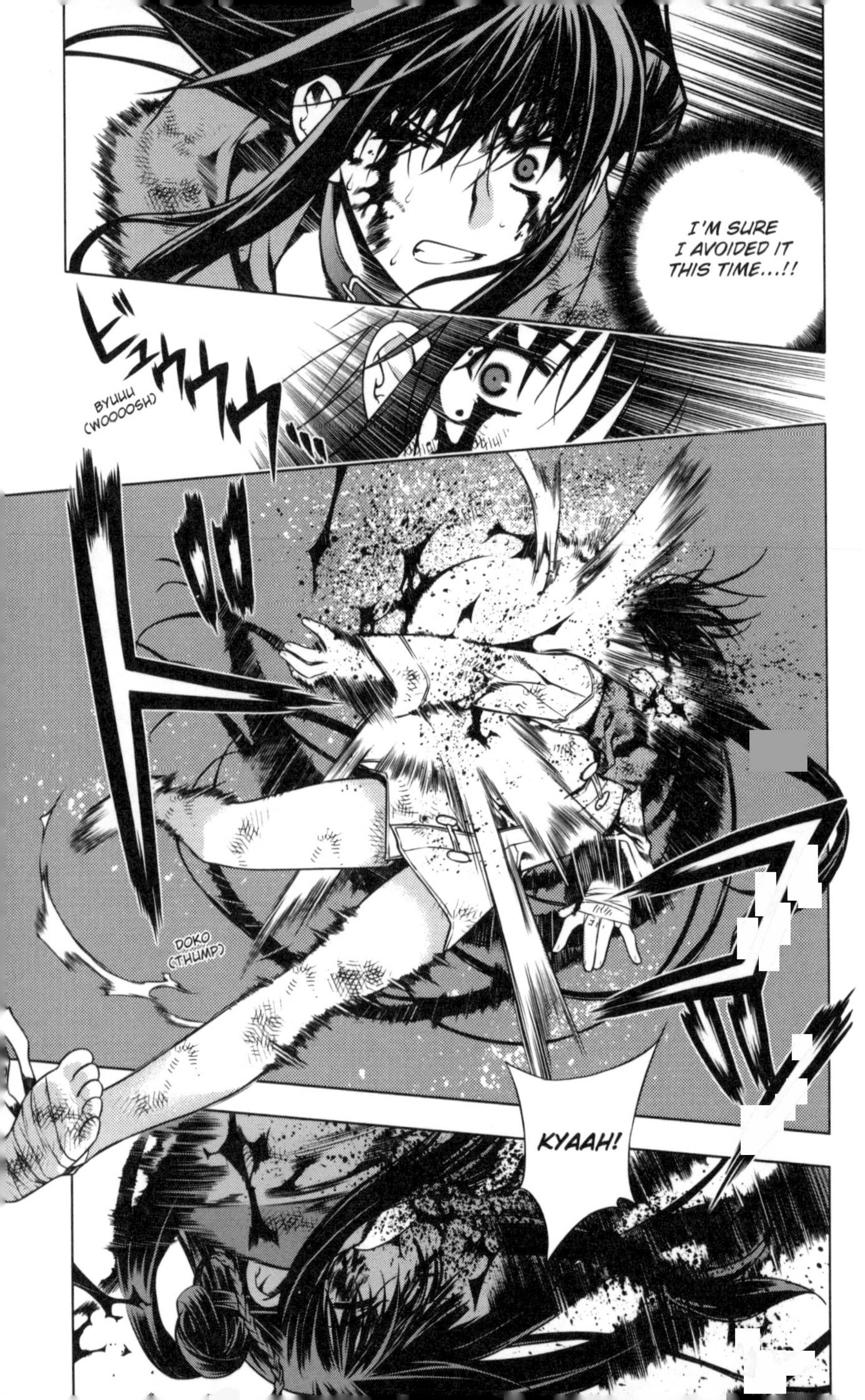
I'M SURE I AVOIDED IT THIS TIME...!!
ビュウウウ…
BYUUU (WOOOOSH)
ドッ
DOKO (THUMP)
KYAAH!

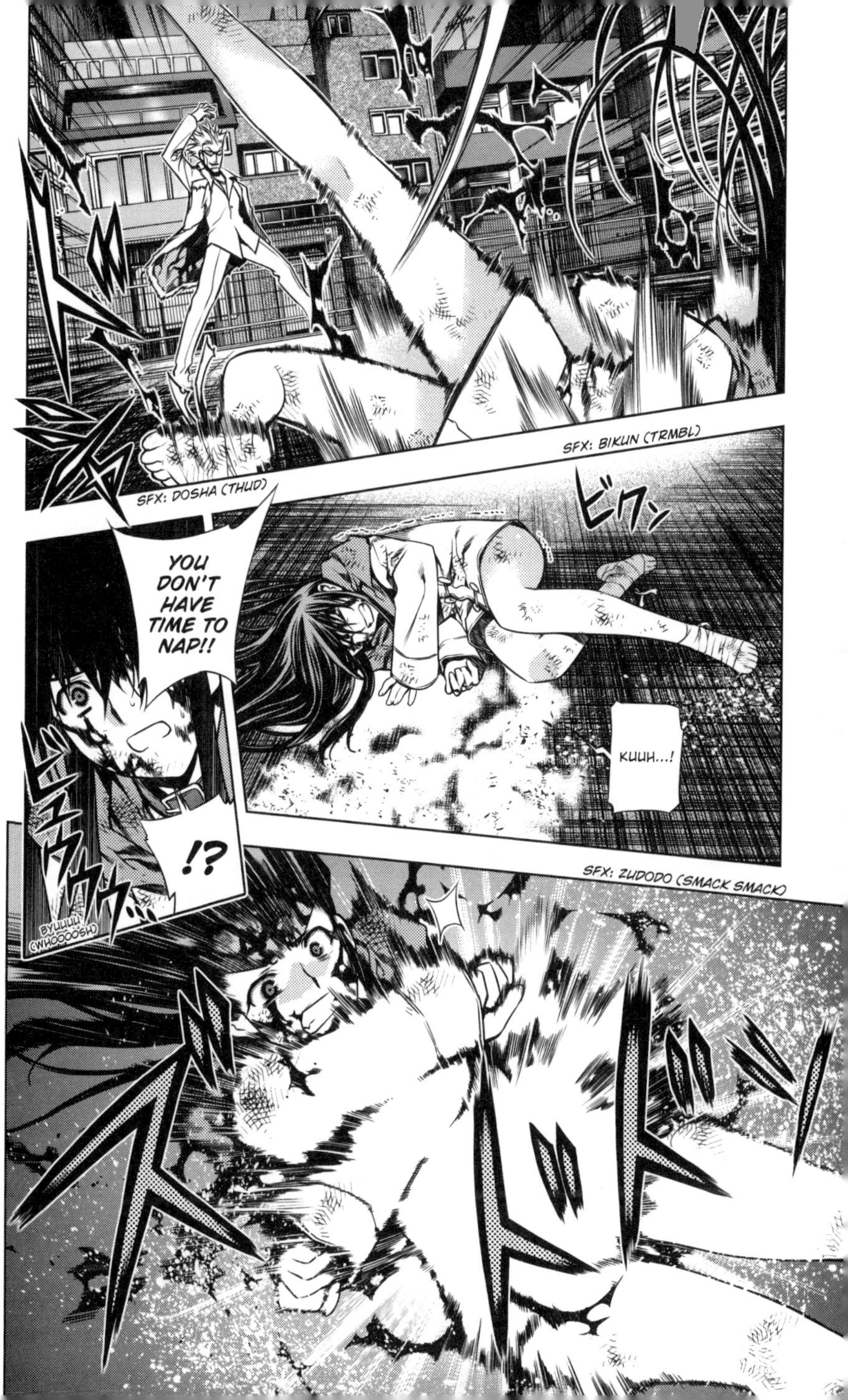
SFX: DOSHA (THUD)
SFX: BIKUN (TRMBL)
KUUH...!
YOU DON'T HAVE TIME TO NAP!!
!?
BYUUUN (WHOOOOSH)
SFX: ZUDODO (SMACK SMACK)

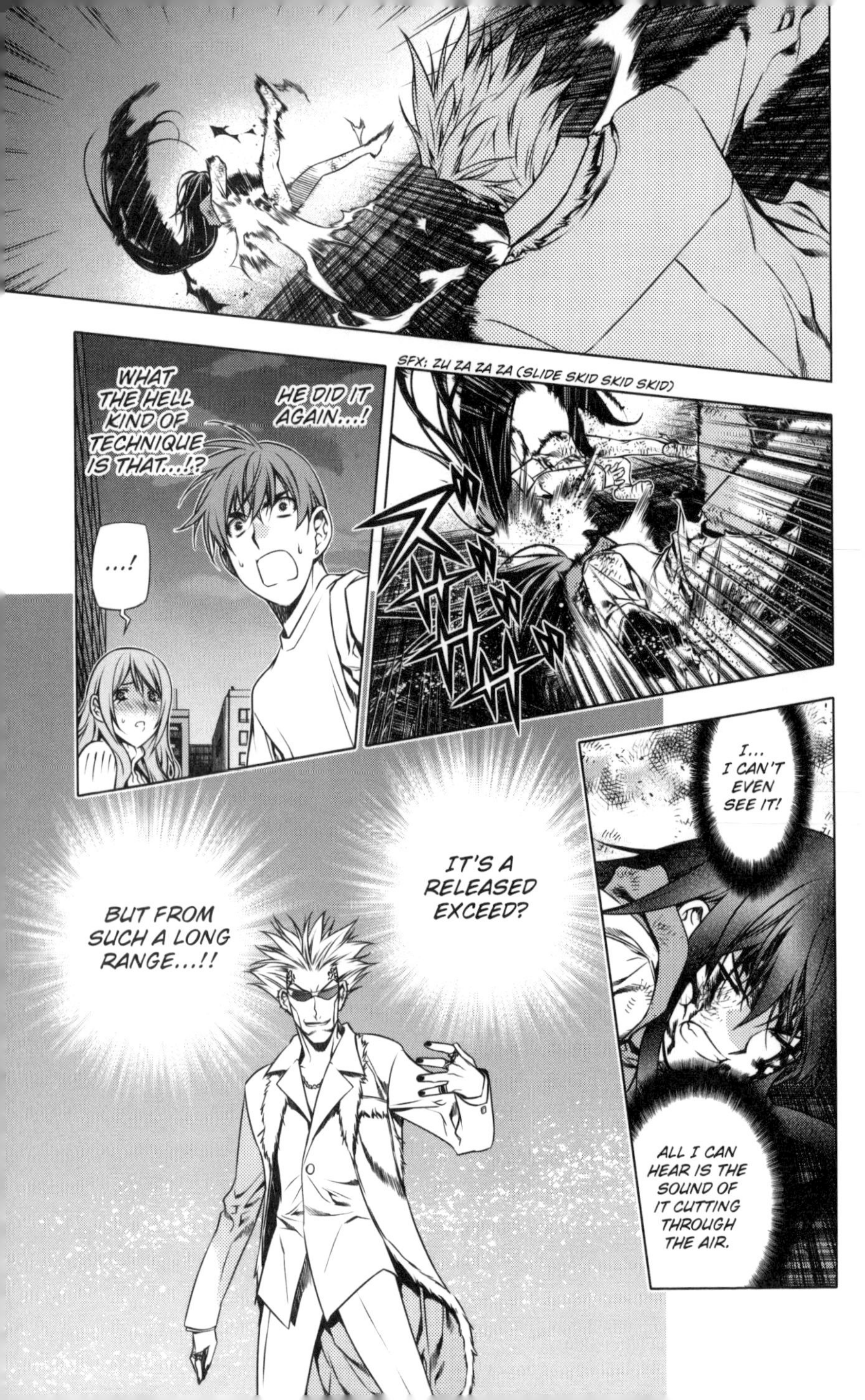
SFX: ZU ZA ZA ZA (SLIDE SKID SKID SKID)
HE DID IT AGAIN...!
WHAT THE HELL KIND OF TECHNIQUE IS THAT...!?
...!
I... I CAN'T EVEN SEE IT!
ALL I CAN HEAR IS THE SOUND OF IT CUTTING THROUGH THE AIR.
IT'S A RELEASED EXCEED?
BUT FROM SUCH A LONG RANGE...!!

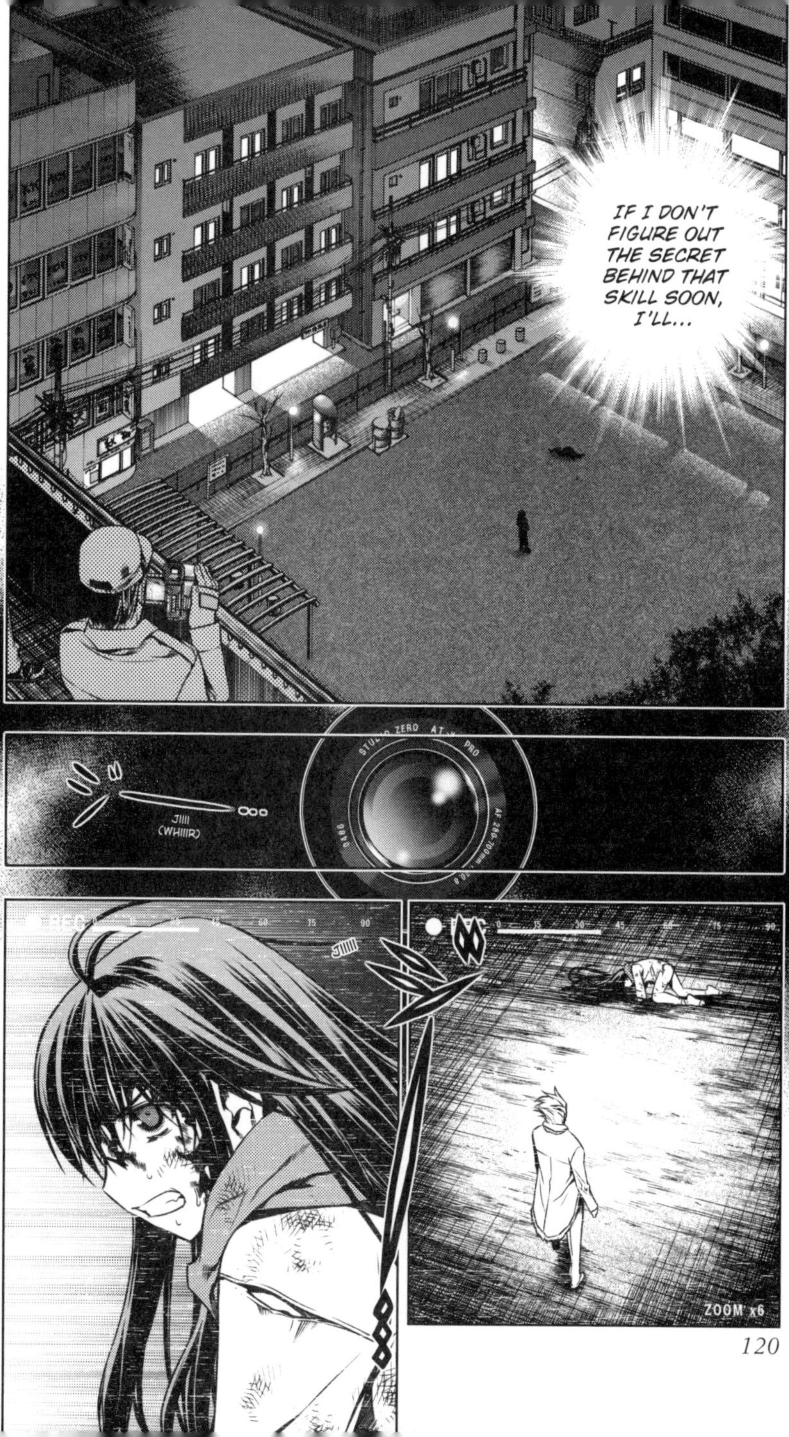
IF I DON'T FIGURE OUT THE SECRET BEHIND THAT SKILL SOON, I'LL...
JIIII
(WHIIIR)
ZOOM x6
JIIII

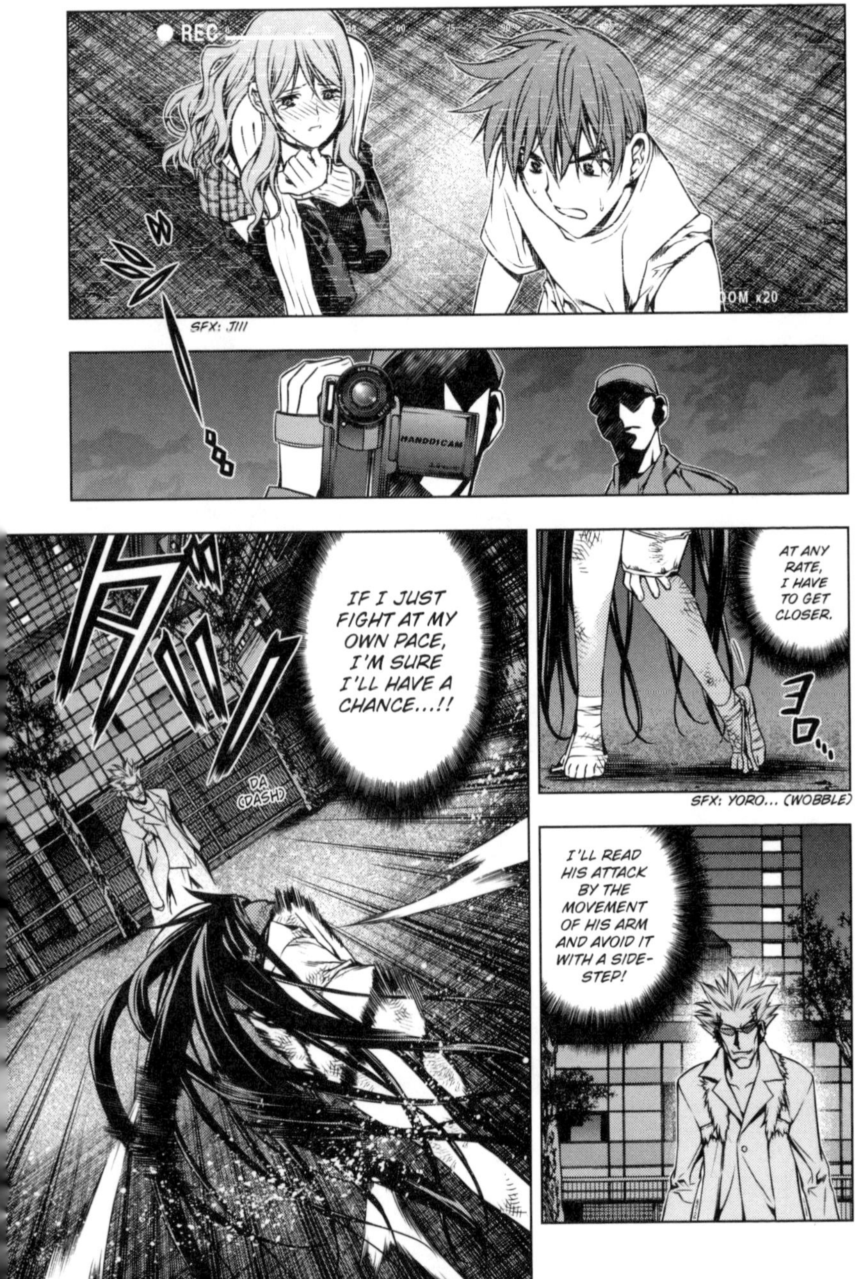
REC
OOM x20
SFX: JIII
HANDDICAM
AT ANY RATE, I HAVE TO GET CLOSER.
SFX: YORO... (WOBBLE)
I'LL READ HIS ATTACK BY THE MOVEMENT OF HIS ARM AND AVOID IT WITH A SIDE-STEP!
IF I JUST FIGHT AT MY OWN PACE, I'M SURE I'LL HAVE A CHANCE...!!
DA (DASH)

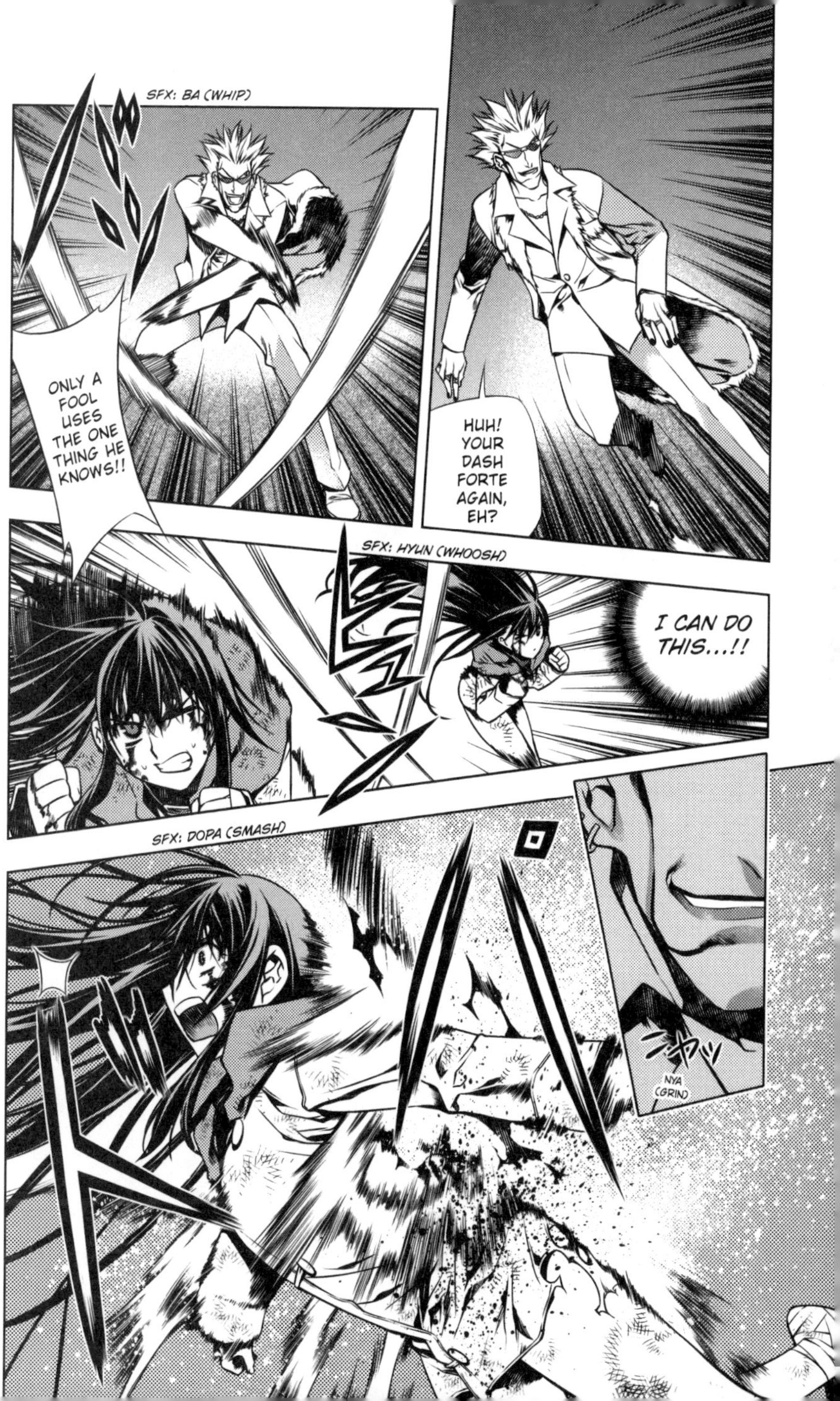
HUH! YOUR DASH FORTE AGAIN, EH?
SFX: BA (WHIP)
ONLY A FOOL USES THE ONE THING HE KNOWS!!
SFX: HYUN (WHOOSH)
I CAN DO THIS...!!
ニヤッ
NYA (GRIN)
SFX: DOPA (SMASH)

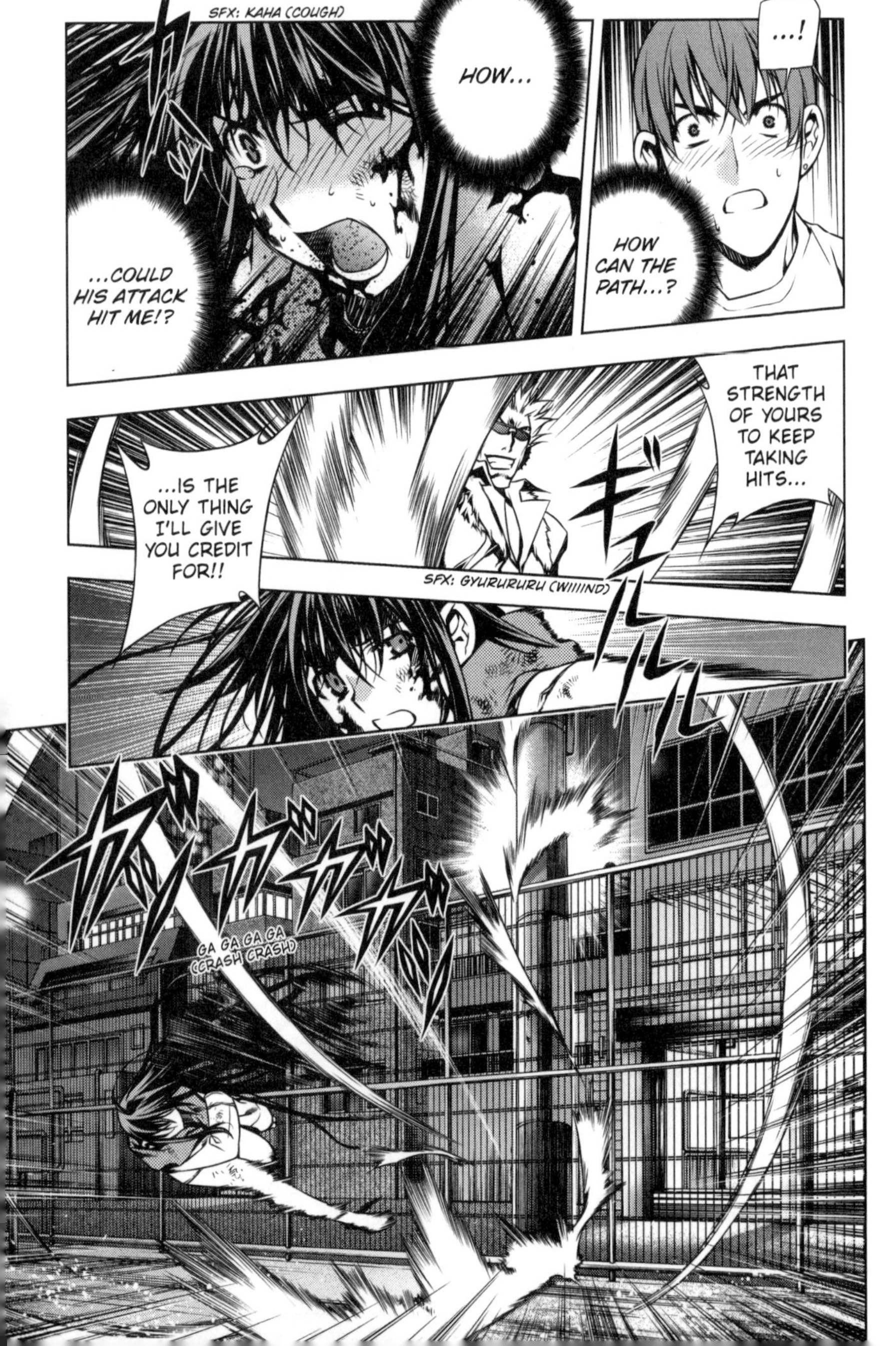
...!
HOW CAN THE PATH...?
SFX: KAHA (COUGH)
HOW...
...COULD HIS ATTACK HIT ME!?
THAT STRENGTH OF YOURS TO KEEP TAKING HITS...
...IS THE ONLY THING I'LL GIVE YOU CREDIT FOR!!
SFX: GYURURURU (WIIIND)
GA GA GA GA (CRASH CRASH)

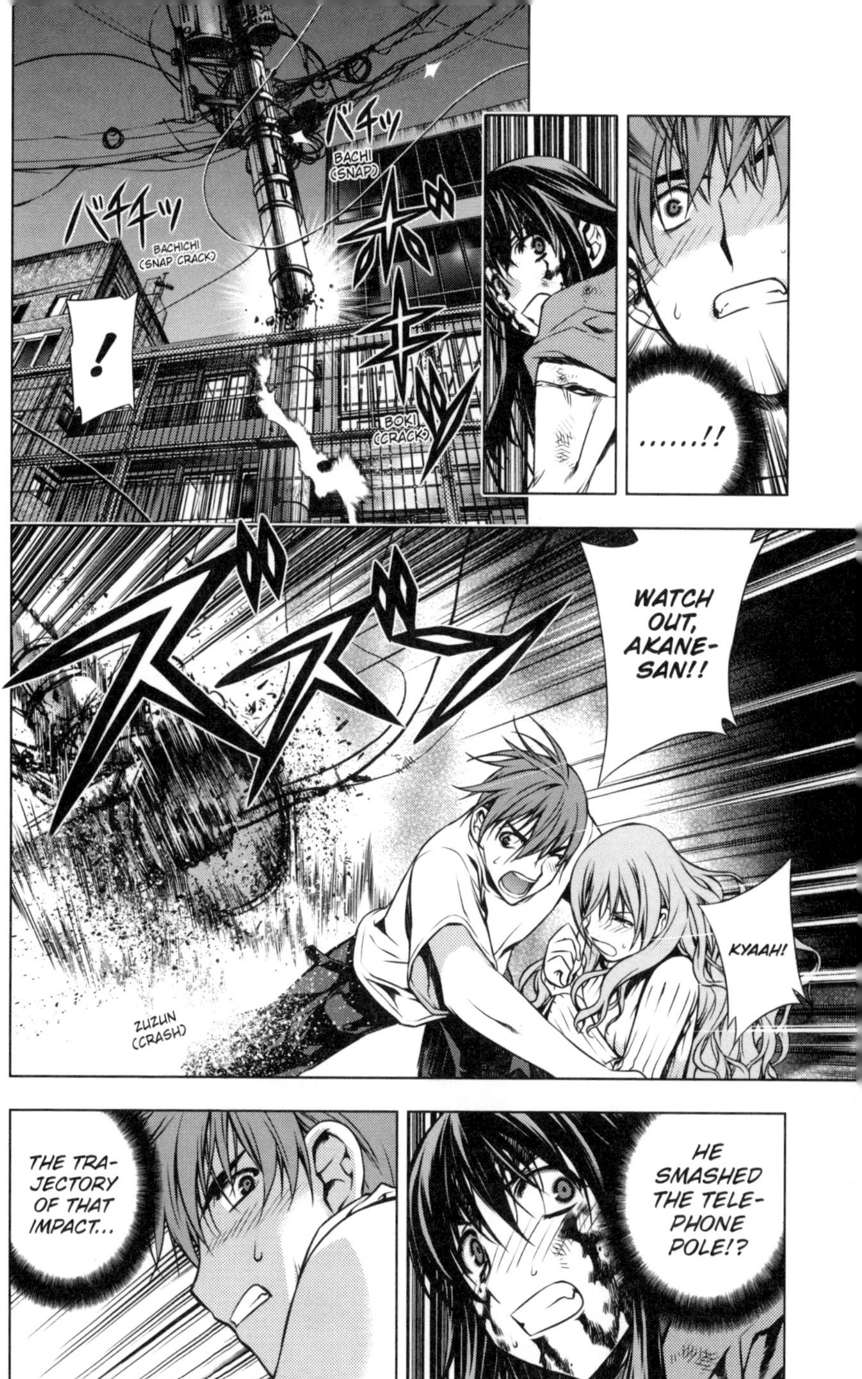
......!!
バチッ
BACHI (SNAP)
バチチッ
BACHICHI (SNAP CRACK)
!
ボキッ
BOKI (CRACK)
WATCH OUT, AKANE-SAN!!
ズズン
KYAAH!
ZUZUN (CRASH)
HE SMASHED THE TELE-PHONE POLE!?
THE TRA-JECTORY OF THAT IMPACT...

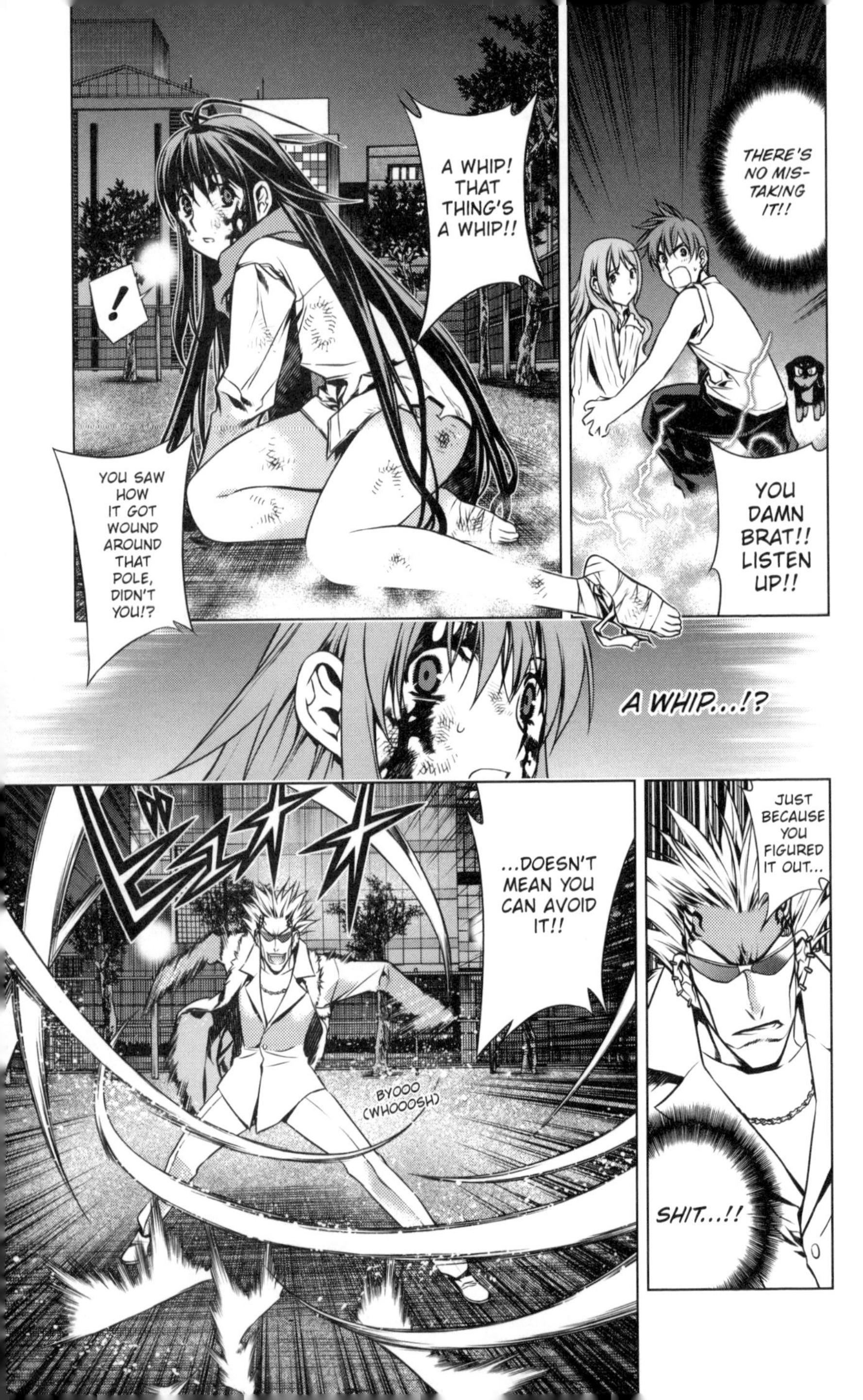
THERE'S NO MIS-TAKING IT!!
YOU DAMN BRAT!! LISTEN UP!!
A WHIP! THAT THING'S A WHIP!!
!
YOU SAW HOW IT GOT WOUND AROUND THAT POLE, DIDN'T YOU!?
A WHIP...!?
JUST BECAUSE YOU FIGURED IT OUT...
SHIT...!!
...DOESN'T MEAN YOU CAN AVOID IT!!
BYOOO (WHOOOSH)

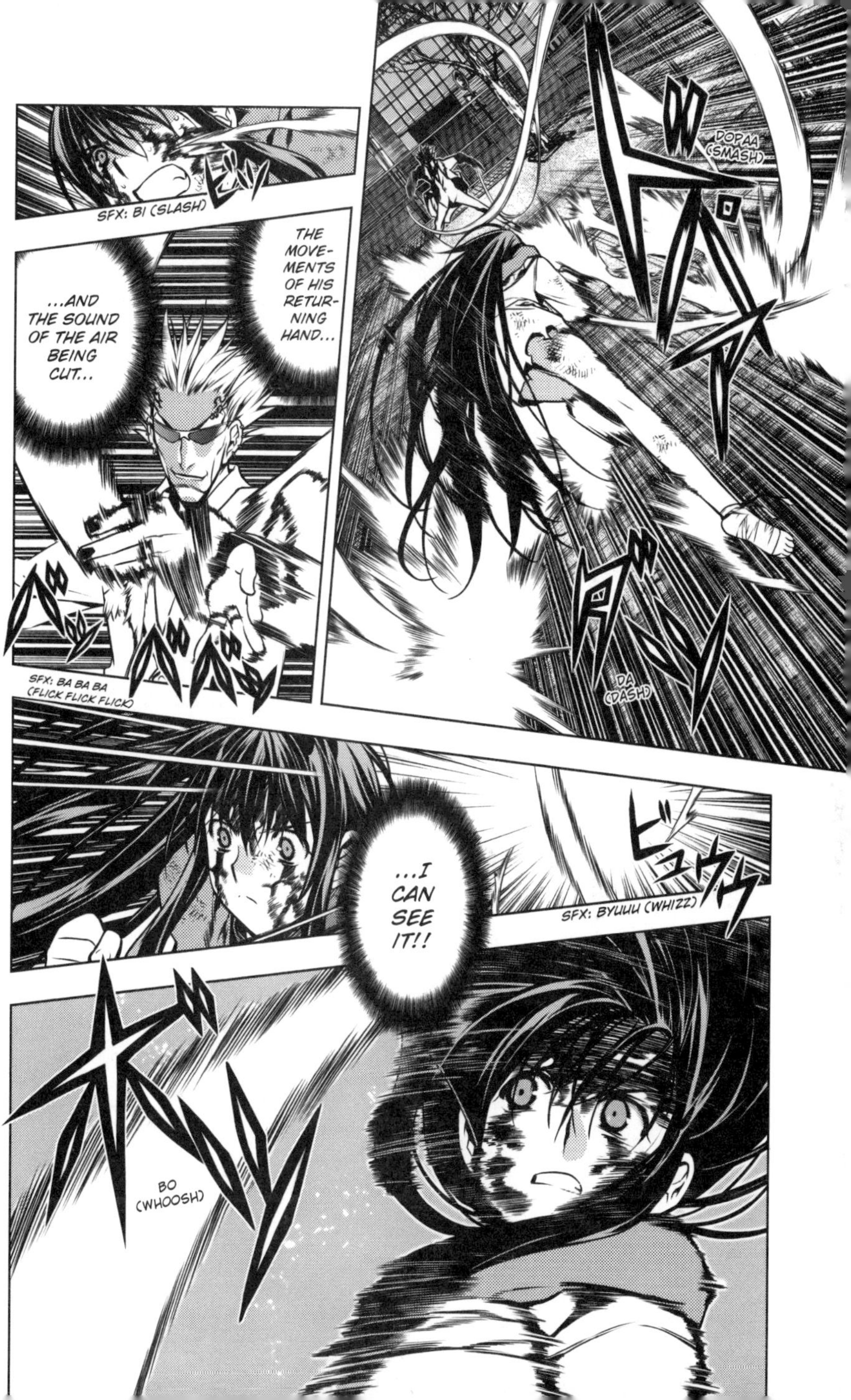
DOPAA (SMASH)
DA (DASH)
SFX: BI (SLASH)
THE MOVEMENTS OF HIS RETURNING HAND...
...AND THE SOUND OF THE AIR BEING CUT...
SFX: BA BA BA (FLICK FLICK FLICK)
SFX: BYUUU (WHIZZ)
...I CAN SEE IT!!
BO (WHOOSH)

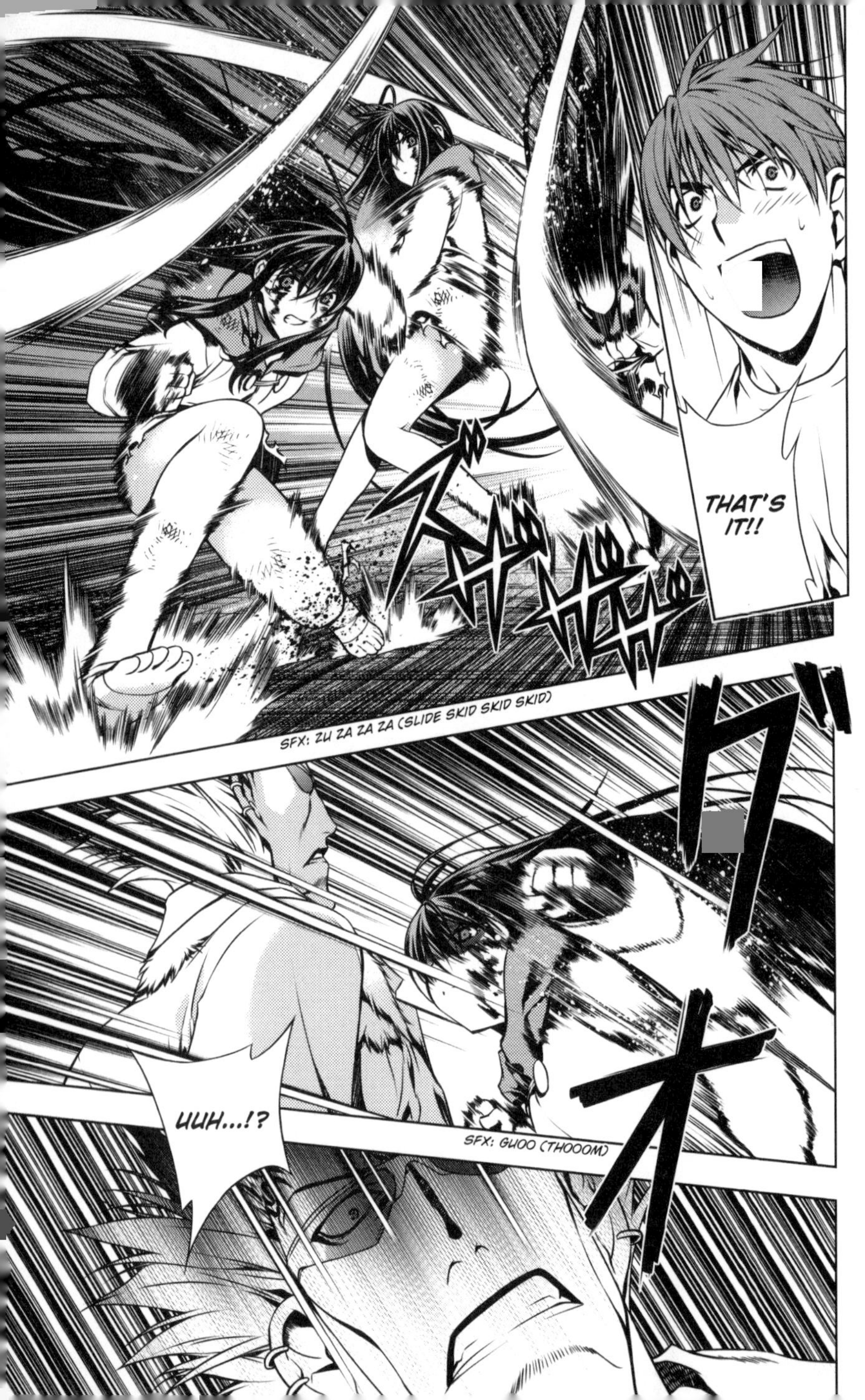
THAT'S IT!!
SFX: ZU ZA ZA ZA (SLIDE SKID SKID SKID)
SFX: GUOO (THOOOM)
UUH...!?

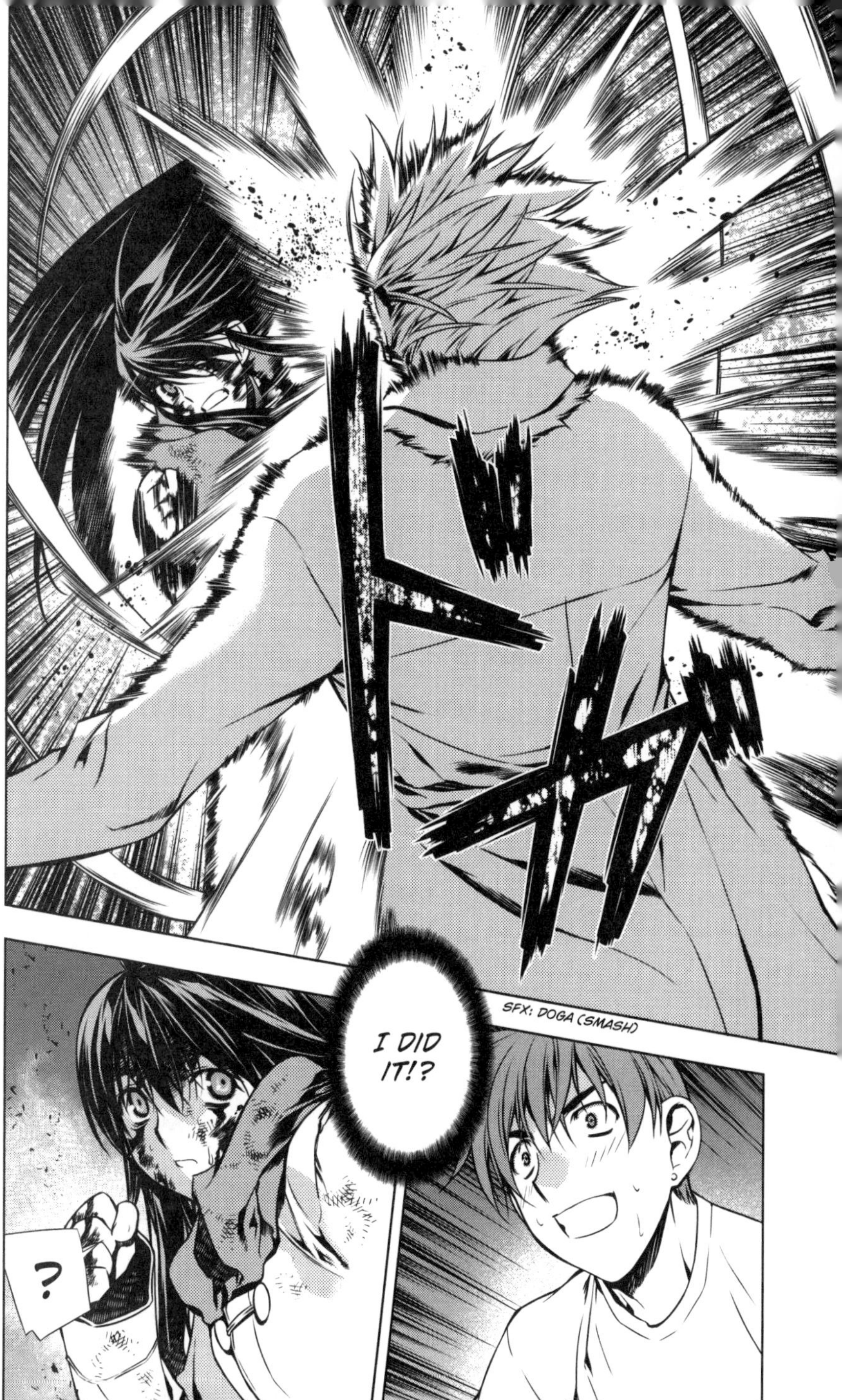
SFX: DOGA (SMASH)
I DID IT!?
?

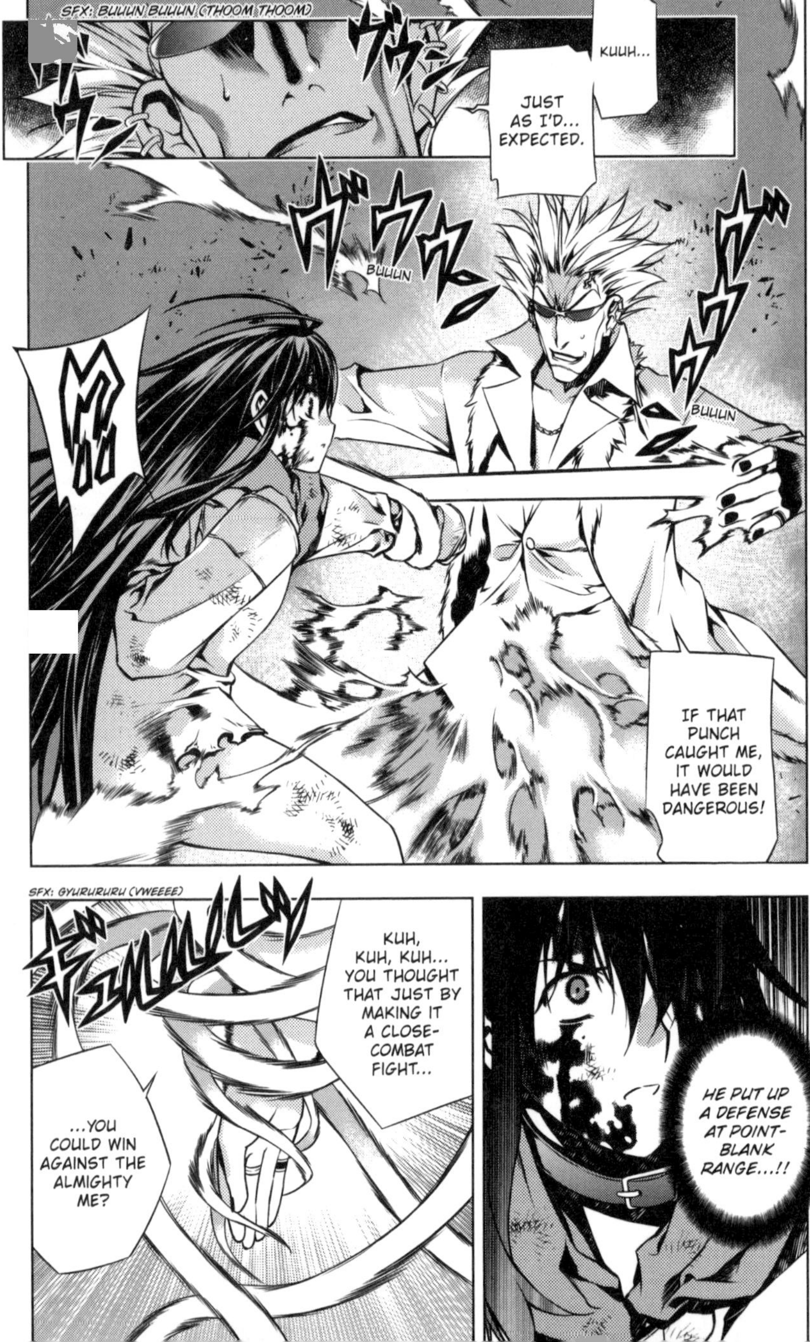
SFX: BUUUN BUUUN (THOOM THOOM)
KUUH...
JUST AS I'D... EXPECTED.
BUUUN
BUUUN
IF THAT PUNCH CAUGHT ME, IT WOULD HAVE BEEN DANGEROUS!
HE PUT UP A DEFENSE AT POINT-BLANK RANGE...!!
SFX: GYURURURU (VWEEEE)
KUH, KUH, KUH... YOU THOUGHT THAT JUST BY MAKING IT A CLOSE-COMBAT FIGHT...
...YOU COULD WIN AGAINST THE ALMIGHTY ME?

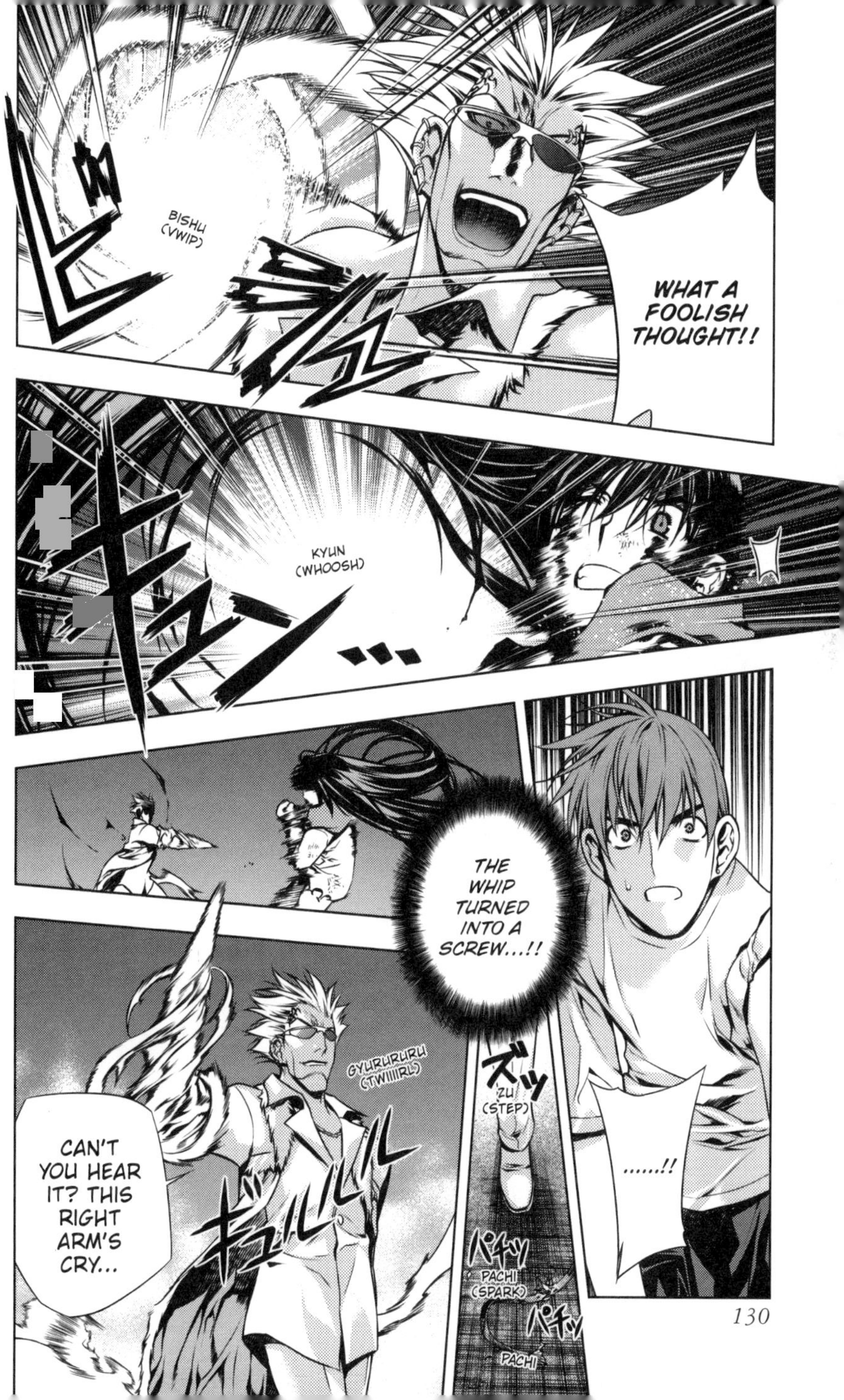
BISHU (VWIP)
WHAT A FOOLISH THOUGHT!!
KYUN (WHOOSH)
THE WHIP TURNED INTO A SCREW...!!
ZU (STEP)
......!!
GYURURURU (TWIIIIRL)
CAN'T YOU HEAR IT? THIS RIGHT ARM'S CRY...
PACHI (SPARK)
PACHI

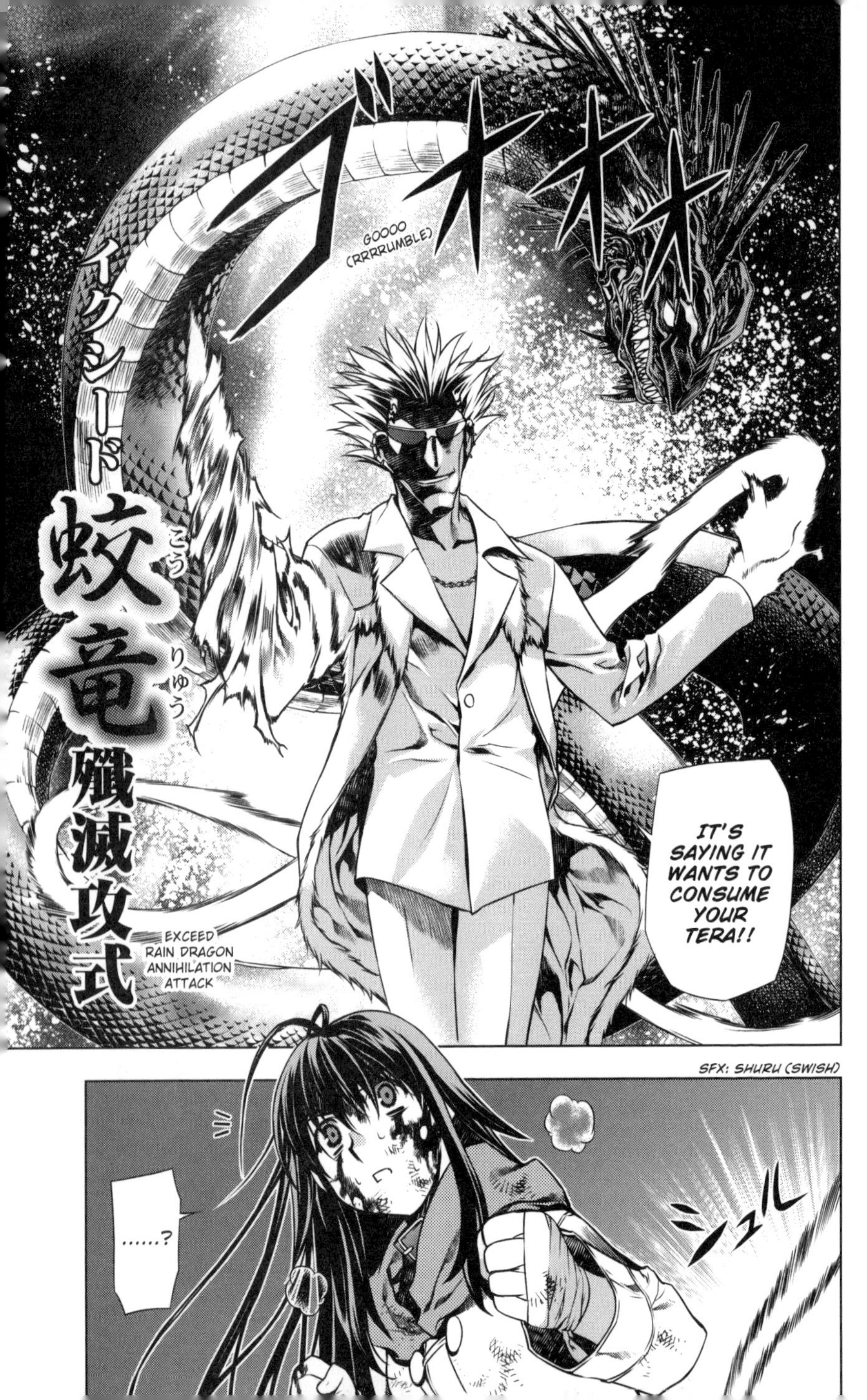
ゴオオオ
GOOOO (RRRRUMBLE)
イクシード蛟竜殲滅攻式
こう りゅう
EXCEED RAIN DRAGON ANNIHILATION ATTACK
IT'S SAYING IT WANTS TO CONSUME YOUR TERA!!
シュル
SFX: SHURU (SWISH)
......?

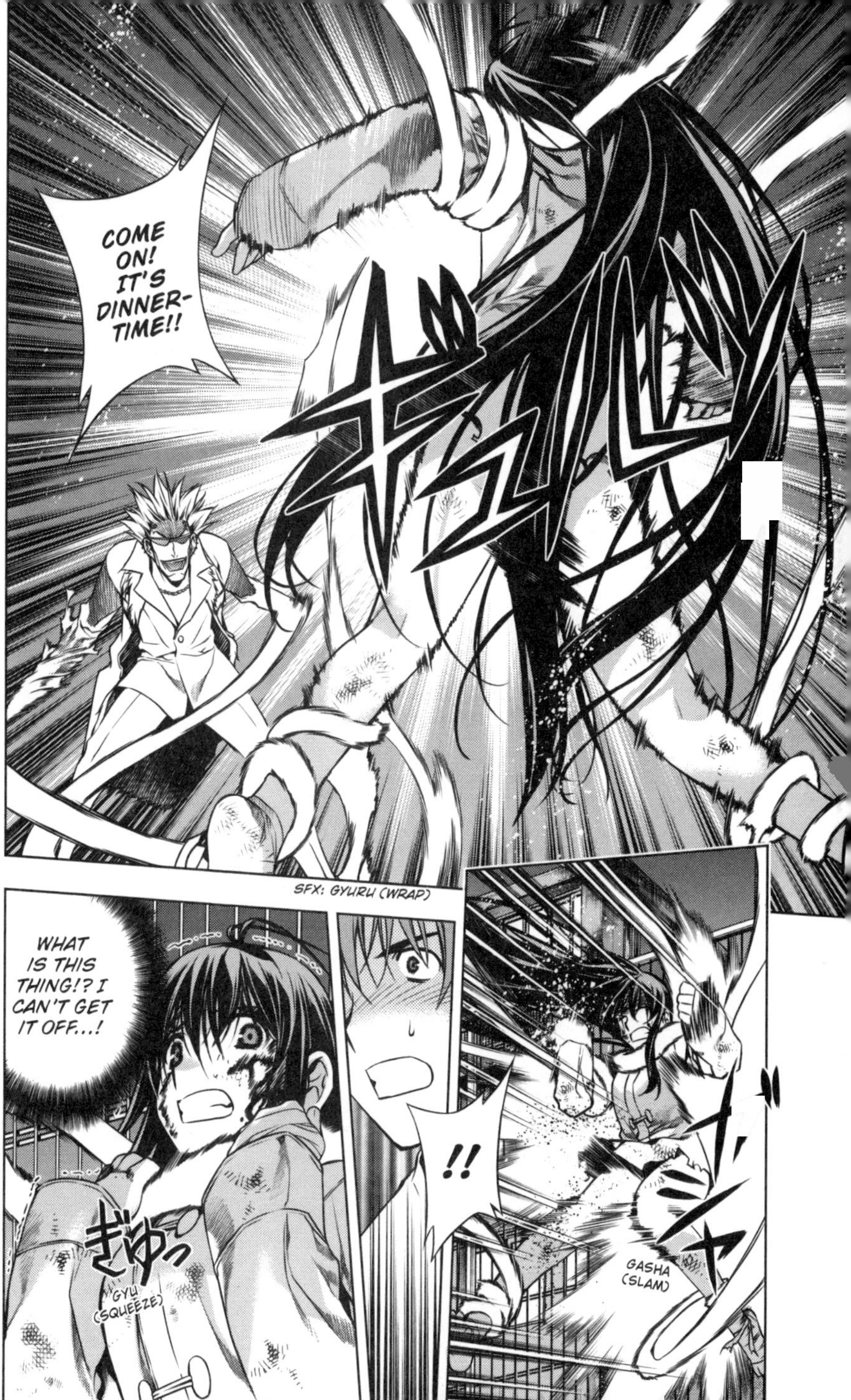
COME ON! IT'S DINNER-TIME!!
SFX: GYURU (WRAP)
GASHA (SLAM)
!!
WHAT IS THIS THING!? I CAN'T GET IT OFF...!
ぎゅっ
GYU (SQUEEZE)

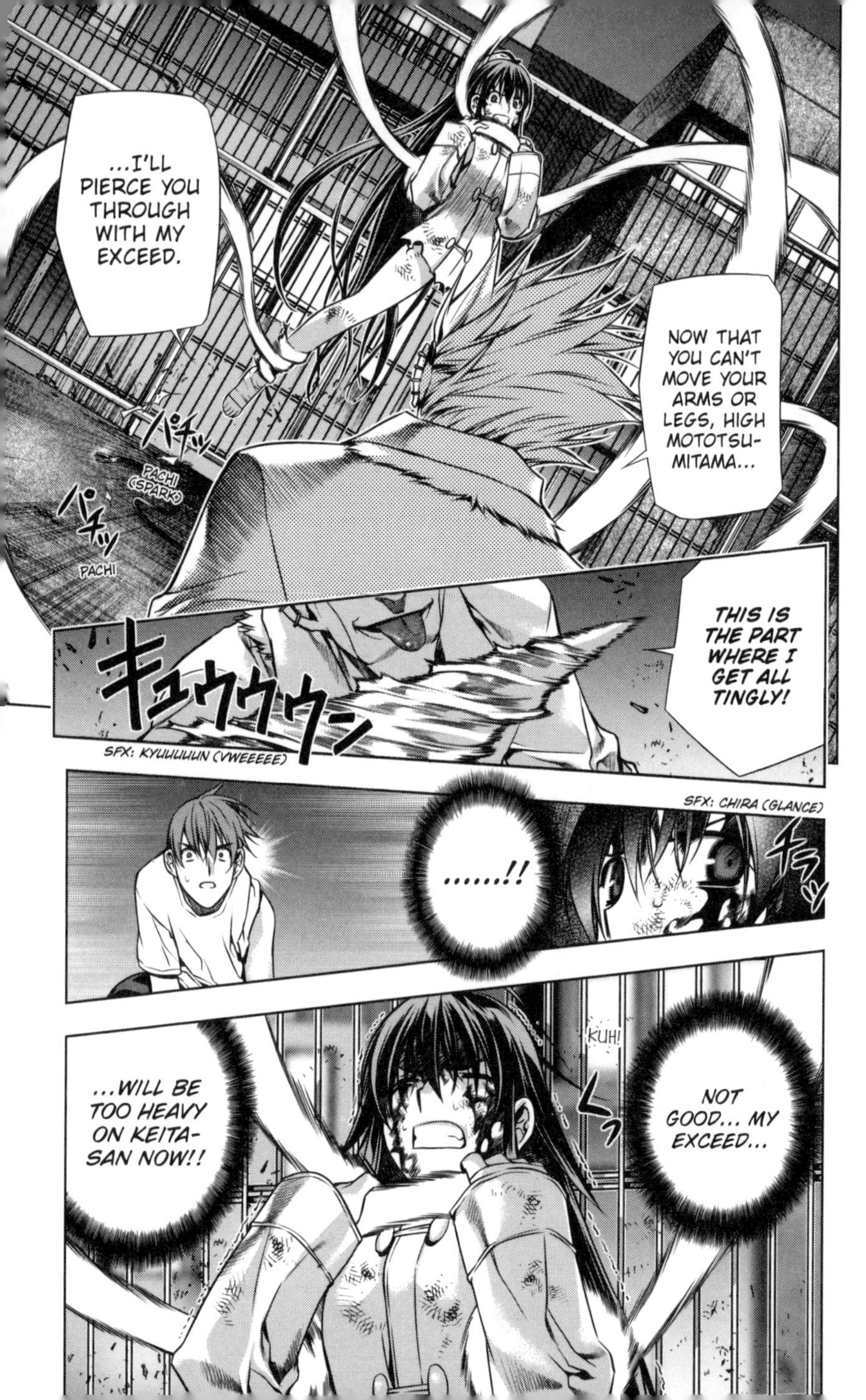
NOW THAT YOU CAN'T MOVE YOUR ARMS OR LEGS, HIGH MOTOTSU-MITAMA...
...I'LL PIERCE YOU THROUGH WITH MY EXCEED.
パチッ
PACHI (SPARK)
パチッ
PACHI
THIS IS THE PART WHERE I GET ALL TINGLY!
キュウウウウン
SFX: KYUUUUUN (VWEEEEE)
SFX: CHIRA (GLANCE)
......!!
NOT GOOD... MY EXCEED...
KUH!
...WILL BE TOO HEAVY ON KEITA-SAN NOW!!

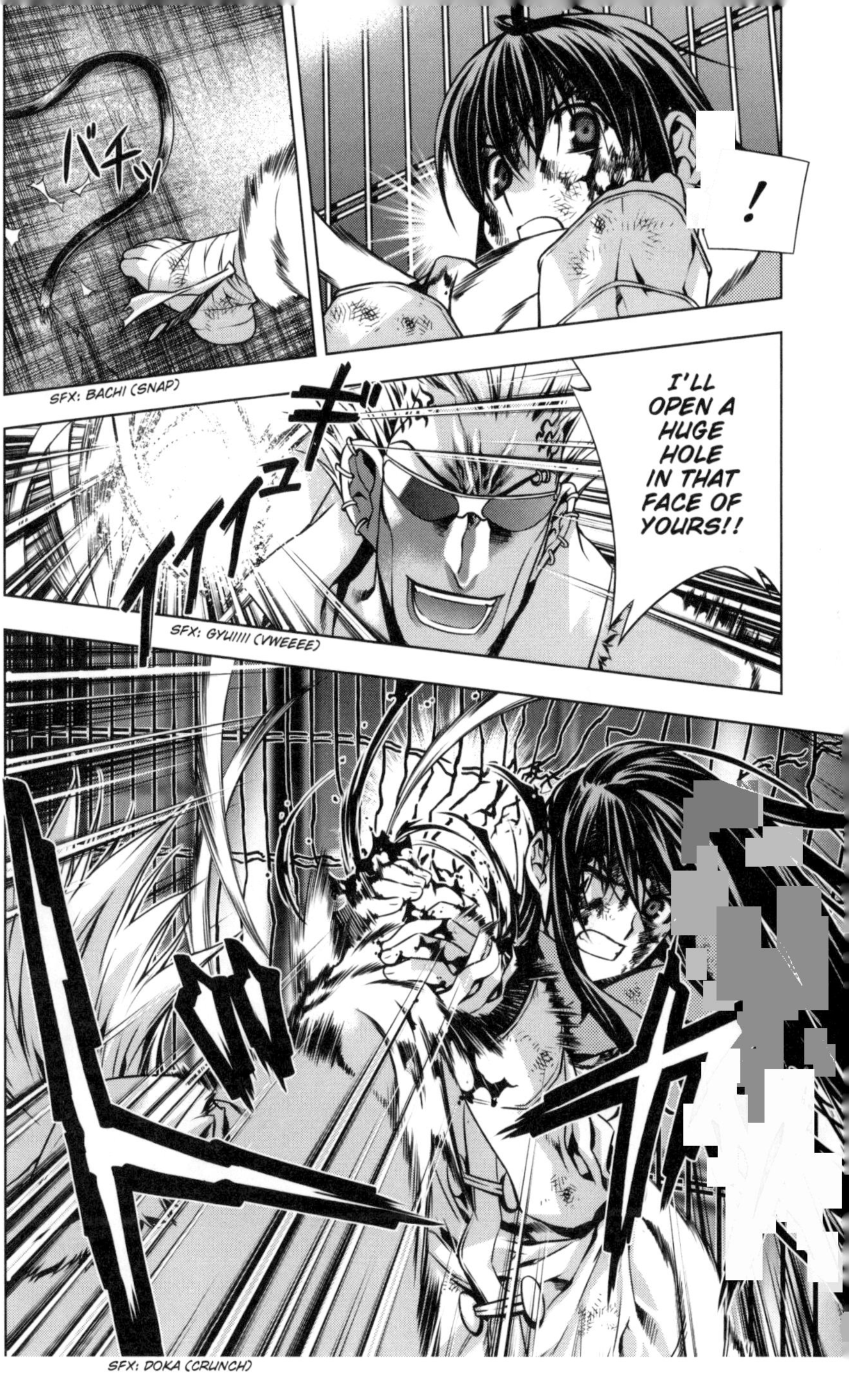
!
SFX: BACHI (SNAP)
I'LL OPEN A HUGE HOLE IN THAT FACE OF YOURS!!
SFX: GYUIIII (VWEEEE)
SFX: DOKA (CRUNCH)

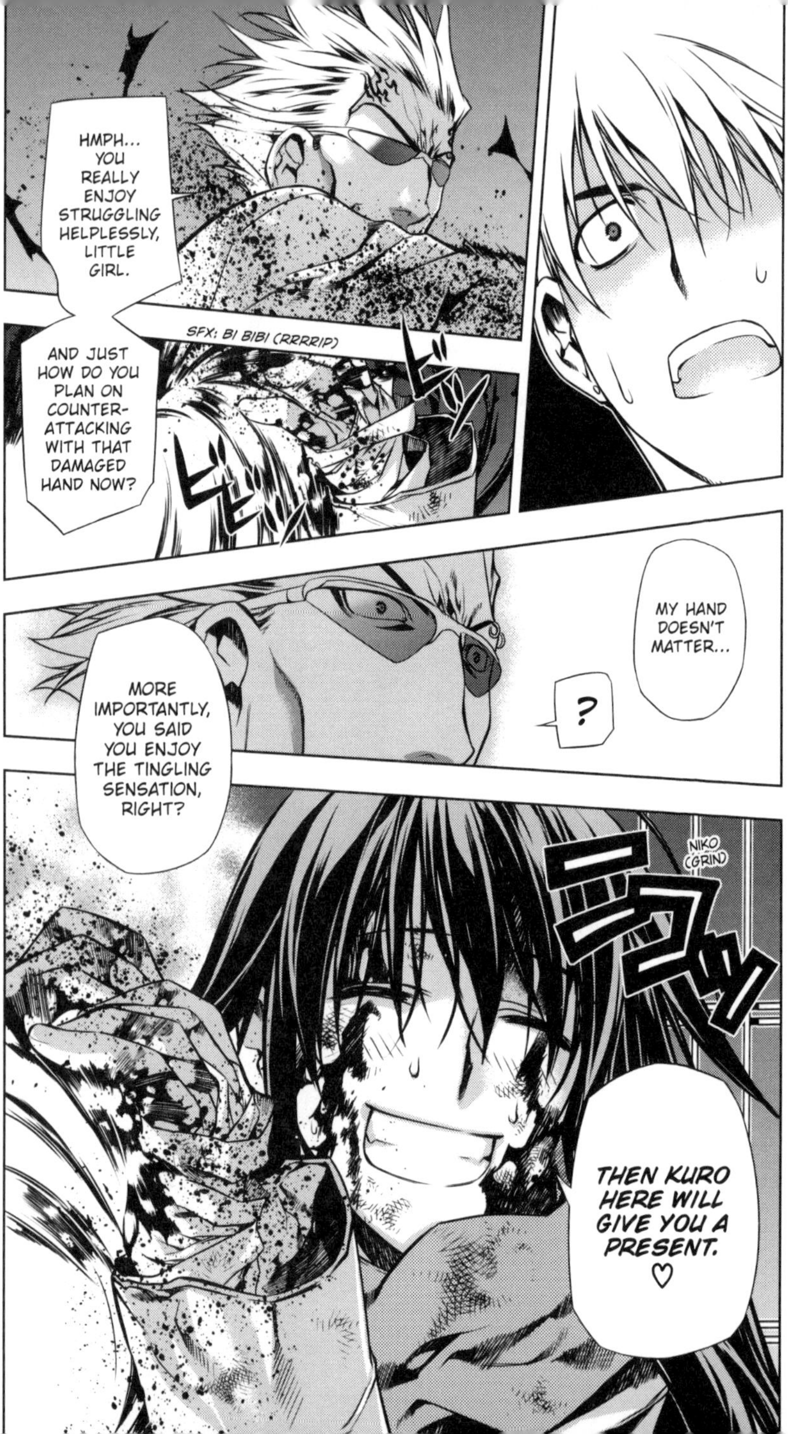
HMPH... YOU REALLY ENJOY STRUGGLING HELPLESSLY, LITTLE GIRL.
SFX: BI BIBI (RRRRIP)
AND JUST HOW DO YOU PLAN ON COUNTER-ATTACKING WITH THAT DAMAGED HAND NOW?
MY HAND DOESN'T MATTER...
?
MORE IMPORTANTLY, YOU SAID YOU ENJOY THE TINGLING SENSATION, RIGHT?
NIKO (GRIN)
THEN KURO HERE WILL GIVE YOU A PRESENT. ♡

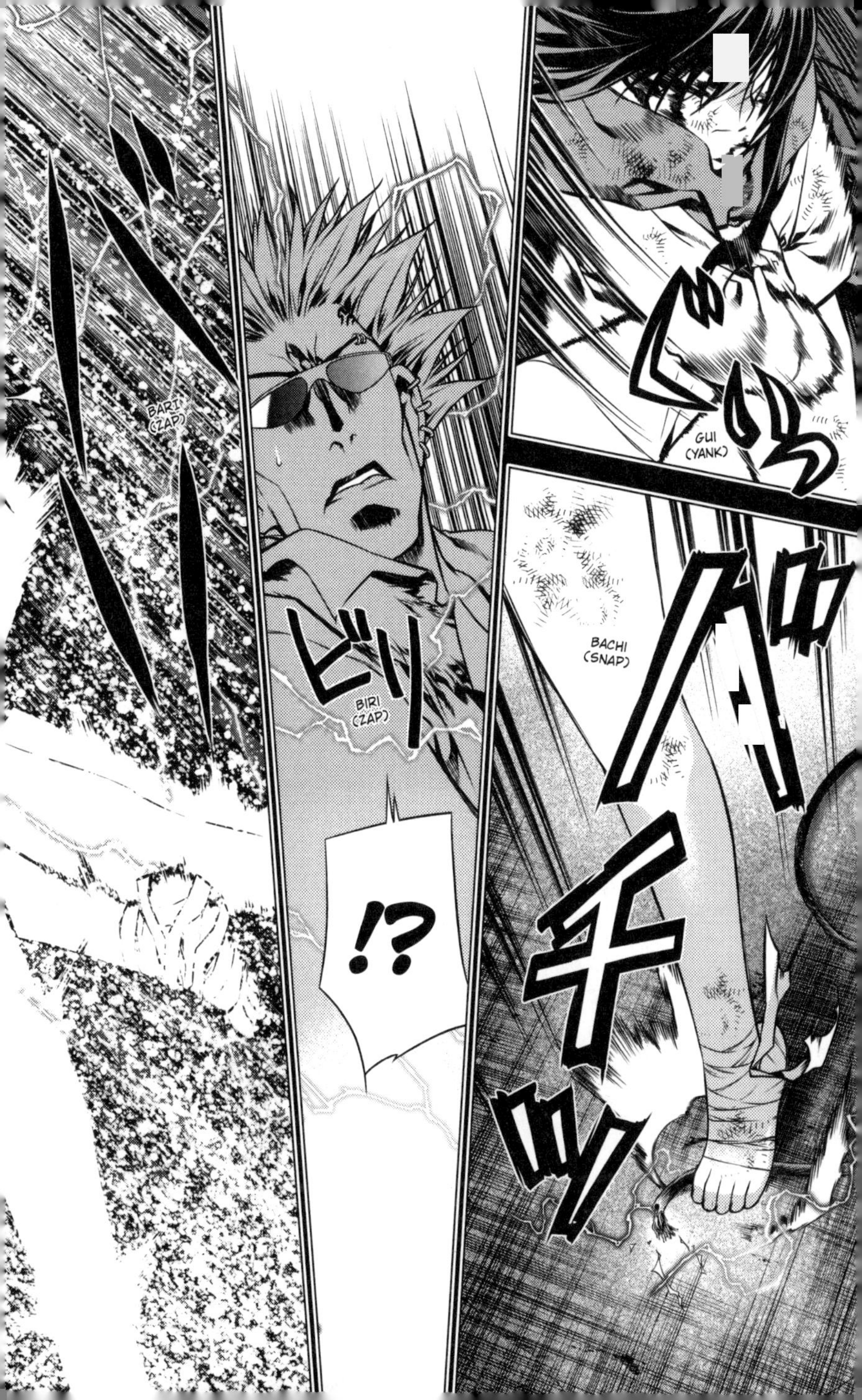
GUI (YANK)
BACHI (SNAP)
ビリ
BIRI (ZAP)
!?
BARI (ZAP)

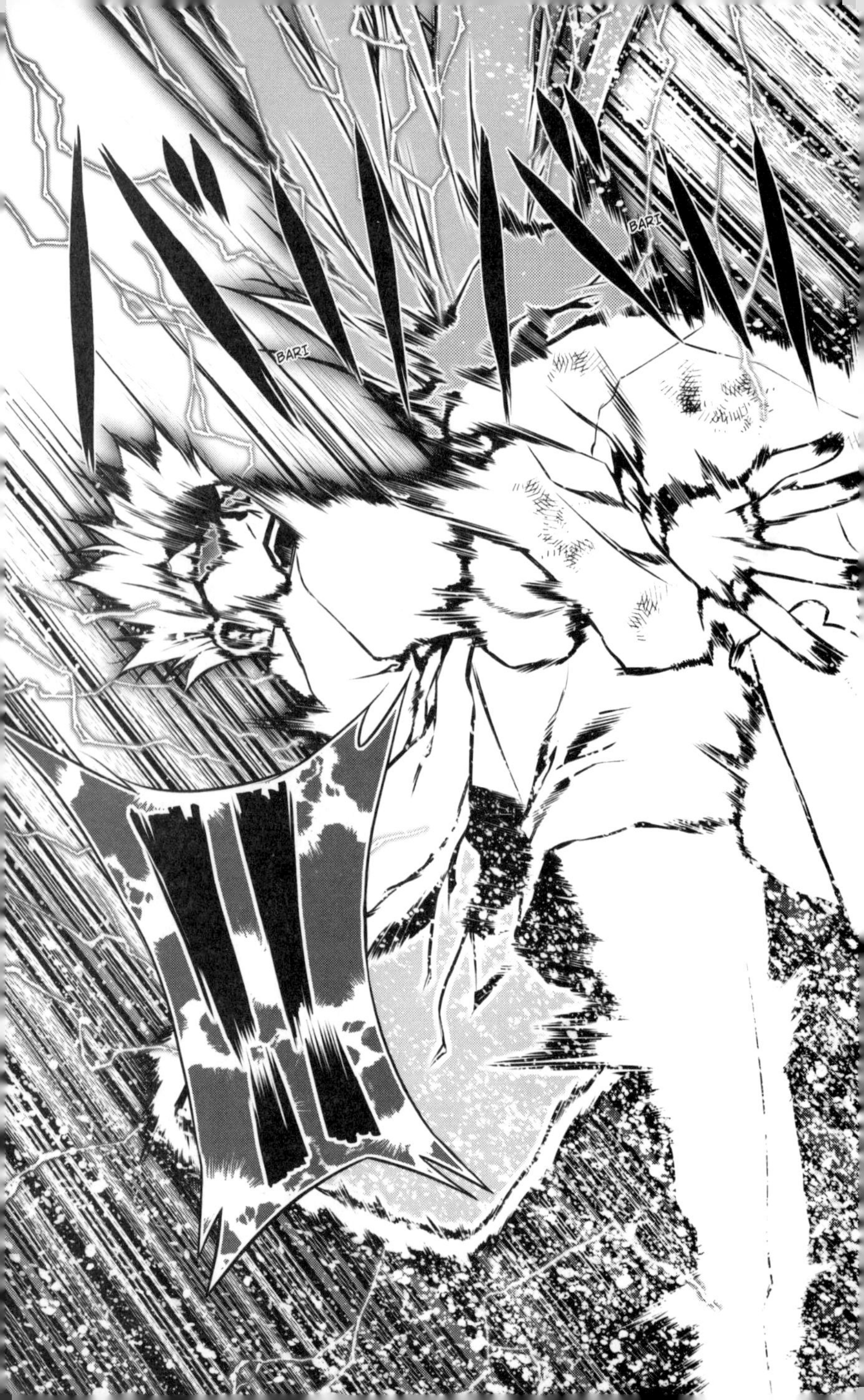
BARI
BARI

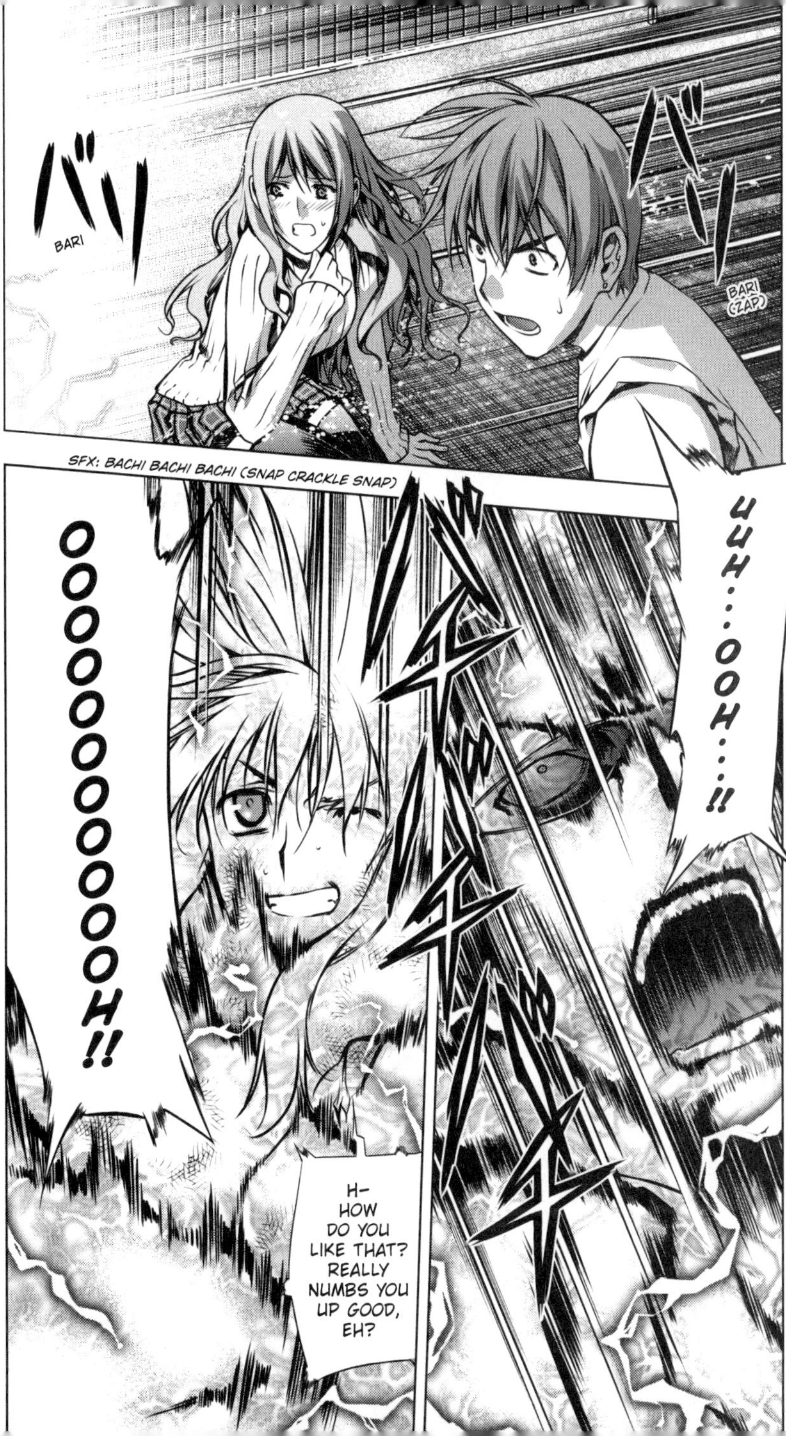
BARI (ZAP)
BARI
SFX: BACHI BACHI BACHI (SNAP CRACKLE SNAP)
UUH...OOH...!!
OOOOOOOOOOOOOH!!
H-HOW DO YOU LIKE THAT? REALLY NUMBS YOU UP GOOD, EH?

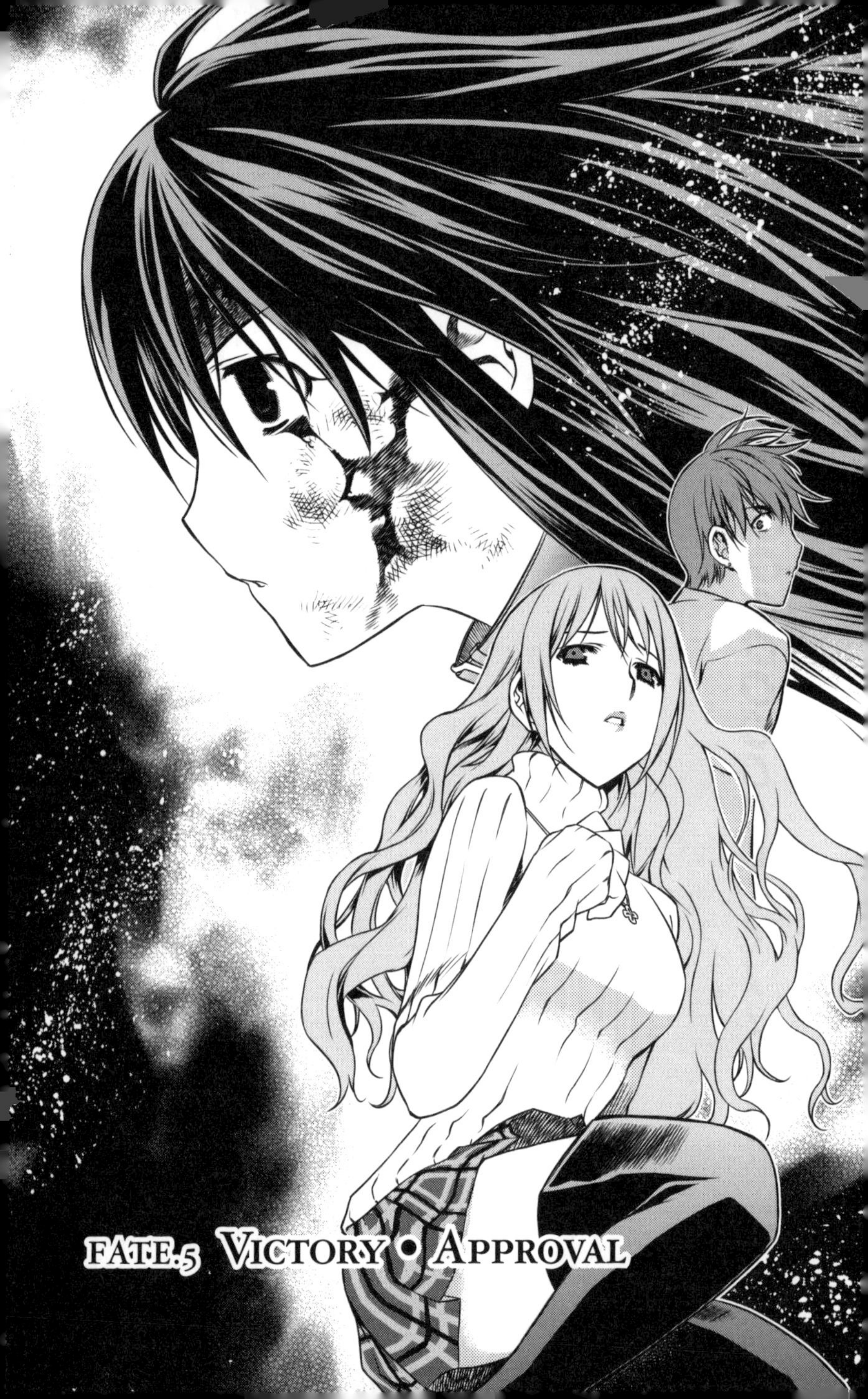
FATE.5 Victory • Approval

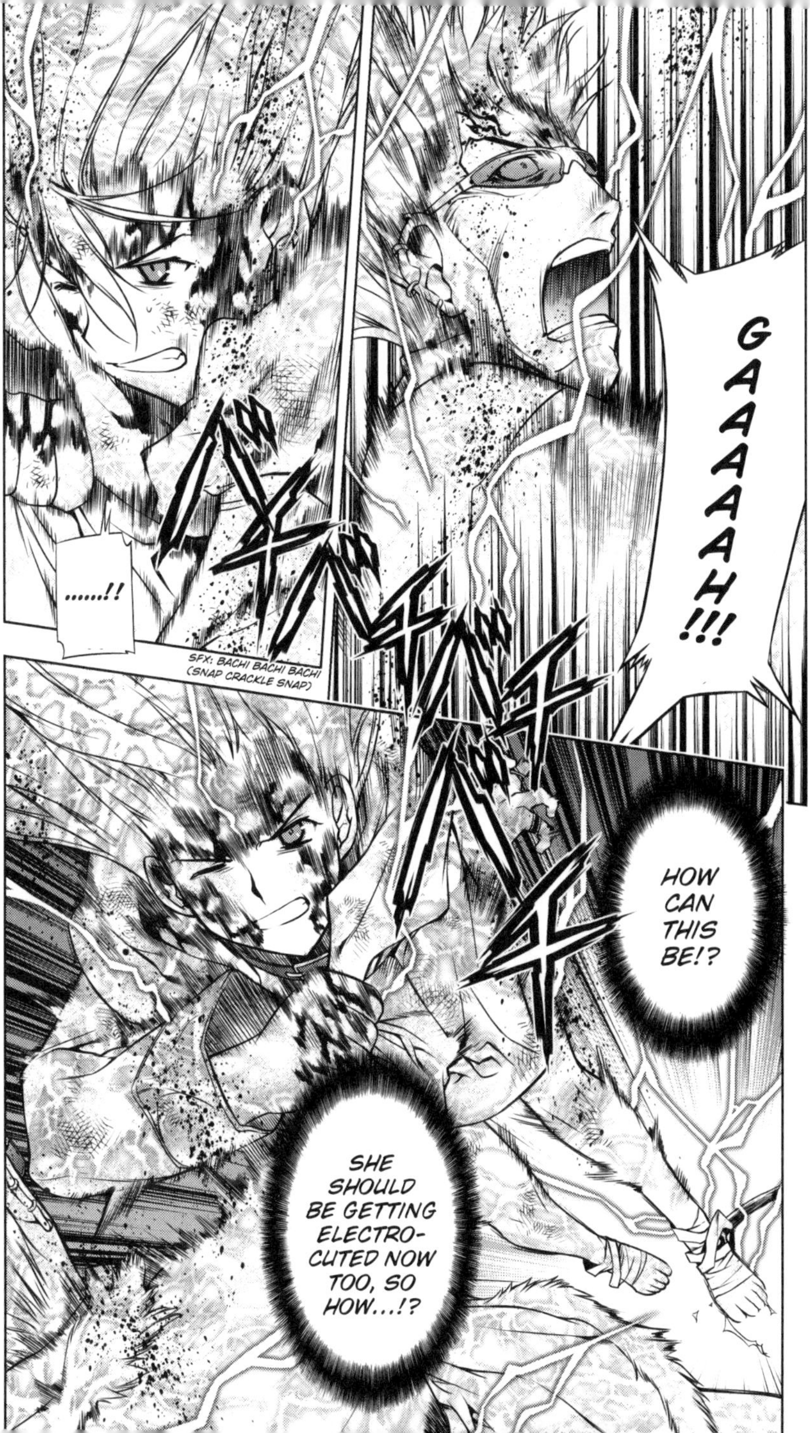
GAAAAAAAH!!!
......!!
SFX: BACHI BACHI BACHI (SNAP CRACKLE SNAP)
HOW CAN THIS BE!?
SHE SHOULD BE GETTING ELECTRO-CUTED NOW TOO, SO HOW...!?

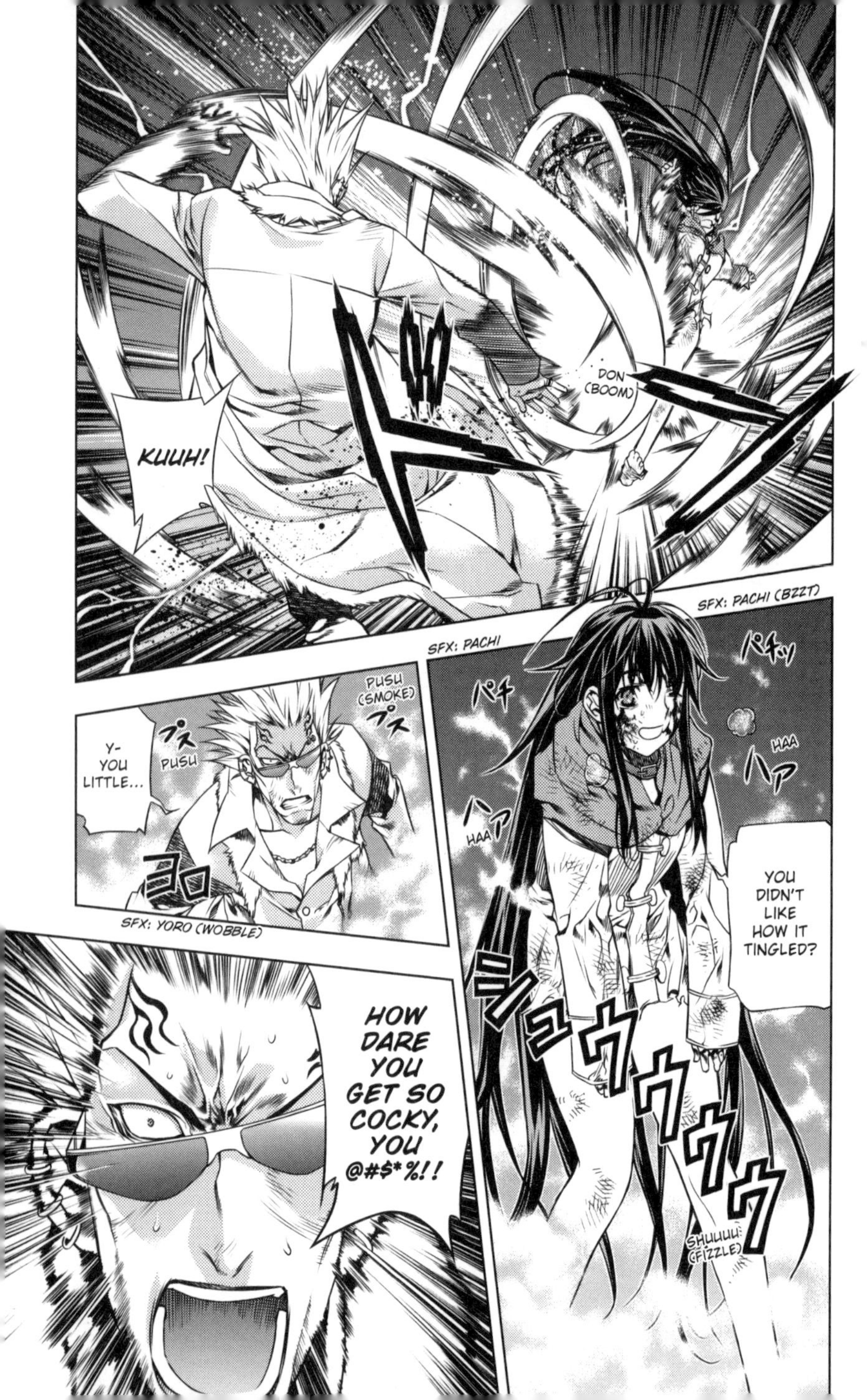
DON (BOOM)
KUUH!
SFX: PACHI (BZZT)
SFX: PACHI
HAA
HAA
YOU DIDN'T LIKE HOW IT TINGLED?
SHUUUU (FIZZLE)
PUSU (SMOKE)
PUSU
Y-YOU LITTLE...
SFX: YORO (WOBBLE)
HOW DARE YOU GET SO COCKY, YOU @#$*%!!

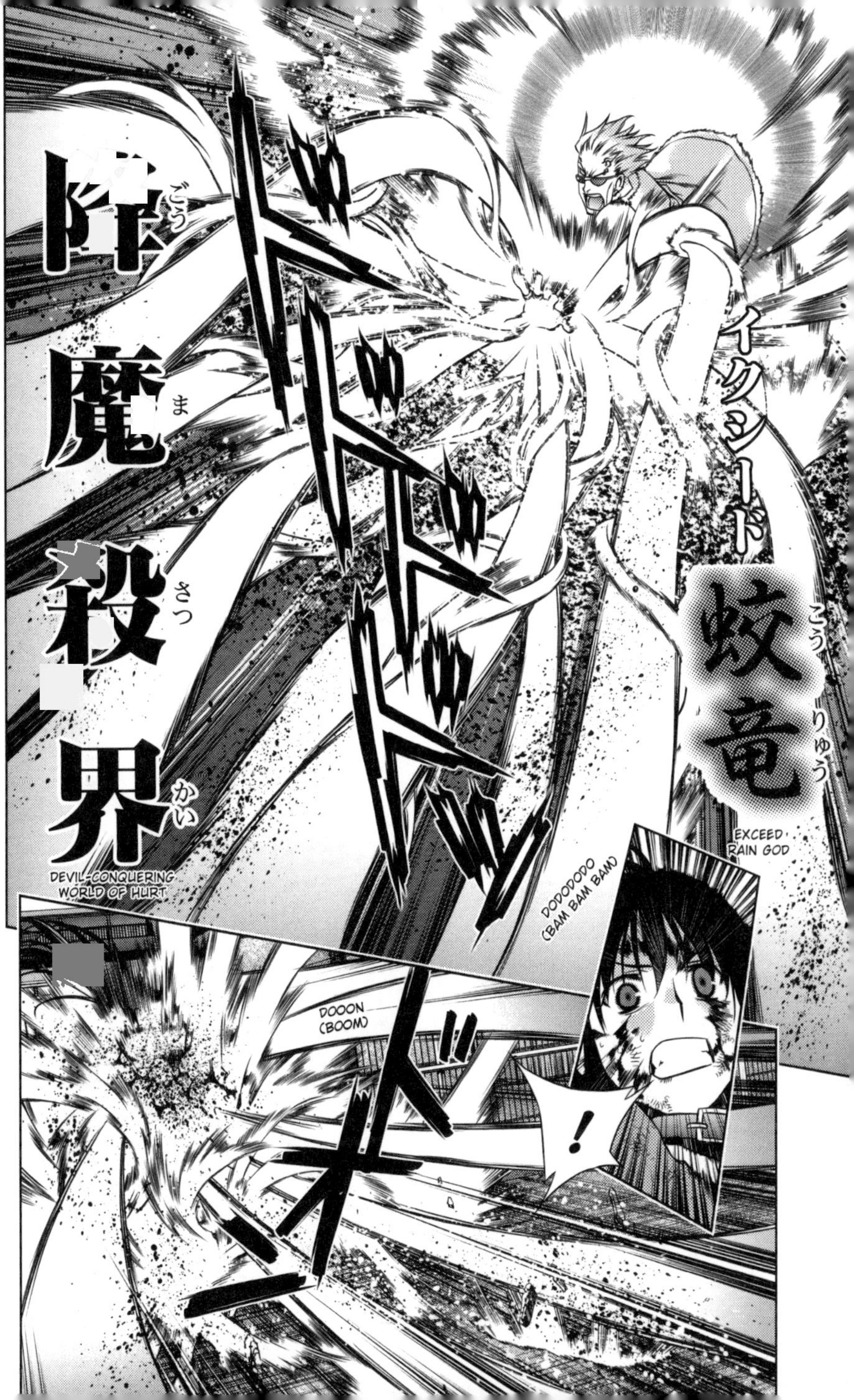
イクシード
蛟竜
EXCEED RAIN GOD
降魔殺界
DEVIL-CONQUERING WORLD OF HURT
DODODODO (BAM BAM BAM)
!
DOOON (BOOM)

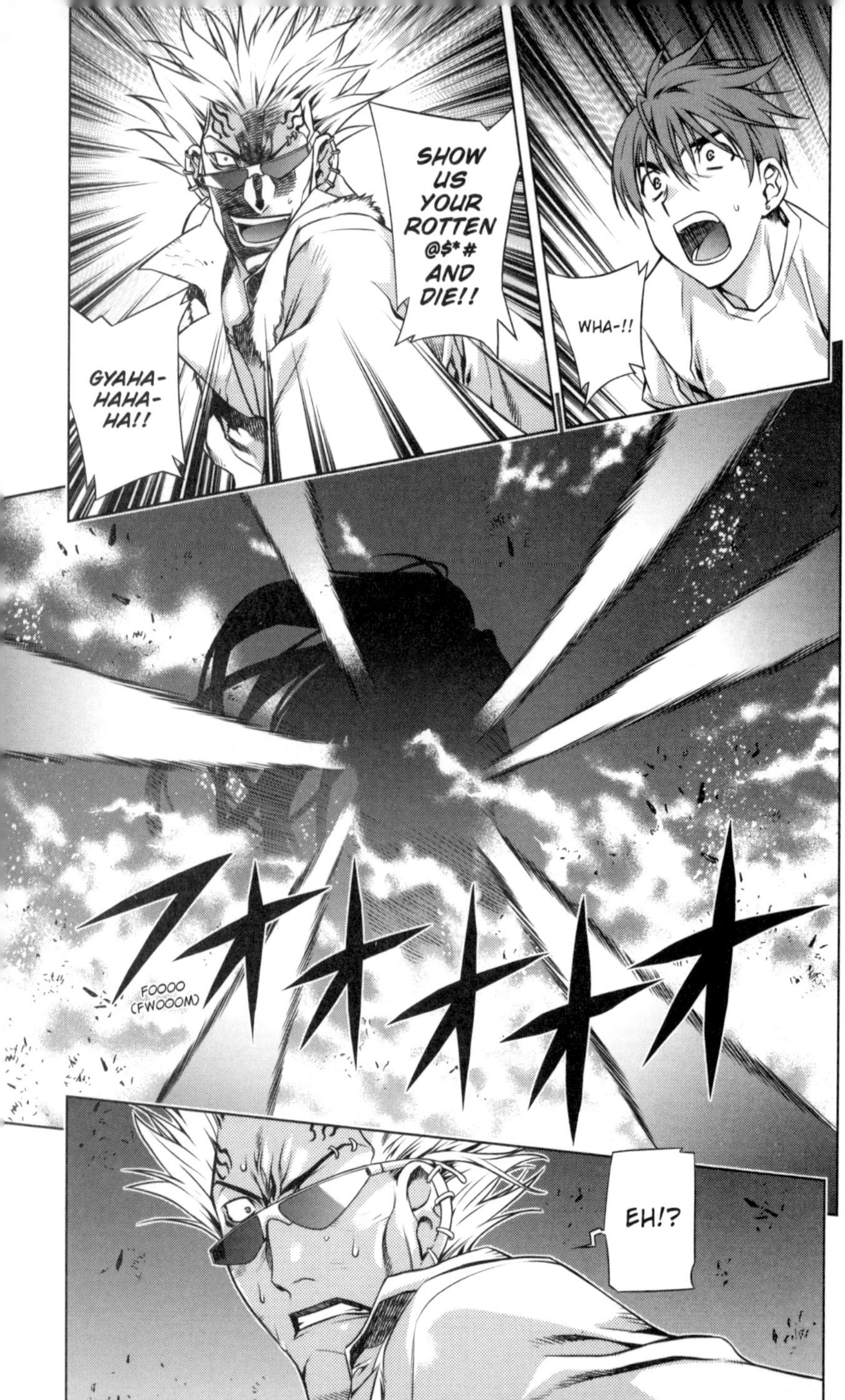
WHA-!!
SHOW US YOUR ROTTEN @$*# AND DIE!!
GYAHA-HAHA-HA!!
FOOOO (FWOOOM)
EH!?

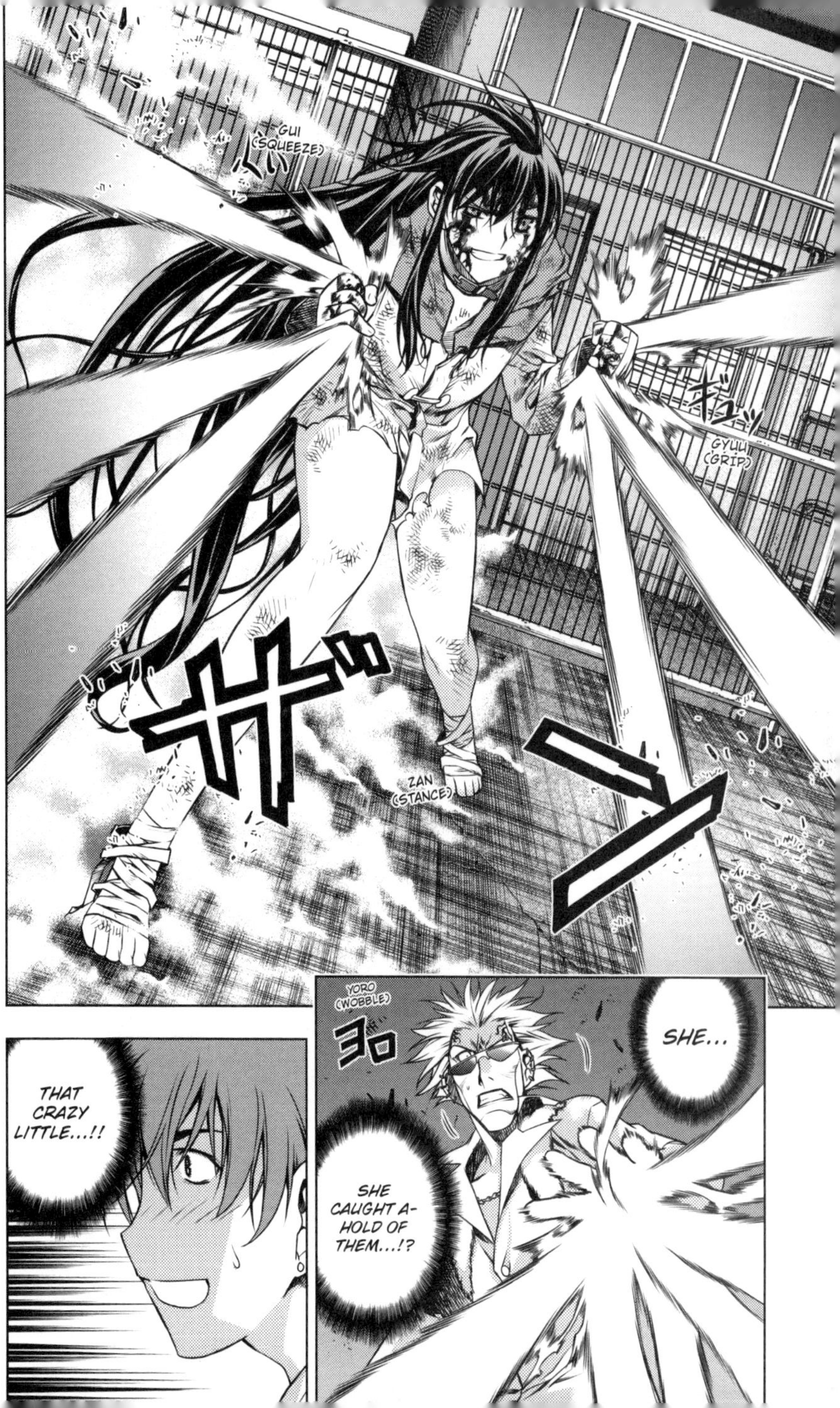
GUI (SQUEEZE)
GYUU (GRIP)
ZAN (STANCE)
YORO (WOBBLE)
SHE...
SHE CAUGHT A-HOLD OF THEM...!?
THAT CRAZY LITTLE...!!

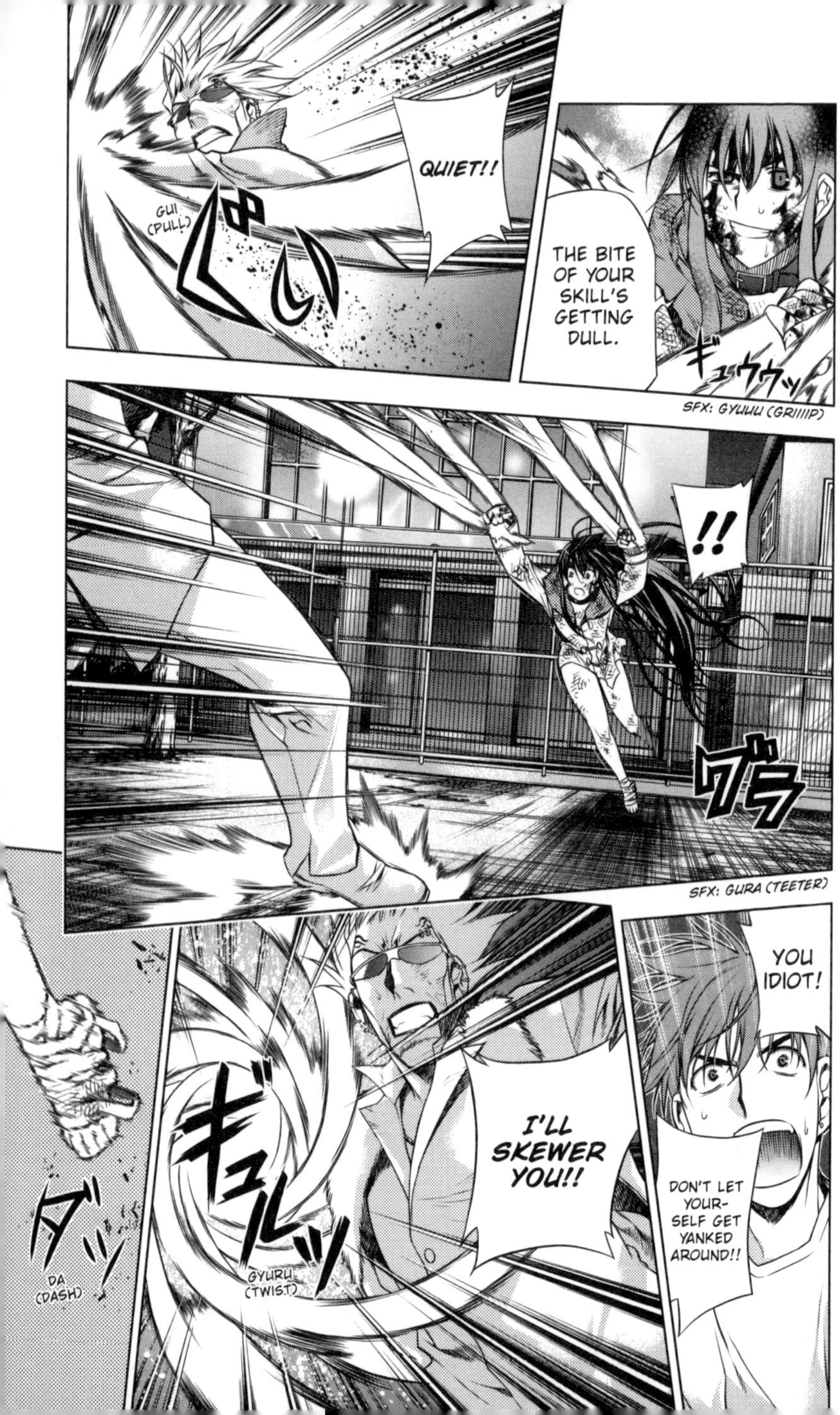
THE BITE OF YOUR SKILL'S GETTING DULL.
SFX: GYUUU (GRIIIIP)
QUIET!!
GUI (PULL)
!!
SFX: GURA (TEETER)
YOU IDIOT!
DON'T LET YOURSELF GET YANKED AROUND!!
I'LL SKEWER YOU!!
GYURU (TWIST)
DA (DASH)

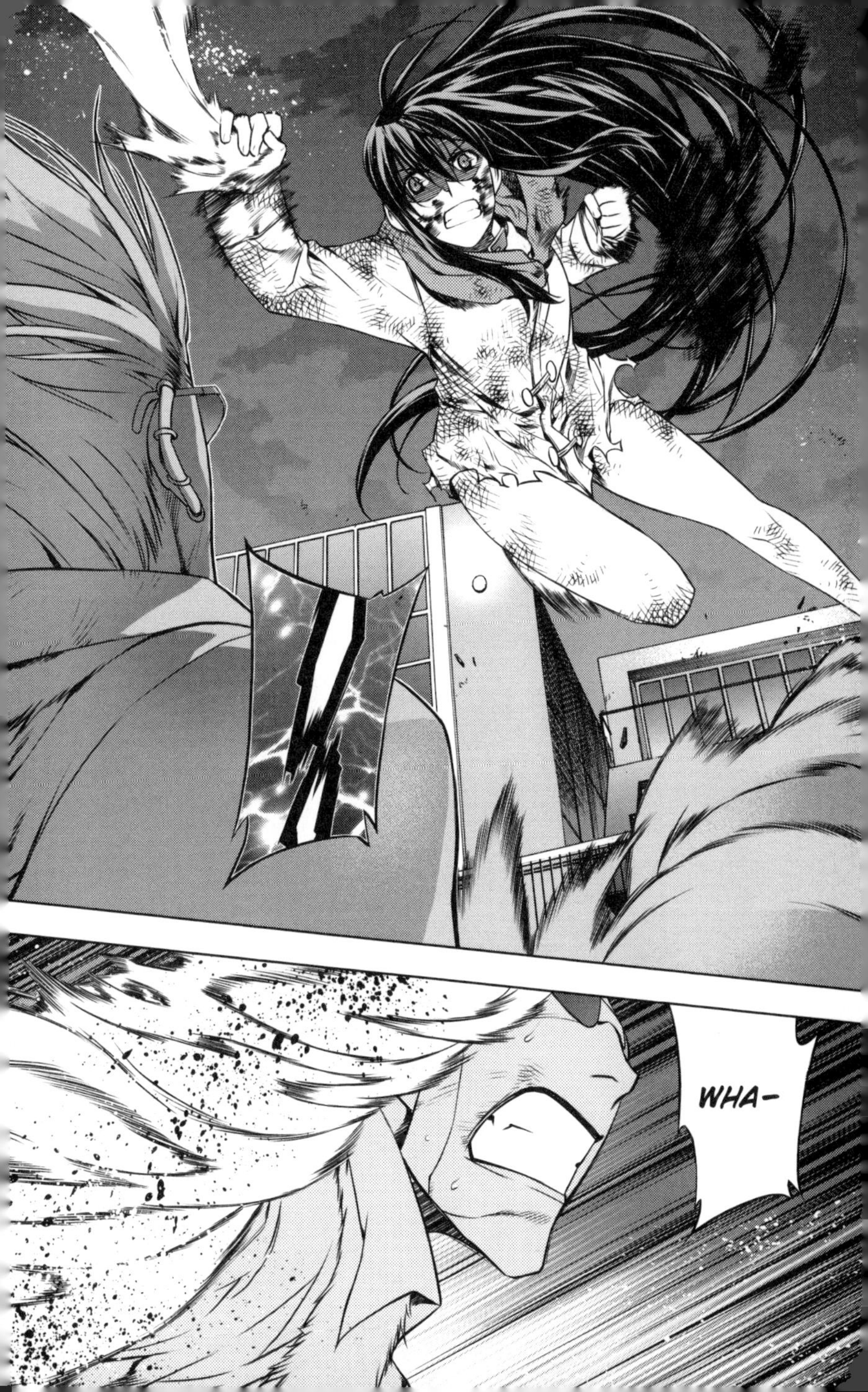
WHA-

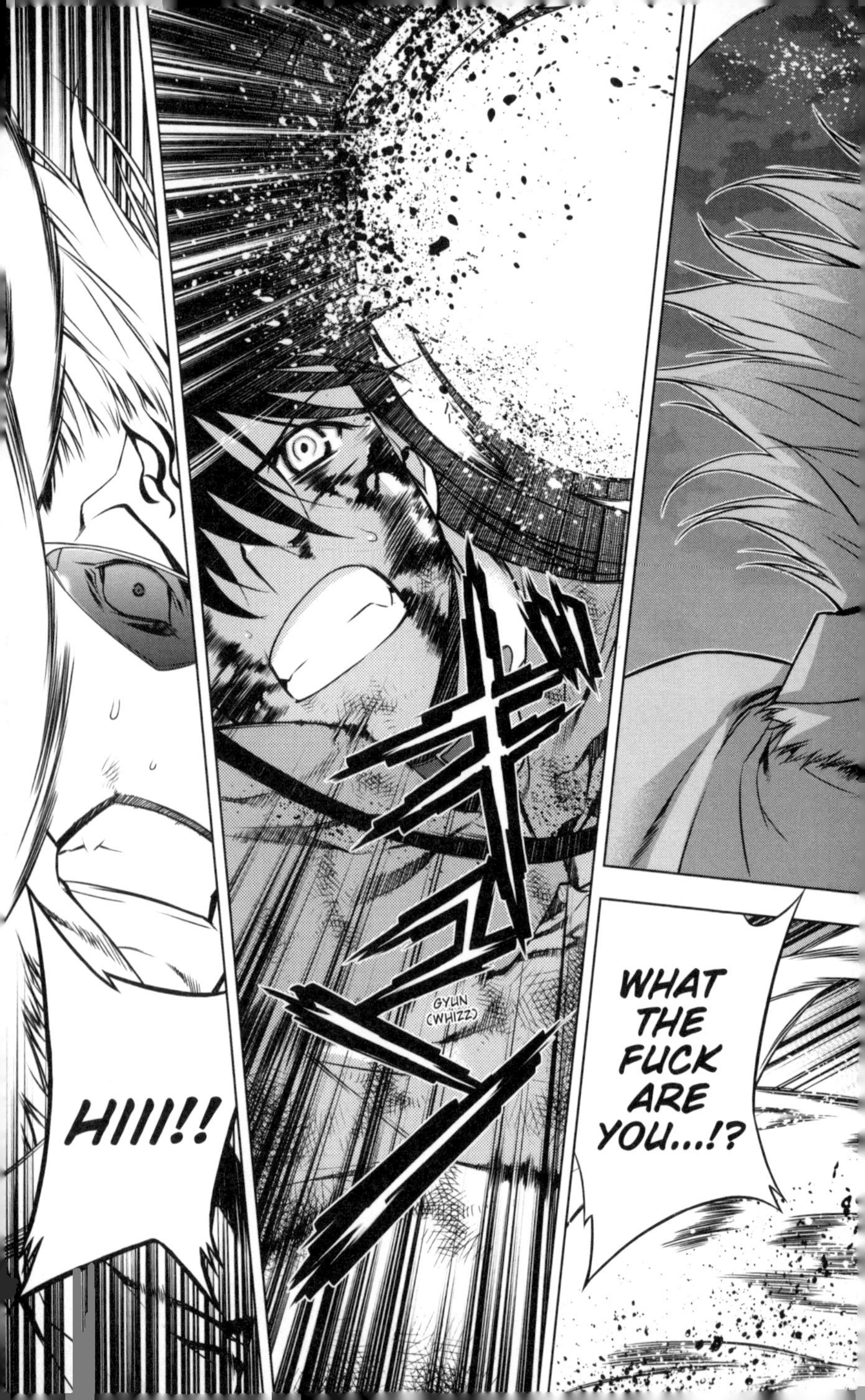
WHAT THE FUCK ARE YOU...!?
GYUN (WHIZZ)
HIII!!

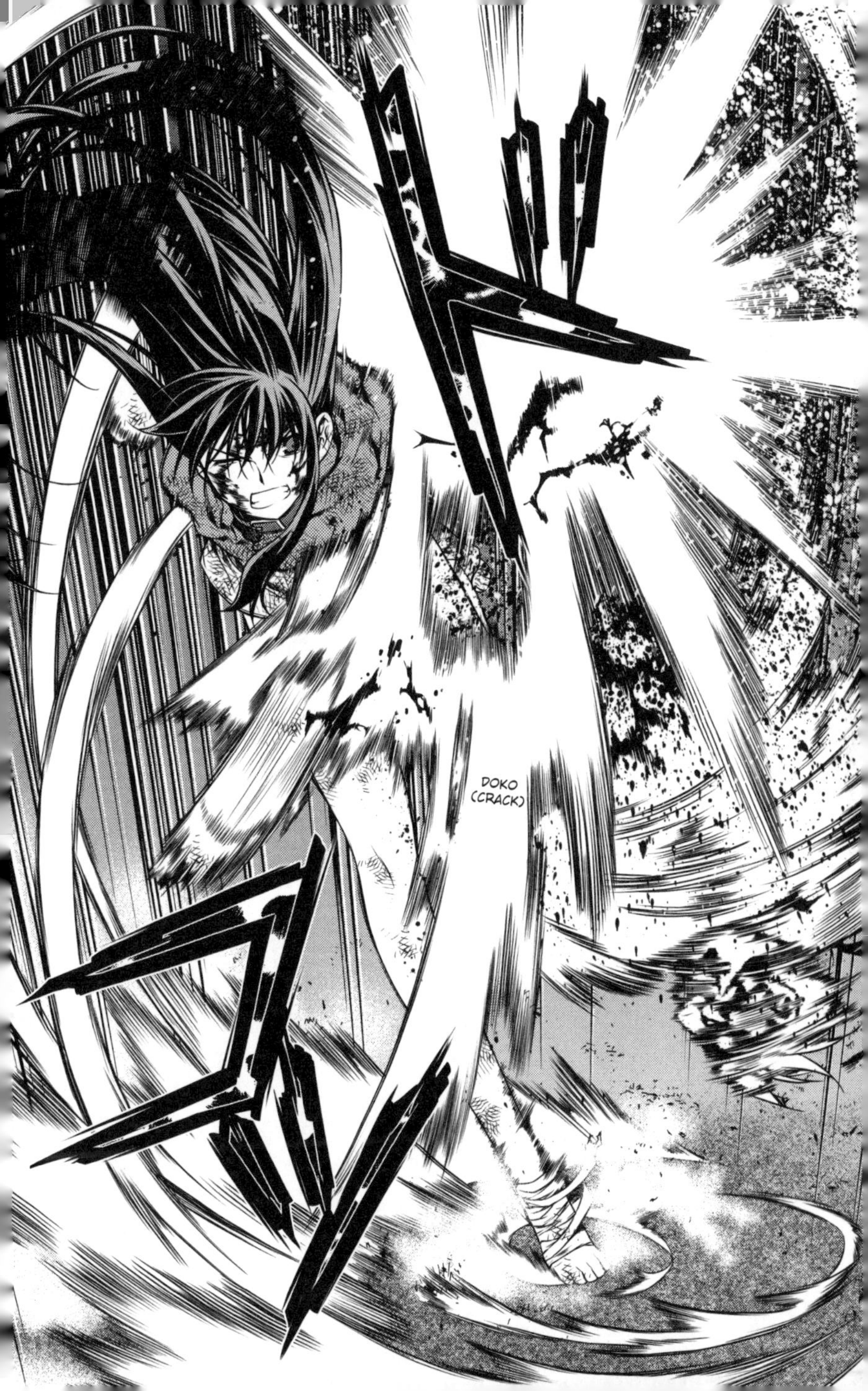
DOKO
(CRACK)

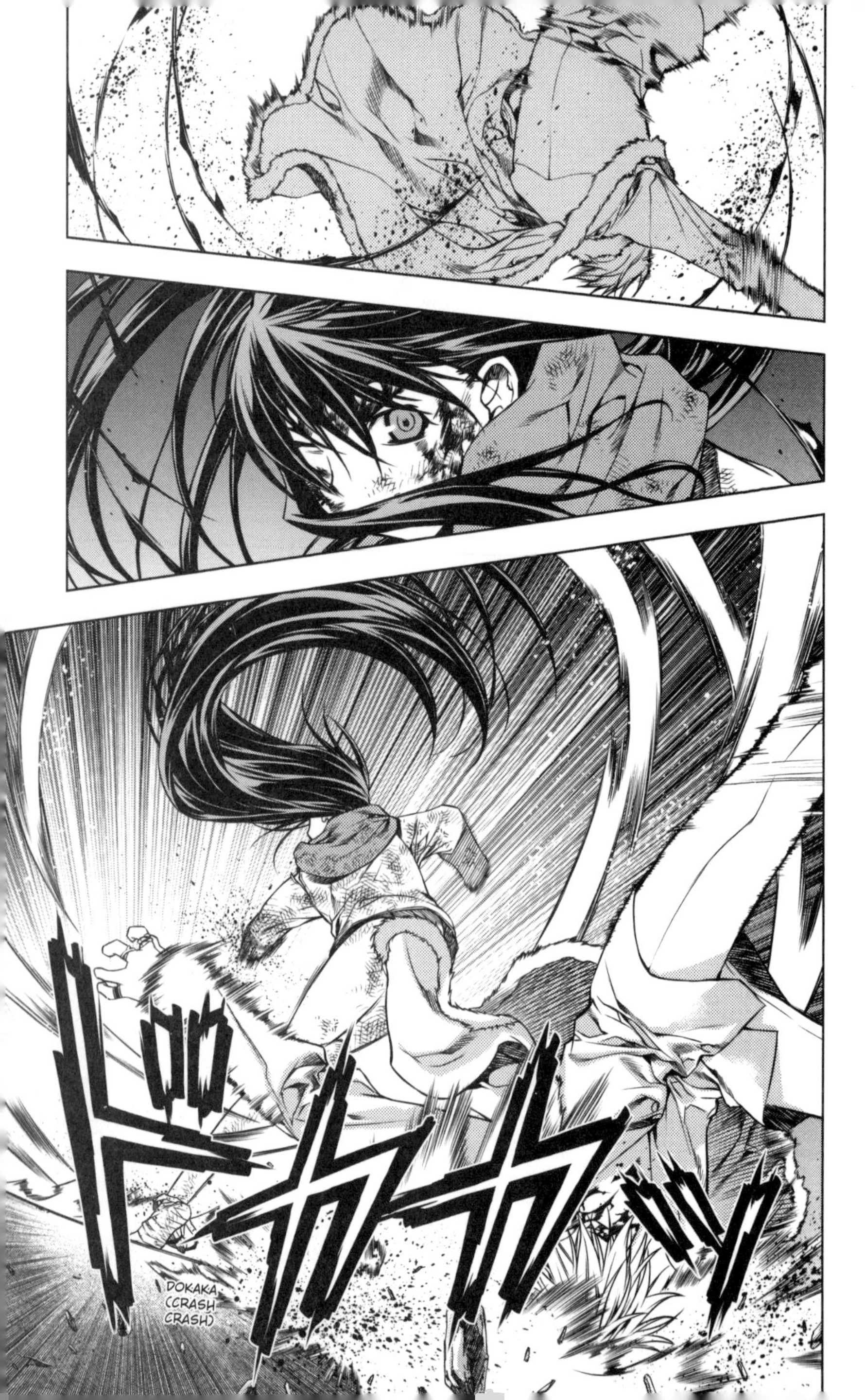
DOKAKA
(CRASH
CRASH)

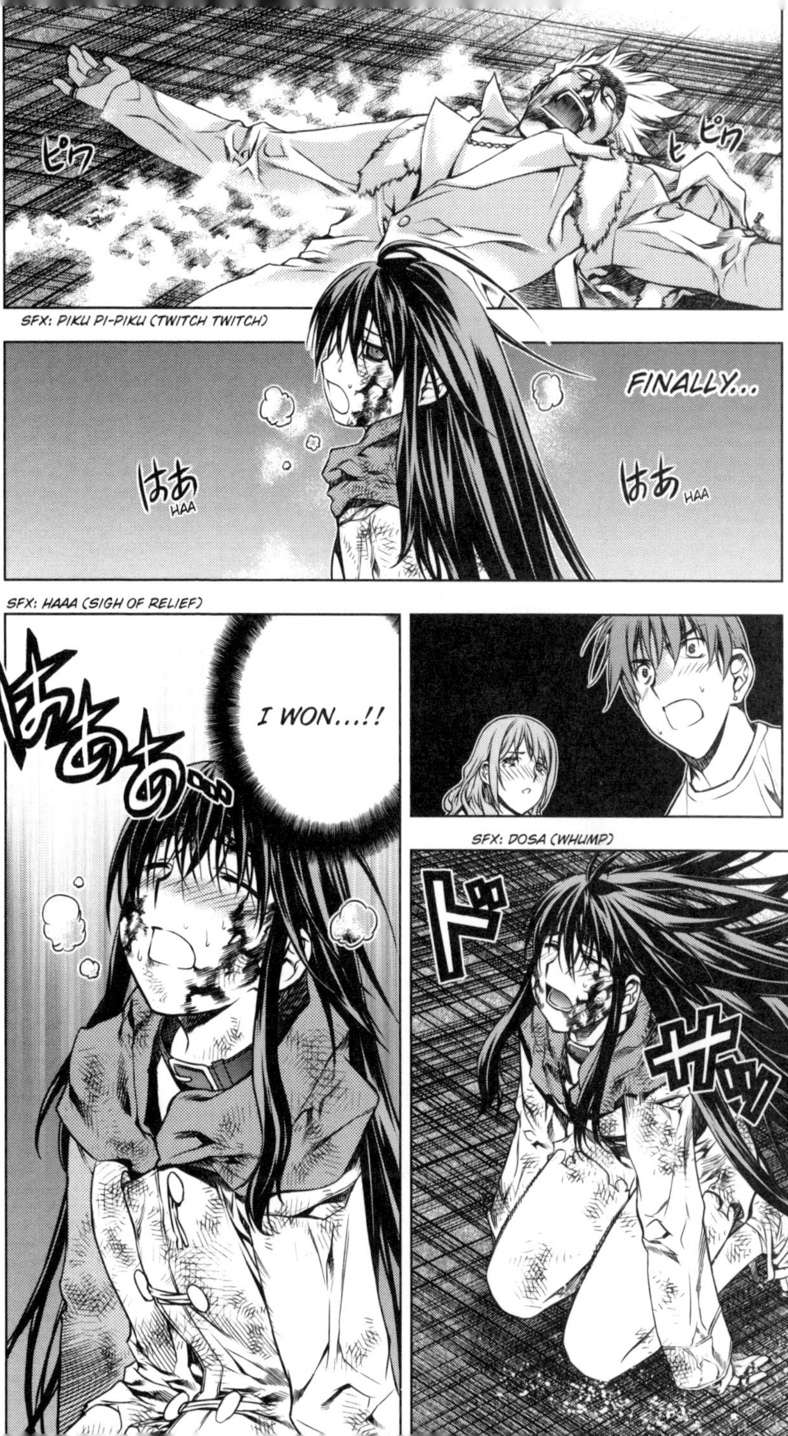
ピピク
ピク
SFX: PIKU PI-PIKU (TWITCH TWITCH)
FINALLY...
はあ HAA
はあ HAA
SFX: HAAA (SIGH OF RELIEF)
SFX: DOSA (WHUMP)
ド
サッ
I WON...!!

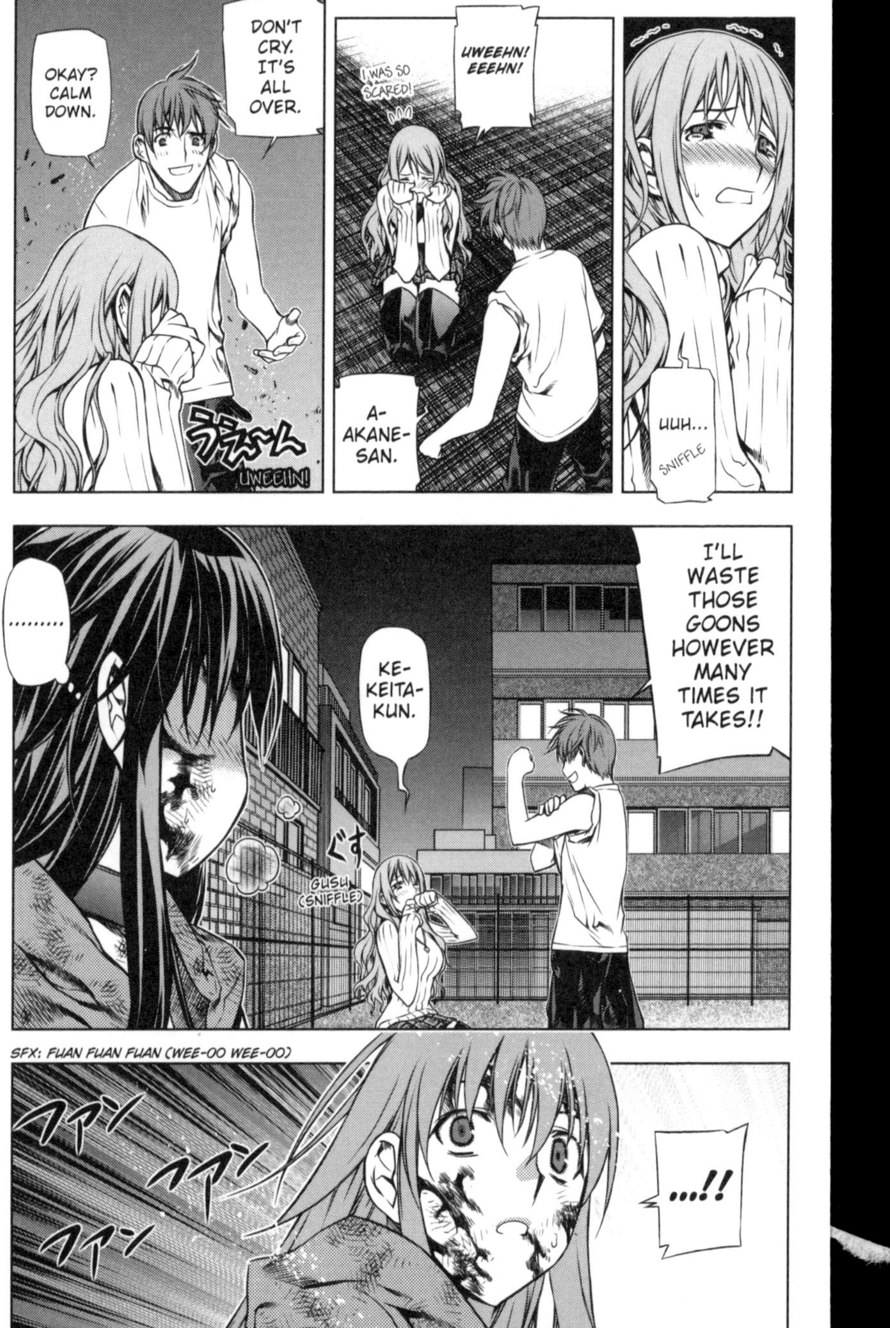
UUH...
SNIFFLE
UWEEHN! EEEHN!
I WAS SO SCARED!
A-AKANE-SAN.
DON'T CRY. IT'S ALL OVER.
OKAY? CALM DOWN.
うえ～ん
UWEEHN!
I'LL WASTE THOSE GOONS HOWEVER MANY TIMES IT TAKES!!
KE-KEITA-KUN.
ぐす
GUSU (SNIFFLE)
....
SFX: FUAN FUAN FUAN (WEE-OO WEE-OO)
...!!
ファン
ファン
ファン

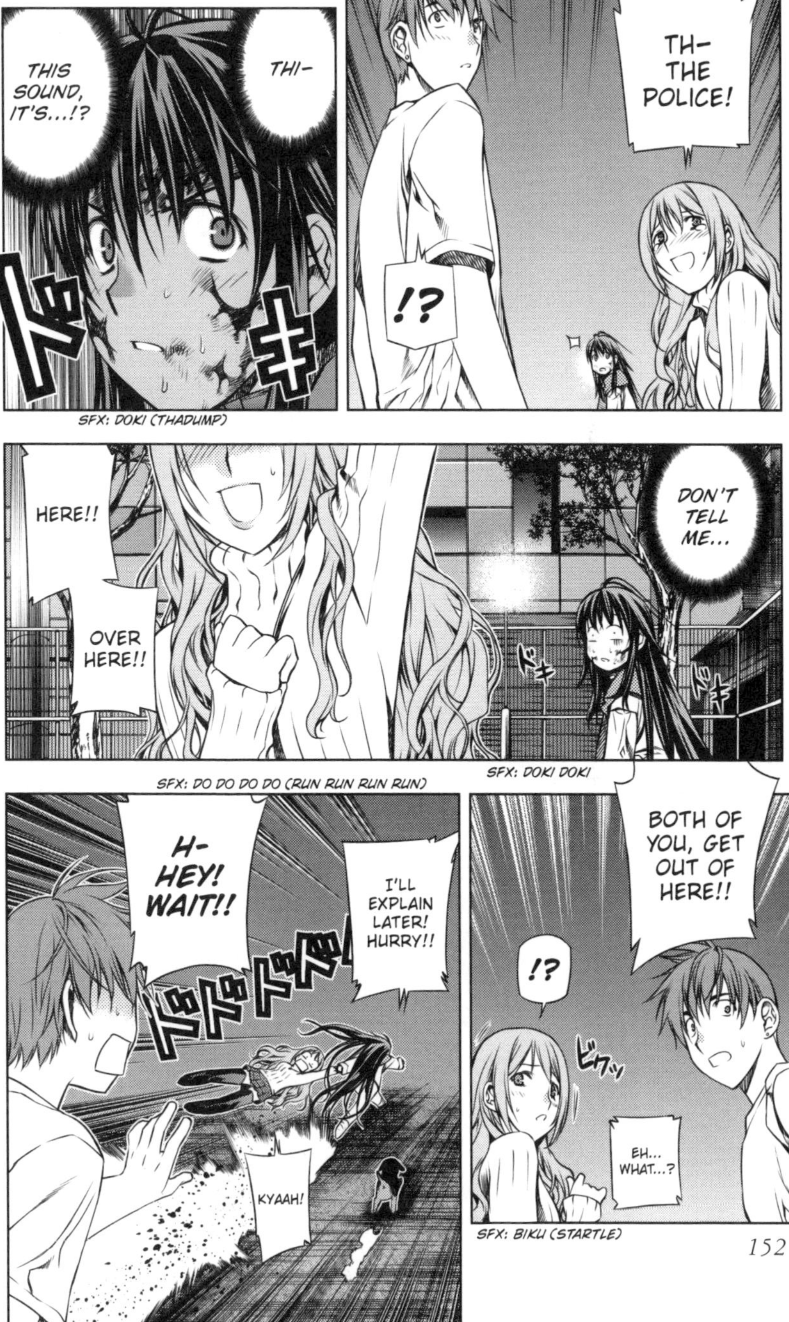
TH- THE POLICE!
!?
THI-
THIS SOUND, IT'S...!?
SFX: DOKI (THADUMP)
DON'T TELL ME...
HERE!!
OVER HERE!!
SFX: DOKI DOKI
SFX: DO DO DO DO (RUN RUN RUN RUN)
BOTH OF YOU, GET OUT OF HERE!!
!?
EH... WHAT...?
SFX: BIKU (STARTLE)
I'LL EXPLAIN LATER! HURRY!!
KYAAH!
H- HEY! WAIT!!

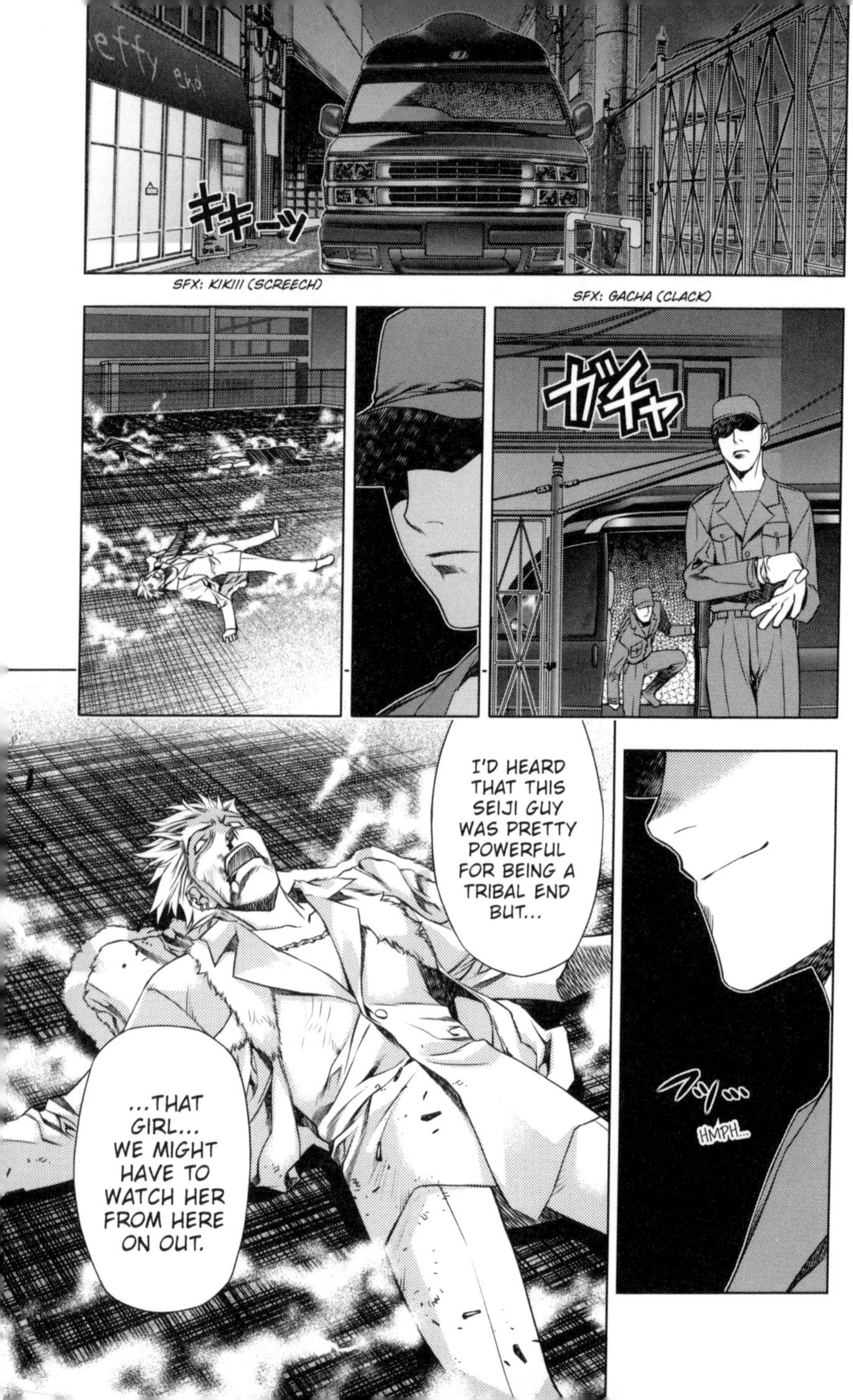

effy end
キキーッ
SFX: KIKIII (SCREECH)
ガチャ
SFX: GACHA (CLACK)
フッ…
HMPH...
I'D HEARD THAT THIS SEIJI GUY WAS PRETTY POWERFUL FOR BEING A TRIBAL END BUT...
...THAT GIRL... WE MIGHT HAVE TO WATCH HER FROM HERE ON OUT.

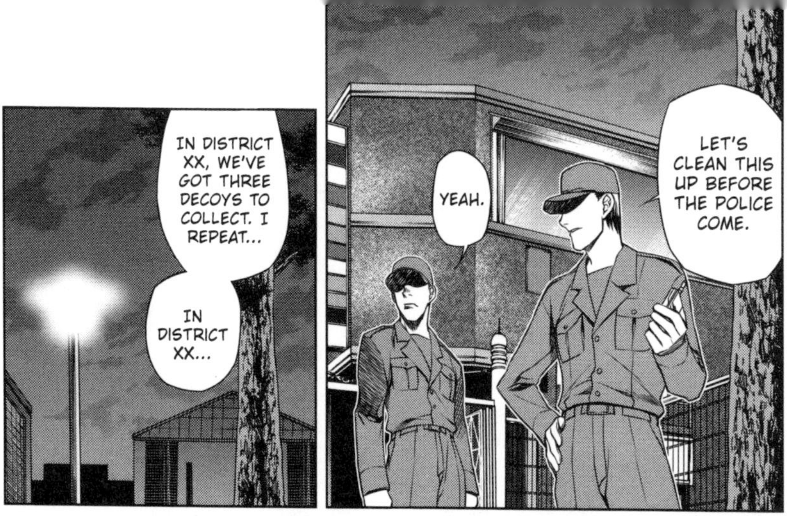
LET'S CLEAN THIS UP BEFORE THE POLICE COME.
YEAH.
IN DISTRICT XX, WE'VE GOT THREE DECOYS TO COLLECT. I REPEAT...
IN DISTRICT XX...

SIGN: SERVICE

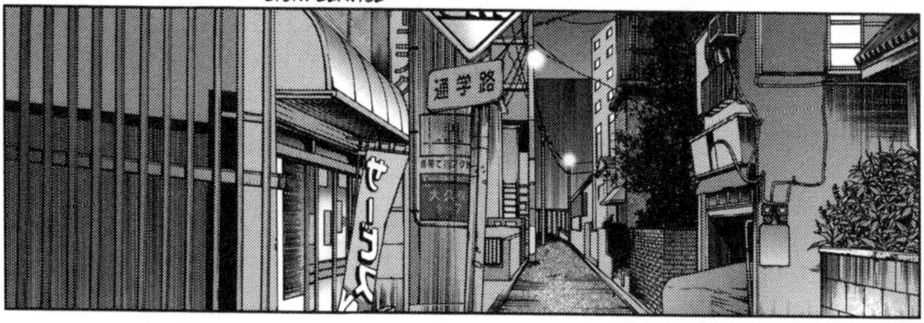
通学路

SFX: HAA HAA HAA

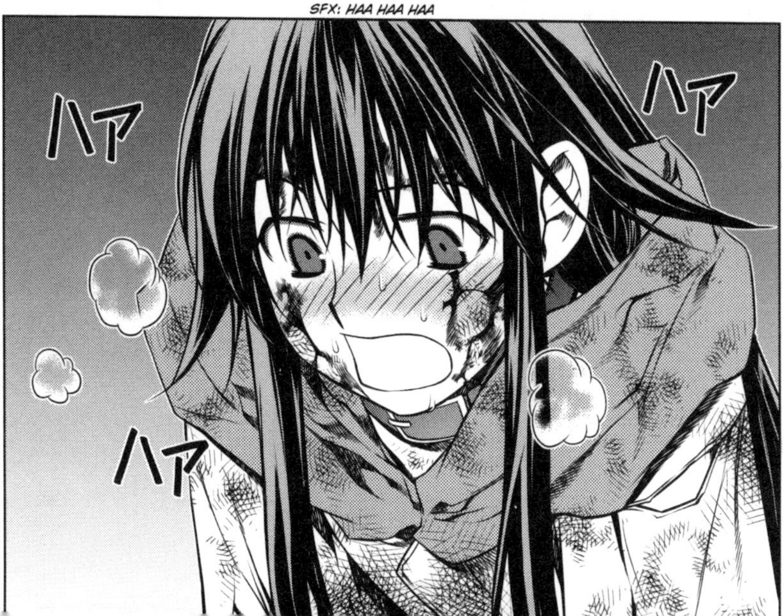
ハア
ハア
ハア

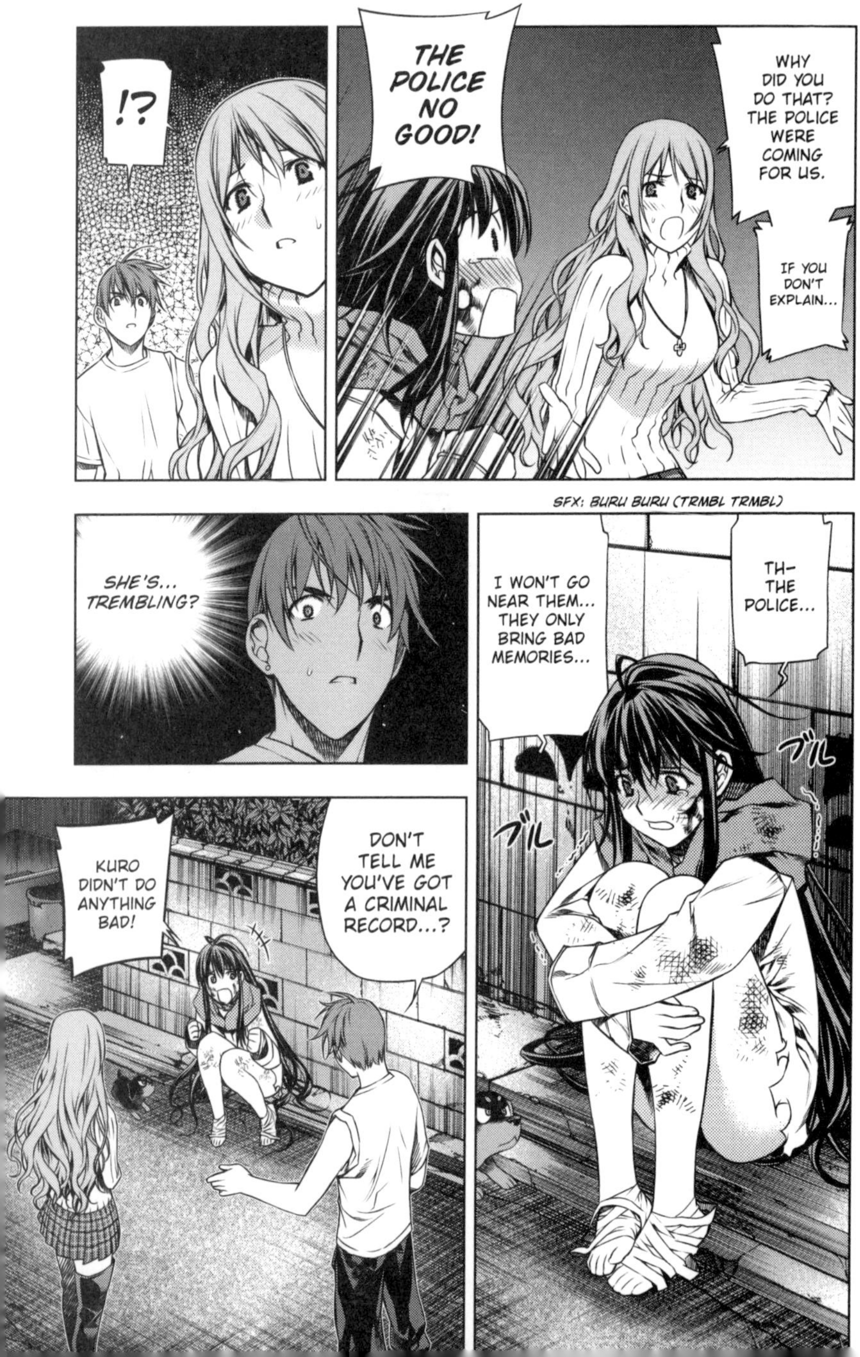
WHY DID YOU DO THAT? THE POLICE WERE COMING FOR US.
IF YOU DON'T EXPLAIN...
THE POLICE NO GOOD!
!?
SFX: BURU BURU (TRMBL TRMBL)
TH- THE POLICE...
I WON'T GO NEAR THEM... THEY ONLY BRING BAD MEMORIES...
ブル
ブル
SHE'S... TREMBLING?
DON'T TELL ME YOU'VE GOT A CRIMINAL RECORD...?
KURO DIDN'T DO ANYTHING BAD!

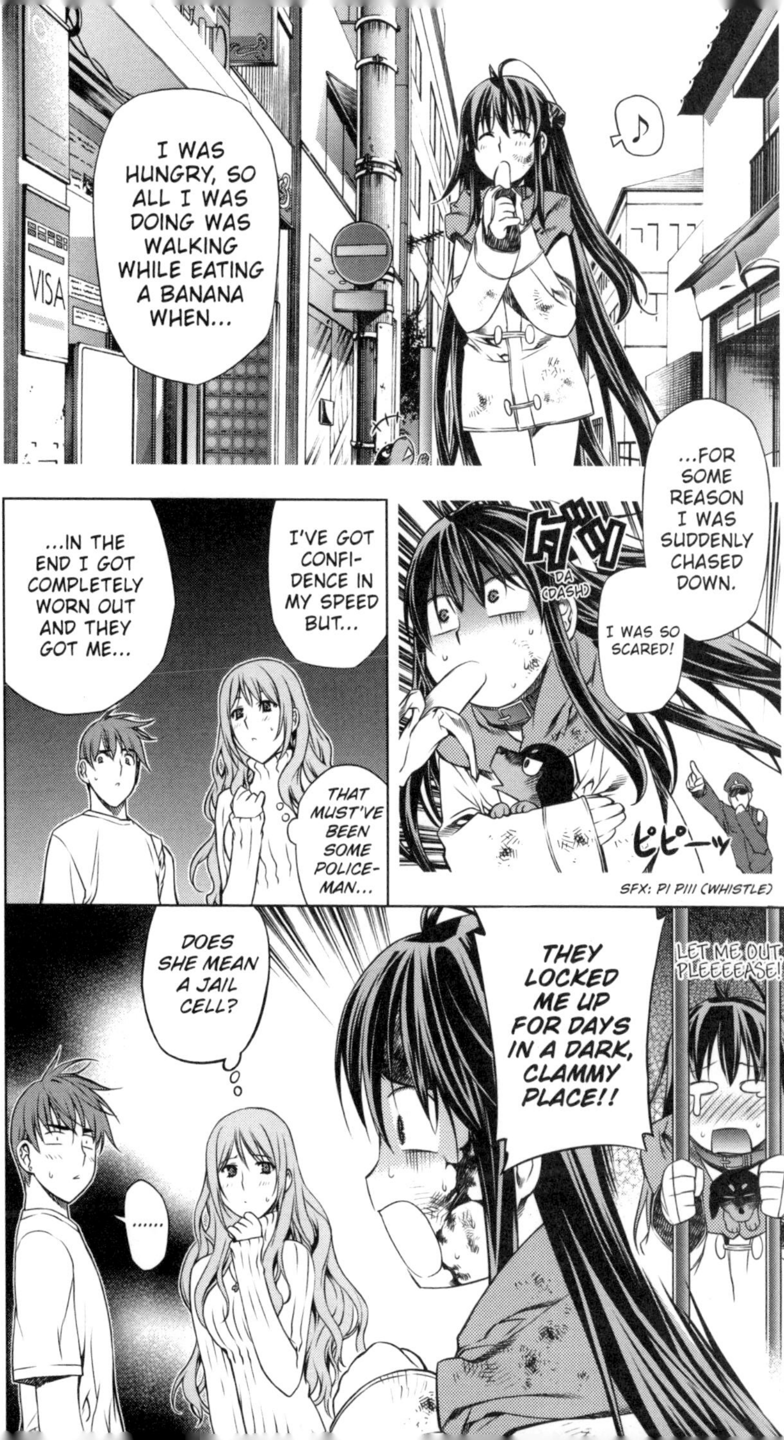
♪
I WAS HUNGRY, SO ALL I WAS DOING WAS WALKING WHILE EATING A BANANA WHEN...
...FOR SOME REASON I WAS SUDDENLY CHASED DOWN.
DA (DASH)
I WAS SO SCARED!
SFX: PI PIII (WHISTLE)
I'VE GOT CONFIDENCE IN MY SPEED BUT...
...IN THE END I GOT COMPLETELY WORN OUT AND THEY GOT ME...
THAT MUST'VE BEEN SOME POLICEMAN...
LET ME OUT, PLEEEEASE!
THEY LOCKED ME UP FOR DAYS IN A DARK, CLAMMY PLACE!!
DOES SHE MEAN A JAIL CELL?
......

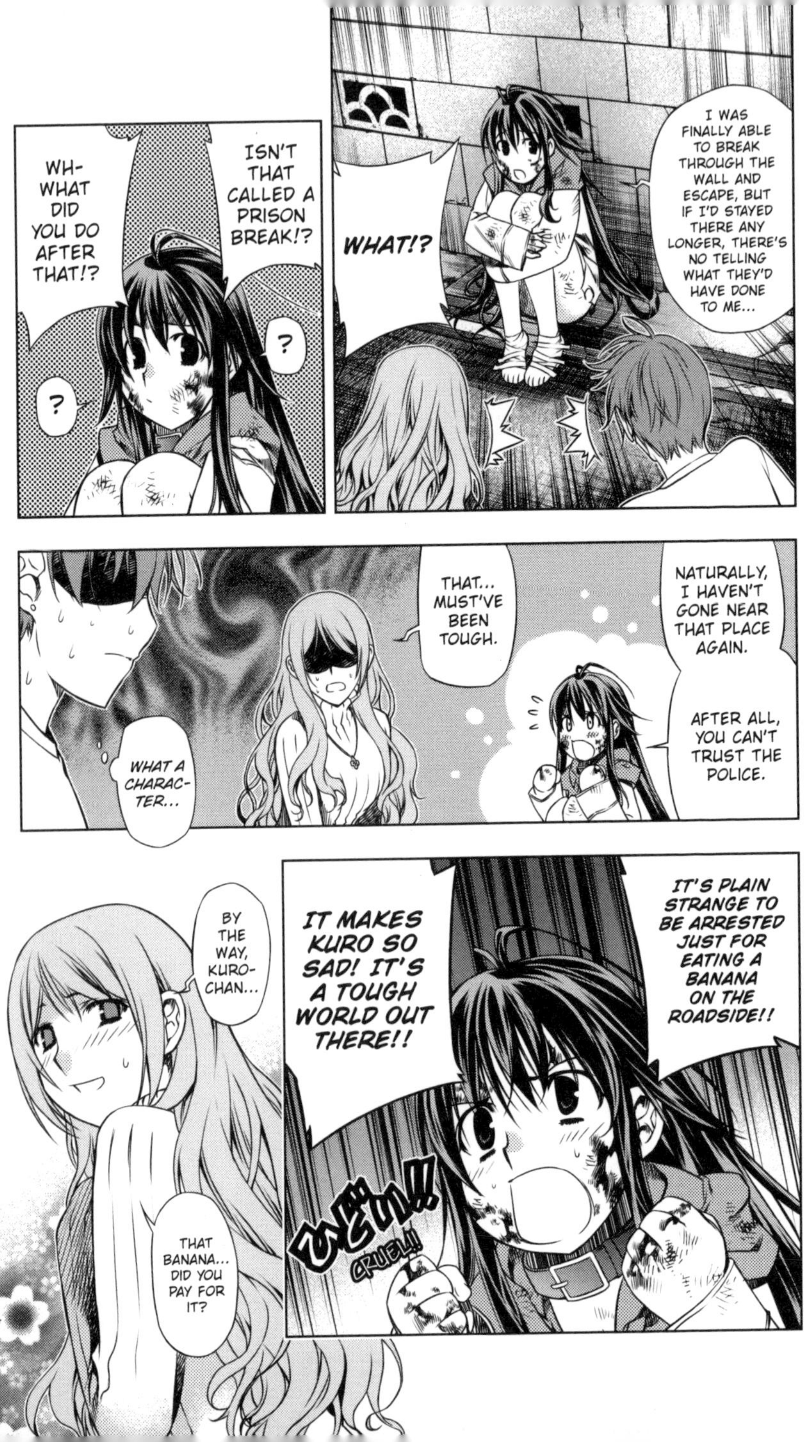
I WAS FINALLY ABLE TO BREAK THROUGH THE WALL AND ESCAPE, BUT IF I'D STAYED THERE ANY LONGER, THERE'S NO TELLING WHAT THEY'D HAVE DONE TO ME...
WHAT!?
ISN'T THAT CALLED A PRISON BREAK!?
WH-WHAT DID YOU DO AFTER THAT!?
?
?
NATURALLY, I HAVEN'T GONE NEAR THAT PLACE AGAIN.
AFTER ALL, YOU CAN'T TRUST THE POLICE.
THAT... MUST'VE BEEN TOUGH.
WHAT A CHARACTER...
IT'S PLAIN STRANGE TO BE ARRESTED JUST FOR EATING A BANANA ON THE ROADSIDE!!
IT MAKES KURO SO SAD! IT'S A TOUGH WORLD OUT THERE!!
CRUEL!!
BY THE WAY, KURO-CHAN...
THAT BANANA... DID YOU PAY FOR IT?

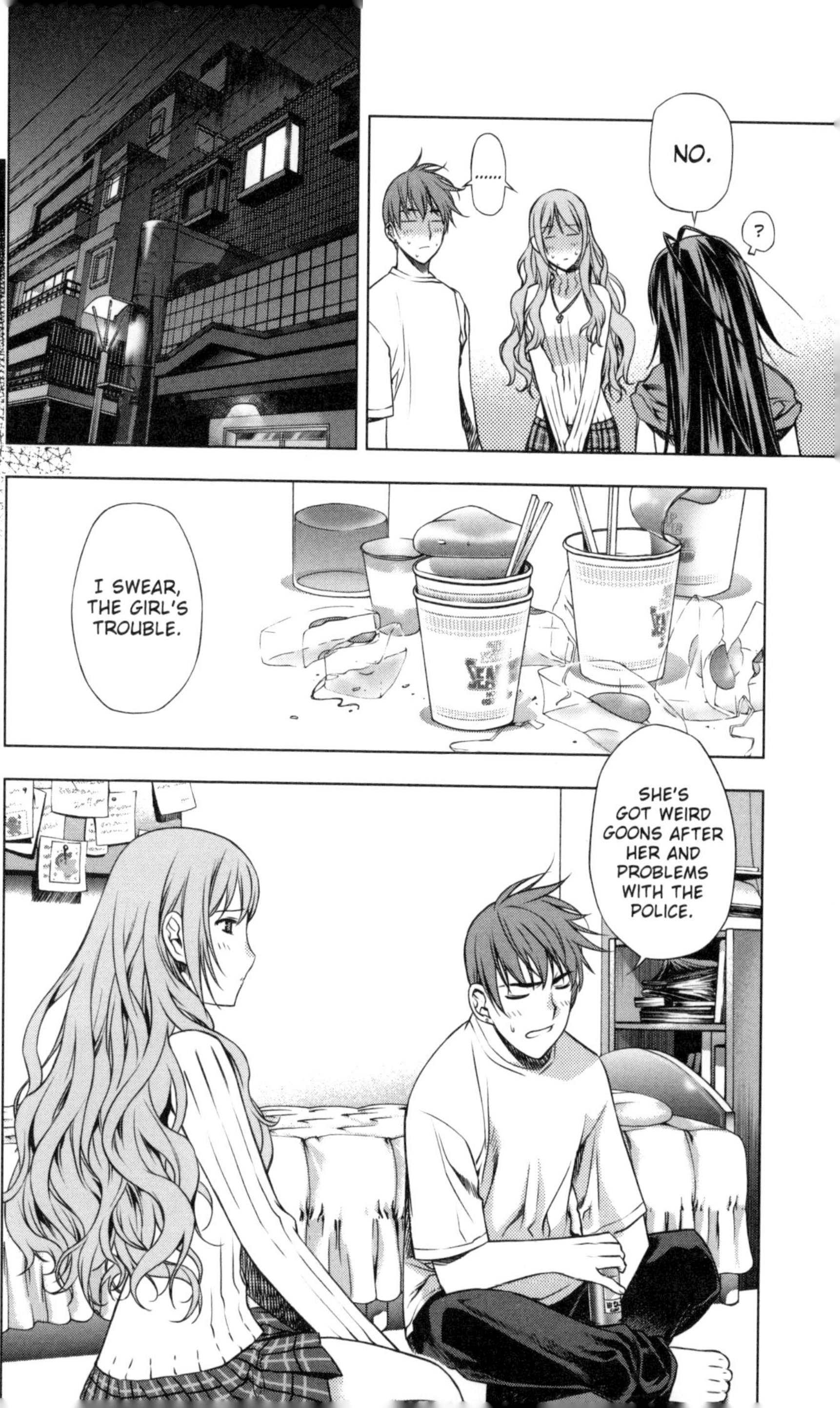
NO.
?
......
I SWEAR, THE GIRL'S TROUBLE.
SHE'S GOT WEIRD GOONS AFTER HER AND PROBLEMS WITH THE POLICE.

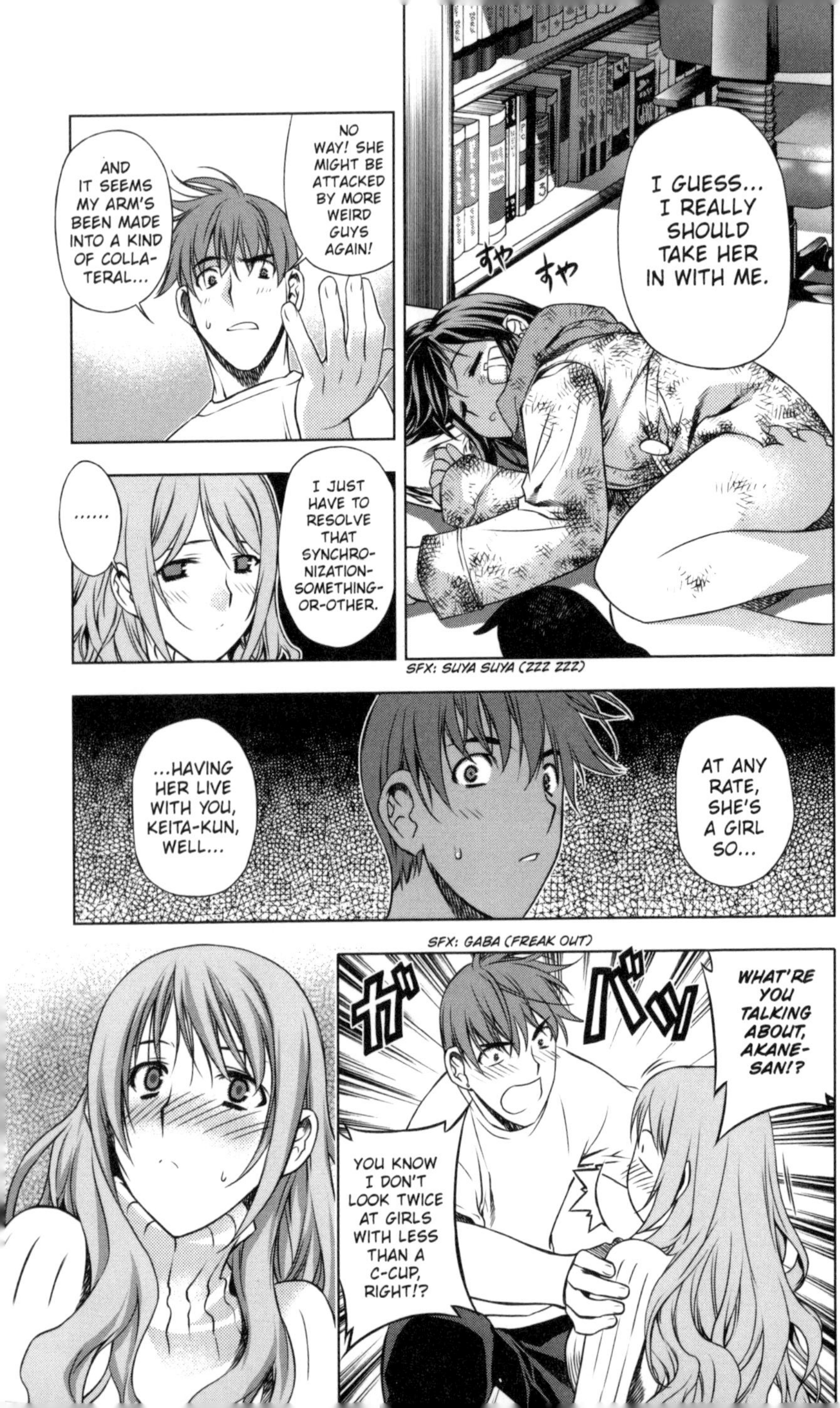
I GUESS... I REALLY SHOULD TAKE HER IN WITH ME.
すや すや
SFX: SUYA SUYA (ZZZ ZZZ)
NO WAY! SHE MIGHT BE ATTACKED BY MORE WEIRD GUYS AGAIN!
AND IT SEEMS MY ARM'S BEEN MADE INTO A KIND OF COLLA-TERAL...
I JUST HAVE TO RESOLVE THAT SYNCHRO-NIZATION-SOMETHING-OR-OTHER.
......
AT ANY RATE, SHE'S A GIRL SO...
...HAVING HER LIVE WITH YOU, KEITA-KUN, WELL...
SFX: GABA (FREAK OUT)
がばっ
WHAT'RE YOU TALKING ABOUT, AKANE-SAN!?
YOU KNOW I DON'T LOOK TWICE AT GIRLS WITH LESS THAN A C-CUP, RIGHT!?

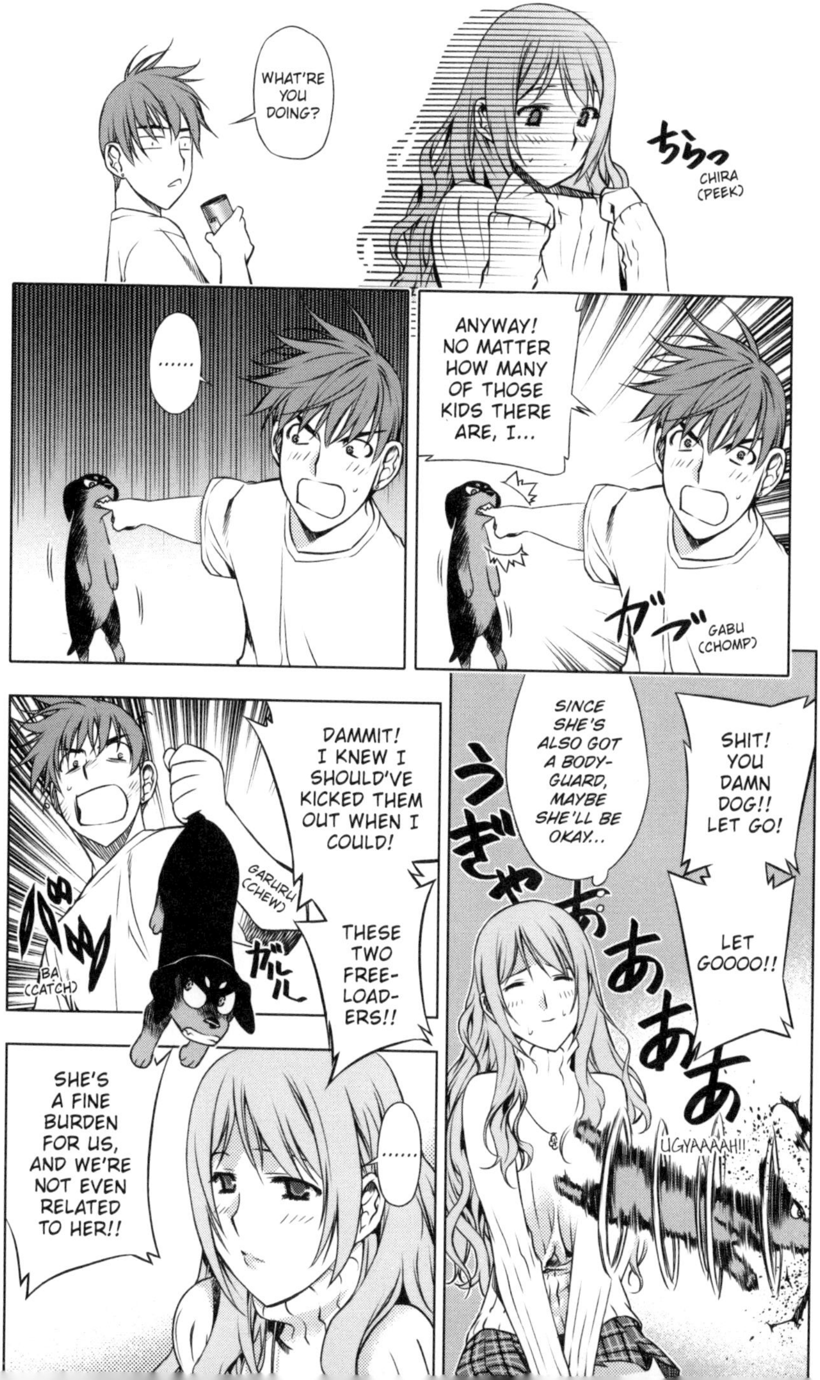

ちらっ
CHIRA (PEEK)
WHAT'RE YOU DOING?
ANYWAY! NO MATTER HOW MANY OF THOSE KIDS THERE ARE, I...
ガブ
GABU (CHOMP)
......
SHIT! YOU DAMN DOG!! LET GO!
SINCE SHE'S ALSO GOT A BODY-GUARD, MAYBE SHE'LL BE OKAY...
LET GOOOO!!
うぎゃあああ
UGYAAAAH!!
DAMMIT! I KNEW I SHOULD'VE KICKED THEM OUT WHEN I COULD!
GARURU (CHEW)
ガルル
ぱっ
BA (CATCH)
THESE TWO FREE-LOAD-ERS!!
SHE'S A FINE BURDEN FOR US, AND WE'RE NOT EVEN RELATED TO HER!!
......

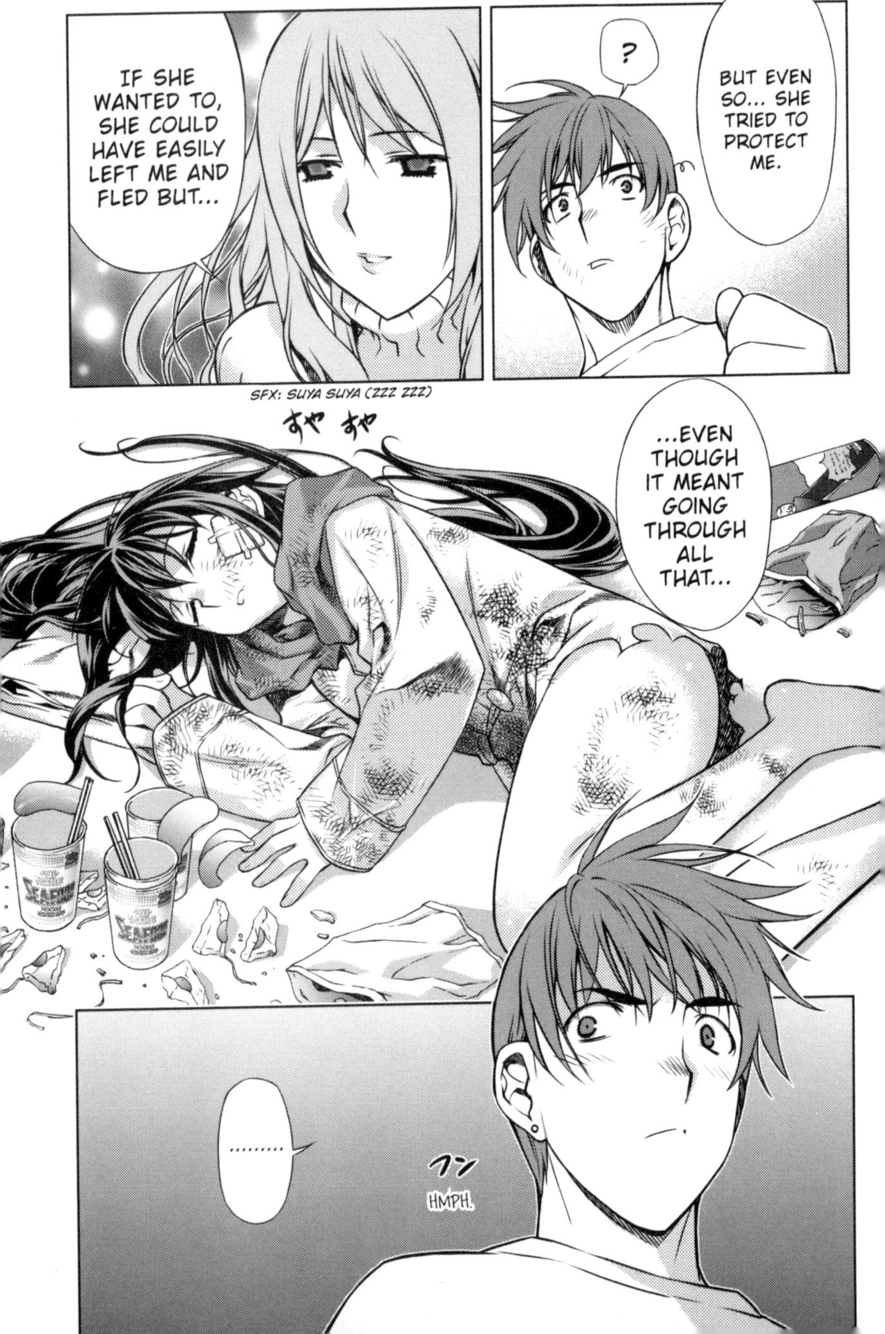
?
BUT EVEN SO... SHE TRIED TO PROTECT ME.
IF SHE WANTED TO, SHE COULD HAVE EASILY LEFT ME AND FLED BUT...
SFX: SUYA SUYA (ZZZ ZZZ)
すや すや
...EVEN THOUGH IT MEANT GOING THROUGH ALL THAT...
フン
HMPH.
....

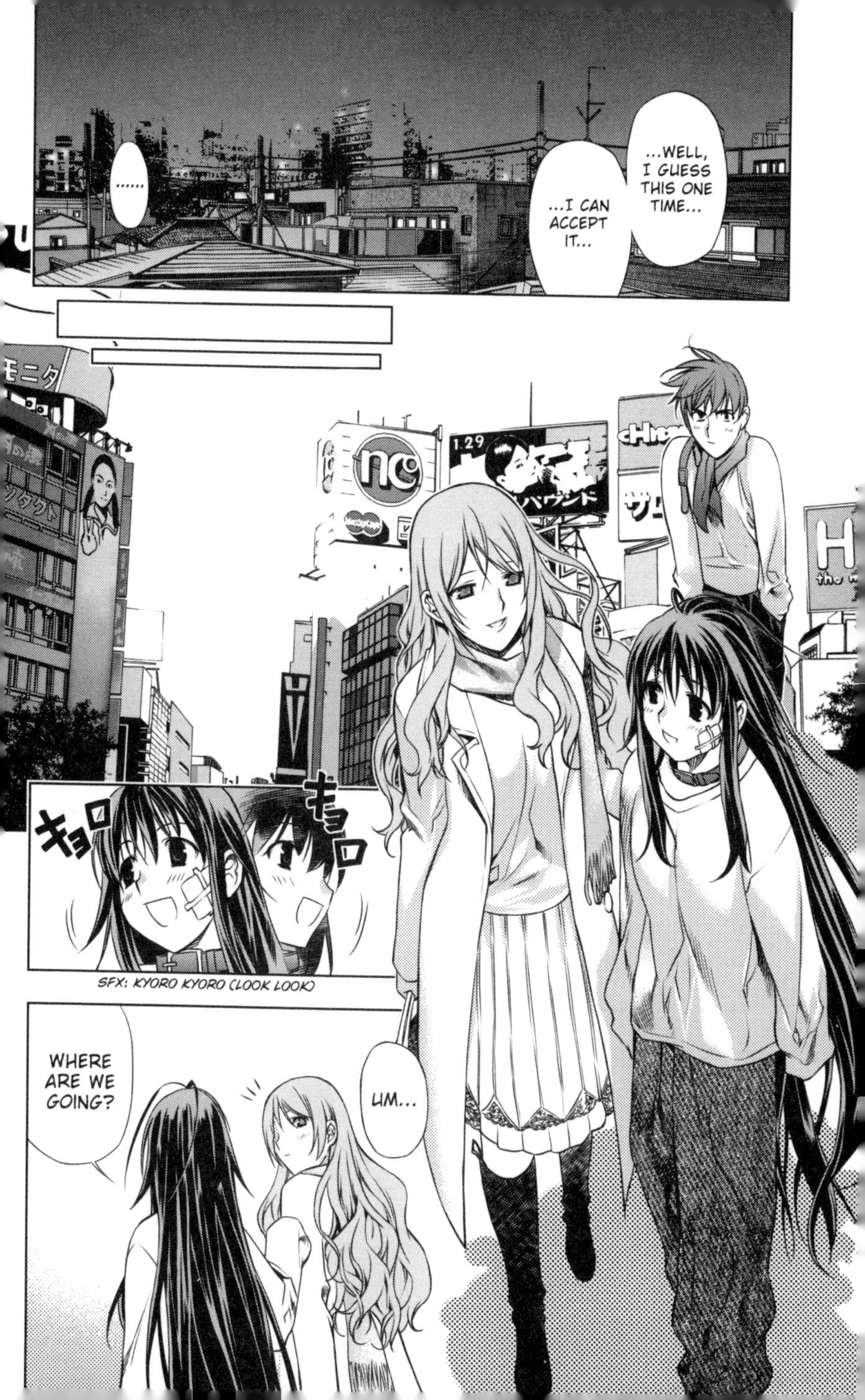
...WELL, I GUESS THIS ONE TIME...
...I CAN ACCEPT IT...
......
キョロ
キョロ
SFX: KYORO KYORO (LOOK LOOK)
UM...
WHERE ARE WE GOING?

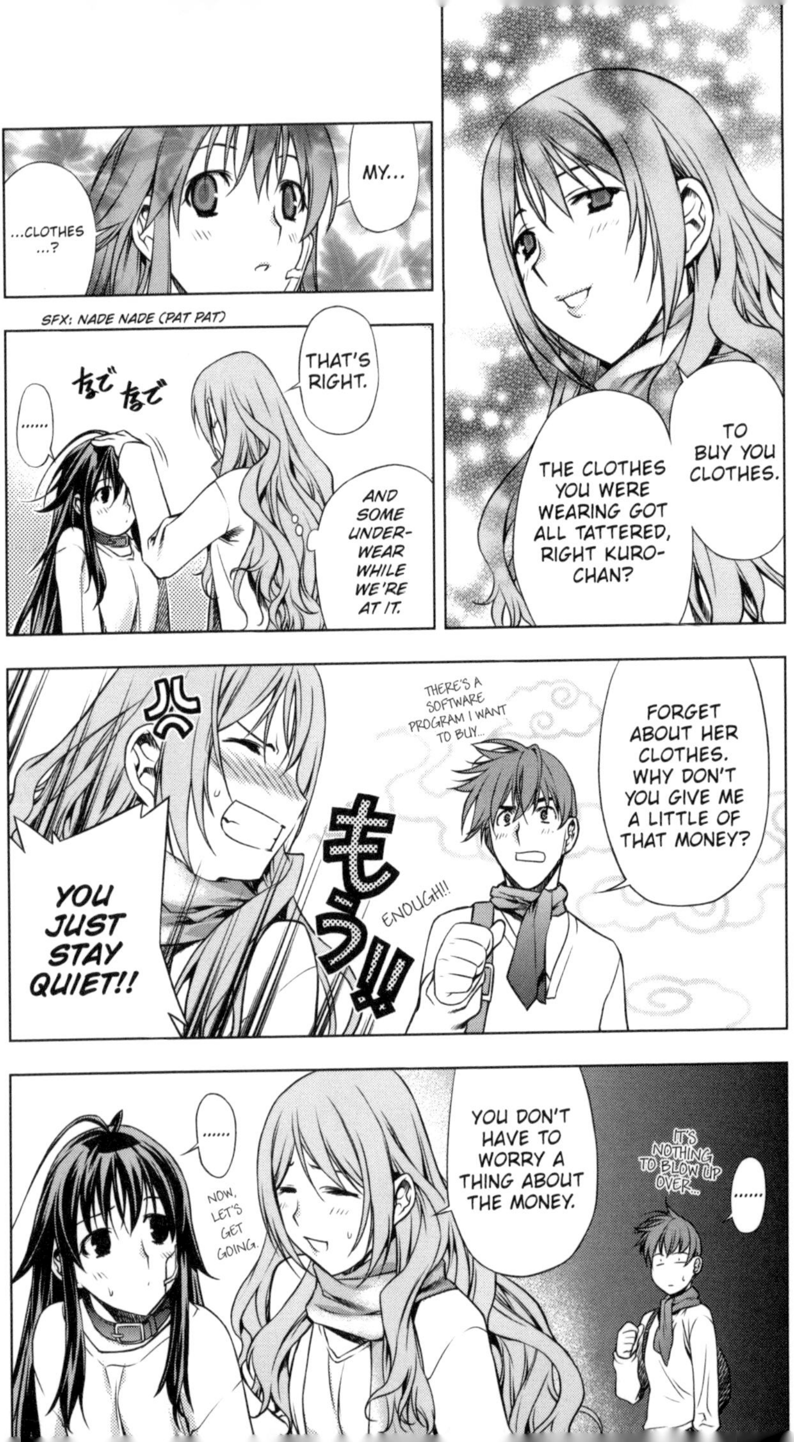
TO BUY YOU CLOTHES.
THE CLOTHES YOU WERE WEARING GOT ALL TATTERED, RIGHT KURO-CHAN?
MY...
...CLOTHES ...?
SFX: NADE NADE (PAT PAT)
THAT'S RIGHT.
AND SOME UNDER-WEAR WHILE WE'RE AT IT.
なでなで
......
FORGET ABOUT HER CLOTHES. WHY DON'T YOU GIVE ME A LITTLE OF THAT MONEY?
THERE'S A SOFTWARE PROGRAM I WANT TO BUY...
もう!!
ENOUGH!!
YOU JUST STAY QUIET!!
......
IT'S NOTHING TO BLOW UP OVER...
YOU DON'T HAVE TO WORRY A THING ABOUT THE MONEY.
NOW, LET'S GET GOING.
......

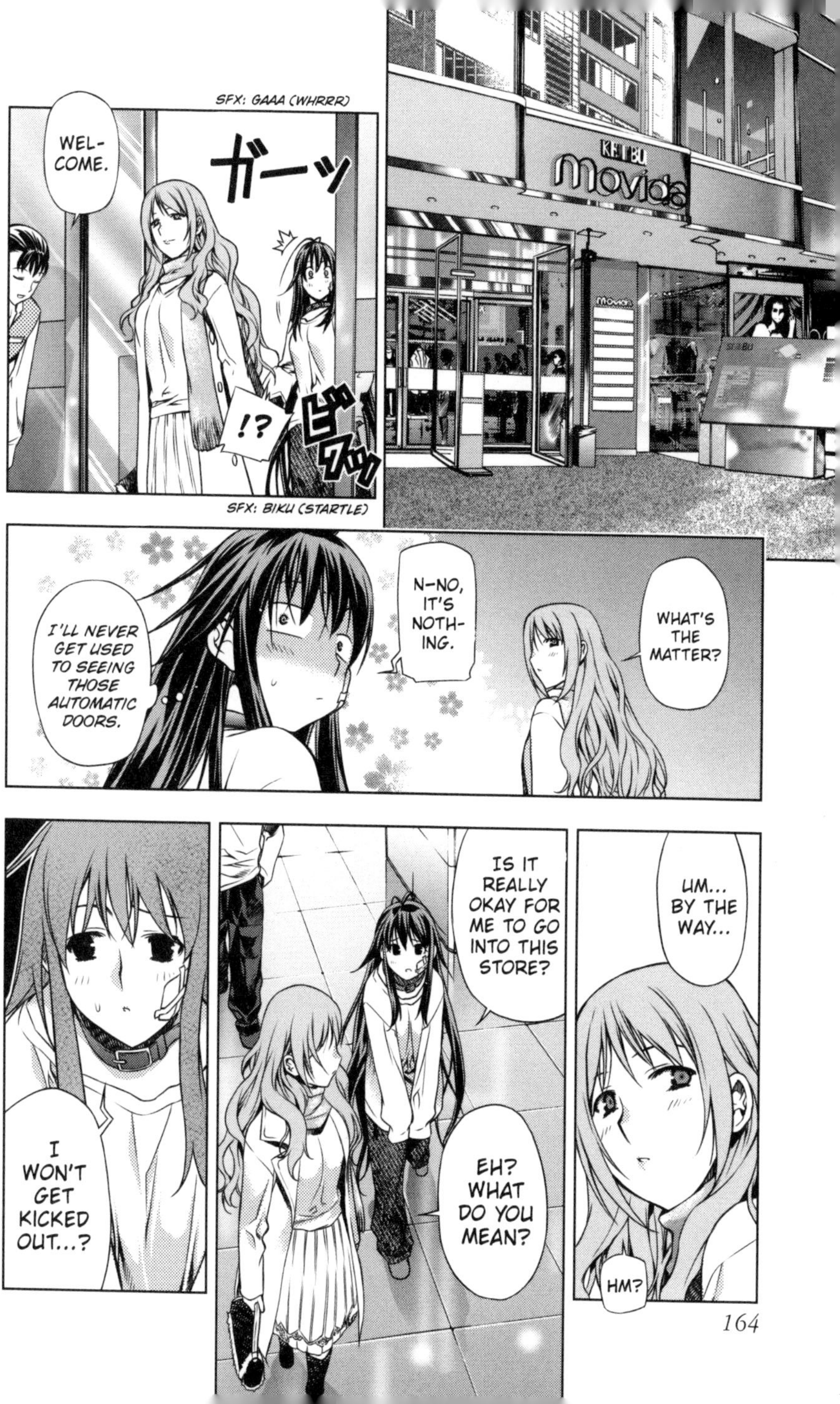
KEI BU
movida
SFX: GAAA (WHRRR)
WEL-COME.
ガーッ
!?
ビクッ
SFX: BIKU (STARTLE)
WHAT'S THE MATTER?
N-NO, IT'S NOTHING.
I'LL NEVER GET USED TO SEEING THOSE AUTOMATIC DOORS.
UM... BY THE WAY...
HM?
IS IT REALLY OKAY FOR ME TO GO INTO THIS STORE?
EH? WHAT DO YOU MEAN?
I WON'T GET KICKED OUT...?

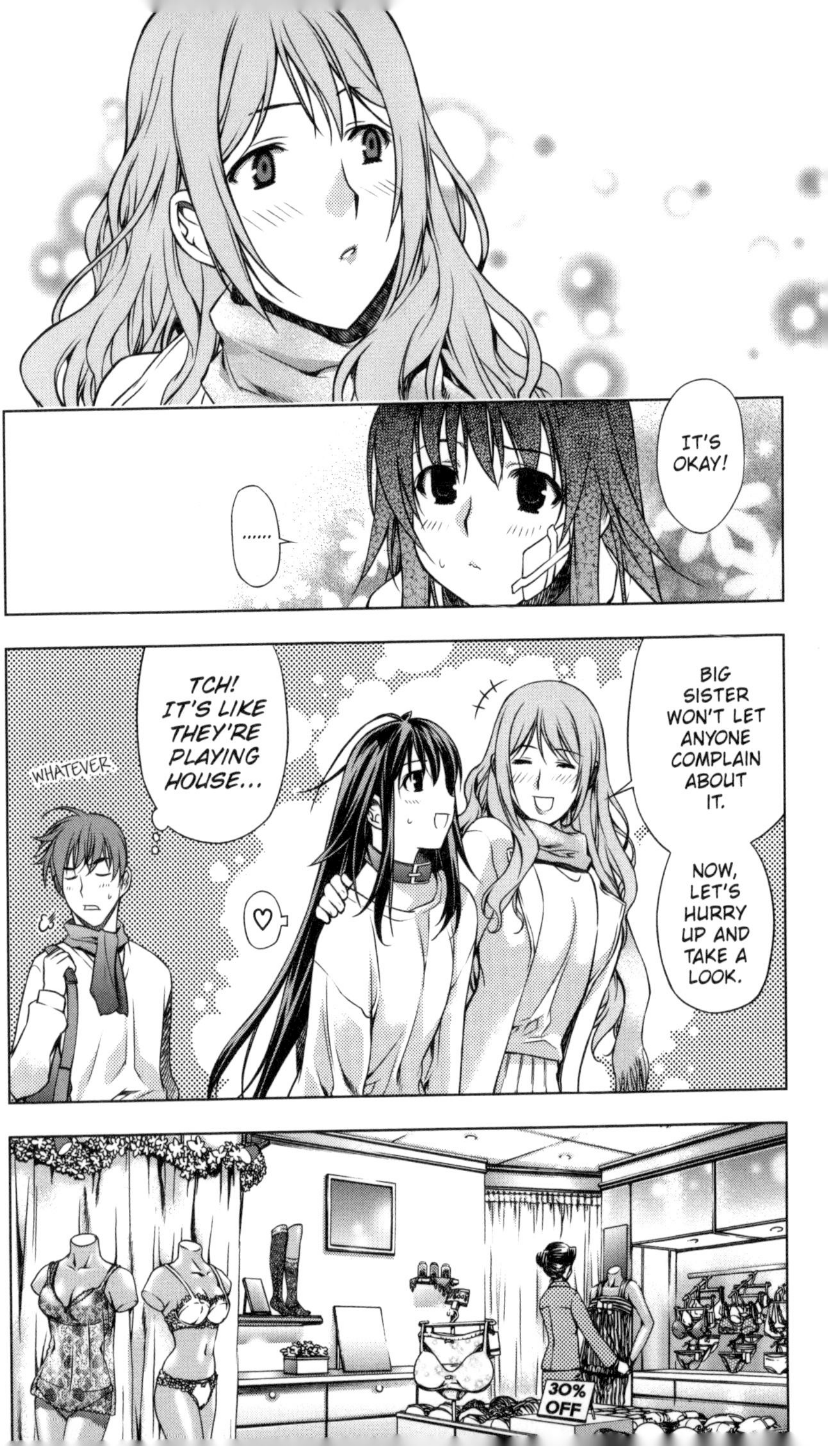
IT'S OKAY!
......
BIG SISTER WON'T LET ANYONE COMPLAIN ABOUT IT.
NOW, LET'S HURRY UP AND TAKE A LOOK.
♡
TCH! IT'S LIKE THEY'RE PLAYING HOUSE...
WHATEVER.
30% OFF

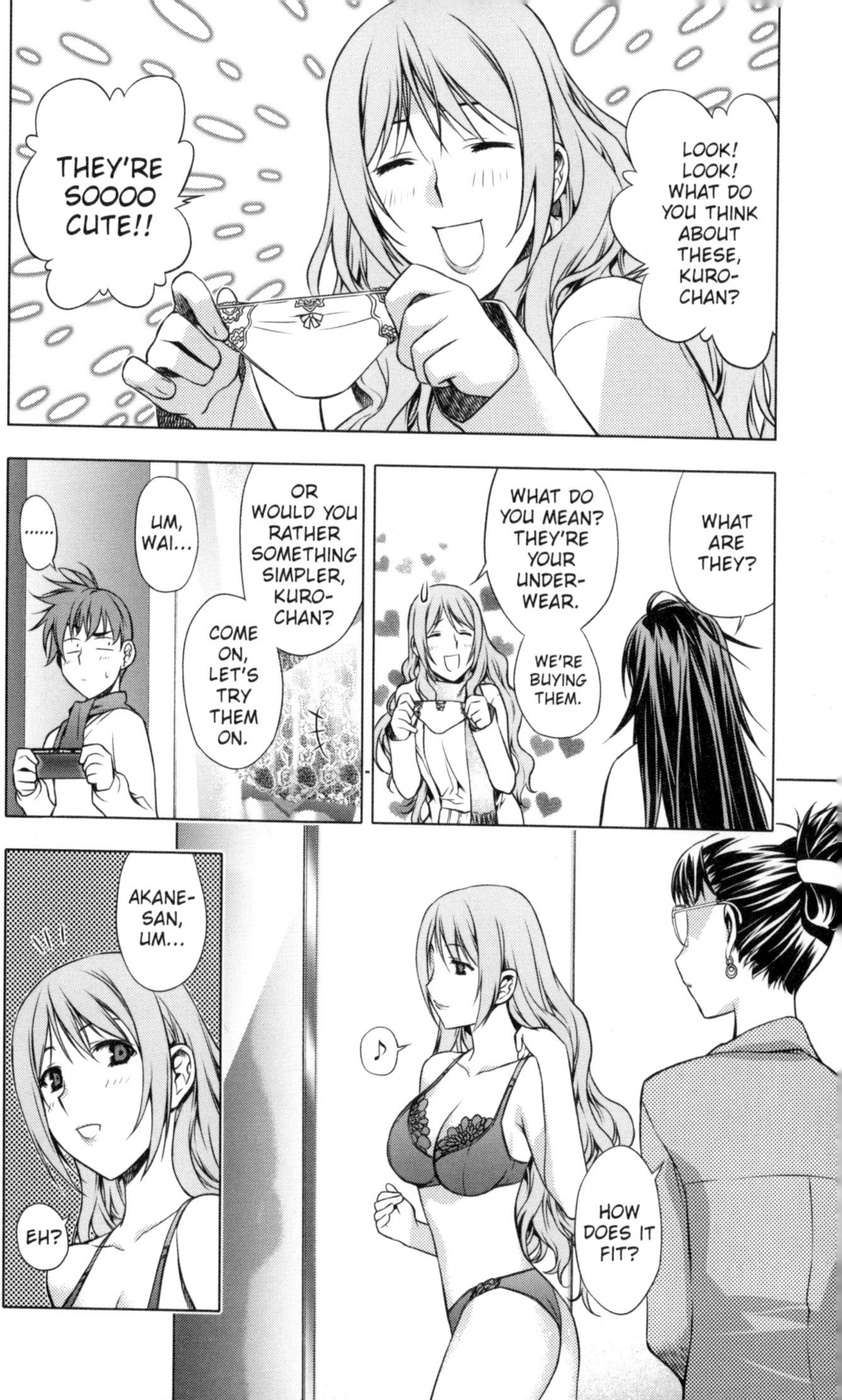
LOOK! LOOK! WHAT DO YOU THINK ABOUT THESE, KURO-CHAN?
THEY'RE SOOOO CUTE!!
WHAT ARE THEY?
WHAT DO YOU MEAN? THEY'RE YOUR UNDER-WEAR.
WE'RE BUYING THEM.
OR WOULD YOU RATHER SOMETHING SIMPLER, KURO-CHAN?
COME ON, LET'S TRY THEM ON.
UM, WAI...
......
♪
HOW DOES IT FIT?
AKANE-SAN, UM...
EH?

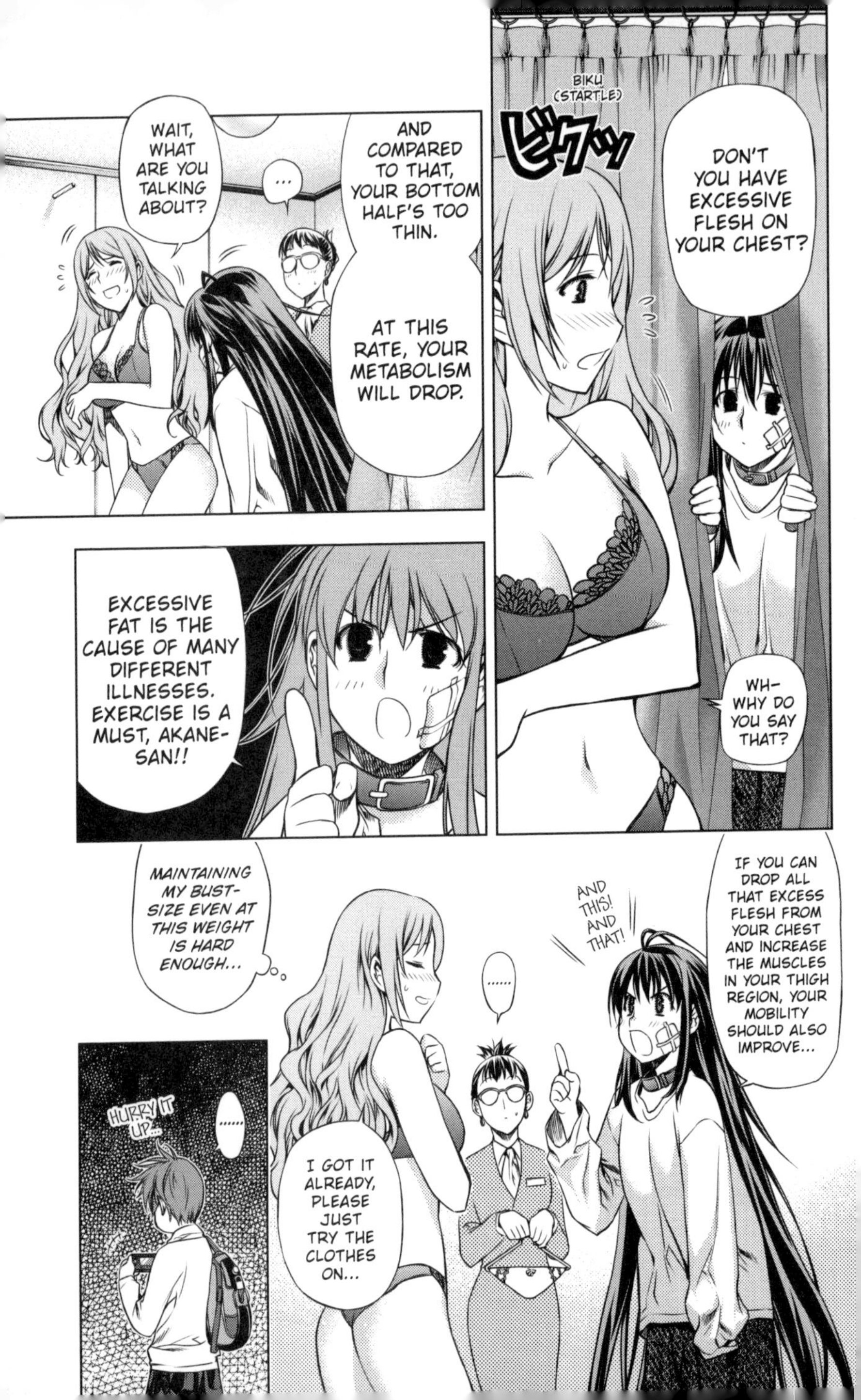
BIKU (STARTLE)
DON'T YOU HAVE EXCESSIVE FLESH ON YOUR CHEST?
WH- WHY DO YOU SAY THAT?
AND COMPARED TO THAT, YOUR BOTTOM HALF'S TOO THIN.
AT THIS RATE, YOUR METABOLISM WILL DROP.
...
WAIT, WHAT ARE YOU TALKING ABOUT?
EXCESSIVE FAT IS THE CAUSE OF MANY DIFFERENT ILLNESSES. EXERCISE IS A MUST, AKANE-SAN!!
IF YOU CAN DROP ALL THAT EXCESS FLESH FROM YOUR CHEST AND INCREASE THE MUSCLES IN YOUR THIGH REGION, YOUR MOBILITY SHOULD ALSO IMPROVE...
AND THIS! AND THAT!
......
MAINTAINING MY BUST-SIZE EVEN AT THIS WEIGHT IS HARD ENOUGH...
I GOT IT ALREADY, PLEASE JUST TRY THE CLOTHES ON...
......
HURRY IT UP...

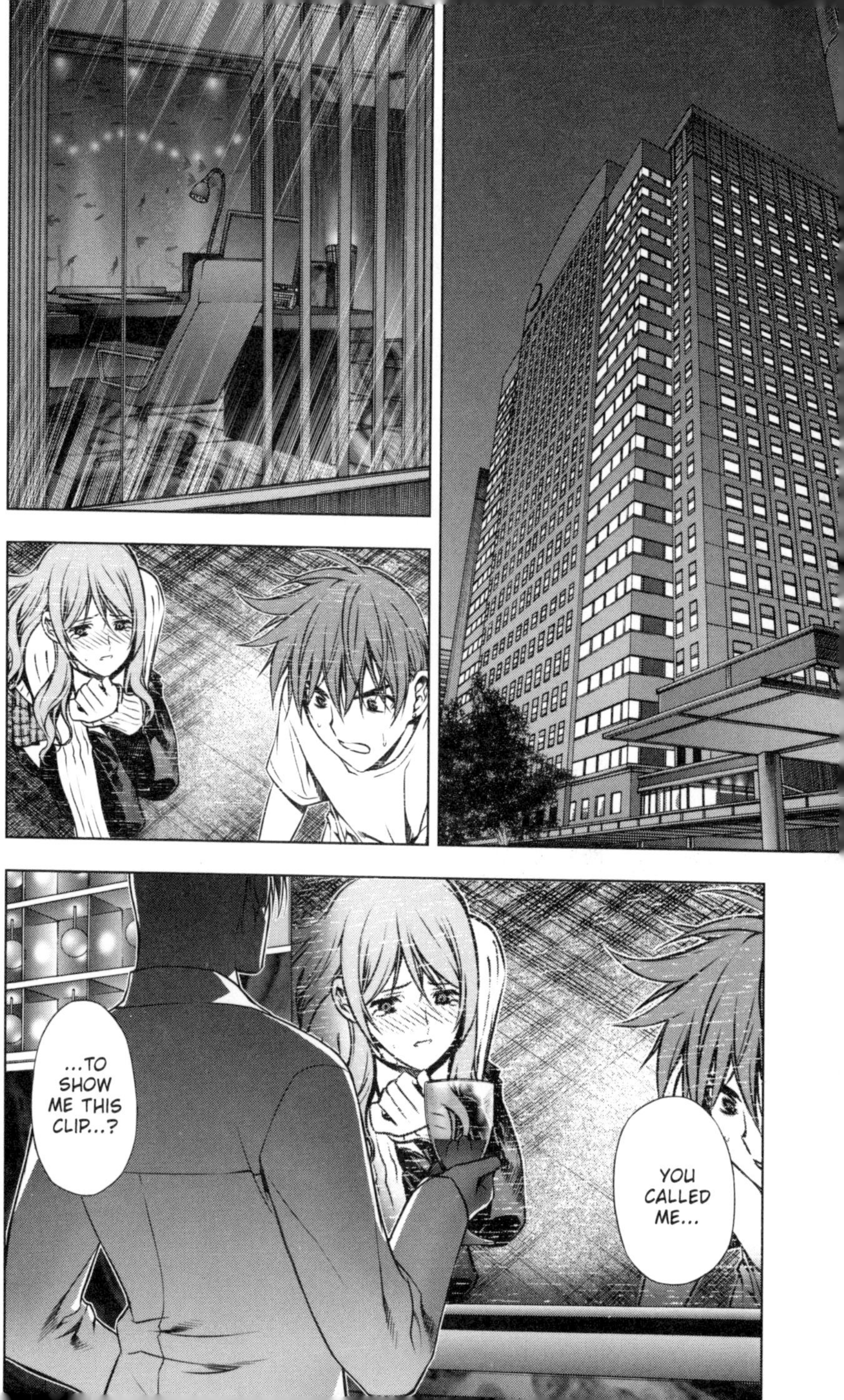
YOU CALLED ME...
...TO SHOW ME THIS CLIP...?

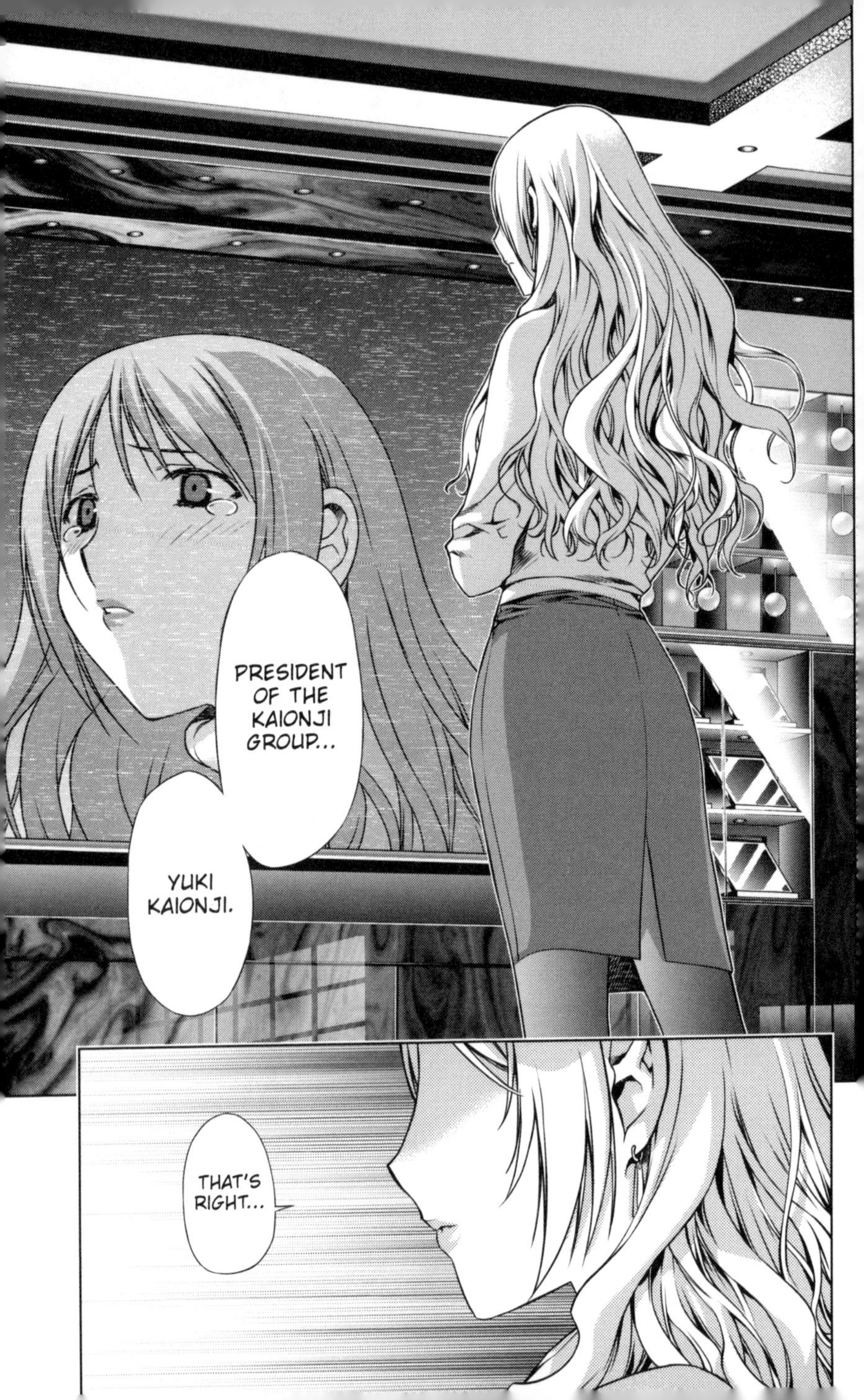
PRESIDENT OF THE KAIONJI GROUP...
YUKI KAIONJI.
THAT'S RIGHT...

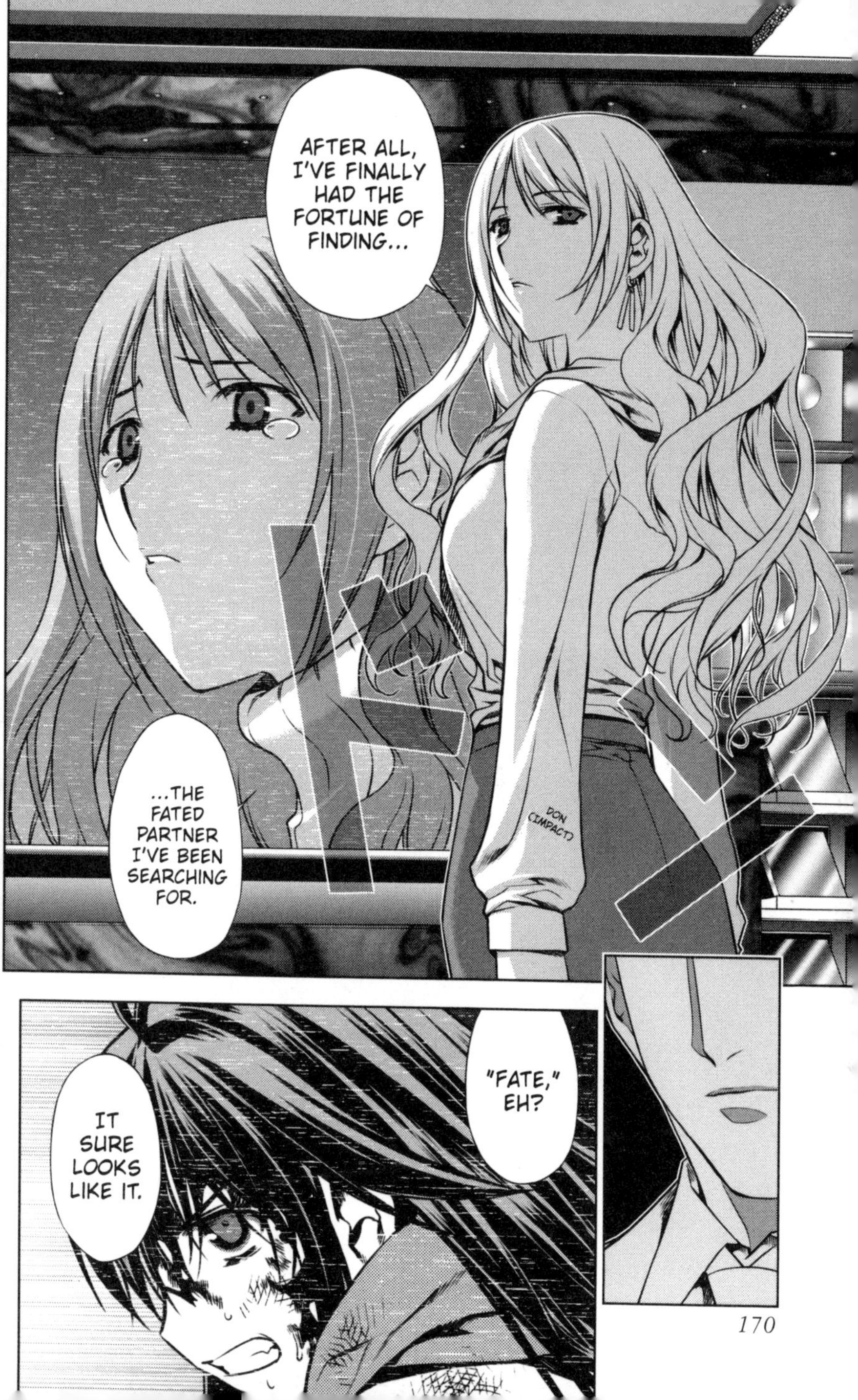
AFTER ALL, I'VE FINALLY HAD THE FORTUNE OF FINDING...
...THE FATED PARTNER I'VE BEEN SEARCHING FOR.
DON (IMPACT)
"FATE," EH?
IT SURE LOOKS LIKE IT.

技

一

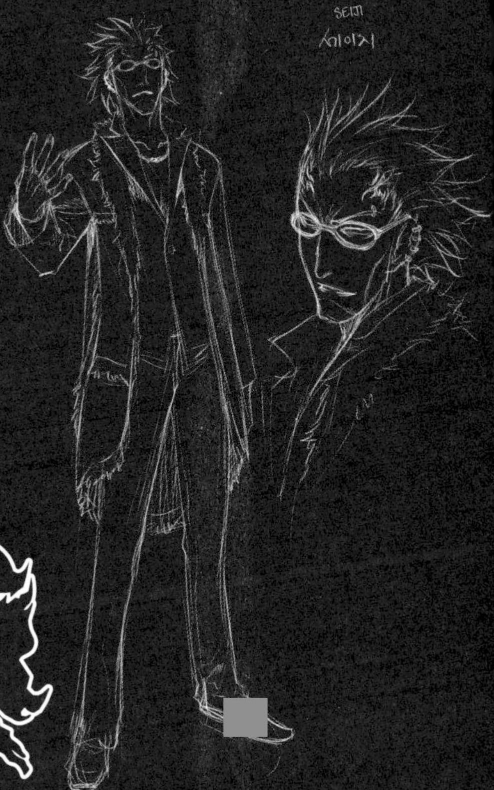
SEIJI
세이지

黒神

BLACK GOD

which maintains balance in the world.

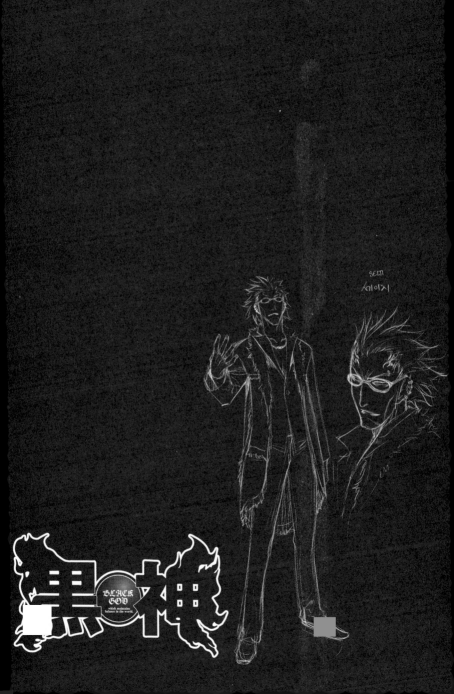

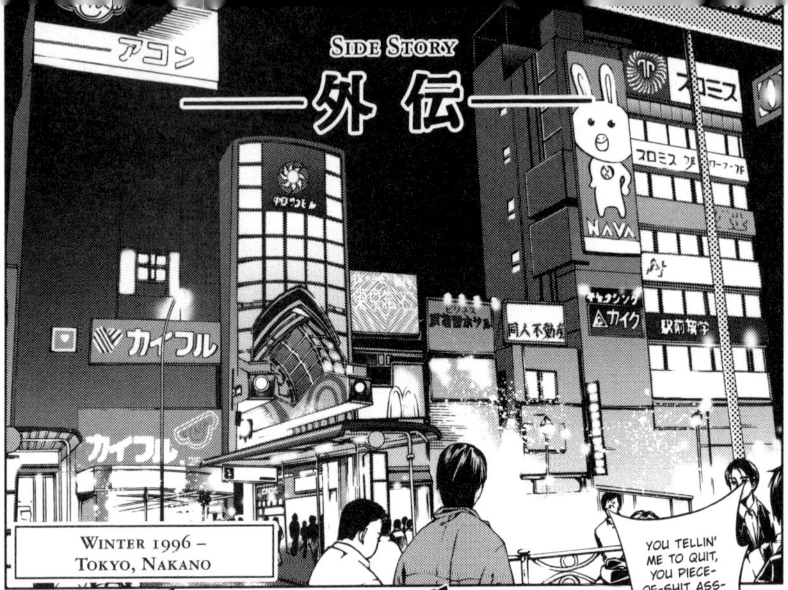
SIDE STORY
—外伝—
WINTER 1996 – TOKYO, NAKANO

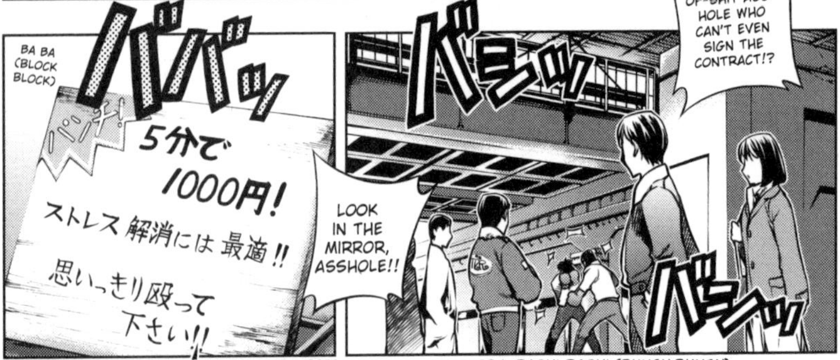
YOU TELLIN' ME TO QUIT, YOU PIECE-OF-SHIT ASS-HOLE WHO CAN'T EVEN SIGN THE CONTRACT!?
LOOK IN THE MIRROR, ASSHOLE!!
BA BA (BLOCK BLOCK)
パンチ!
5分で 1000円!
ストレス 解消には 最適!!
思いっきり殴って 下さい!!

SIGN: PUNCH! ¥1000 FOR 5 MINUTES! BEST FOR STRESS RELIEF!! PLEASE PUNCH ME WITH ALL YOU'VE GOT!!

SFX: BASHI BASHI (PUNCH PUNCH)

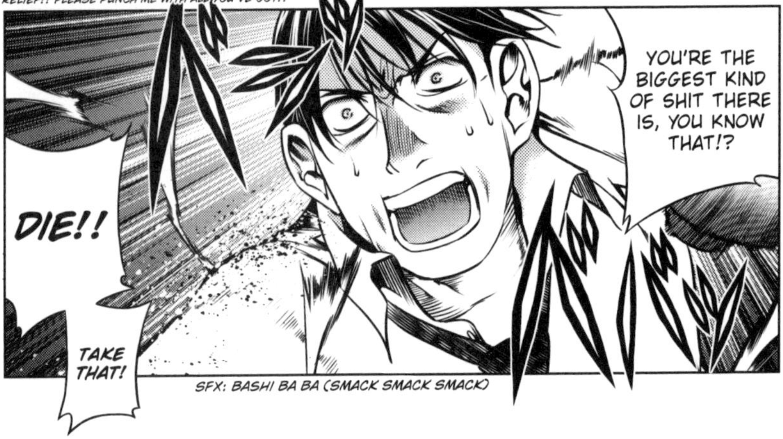
YOU'RE THE BIGGEST KIND OF SHIT THERE IS, YOU KNOW THAT!?
DIE!!
TAKE THAT!

SFX: BASHI BA BA (SMACK SMACK SMACK)

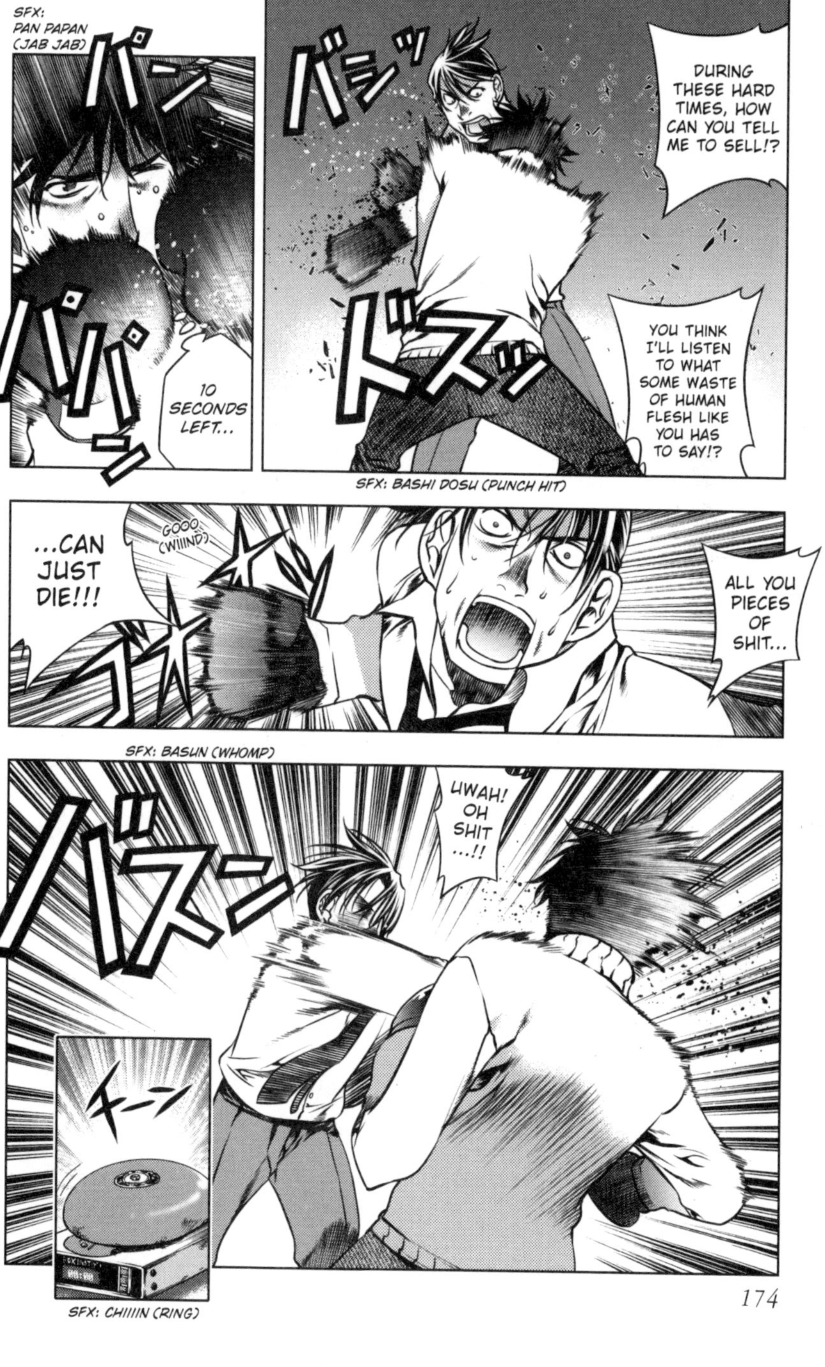
DURING THESE HARD TIMES, HOW CAN YOU TELL ME TO SELL!?
YOU THINK I'LL LISTEN TO WHAT SOME WASTE OF HUMAN FLESH LIKE YOU HAS TO SAY!?
SFX: BASHI DOSU (PUNCH HIT)
SFX: PAN PAPAN (JAB JAB)
10 SECONDS LEFT...
ALL YOU PIECES OF SHIT...
...CAN JUST DIE!!!
GOOO (WIIIND)
SFX: BASUN (WHOMP)
UWAH! OH SHIT ...!!
SFX: CHIIIIN (RING)

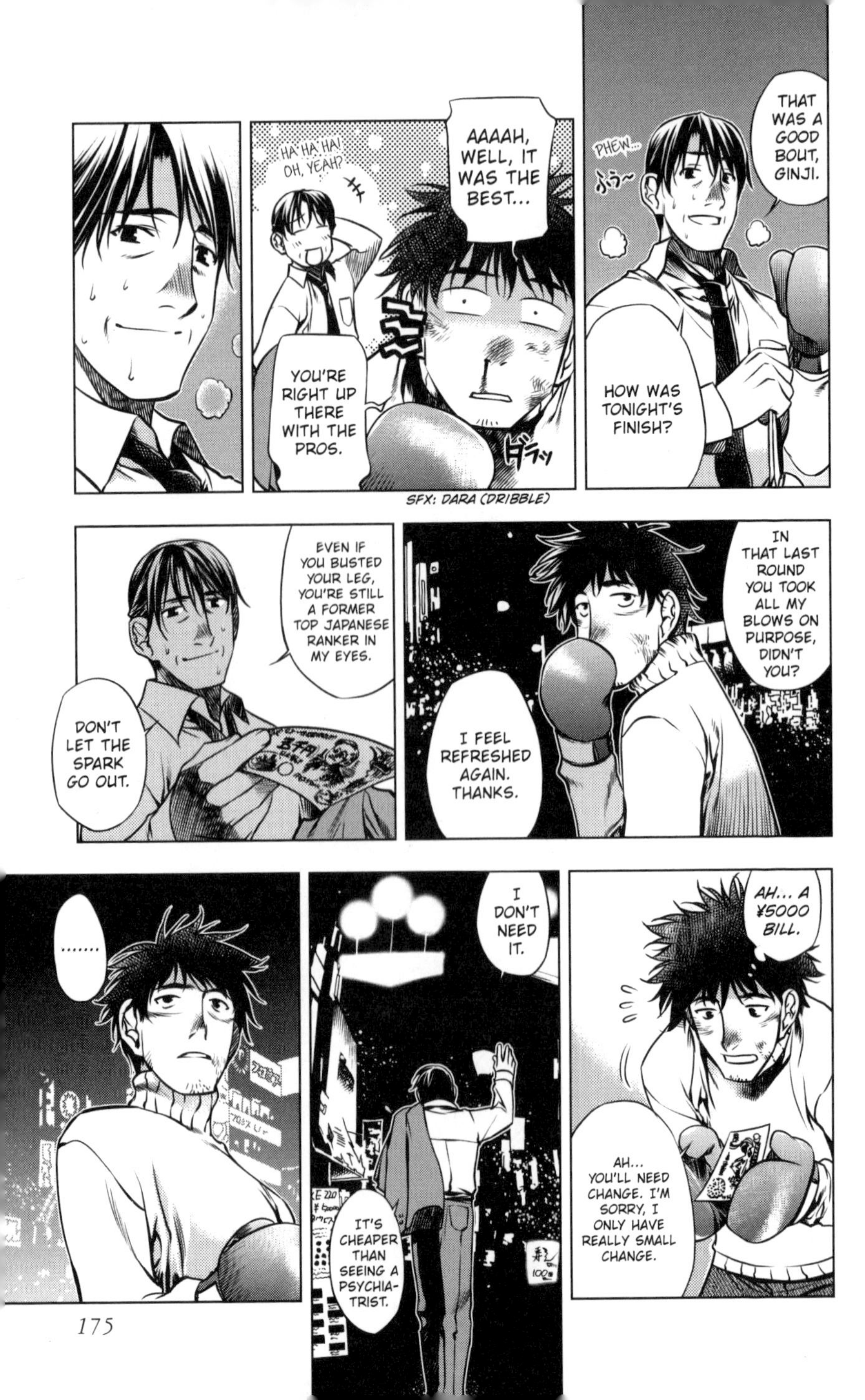
PHEW...
ふぅ~
THAT WAS A GOOD BOUT, GINJI.
HOW WAS TONIGHT'S FINISH?
AAAAH, WELL, IT WAS THE BEST...
HA HA HA! OH, YEAH?
YOU'RE RIGHT UP THERE WITH THE PROS.
ダラッ
SFX: DARA (DRIBBLE)
IN THAT LAST ROUND YOU TOOK ALL MY BLOWS ON PURPOSE, DIDN'T YOU?
I FEEL REFRESHED AGAIN. THANKS.
EVEN IF YOU BUSTED YOUR LEG, YOU'RE STILL A FORMER TOP JAPANESE RANKER IN MY EYES.
DON'T LET THE SPARK GO OUT.
AH... A ¥5000 BILL.
AH... YOU'LL NEED CHANGE. I'M SORRY, I ONLY HAVE REALLY SMALL CHANGE.
I DON'T NEED IT.
IT'S CHEAPER THAN SEEING A PSYCHIATRIST.
....

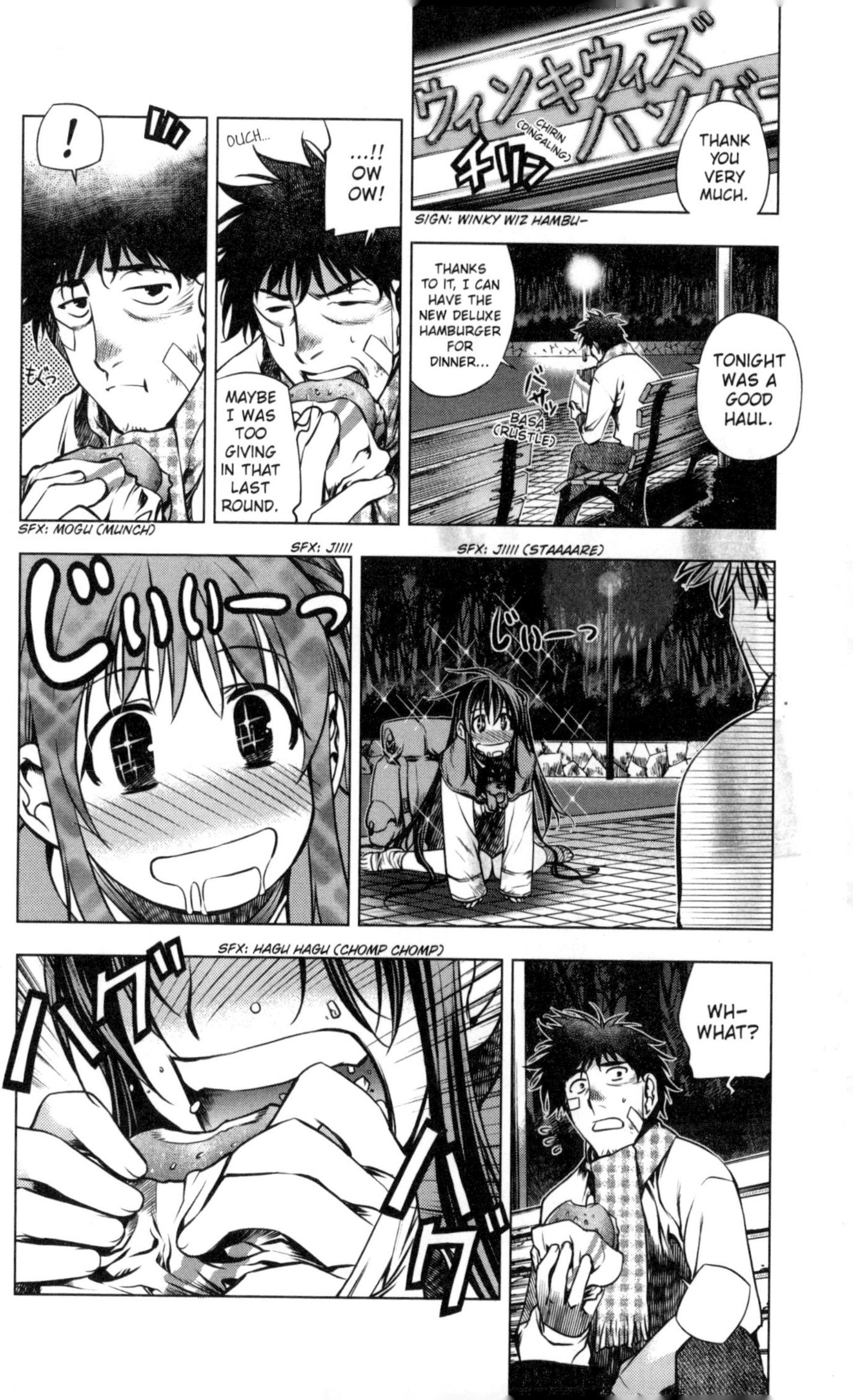
CHIRIN (DINGALING)
THANK YOU VERY MUCH.
SIGN: WINKY WIZ HAMBU-
TONIGHT WAS A GOOD HAUL.
THANKS TO IT, I CAN HAVE THE NEW DELUXE HAMBURGER FOR DINNER...
BASA (RUSTLE)
...!! OW OW!
OUCH...
MAYBE I WAS TOO GIVING IN THAT LAST ROUND.
!
SFX: MOGU (MUNCH)
SFX: JIIII (STAAAARE)
SFX: JIIII
WH- WHAT?
SFX: HAGU HAGU (CHOMP CHOMP)

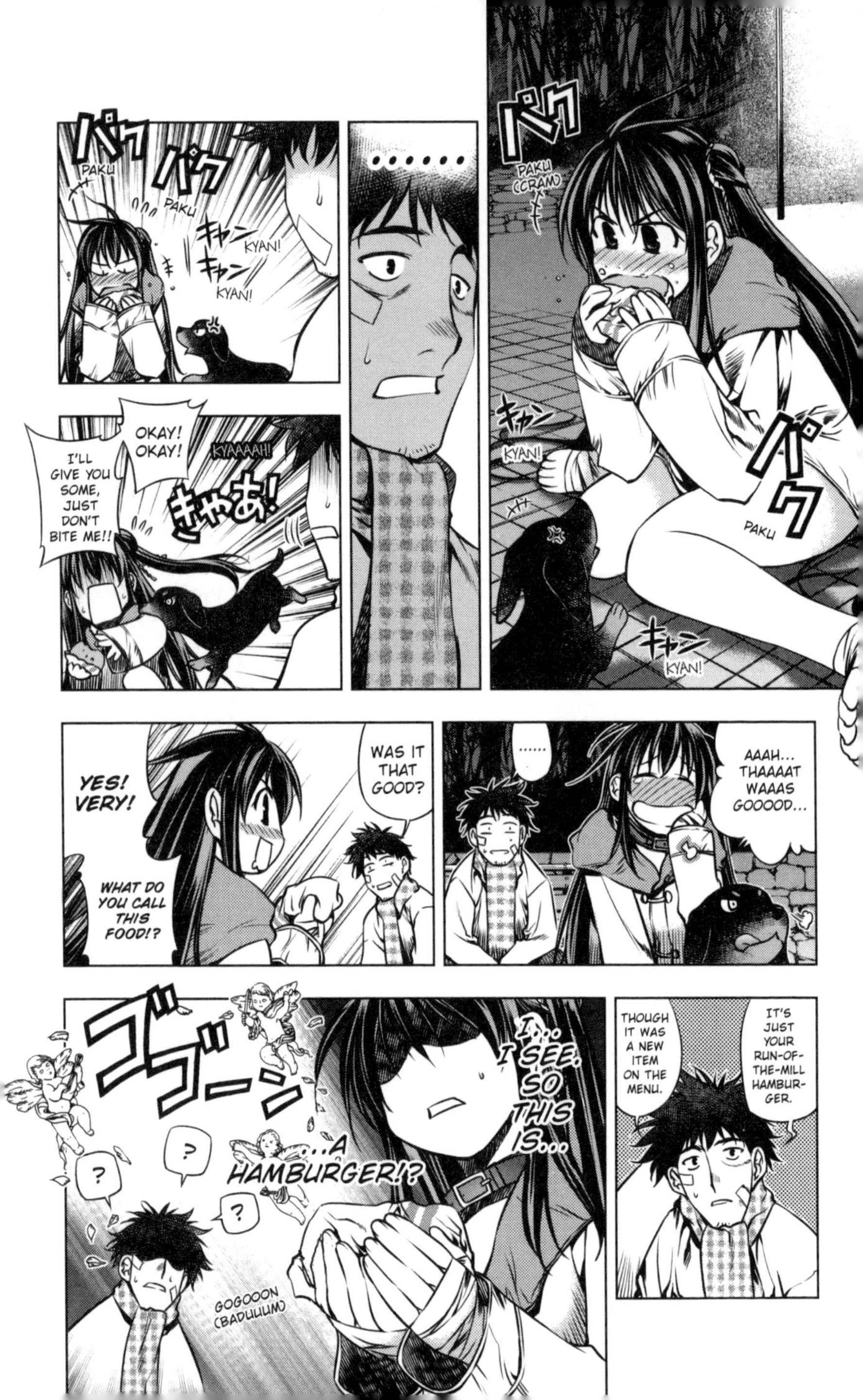
パク
PAKU (CRAM)
キャン
KYAN!
パク
PAKU
キャン
KYAN!
......
パク
PAKU
パク
PAKU
キャン
KYAN!
キャン
KYAN!
KYAAAH!
きゃあ!
OKAY! OKAY!
I'LL GIVE YOU SOME, JUST DON'T BITE ME!!
AAAH... THAAAAT WAAAS GOOOOD...
......
WAS IT THAT GOOD?
YES! VERY!
WHAT DO YOU CALL THIS FOOD!?
IT'S JUST YOUR RUN-OF-THE-MILL HAMBUR-GER.
THOUGH IT WAS A NEW ITEM ON THE MENU.
I... I SEE. SO THIS IS...
ゴゴーン
...A HAMBURGER!?
?
?
?
GOGOOON (BADUUUM)

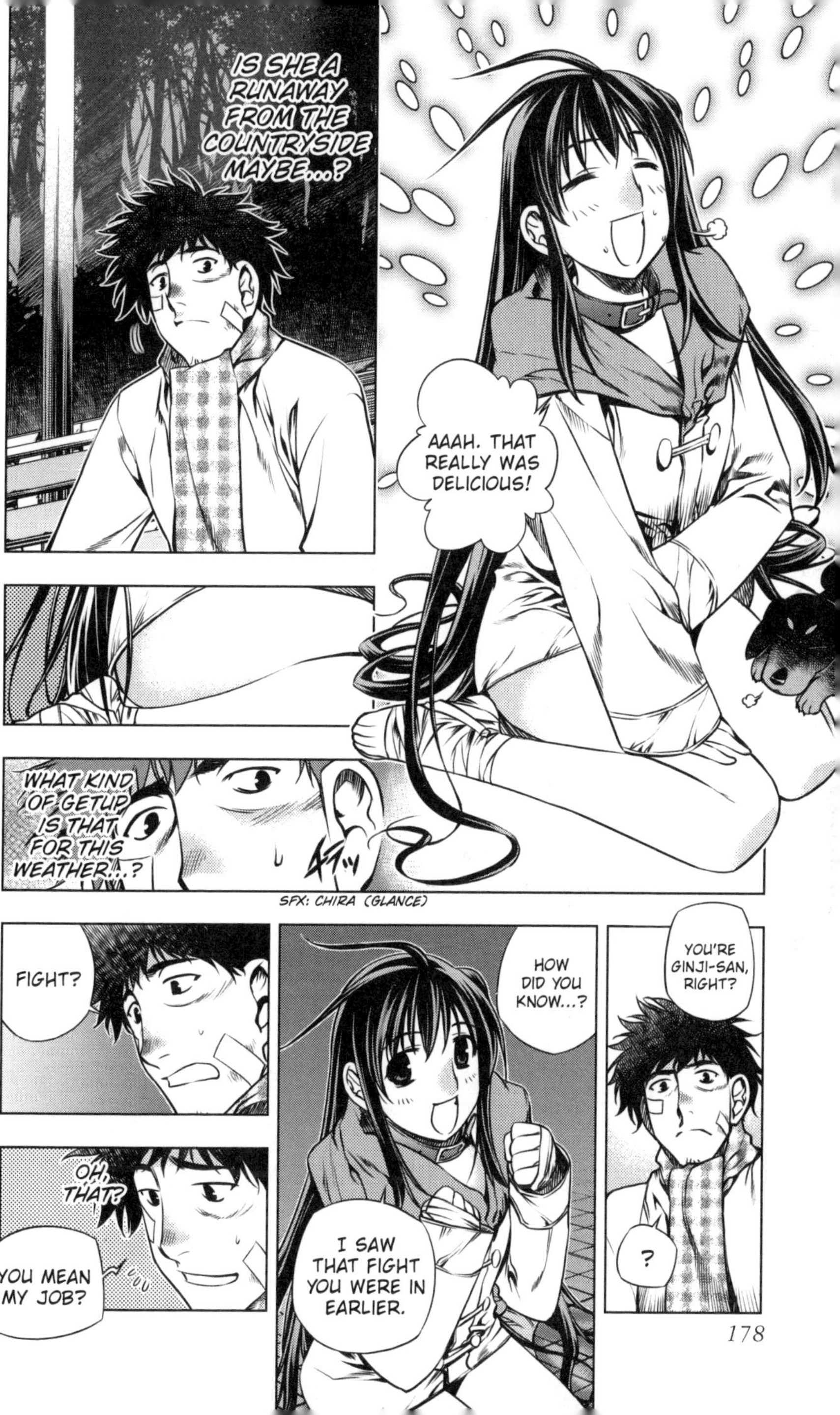
AAAH. THAT REALLY WAS DELICIOUS!
IS SHE A RUNAWAY FROM THE COUNTRYSIDE MAYBE...?
WHAT KIND OF GETUP IS THAT FOR THIS WEATHER...?
SFX: CHIRA (GLANCE)
YOU'RE GINJI-SAN, RIGHT?
?
HOW DID YOU KNOW...?
I SAW THAT FIGHT YOU WERE IN EARLIER.
FIGHT?
OH, THAT?
YOU MEAN MY JOB?

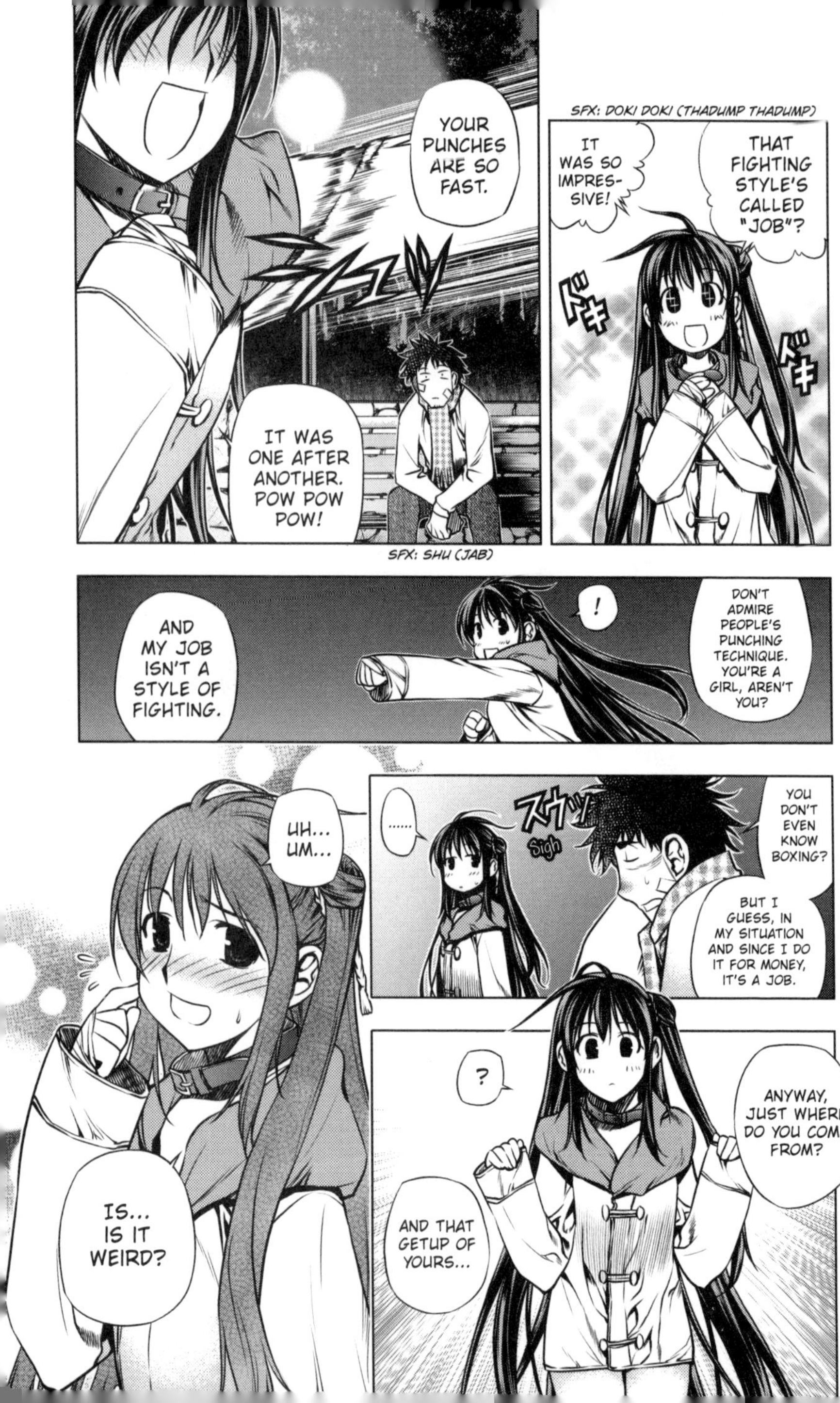
SFX: DOKI DOKI (THADUMP THADUMP)
THAT FIGHTING STYLE'S CALLED "JOB"?
IT WAS SO IMPRES- SIVE!
YOUR PUNCHES ARE SO FAST.
IT WAS ONE AFTER ANOTHER. POW POW POW!
SFX: SHU (JAB)
DON'T ADMIRE PEOPLE'S PUNCHING TECHNIQUE. YOU'RE A GIRL, AREN'T YOU?
!
AND MY JOB ISN'T A STYLE OF FIGHTING.
YOU DON'T EVEN KNOW BOXING?
Sigh
......
BUT I GUESS, IN MY SITUATION AND SINCE I DO IT FOR MONEY, IT'S A JOB.
ANYWAY, JUST WHERE DO YOU COME FROM?
?
AND THAT GETUP OF YOURS...
UH... UM...
IS... IS IT WEIRD?

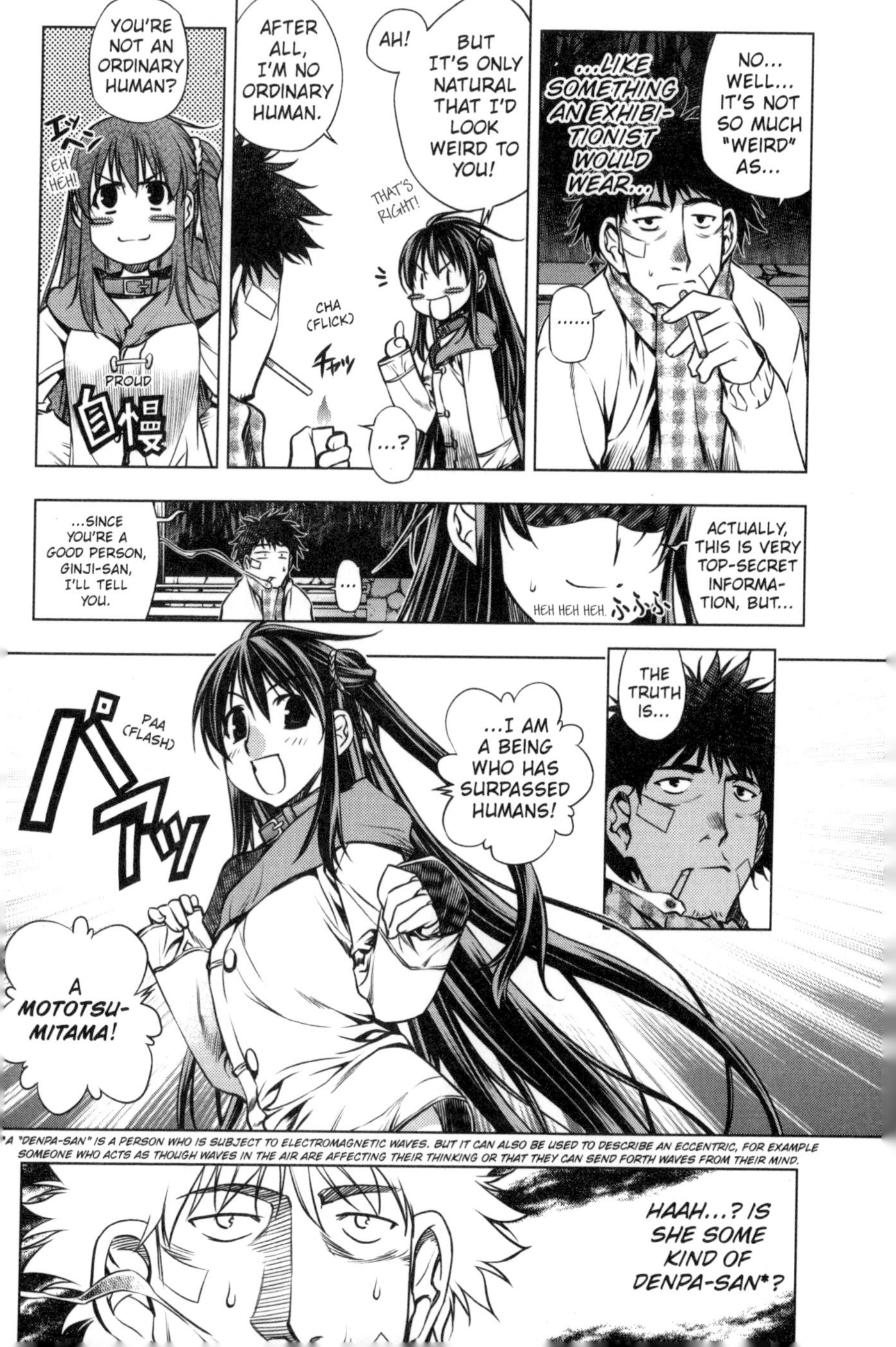
NO... WELL... IT'S NOT SO MUCH "WEIRD" AS...
...LIKE SOMETHING AN EXHIBITIONIST WOULD WEAR...
......
AH!
BUT IT'S ONLY NATURAL THAT I'D LOOK WEIRD TO YOU!
THAT'S RIGHT!
...?
CHA (FLICK)
AFTER ALL, I'M NO ORDINARY HUMAN.
YOU'RE NOT AN ORDINARY HUMAN?
EH HEH!
PROUD
ACTUALLY, THIS IS VERY TOP-SECRET INFORMATION, BUT...
HEH HEH HEH.
...
...SINCE YOU'RE A GOOD PERSON, GINJI-SAN, I'LL TELL YOU.
THE TRUTH IS...
...I AM A BEING WHO HAS SURPASSED HUMANS!
PAA (FLASH)
A MOTOTSU-MITAMA!
HAAH...? IS SHE SOME KIND OF DENPA-SAN*?

*A "DENPA-SAN" IS A PERSON WHO IS SUBJECT TO ELECTROMAGNETIC WAVES. BUT IT CAN ALSO BE USED TO DESCRIBE AN ECCENTRIC, FOR EXAMPLE SOMEONE WHO ACTS AS THOUGH WAVES IN THE AIR ARE AFFECTING THEIR THINKING OR THAT THEY CAN SEND FORTH WAVES FROM THEIR MIND.

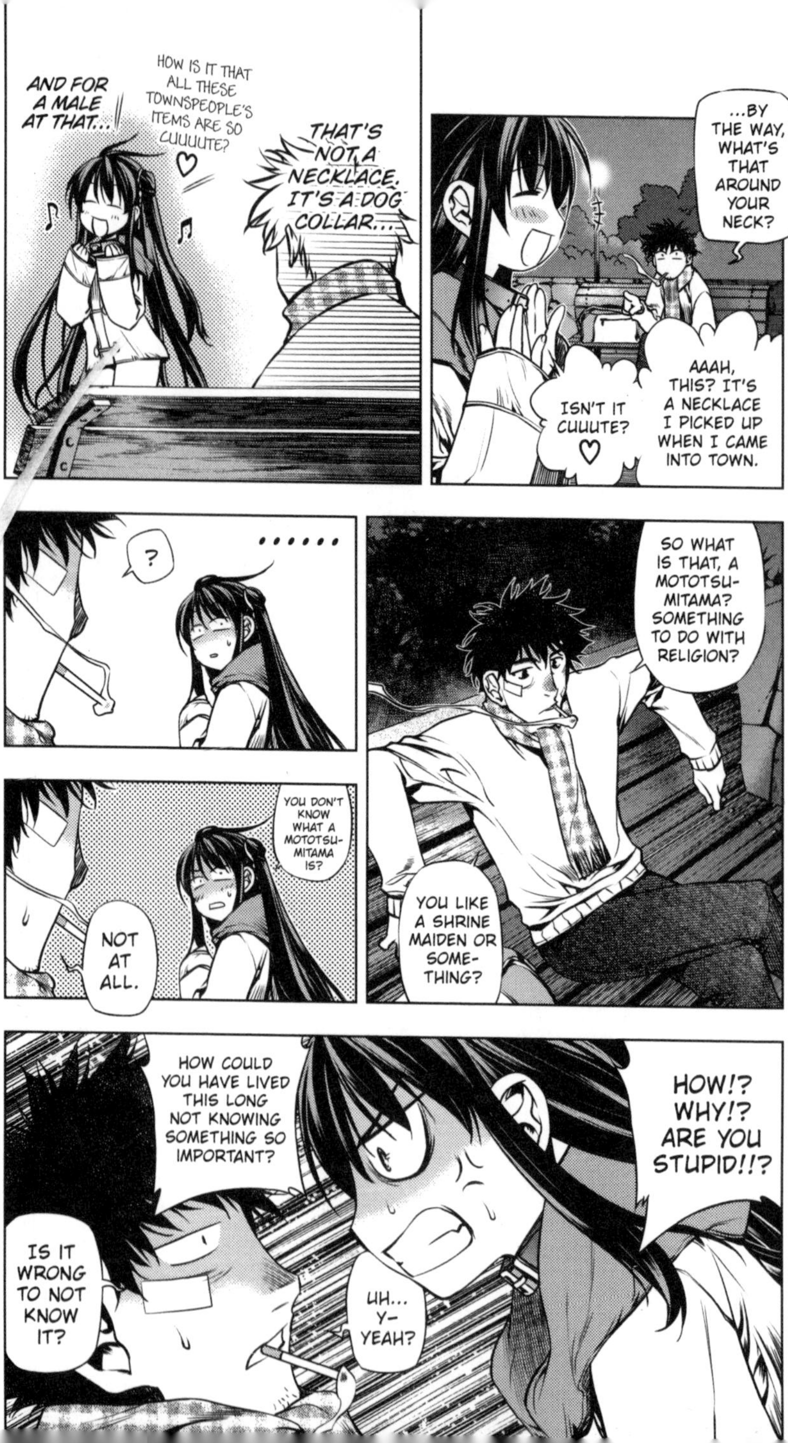
...BY THE WAY, WHAT'S THAT AROUND YOUR NECK?
AAAH, THIS? IT'S A NECKLACE I PICKED UP WHEN I CAME INTO TOWN.
ISN'T IT CUUUTE? ♡
THAT'S NOT A NECKLACE. IT'S A DOG COLLAR...
HOW IS IT THAT ALL THESE TOWNSPEOPLE'S ITEMS ARE SO CUUUUTE? ♡
AND FOR A MALE AT THAT...
SO WHAT IS THAT, A MOTOTSU-MITAMA? SOMETHING TO DO WITH RELIGION?
YOU LIKE A SHRINE MAIDEN OR SOME-THING?
......
?
YOU DON'T KNOW WHAT A MOTOTSU-MITAMA IS?
NOT AT ALL.
HOW!? WHY!? ARE YOU STUPID!!?
HOW COULD YOU HAVE LIVED THIS LONG NOT KNOWING SOMETHING SO IMPORTANT?
IS IT WRONG TO NOT KNOW IT?
UH... Y-YEAH?

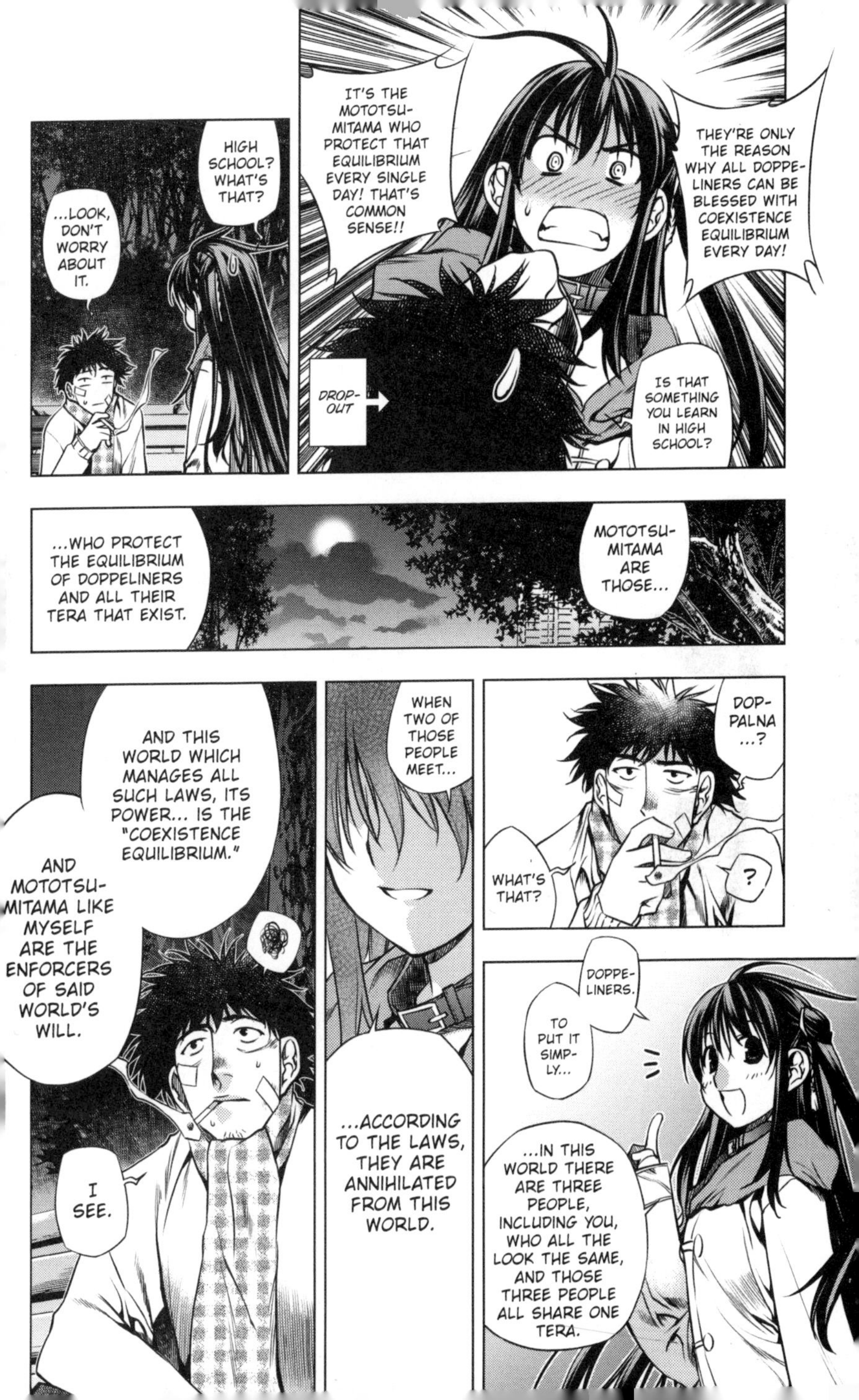
THEY'RE ONLY THE REASON WHY ALL DOPPE-LINERS CAN BE BLESSED WITH COEXISTENCE EQUILIBRIUM EVERY DAY!
IT'S THE MOTOTSU-MITAMA WHO PROTECT THAT EQUILIBRIUM EVERY SINGLE DAY! THAT'S COMMON SENSE!!
IS THAT SOMETHING YOU LEARN IN HIGH SCHOOL?
DROP-OUT
HIGH SCHOOL? WHAT'S THAT?
...LOOK, DON'T WORRY ABOUT IT.
MOTOTSU-MITAMA ARE THOSE...
...WHO PROTECT THE EQUILIBRIUM OF DOPPELINERS AND ALL THEIR TERA THAT EXIST.
DOP-PALNA ...?
?
WHAT'S THAT?
DOPPE-LINERS.
TO PUT IT SIMP-LY...
...IN THIS WORLD THERE ARE THREE PEOPLE, INCLUDING YOU, WHO ALL THE LOOK THE SAME, AND THOSE THREE PEOPLE ALL SHARE ONE TERA.
WHEN TWO OF THOSE PEOPLE MEET...
...ACCORDING TO THE LAWS, THEY ARE ANNIHILATED FROM THIS WORLD.
AND THIS WORLD WHICH MANAGES ALL SUCH LAWS, ITS POWER... IS THE "COEXISTENCE EQUILIBRIUM."
AND MOTOTSU-MITAMA LIKE MYSELF ARE THE ENFORCERS OF SAID WORLD'S WILL.
I SEE.

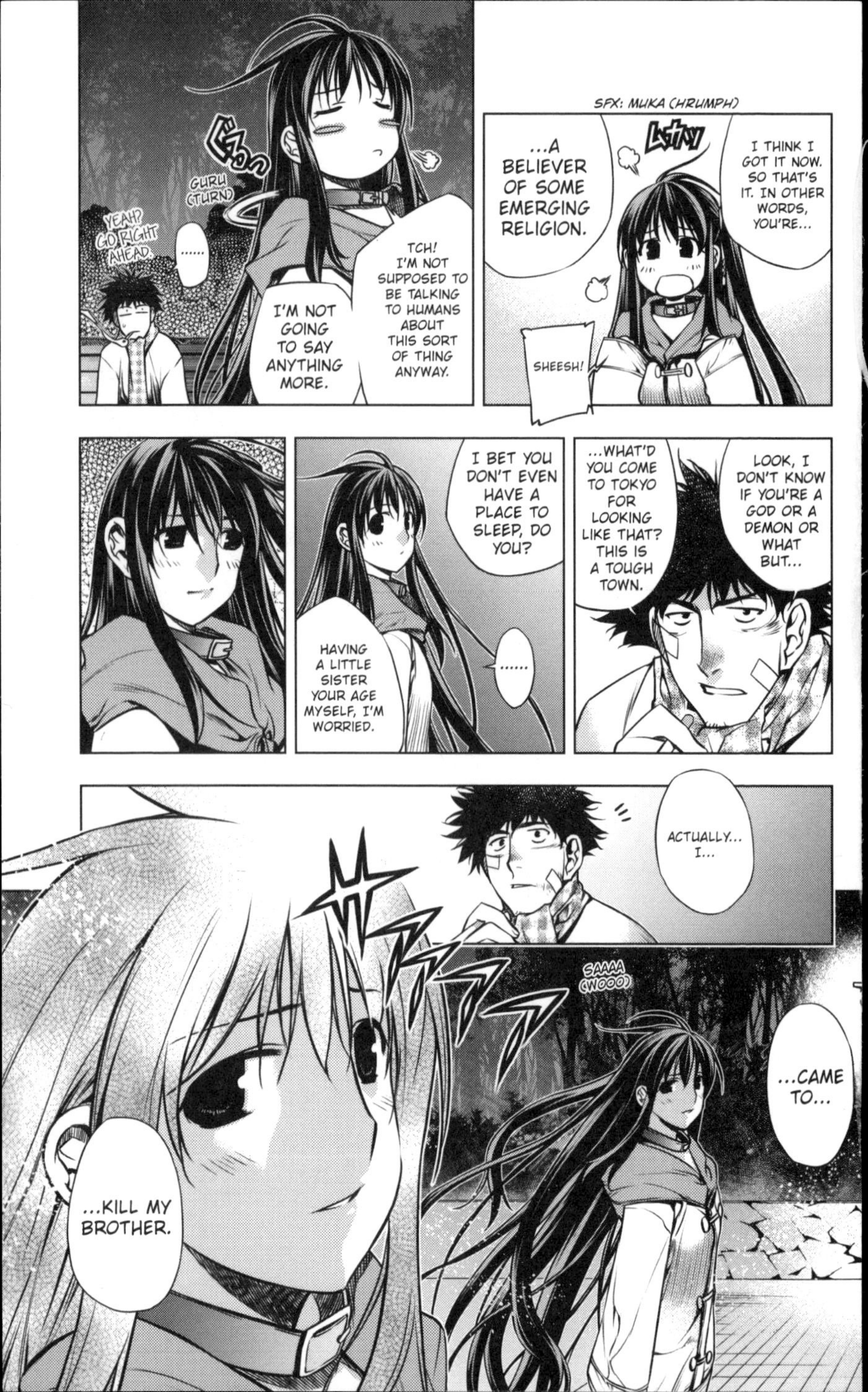
SFX: MUKA (HRUMPH)
I THINK I GOT IT NOW. SO THAT'S IT. IN OTHER WORDS, YOU'RE...
...A BELIEVER OF SOME EMERGING RELIGION.
SHEESH!
TCH! I'M NOT SUPPOSED TO BE TALKING TO HUMANS ABOUT THIS SORT OF THING ANYWAY.
I'M NOT GOING TO SAY ANYTHING MORE.
GURU (TURN)
......
YEAH? GO RIGHT AHEAD.
LOOK, I DON'T KNOW IF YOU'RE A GOD OR A DEMON OR WHAT BUT...
...WHAT'D YOU COME TO TOKYO FOR LOOKING LIKE THAT? THIS IS A TOUGH TOWN.
I BET YOU DON'T EVEN HAVE A PLACE TO SLEEP, DO YOU?
......
HAVING A LITTLE SISTER YOUR AGE MYSELF, I'M WORRIED.
ACTUALLY... I...
SAAAA (WOOO)
...CAME TO...
...KILL MY BROTHER.

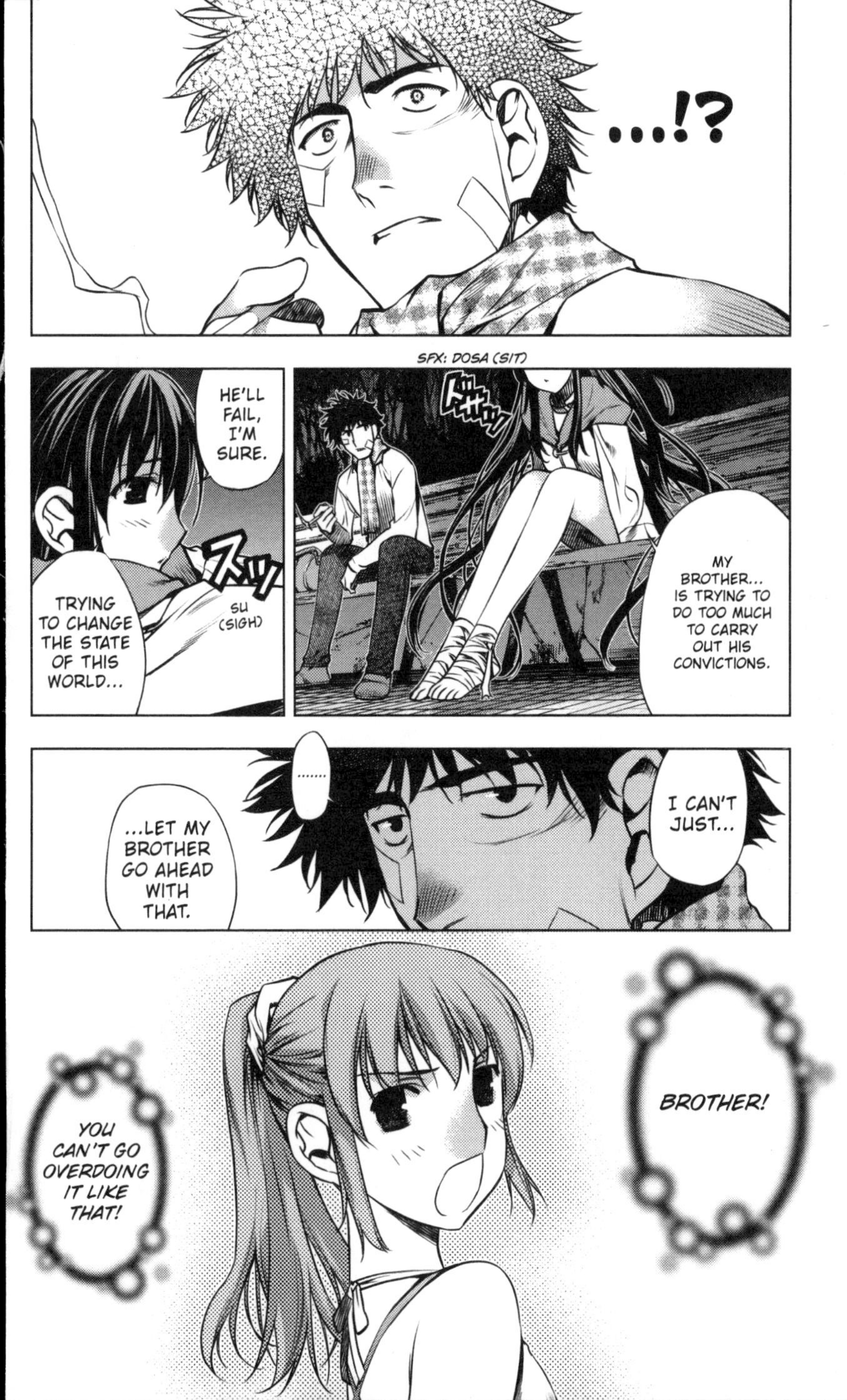
...!?
SFX: DOSA (SIT)
MY BROTHER... IS TRYING TO DO TOO MUCH TO CARRY OUT HIS CONVICTIONS.
HE'LL FAIL, I'M SURE.
TRYING TO CHANGE THE STATE OF THIS WORLD...
SU (SIGH)
....
I CAN'T JUST...
...LET MY BROTHER GO AHEAD WITH THAT.
BROTHER!
YOU CAN'T GO OVERDOING IT LIKE THAT!

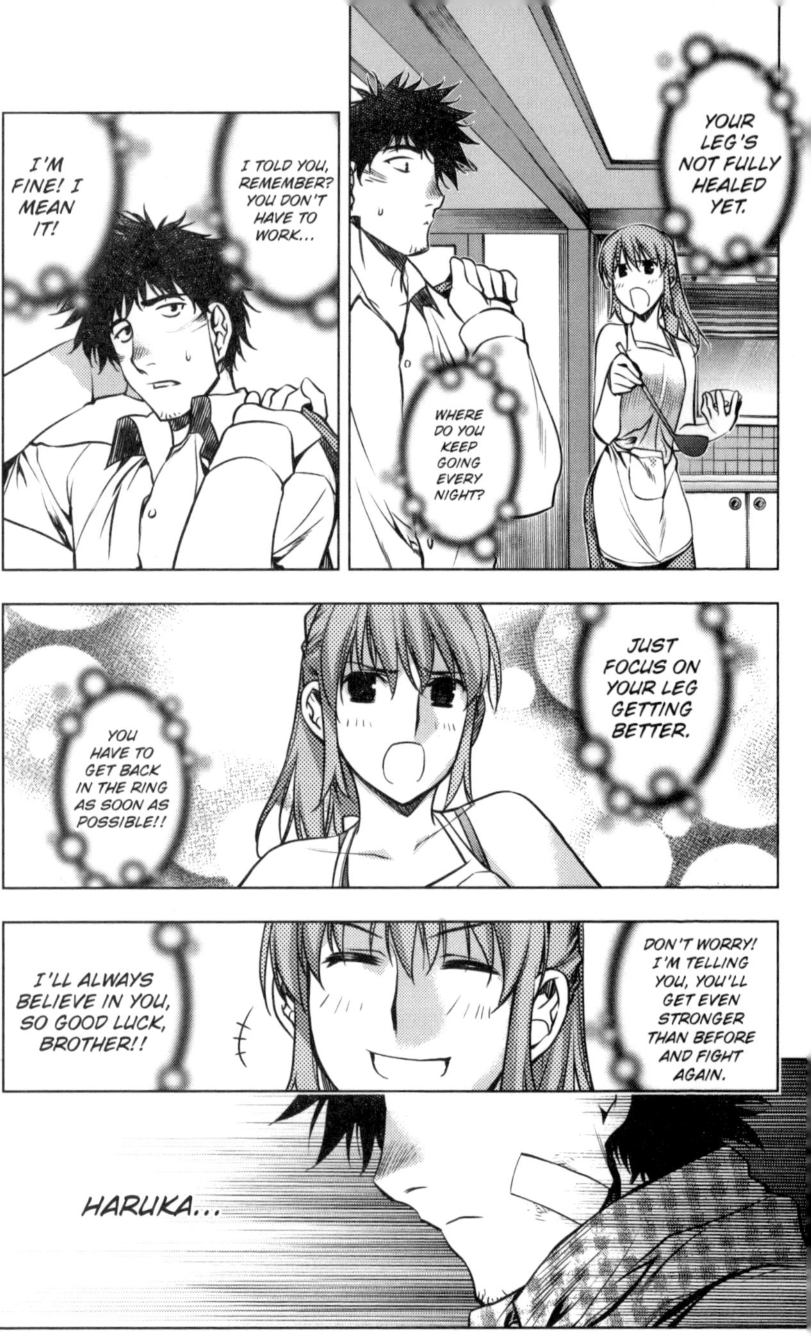
YOUR LEG'S NOT FULLY HEALED YET.
WHERE DO YOU KEEP GOING EVERY NIGHT?
I TOLD YOU, REMEMBER? YOU DON'T HAVE TO WORK...
I'M FINE! I MEAN IT!
JUST FOCUS ON YOUR LEG GETTING BETTER.
YOU HAVE TO GET BACK IN THE RING AS SOON AS POSSIBLE!!
DON'T WORRY! I'M TELLING YOU, YOU'LL GET EVEN STRONGER THAN BEFORE AND FIGHT AGAIN.
I'LL ALWAYS BELIEVE IN YOU, SO GOOD LUCK, BROTHER!!
HARUKA...

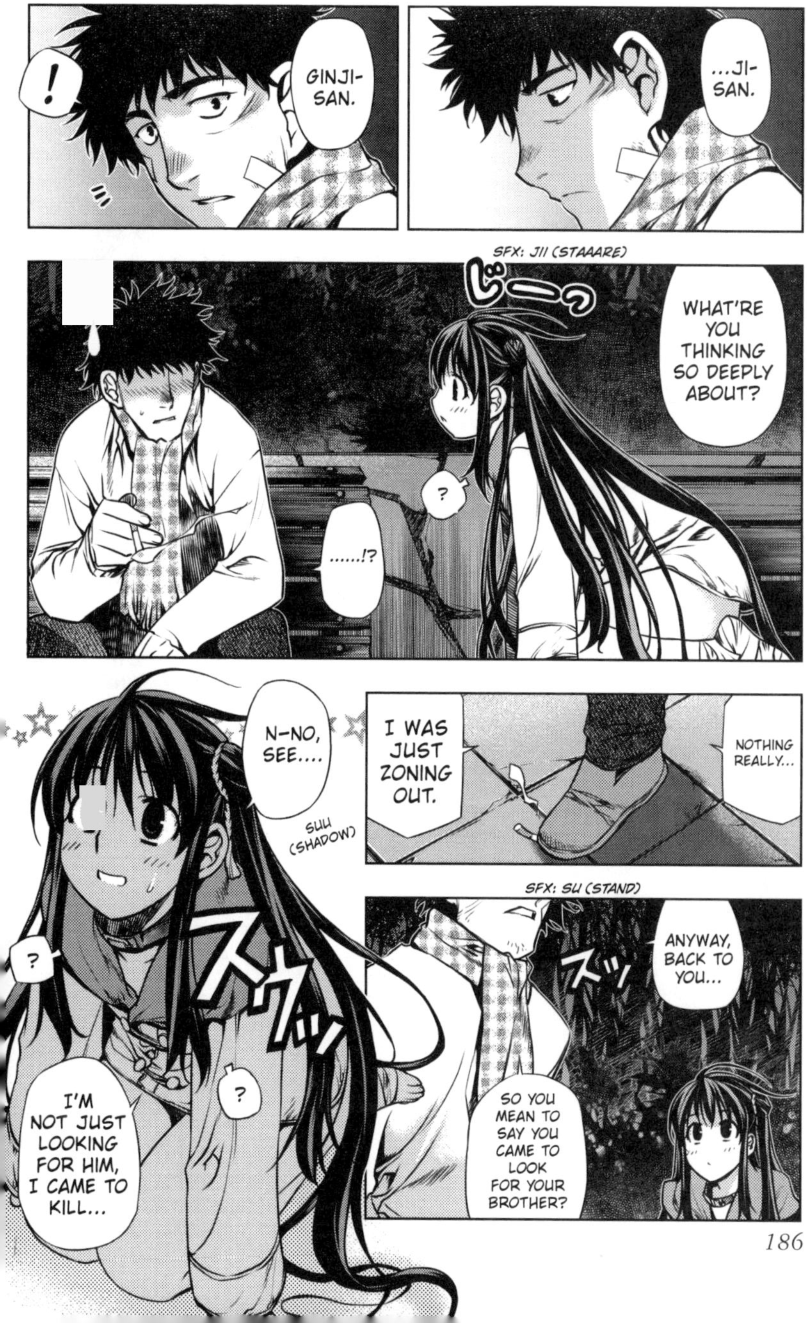
...JI- SAN.
!
GINJI- SAN.
SFX: JII (STAARE)
WHAT'RE YOU THINKING SO DEEPLY ABOUT?
?
......!?
NOTHING REALLY...
I WAS JUST ZONING OUT.
SFX: SU (STAND)
ANYWAY, BACK TO YOU...
SO YOU MEAN TO SAY YOU CAME TO LOOK FOR YOUR BROTHER?
N-NO, SEE....
SUU (SHADOW)
?
?
I'M NOT JUST LOOKING FOR HIM, I CAME TO KILL...

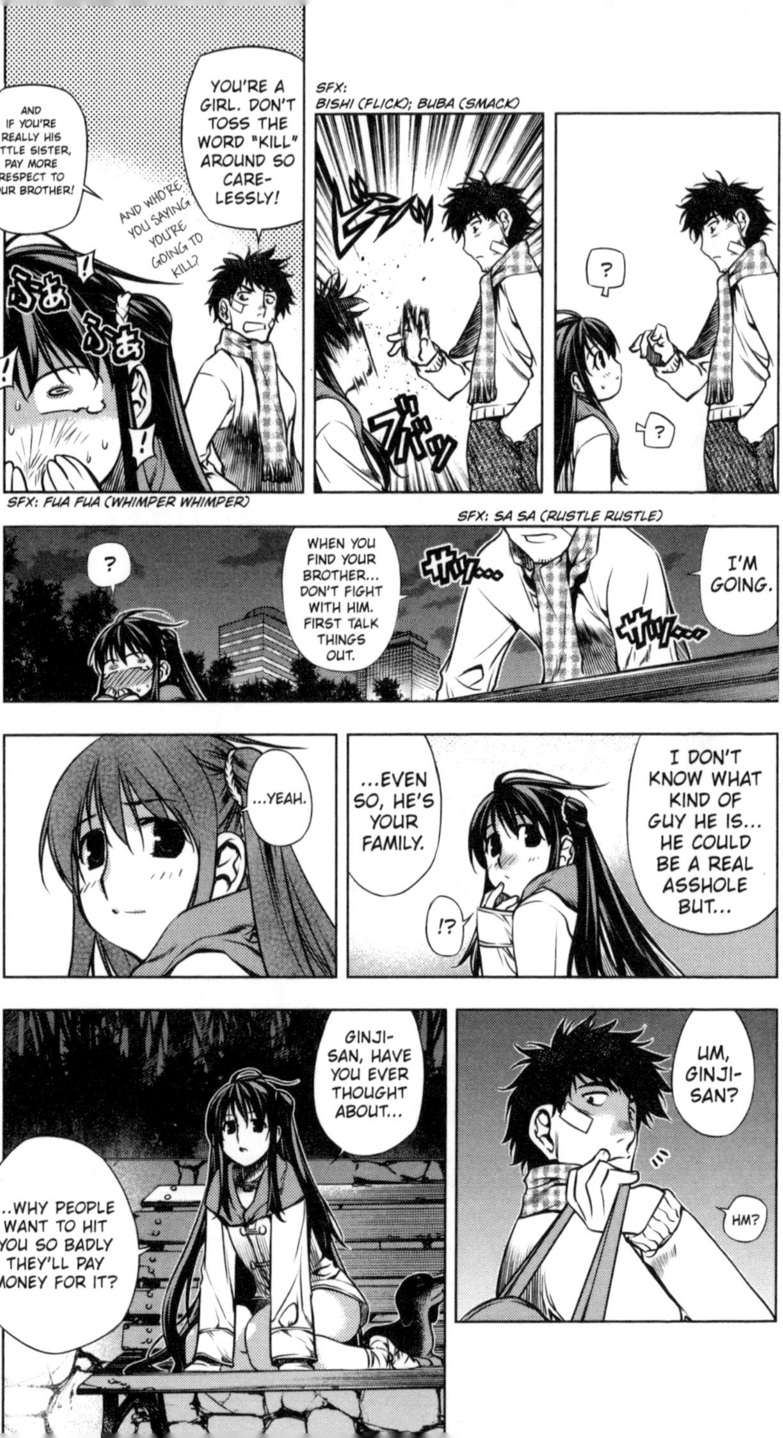
?
?
SFX: BISHI (FLICK); BUBA (SMACK)
YOU'RE A GIRL. DON'T TOSS THE WORD "KILL" AROUND SO CARE-LESSLY!
AND WHO'RE YOU SAYING YOU'RE GOING TO KILL?
AND IF YOU'RE REALLY HIS LITTLE SISTER, PAY MORE RESPECT TO YOUR BROTHER!
SFX: FUA FUA (WHIMPER WHIMPER)
I'M GOING.
SFX: SA SA (RUSTLE RUSTLE)
WHEN YOU FIND YOUR BROTHER... DON'T FIGHT WITH HIM. FIRST TALK THINGS OUT.
?
I DON'T KNOW WHAT KIND OF GUY HE IS... HE COULD BE A REAL ASSHOLE BUT...
!?
...EVEN SO, HE'S YOUR FAMILY.
...YEAH.
UM, GINJI-SAN?
HM?
GINJI-SAN, HAVE YOU EVER THOUGHT ABOUT...
...WHY PEOPLE WANT TO HIT YOU SO BADLY THEY'LL PAY MONEY FOR IT?

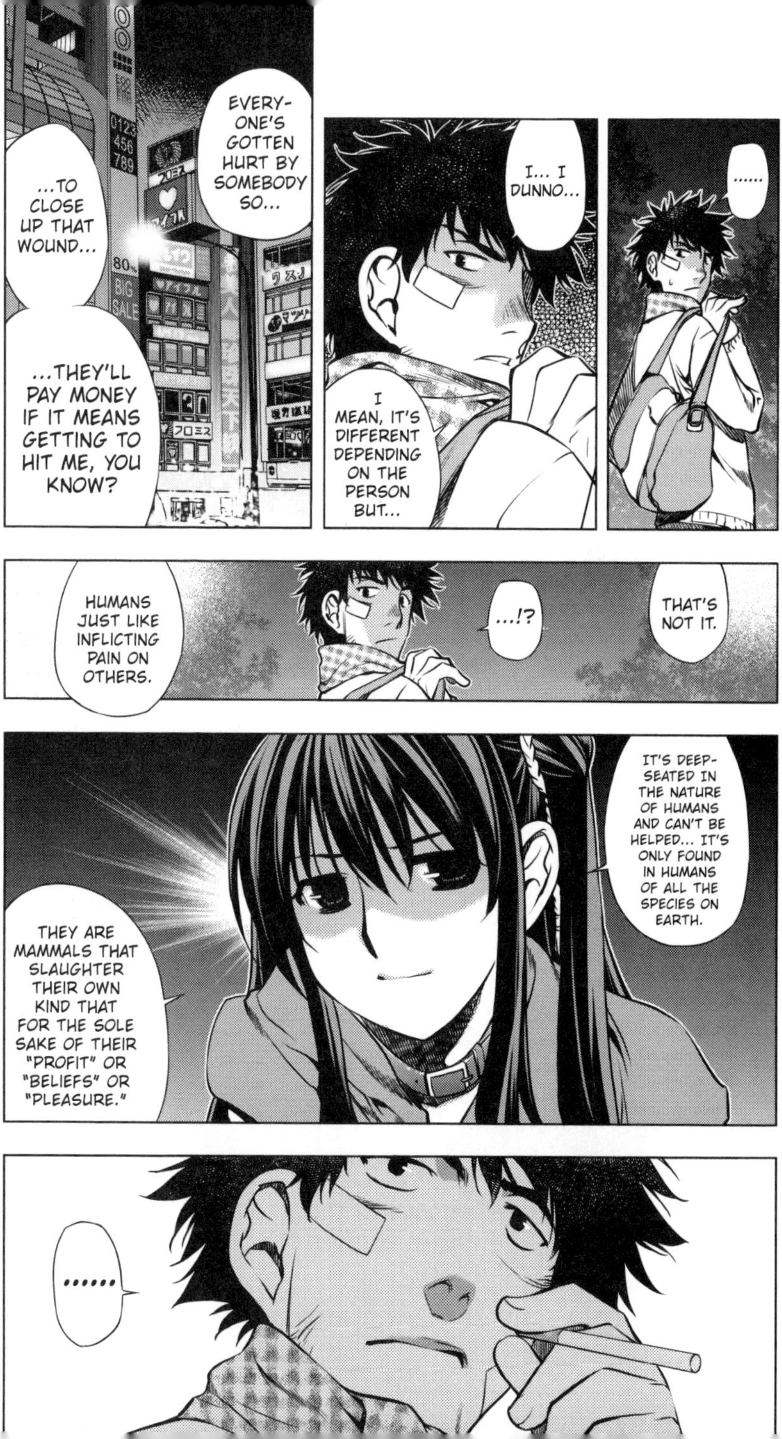
......
I... I DUNNO...
I MEAN, IT'S DIFFERENT DEPENDING ON THE PERSON BUT...
EVERY-ONE'S GOTTEN HURT BY SOMEBODY SO...
...TO CLOSE UP THAT WOUND...
...THEY'LL PAY MONEY IF IT MEANS GETTING TO HIT ME, YOU KNOW?
THAT'S NOT IT.
...!?
HUMANS JUST LIKE INFLICTING PAIN ON OTHERS.
IT'S DEEP-SEATED IN THE NATURE OF HUMANS AND CAN'T BE HELPED... IT'S ONLY FOUND IN HUMANS OF ALL THE SPECIES ON EARTH.
THEY ARE MAMMALS THAT SLAUGHTER THEIR OWN KIND THAT FOR THE SOLE SAKE OF THEIR "PROFIT" OR "BELIEFS" OR "PLEASURE."
......

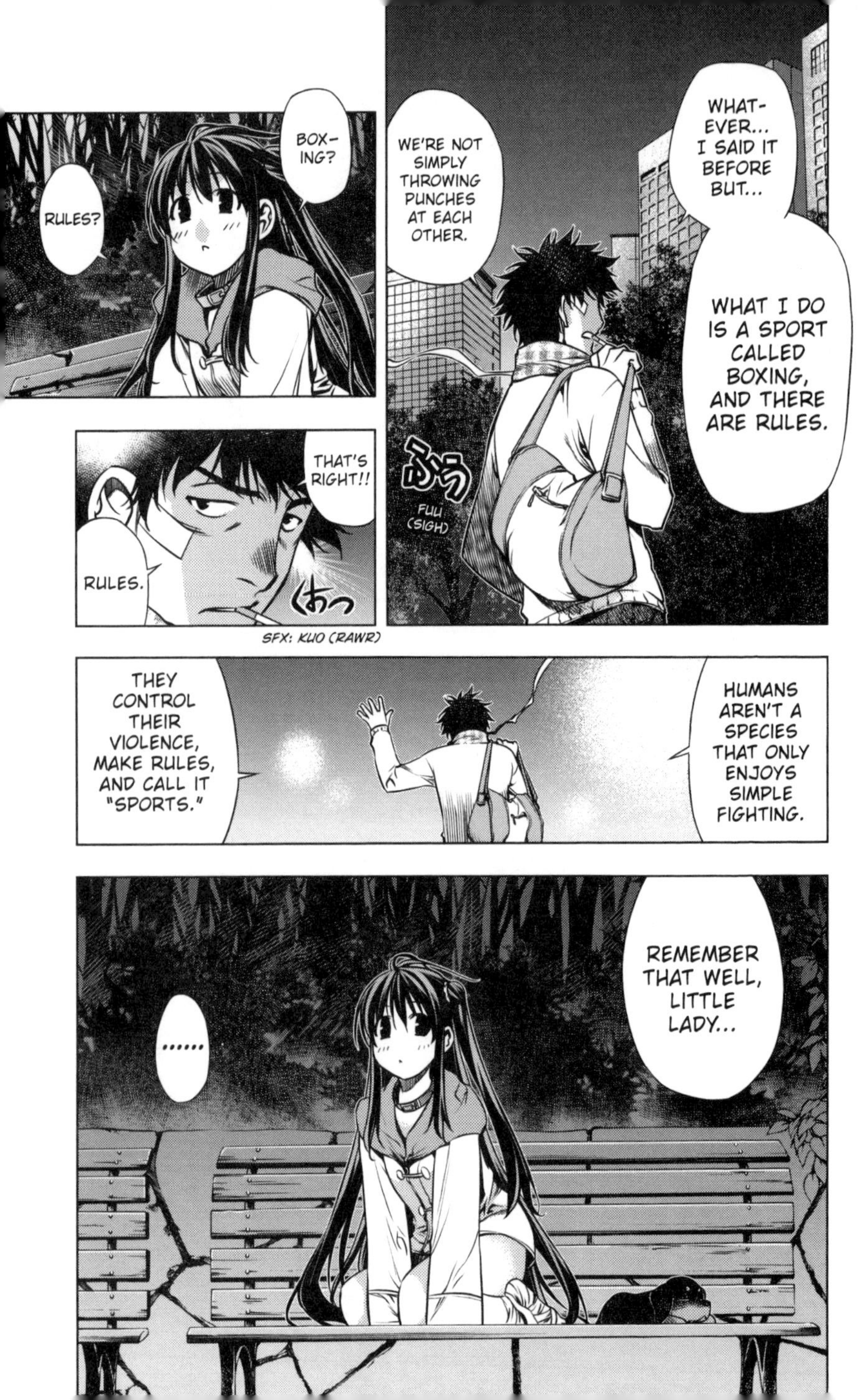
WHAT-EVER... I SAID IT BEFORE BUT...
WHAT I DO IS A SPORT CALLED BOXING, AND THERE ARE RULES.
WE'RE NOT SIMPLY THROWING PUNCHES AT EACH OTHER.
ふう
FUU (SIGH)
BOX-ING?
RULES?
THAT'S RIGHT!!
RULES.
くあっ
SFX: KUO (RAWR)
HUMANS AREN'T A SPECIES THAT ONLY ENJOYS SIMPLE FIGHTING.
THEY CONTROL THEIR VIOLENCE, MAKE RULES, AND CALL IT "SPORTS."
REMEMBER THAT WELL, LITTLE LADY...
......

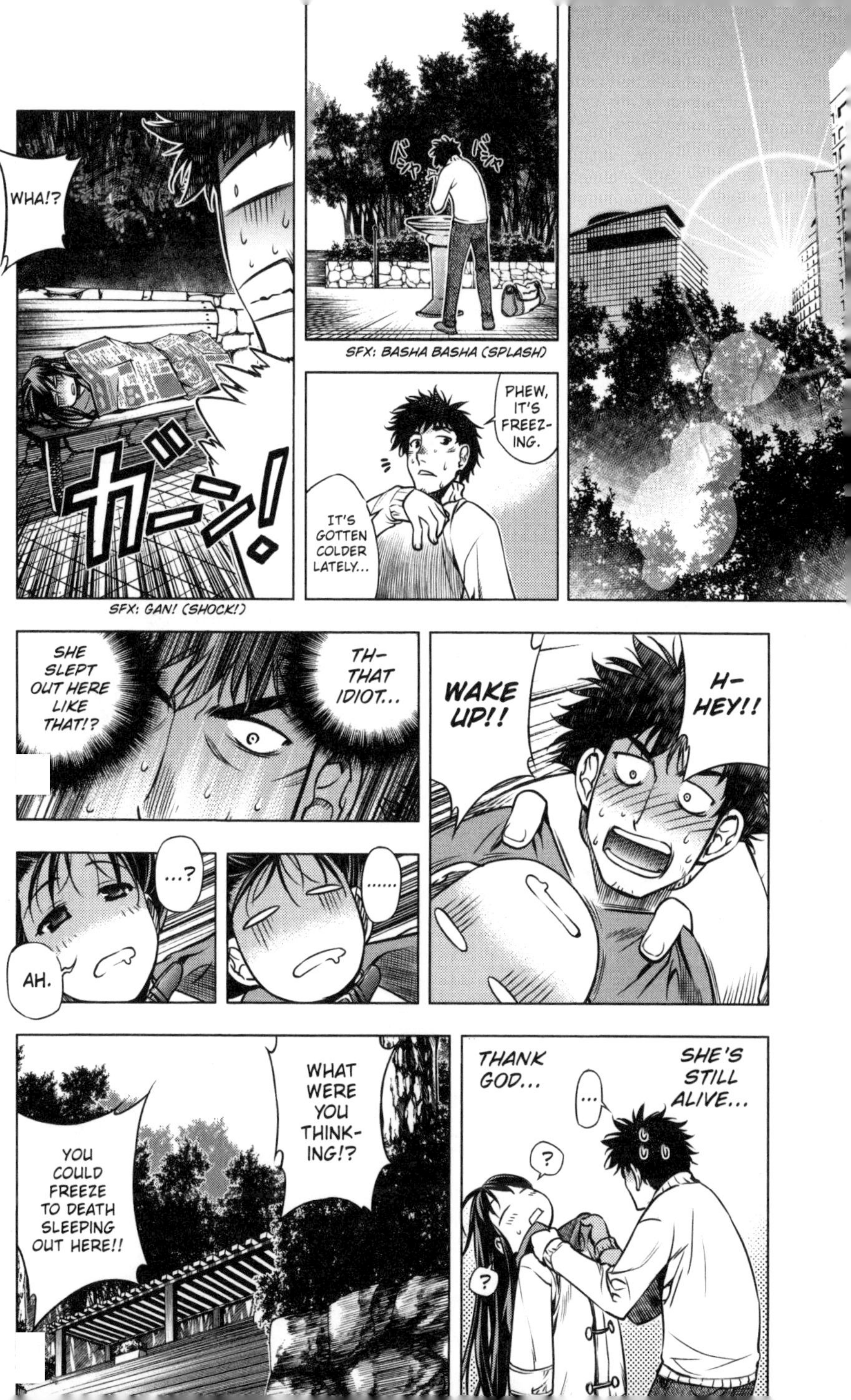

バシャ バシャ
SFX: BASHA BASHA (SPLASH)
PHEW, IT'S FREEZ-ING.
IT'S GOTTEN COLDER LATELY...
WHA!?
ガーン!
SFX: GAN! (SHOCK!)
H-HEY!!
WAKE UP!!
TH-THAT IDIOT...
SHE SLEPT OUT HERE LIKE THAT!?
......
...?
AH.
SHE'S STILL ALIVE...
THANK GOD...
...
?
?
WHAT WERE YOU THINK-ING!?
YOU COULD FREEZE TO DEATH SLEEPING OUT HERE!!

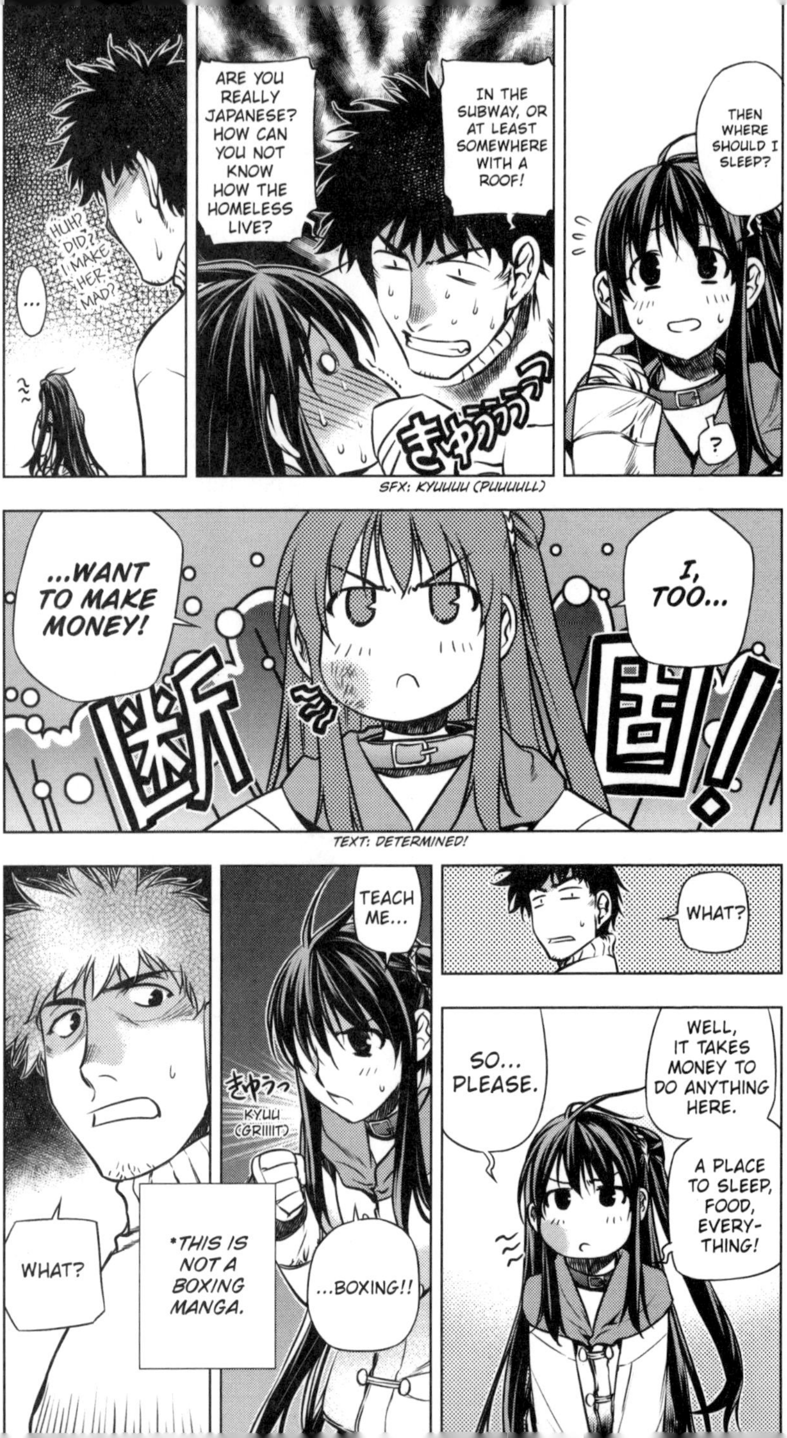

THEN WHERE SHOULD I SLEEP?
IN THE SUBWAY, OR AT LEAST SOMEWHERE WITH A ROOF!
ARE YOU REALLY JAPANESE? HOW CAN YOU NOT KNOW HOW THE HOMELESS LIVE?
きゅううう
SFX: KYUUUU (PUUUULL)
HUH? DID I MAKE HER MAD?
...
I, TOO...
...WANT TO MAKE MONEY!
断固!
TEXT: DETERMINED!
WHAT?
WELL, IT TAKES MONEY TO DO ANYTHING HERE.
A PLACE TO SLEEP, FOOD, EVERY-THING!
SO... PLEASE.
TEACH ME...
きゅうっ
KYUU (GRIIIIT)
...BOXING!!
WHAT?
*THIS IS NOT A BOXING MANGA.

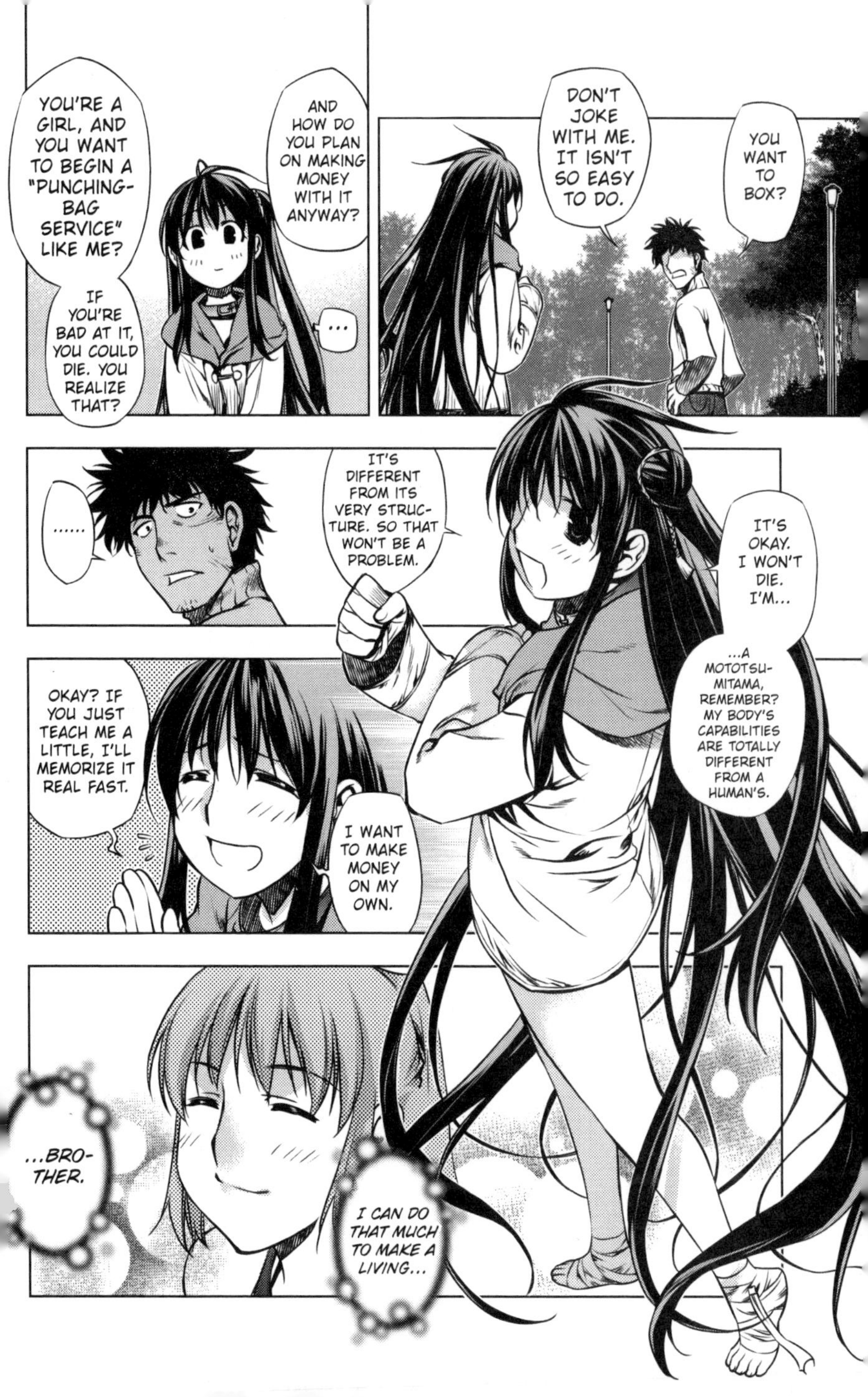
YOU WANT TO BOX?
DON'T JOKE WITH ME. IT ISN'T SO EASY TO DO.
AND HOW DO YOU PLAN ON MAKING MONEY WITH IT ANYWAY?
YOU'RE A GIRL, AND YOU WANT TO BEGIN A "PUNCHING-BAG SERVICE" LIKE ME?
IF YOU'RE BAD AT IT, YOU COULD DIE. YOU REALIZE THAT?
...
IT'S OKAY. I WON'T DIE. I'M...
...A MOTOTSU-MITAMA, REMEMBER? MY BODY'S CAPABILITIES ARE TOTALLY DIFFERENT FROM A HUMAN'S.
IT'S DIFFERENT FROM ITS VERY STRUC-TURE. SO THAT WON'T BE A PROBLEM.
......
I WANT TO MAKE MONEY ON MY OWN.
OKAY? IF YOU JUST TEACH ME A LITTLE, I'LL MEMORIZE IT REAL FAST.
I CAN DO THAT MUCH TO MAKE A LIVING...
...BRO-THER.

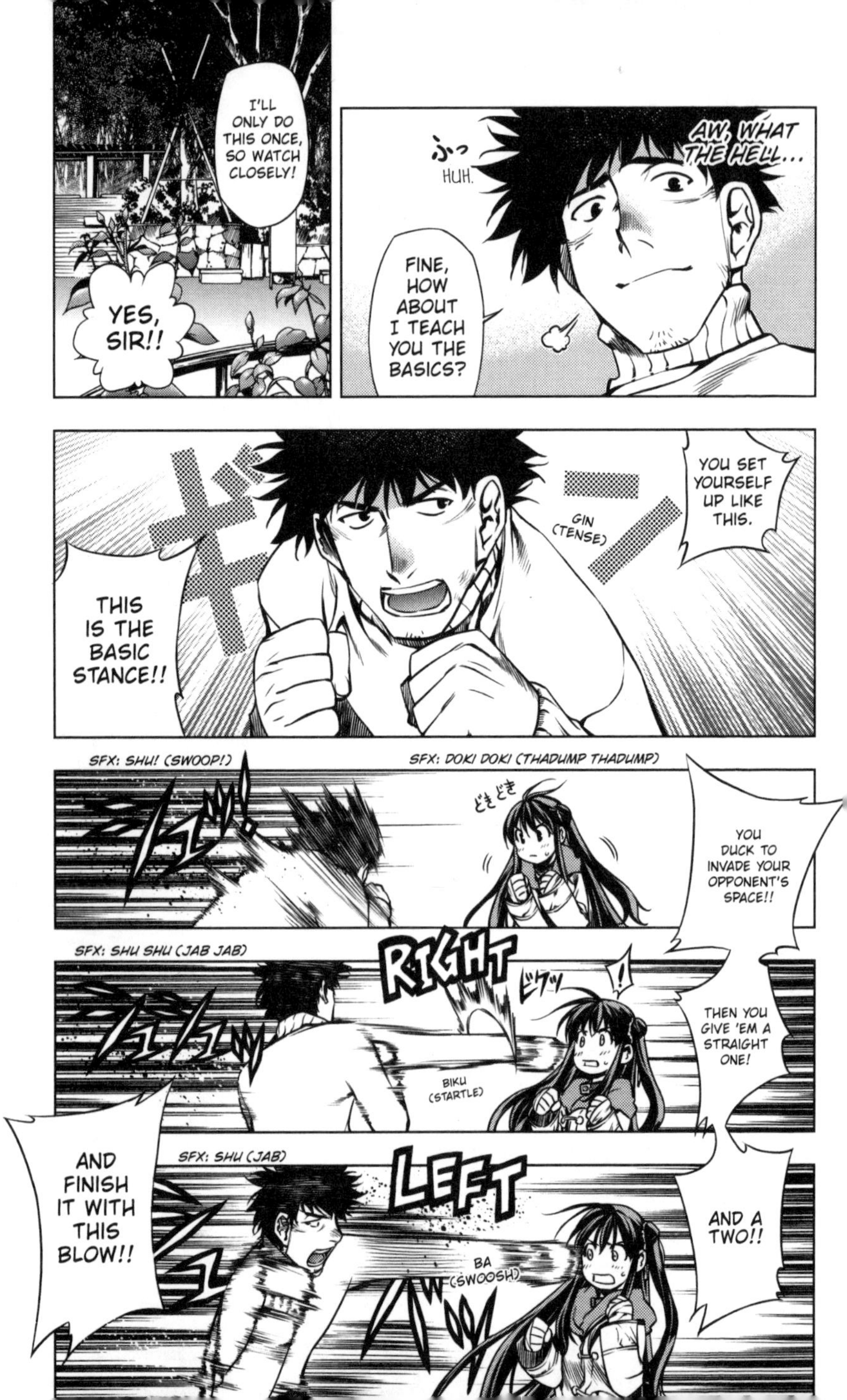
ふっ
HUH.
AW, WHAT THE HELL...
FINE, HOW ABOUT I TEACH YOU THE BASICS?
I'LL ONLY DO THIS ONCE, SO WATCH CLOSELY!
YES, SIR!!
YOU SET YOURSELF UP LIKE THIS.
GIN (TENSE)
THIS IS THE BASIC STANCE!!
YOU DUCK TO INVADE YOUR OPPONENT'S SPACE!!
SFX: DOKI DOKI (THADUMP THADUMP)
どきどき
SFX: SHU! (SWOOP!)
THEN YOU GIVE 'EM A STRAIGHT ONE!
!
ビクッ
BIKU (STARTLE)
RIGHT
SFX: SHU SHU (JAB JAB)
AND A TWO!!
LEFT
BA (SWOOSH)
SFX: SHU (JAB)
AND FINISH IT WITH THIS BLOW!!

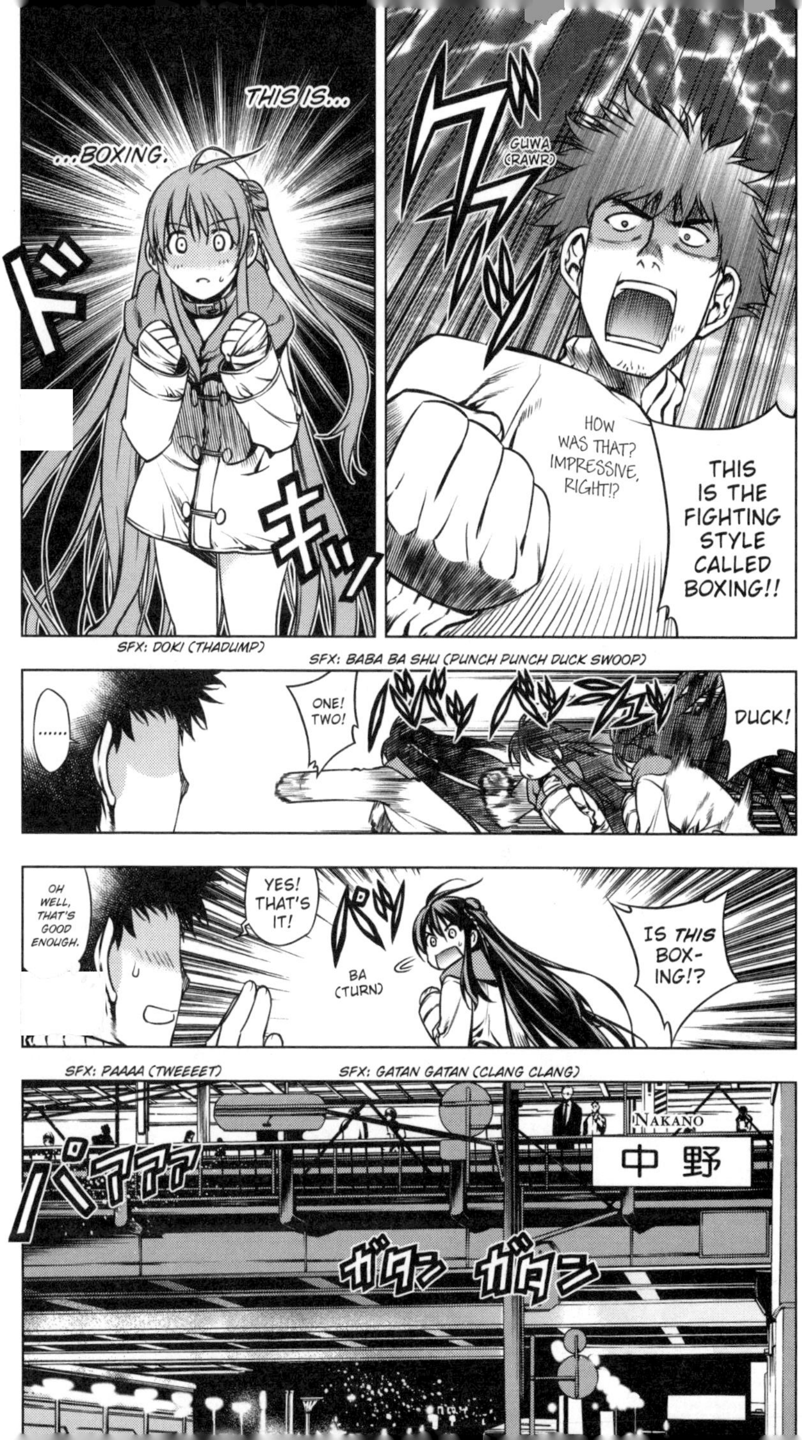
GUWA (RAWR)
THIS IS THE FIGHTING STYLE CALLED BOXING!!
HOW WAS THAT? IMPRESSIVE, RIGHT!?
THIS IS...
...BOXING.
SFX: DOKI (THADUMP)
SFX: BABA BA SHU (PUNCH PUNCH DUCK SWOOP)
DUCK!
ONE! TWO!
......
IS *THIS* BOXING!?
BA (TURN)
YES! THAT'S IT!
OH WELL, THAT'S GOOD ENOUGH.
SFX: PAAAA (TWEEEET)
SFX: GATAN GATAN (CLANG CLANG)
NAKANO
中野

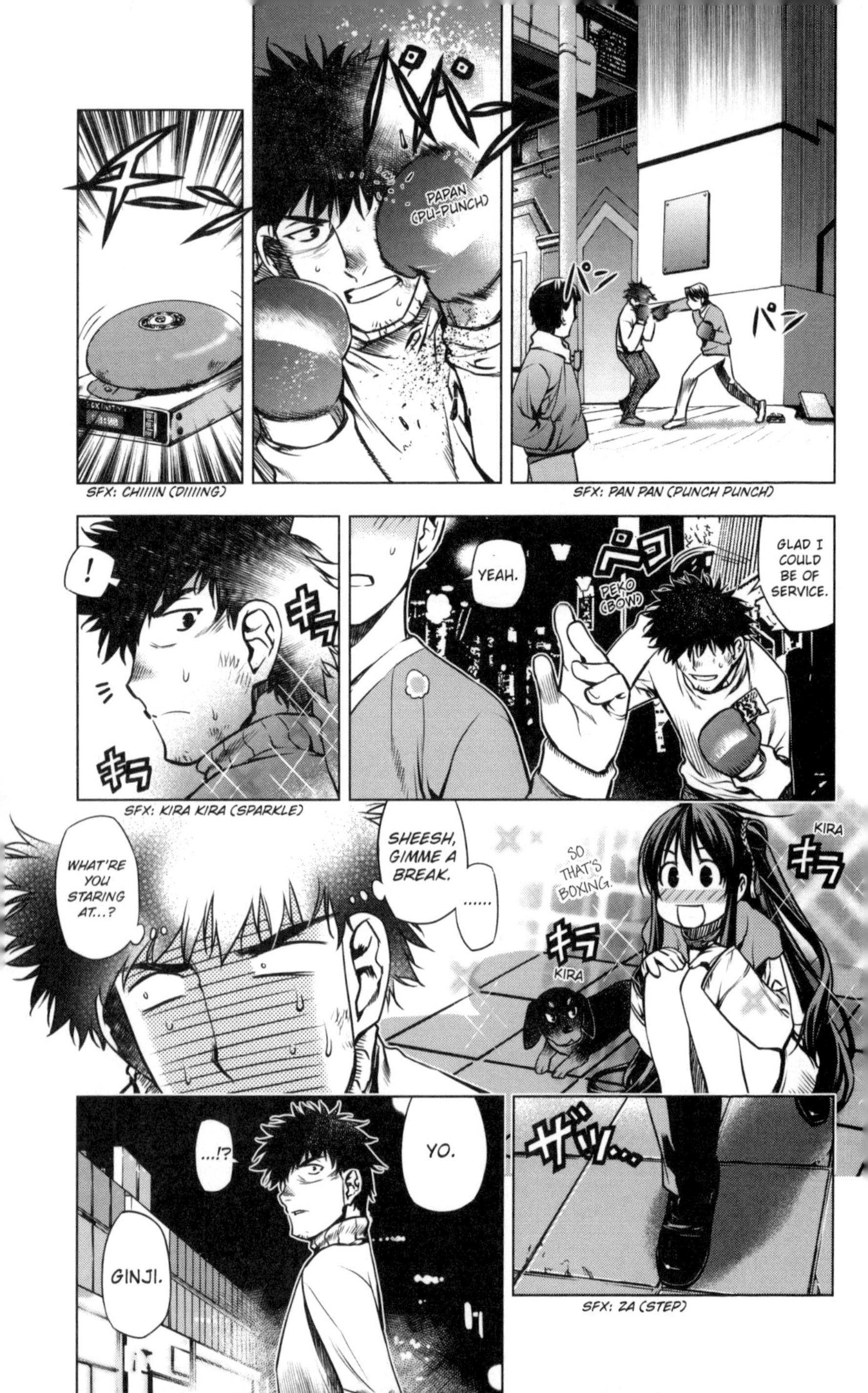
SFX: PAN PAN (PUNCH PUNCH)
PAPAN (PU-PUNCH)
SFX: CHIIIIN (DIIIING)
GLAD I COULD BE OF SERVICE.
PEKO (BOW)
YEAH.
!
SFX: KIRA KIRA (SPARKLE)
KIRA
SO THAT'S BOXING.
KIRA
SHEESH, GIMME A BREAK.
......
WHAT'RE YOU STARING AT...?
SFX: ZA (STEP)
YO.
...!?
GINJI.

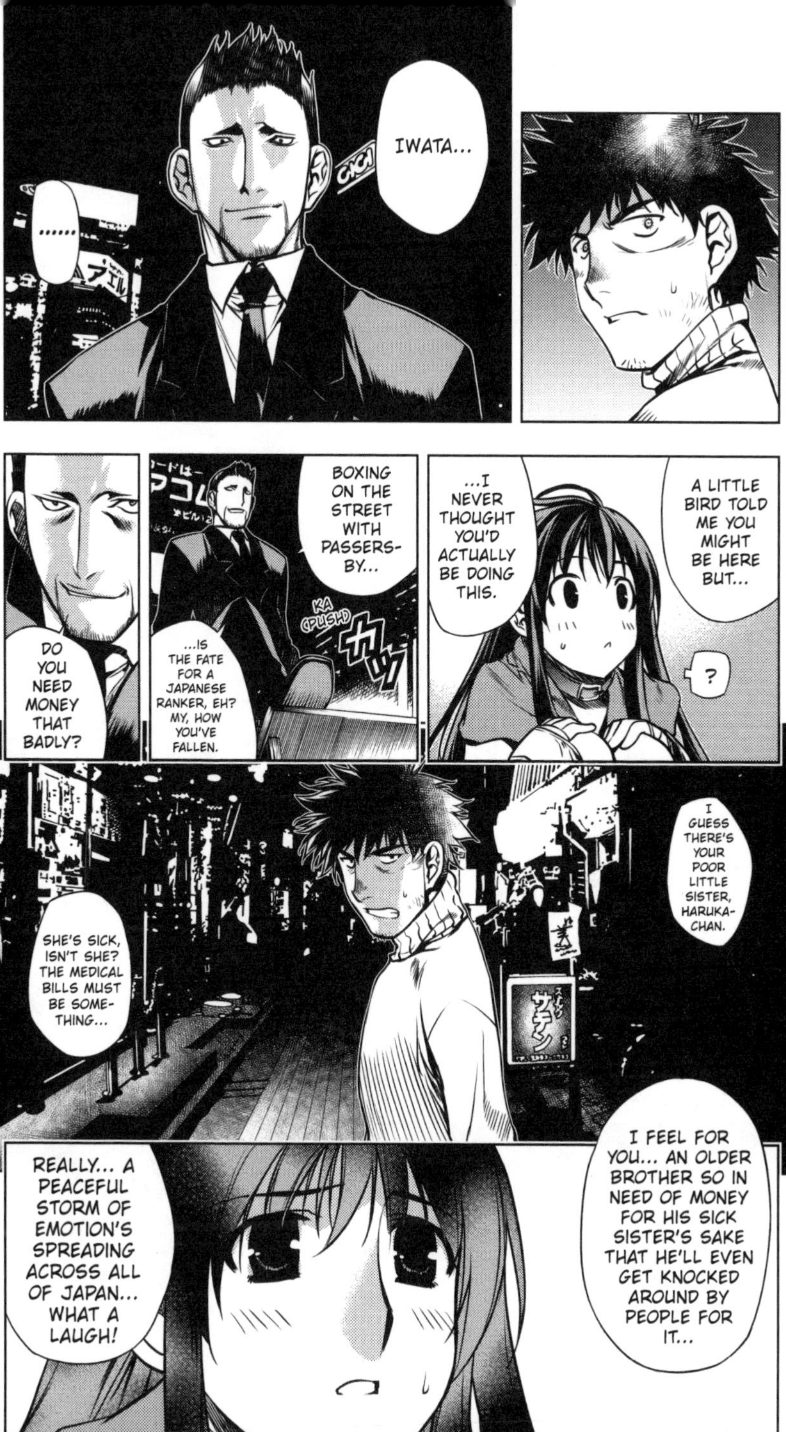
IWATA...
......
A LITTLE BIRD TOLD ME YOU MIGHT BE HERE BUT...
...I NEVER THOUGHT YOU'D ACTUALLY BE DOING THIS.
?
BOXING ON THE STREET WITH PASSERS-BY...
KA (PUSH)
...IS THE FATE FOR A JAPANESE RANKER, EH? MY, HOW YOU'VE FALLEN.
DO YOU NEED MONEY THAT BADLY?
I GUESS THERE'S YOUR POOR LITTLE SISTER, HARUKA-CHAN.
SHE'S SICK, ISN'T SHE? THE MEDICAL BILLS MUST BE SOME-THING...
I FEEL FOR YOU... AN OLDER BROTHER SO IN NEED OF MONEY FOR HIS SICK SISTER'S SAKE THAT HE'LL EVEN GET KNOCKED AROUND BY PEOPLE FOR IT...
REALLY... A PEACEFUL STORM OF EMOTION'S SPREADING ACROSS ALL OF JAPAN... WHAT A LAUGH!

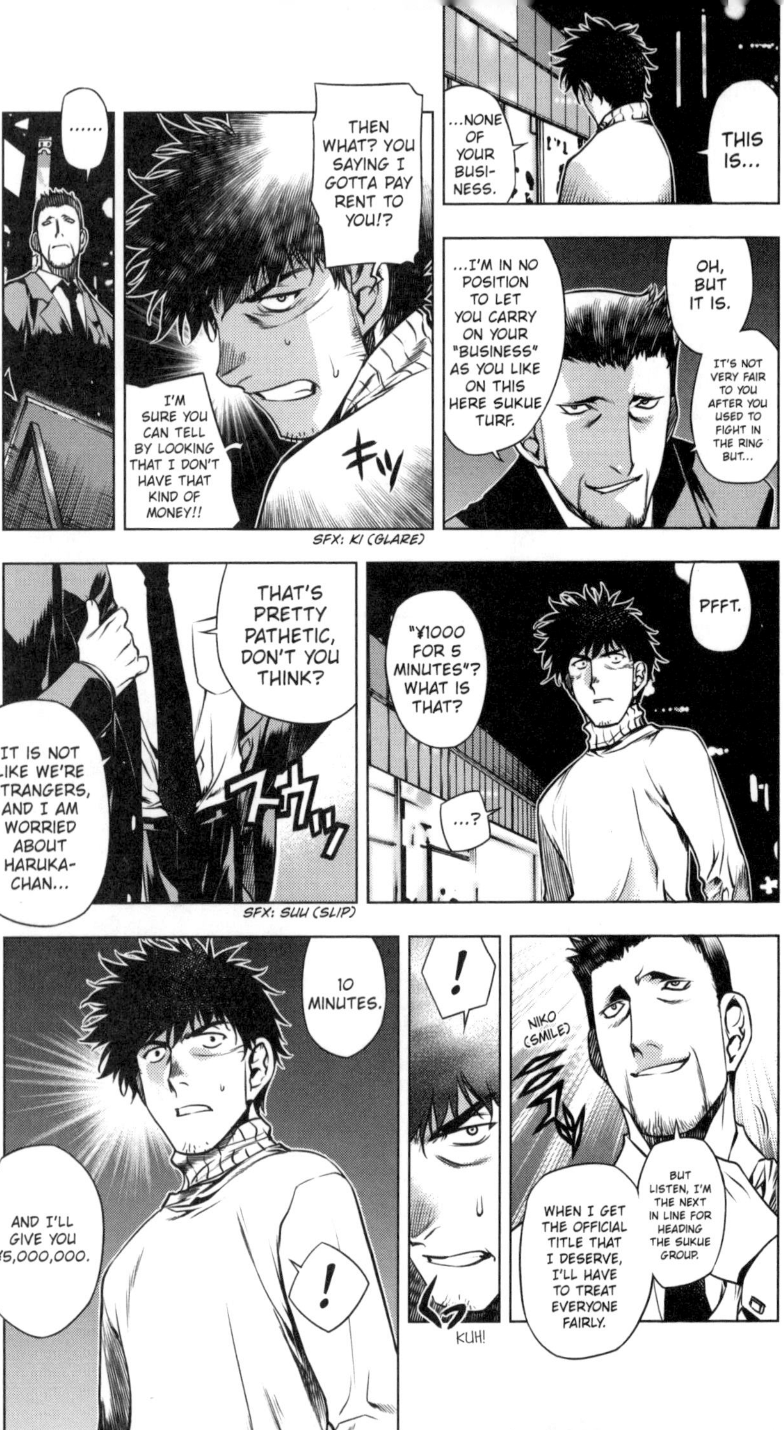
THIS IS...
...NONE OF YOUR BUSI- NESS.
OH, BUT IT IS.
IT'S NOT VERY FAIR TO YOU AFTER YOU USED TO FIGHT IN THE RING BUT...
...I'M IN NO POSITION TO LET YOU CARRY ON YOUR "BUSINESS" AS YOU LIKE ON THIS HERE SUKUE TURF.
THEN WHAT? YOU SAYING I GOTTA PAY RENT TO YOU!?
I'M SURE YOU CAN TELL BY LOOKING THAT I DON'T HAVE THAT KIND OF MONEY!!
......
SFX: KI (GLARE)
PFFT.
"¥1000 FOR 5 MINUTES"? WHAT IS THAT?
...?
THAT'S PRETTY PATHETIC, DON'T YOU THINK?
IT IS NOT LIKE WE'RE STRANGERS, AND I AM WORRIED ABOUT HARUKA- CHAN...
SFX: SUU (SLIP)
NIKO (SMILE)
BUT LISTEN, I'M THE NEXT IN LINE FOR HEADING THE SUKUE GROUP.
WHEN I GET THE OFFICIAL TITLE THAT I DESERVE, I'LL HAVE TO TREAT EVERYONE FAIRLY.
!
KUH!
10 MINUTES.
AND I'LL GIVE YOU ¥5,000,000.
!

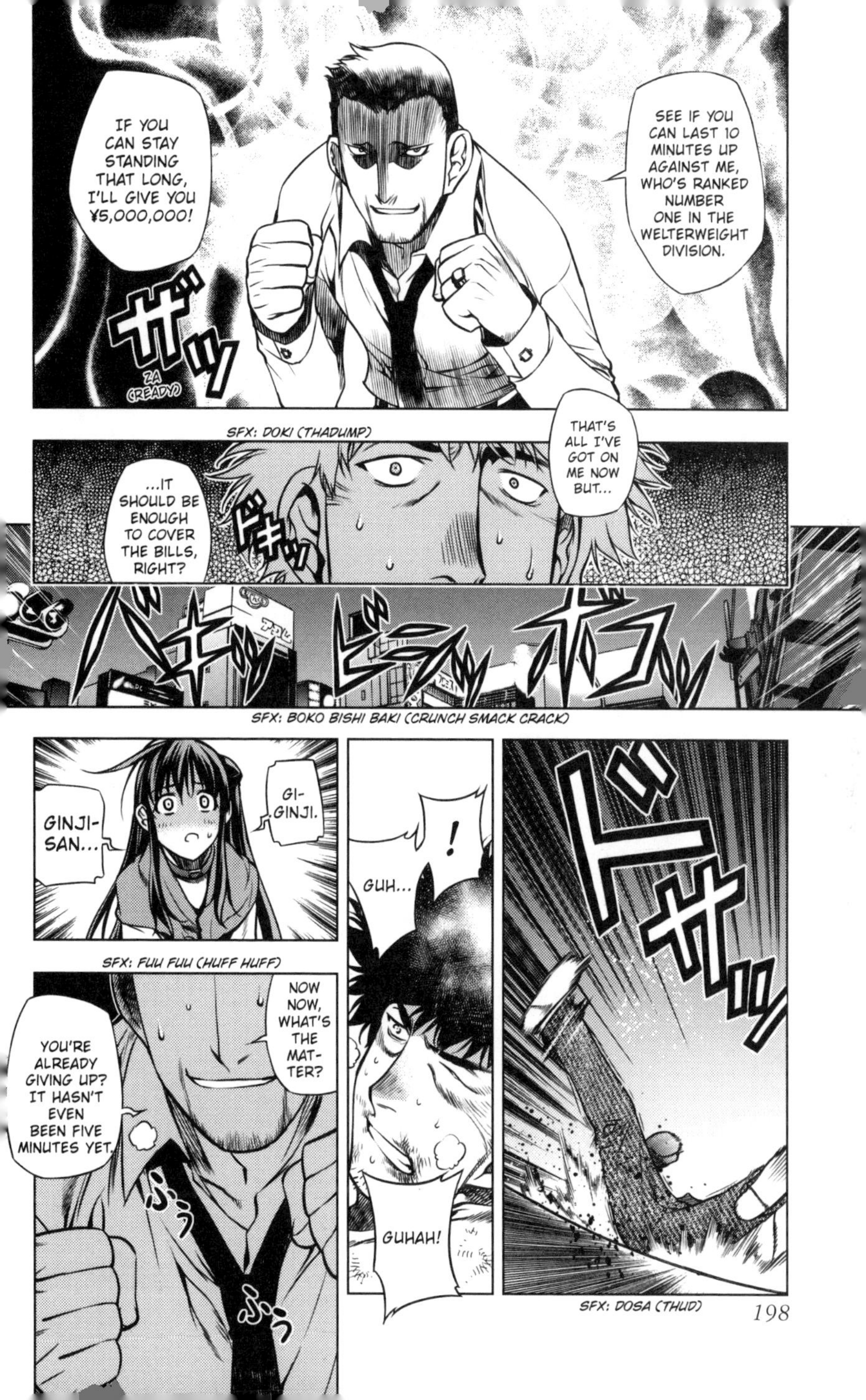
SEE IF YOU CAN LAST 10 MINUTES UP AGAINST ME, WHO'S RANKED NUMBER ONE IN THE WELTERWEIGHT DIVISION.
IF YOU CAN STAY STANDING THAT LONG, I'LL GIVE YOU ¥5,000,000!
ZA (READY)
SFX: DOKI (THADUMP)
THAT'S ALL I'VE GOT ON ME NOW BUT...
...IT SHOULD BE ENOUGH TO COVER THE BILLS, RIGHT?
SFX: BOKO BISHI BAKI (CRUNCH SMACK CRACK)
SFX: DOSA (THUD)
!
GUH...
GUHAH!
GI-GINJI.
GINJI-SAN...
SFX: FUU FUU (HUFF HUFF)
NOW NOW, WHAT'S THE MAT-TER?
YOU'RE ALREADY GIVING UP? IT HASN'T EVEN BEEN FIVE MINUTES YET.

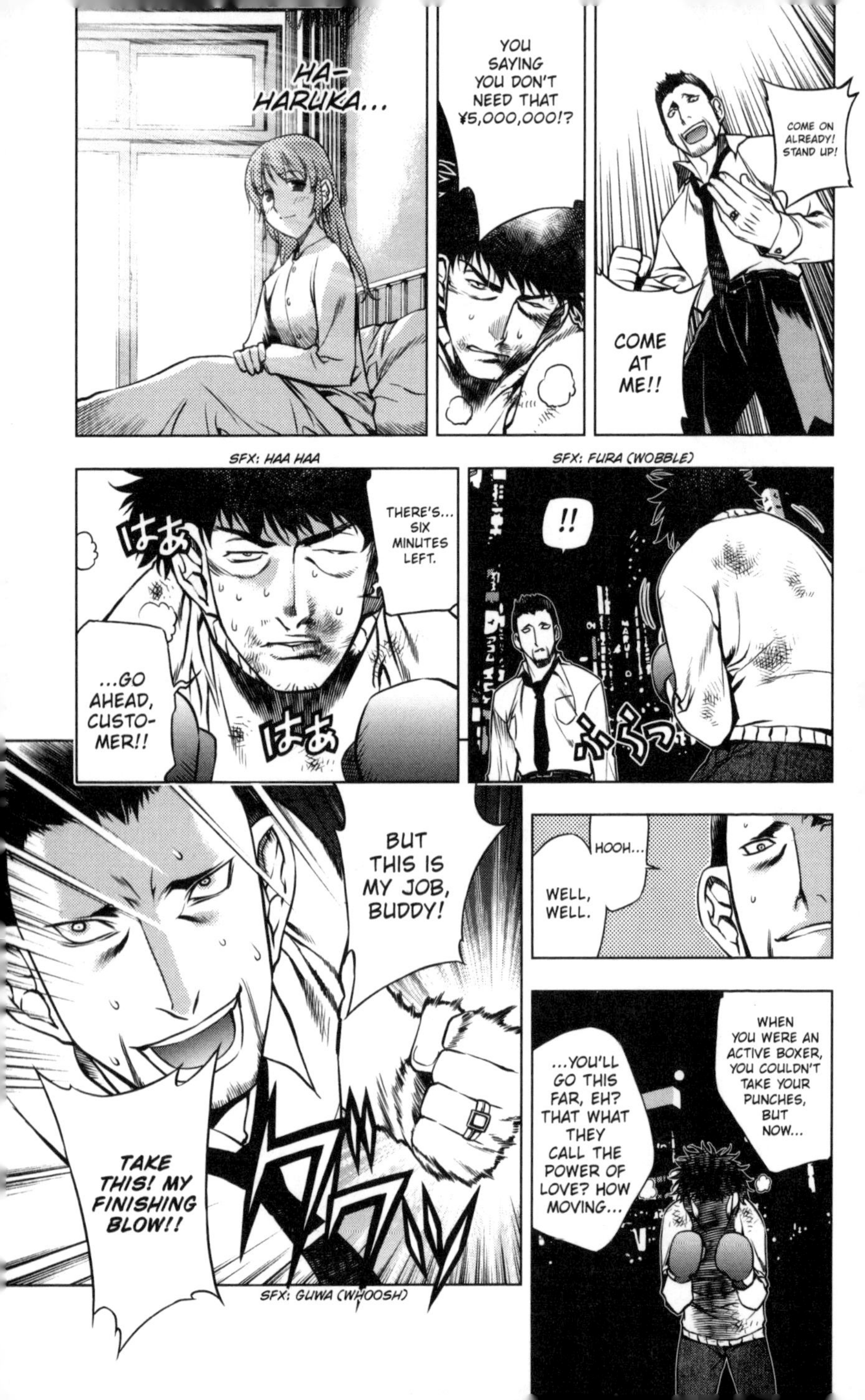
COME ON ALREADY! STAND UP!
COME AT ME!!
YOU SAYING YOU DON'T NEED THAT ¥5,000,000!?
HA- HARUKA...
SFX: FURA (WOBBLE)
!!
ふらっ
SFX: HAA HAA
THERE'S... SIX MINUTES LEFT.
...GO AHEAD, CUSTOMER!!
はあ
はあ
HOOH...
WELL, WELL.
WHEN YOU WERE AN ACTIVE BOXER, YOU COULDN'T TAKE YOUR PUNCHES, BUT NOW...
...YOU'LL GO THIS FAR, EH? THAT WHAT THEY CALL THE POWER OF LOVE? HOW MOVING...
BUT THIS IS MY JOB, BUDDY!
TAKE THIS! MY FINISHING BLOW!!
SFX: GUWA (WHOOSH)

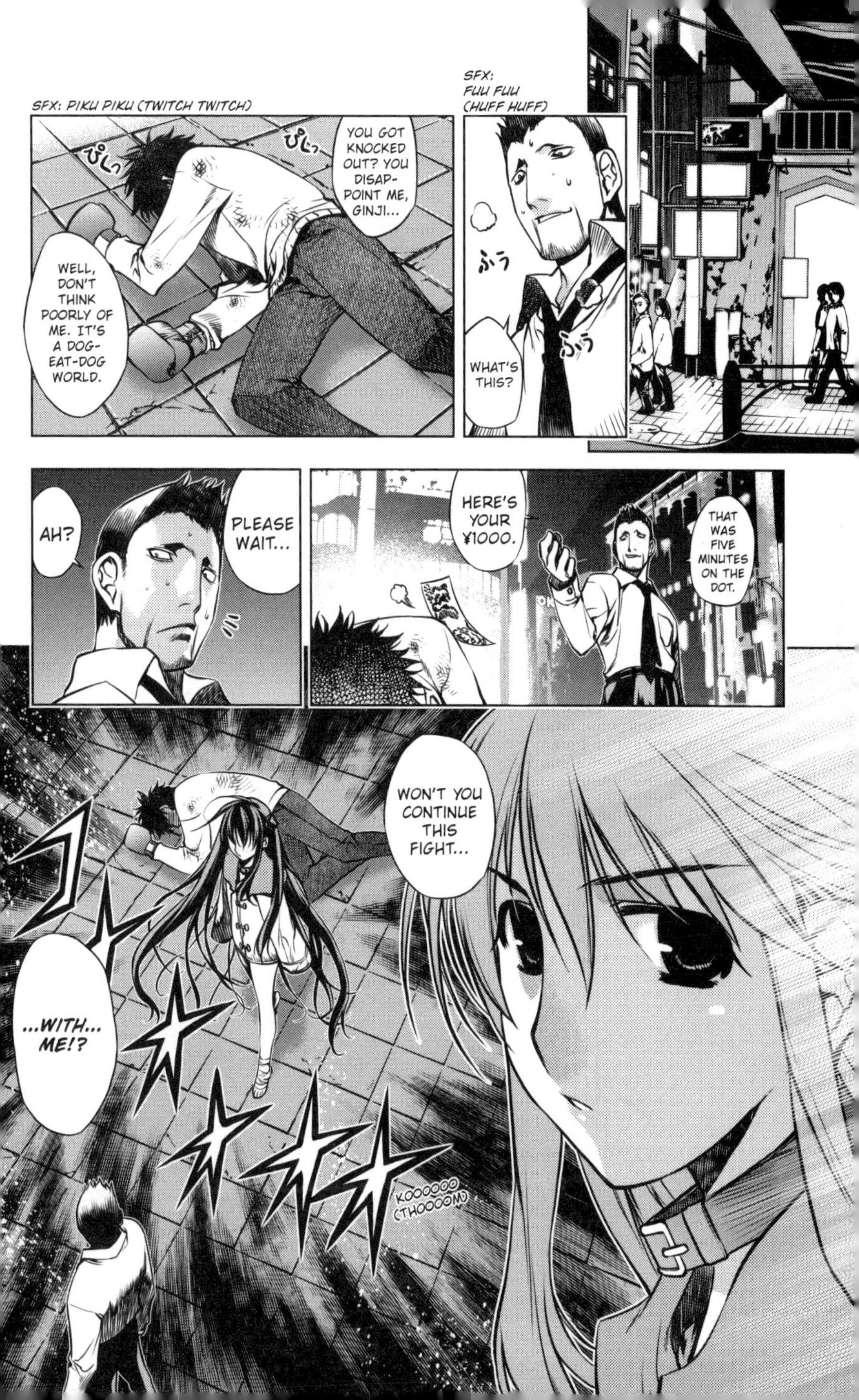
SFX: FUU FUU (HUFF HUFF)
WHAT'S THIS?
YOU GOT KNOCKED OUT? YOU DISAP-POINT ME, GINJI...
SFX: PIKU PIKU (TWITCH TWITCH)
WELL, DON'T THINK POORLY OF ME. IT'S A DOG-EAT-DOG WORLD.
HERE'S YOUR ¥1000.
THAT WAS FIVE MINUTES ON THE DOT.
PLEASE WAIT...
AH?
WON'T YOU CONTINUE THIS FIGHT...
...WITH... ME!?
KOOOOOO (THOOOOM)

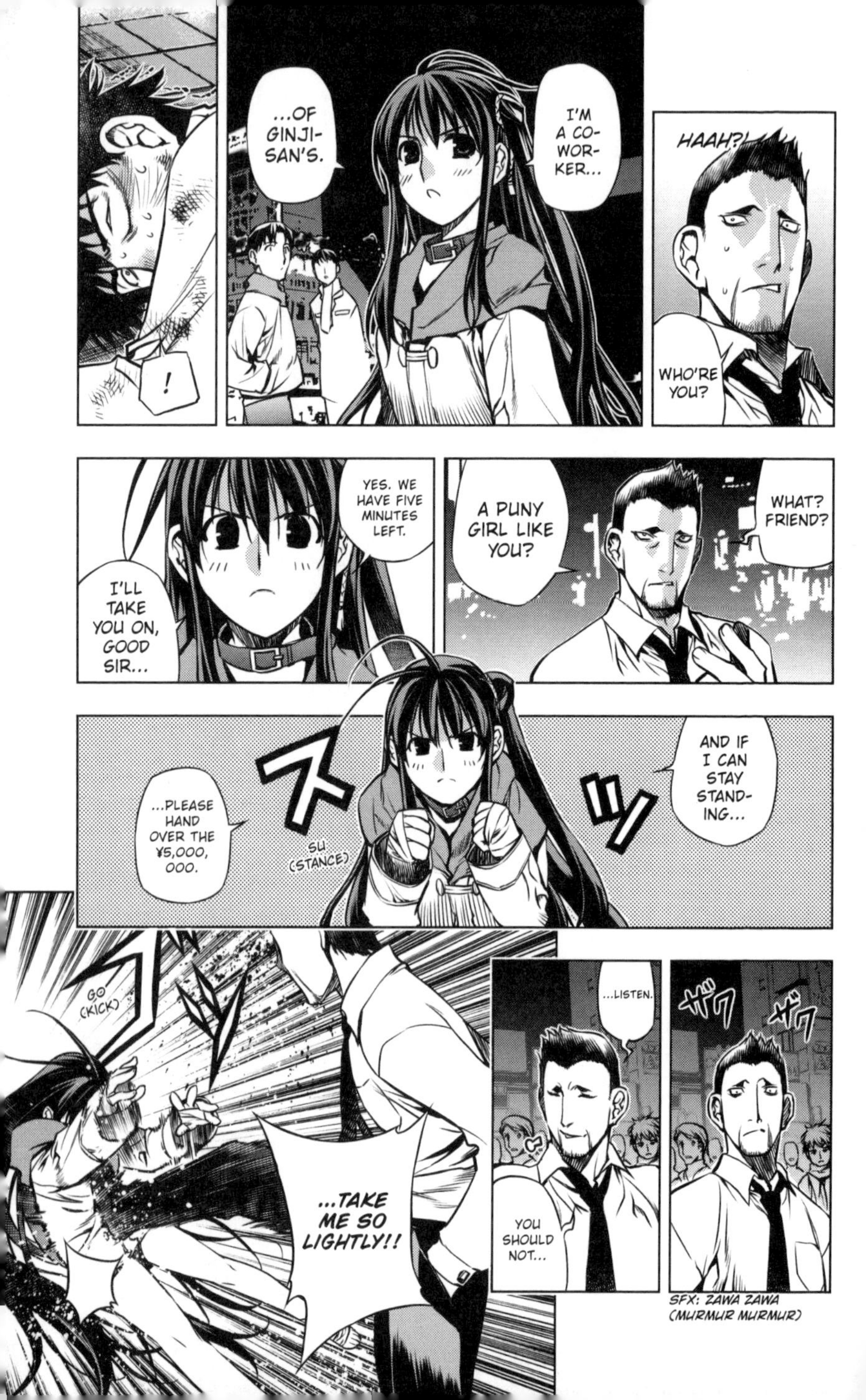
HAAH?!
WHO'RE YOU?
I'M A CO-WORKER...
...OF GINJI-SAN'S.
!
WHAT? FRIEND?
A PUNY GIRL LIKE YOU?
YES. WE HAVE FIVE MINUTES LEFT.
I'LL TAKE YOU ON, GOOD SIR...
AND IF I CAN STAY STANDING...
SU (STANCE)
...PLEASE HAND OVER THE ¥5,000,000.
SFX: ZAWA ZAWA (MURMUR MURMUR)
...LISTEN.
YOU SHOULD NOT...
GO (KICK)
...TAKE ME SO LIGHTLY!!

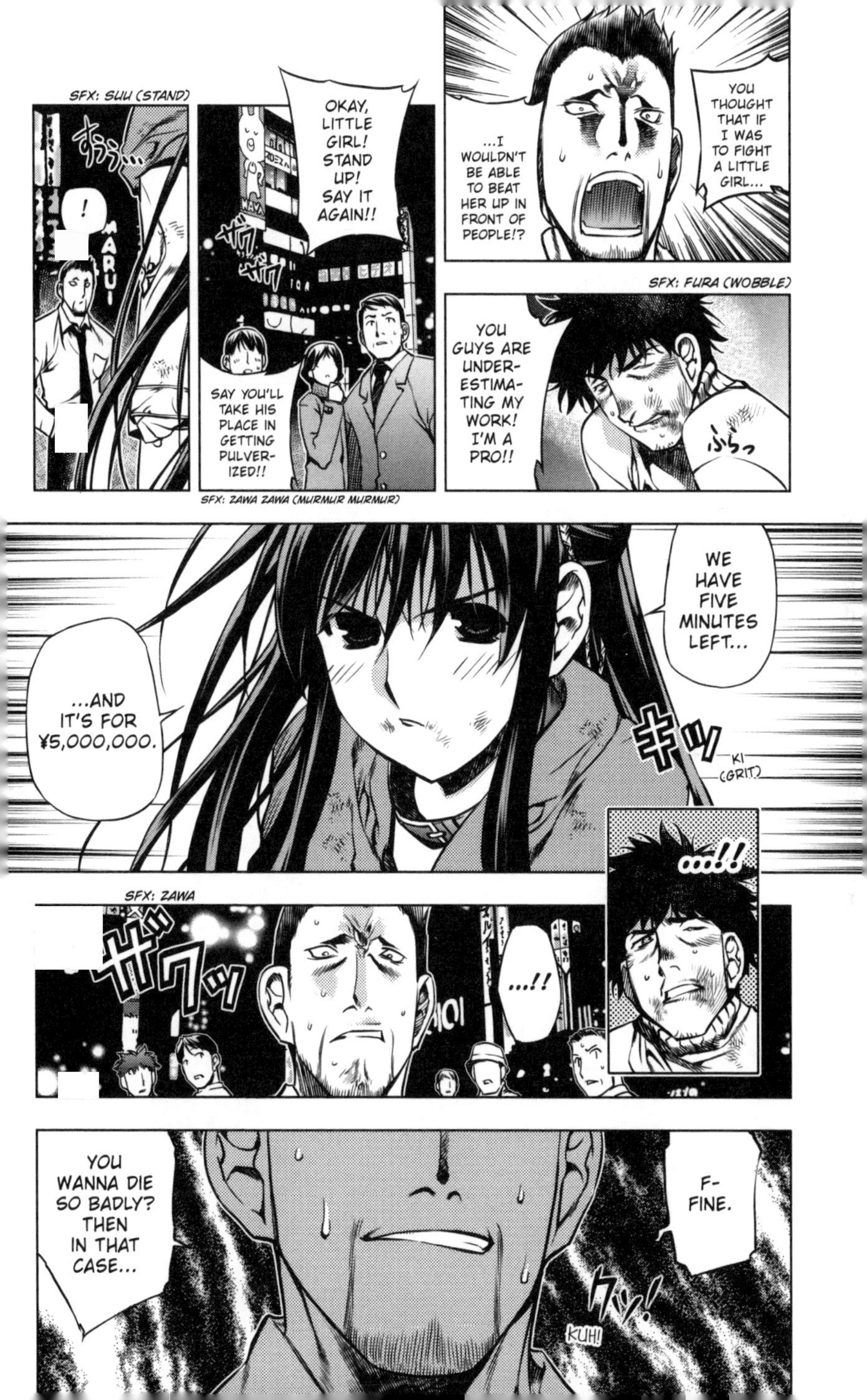
YOU THOUGHT THAT IF I WAS TO FIGHT A LITTLE GIRL...
...I WOULDN'T BE ABLE TO BEAT HER UP IN FRONT OF PEOPLE!?
SFX: FURA (WOBBLE)
YOU GUYS ARE UNDER-ESTIMATING MY WORK! I'M A PRO!!
OKAY, LITTLE GIRL! STAND UP! SAY IT AGAIN!!
SAY YOU'LL TAKE HIS PLACE IN GETTING PULVER-IZED!!
SFX: ZAWA ZAWA (MURMUR MURMUR)
SFX: SUU (STAND)
!
WE HAVE FIVE MINUTES LEFT...
KI (GRIT)
...AND IT'S FOR ¥5,000,000.
ooo!!
...!!
SFX: ZAWA
F-FINE.
KUH!
YOU WANNA DIE SO BADLY? THEN IN THAT CASE...

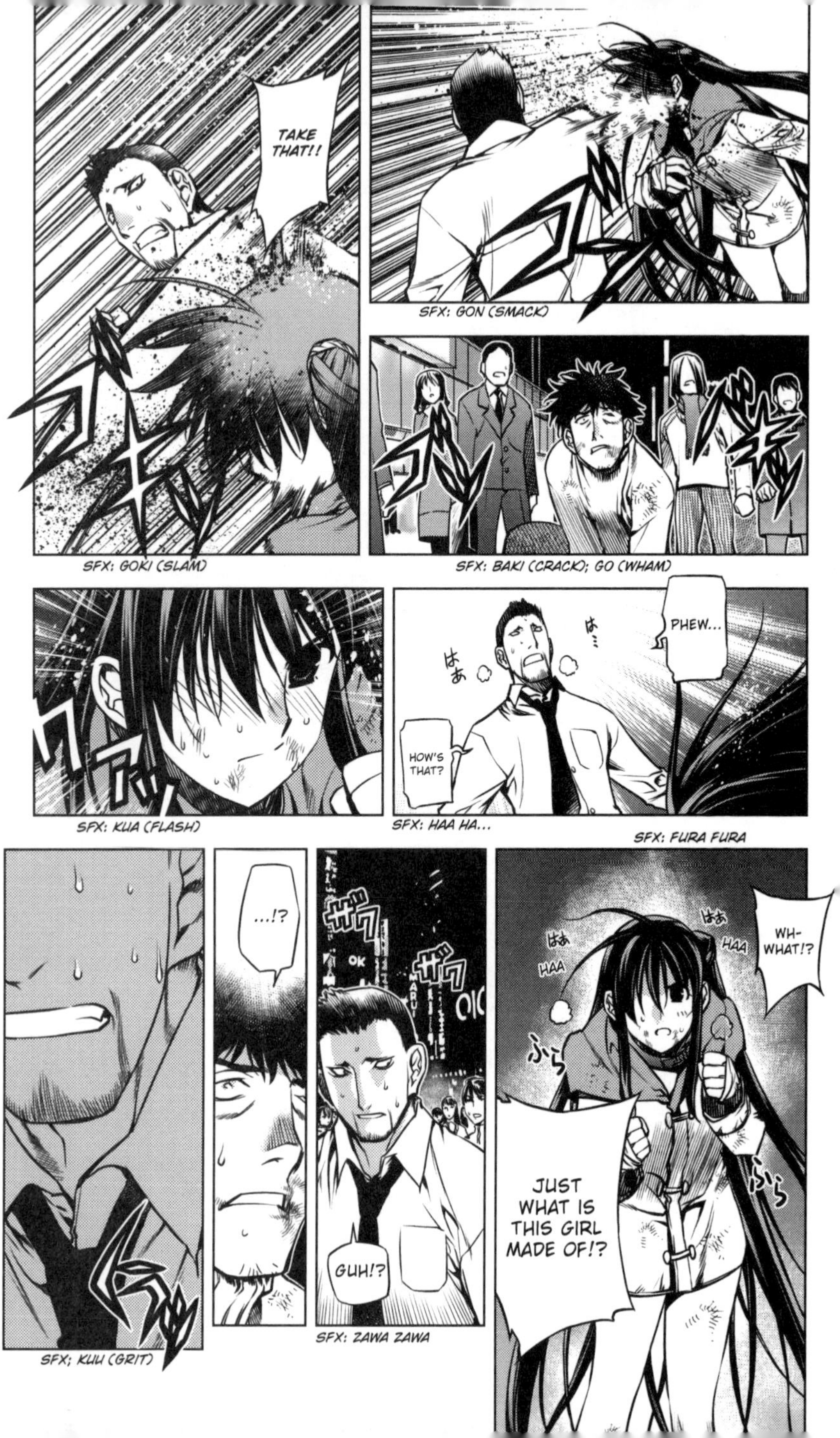
SFX: GON (SMACK)
SFX: BAKI (CRACK); GO (WHAM)
TAKE THAT!!
SFX: GOKI (SLAM)
PHEW...
は…
はあ
HOW'S THAT?
SFX: HAA HA...
SFX: KUA (FLASH)
WH-WHAT!?
はあ HAA
はあ HAA
ふら
JUST WHAT IS THIS GIRL MADE OF!?
ふら
SFX: FURA FURA
GUH!?
SFX: ZAWA ZAWA
...!?
SFX; KUU (GRIT)

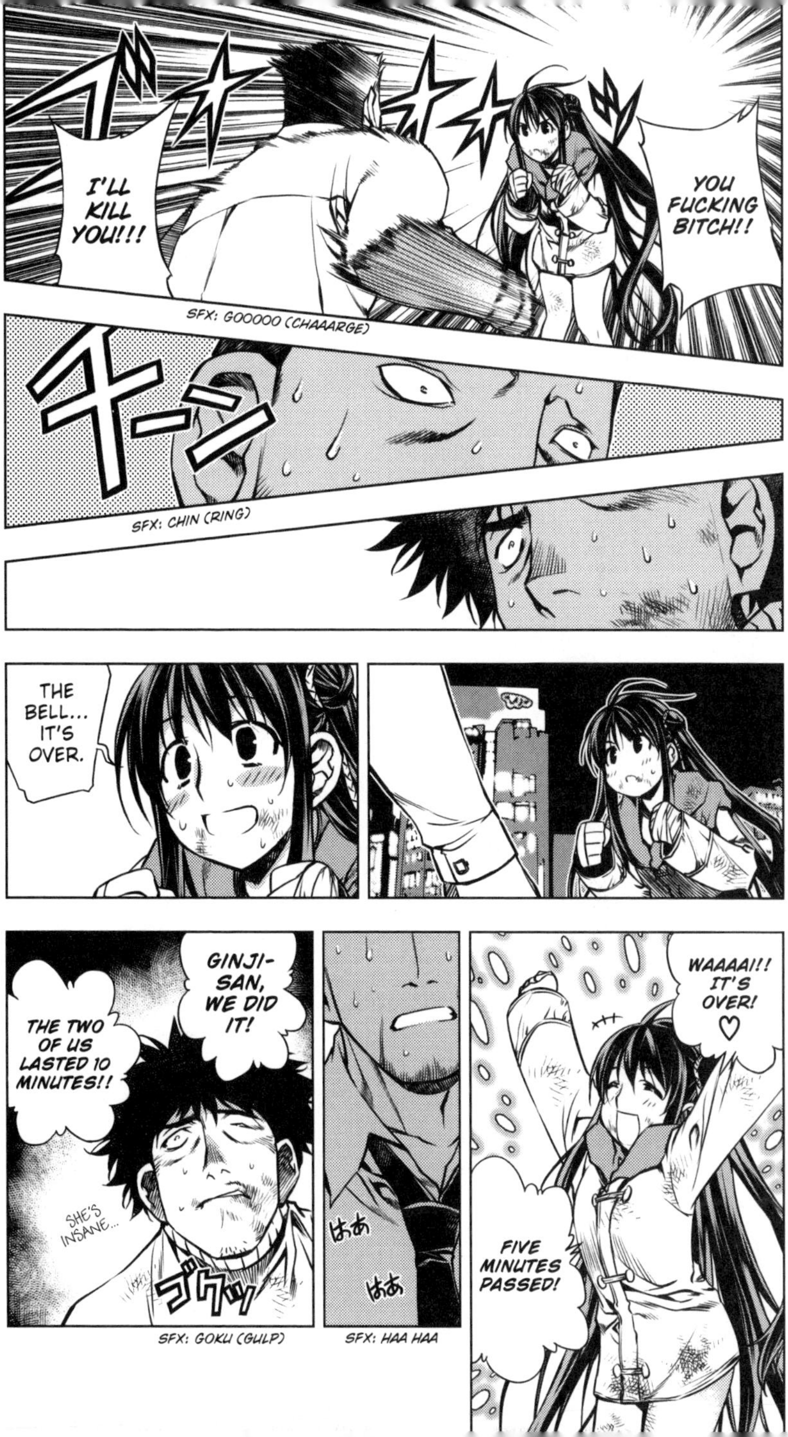
YOU FUCKING BITCH!!
I'LL KILL YOU!!!
SFX: GOOOOO (CHAAARGE)
SFX: CHIN (RING)
THE BELL... IT'S OVER.
WAAAAI!! IT'S OVER! ♡
FIVE MINUTES PASSED!
はあ
はあ
SFX: HAA HAA
GINJI-SAN, WE DID IT!
THE TWO OF US LASTED 10 MINUTES!!
SHE'S INSANE...
SFX: GOKU (GULP)

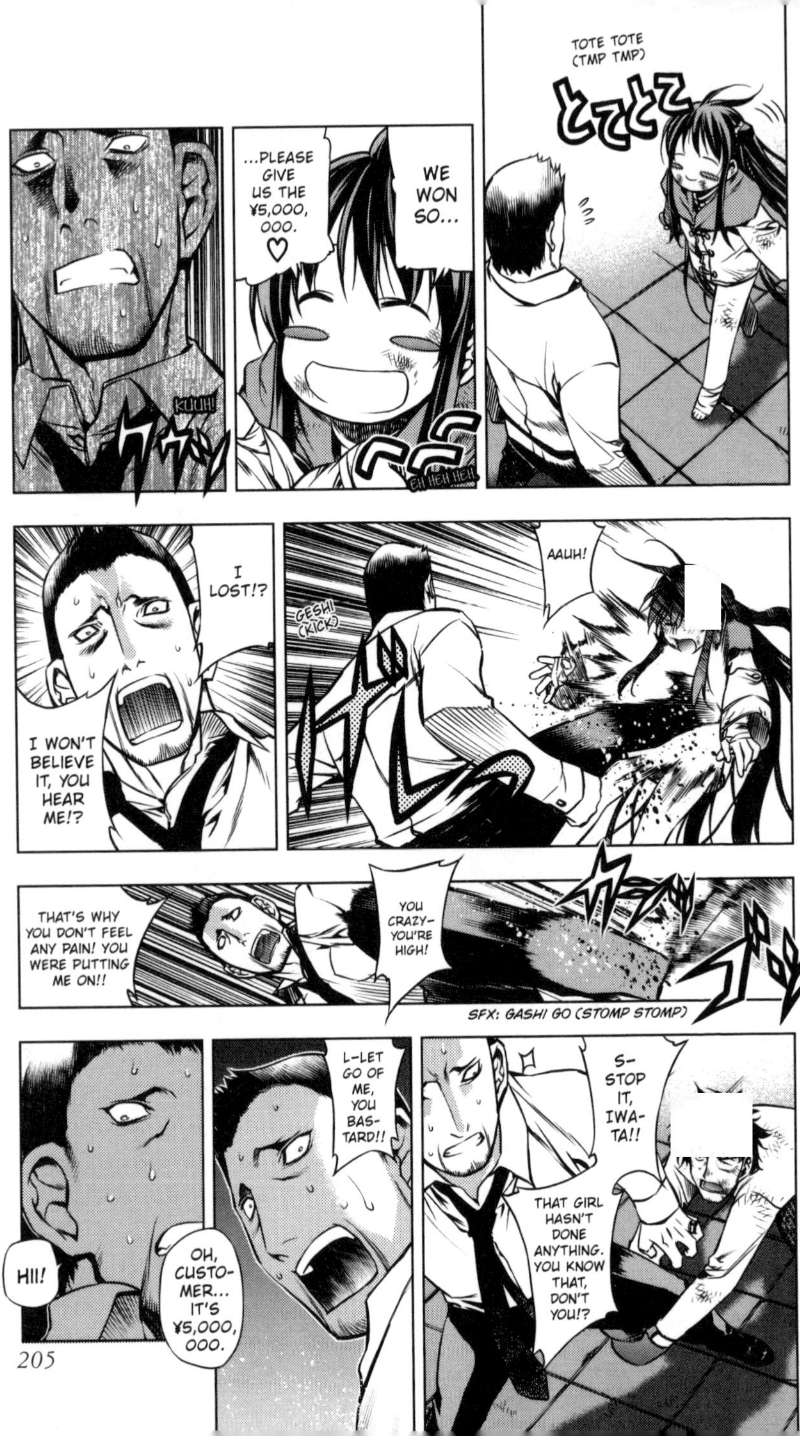
TOTE TOTE (TMP TMP)
WE WON SO...
...PLEASE GIVE US THE ¥5,000,000. ♡
EH HEH HEH
KUUH!
AAUH!
GESHI (KICK)
I LOST!?
I WON'T BELIEVE IT, YOU HEAR ME!?
YOU CRAZY-YOU'RE HIGH!
THAT'S WHY YOU DON'T FEEL ANY PAIN! YOU WERE PUTTING ME ON!!
SFX: GASHI GO (STOMP STOMP)
S-STOP IT, IWATA!!
THAT GIRL HASN'T DONE ANYTHING. YOU KNOW THAT, DON'T YOU!?
L-LET GO OF ME, YOU BASTARD!!
OH, CUSTOMER... IT'S ¥5,000,000.
HII!

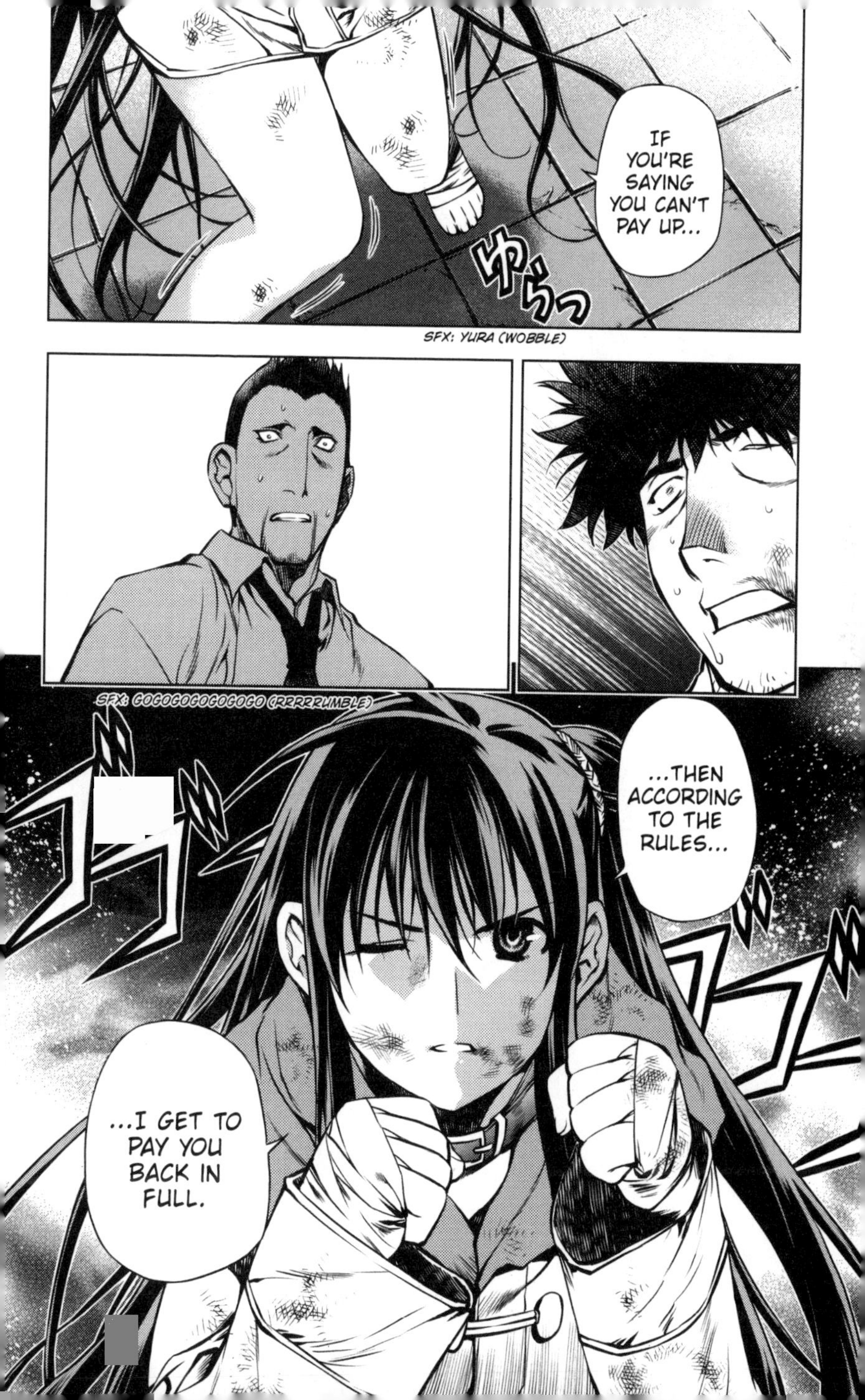
IF YOU'RE SAYING YOU CAN'T PAY UP...
ゆらっ
SFX: YURA (WOBBLE)
SFX: GOGOGOGOGOGOGO (RRRRRUMBLE)
...THEN ACCORDING TO THE RULES...
...I GET TO PAY YOU BACK IN FULL.

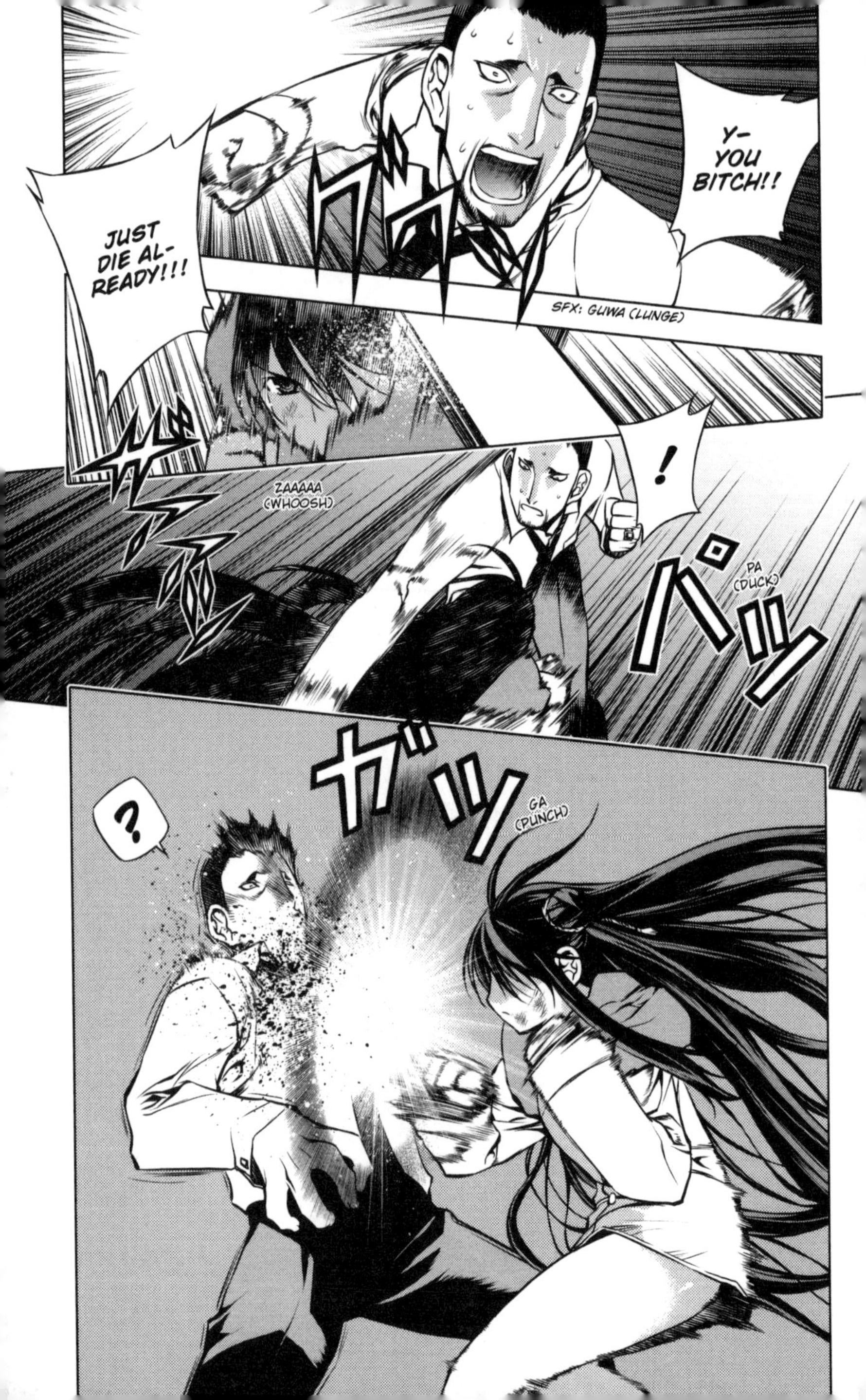
Y-
YOU
BITCH!!
SFX: GUWA (LUNGE)
JUST
DIE AL-
READY!!!
!
PA
(DUCK)
ZAAAAA
(WHOOSH)
GA
(PUNCH)
?

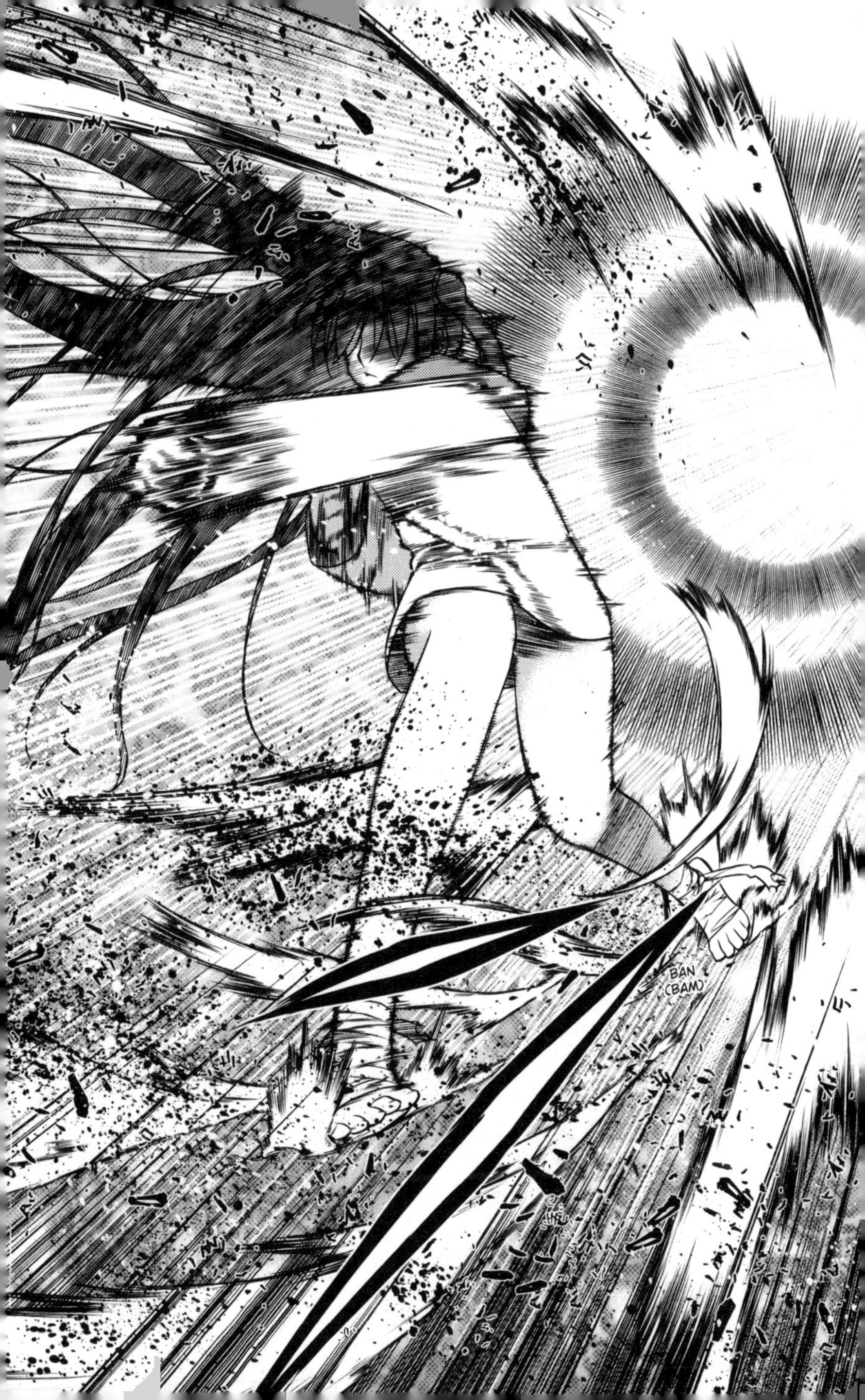
BAN
(BAM)

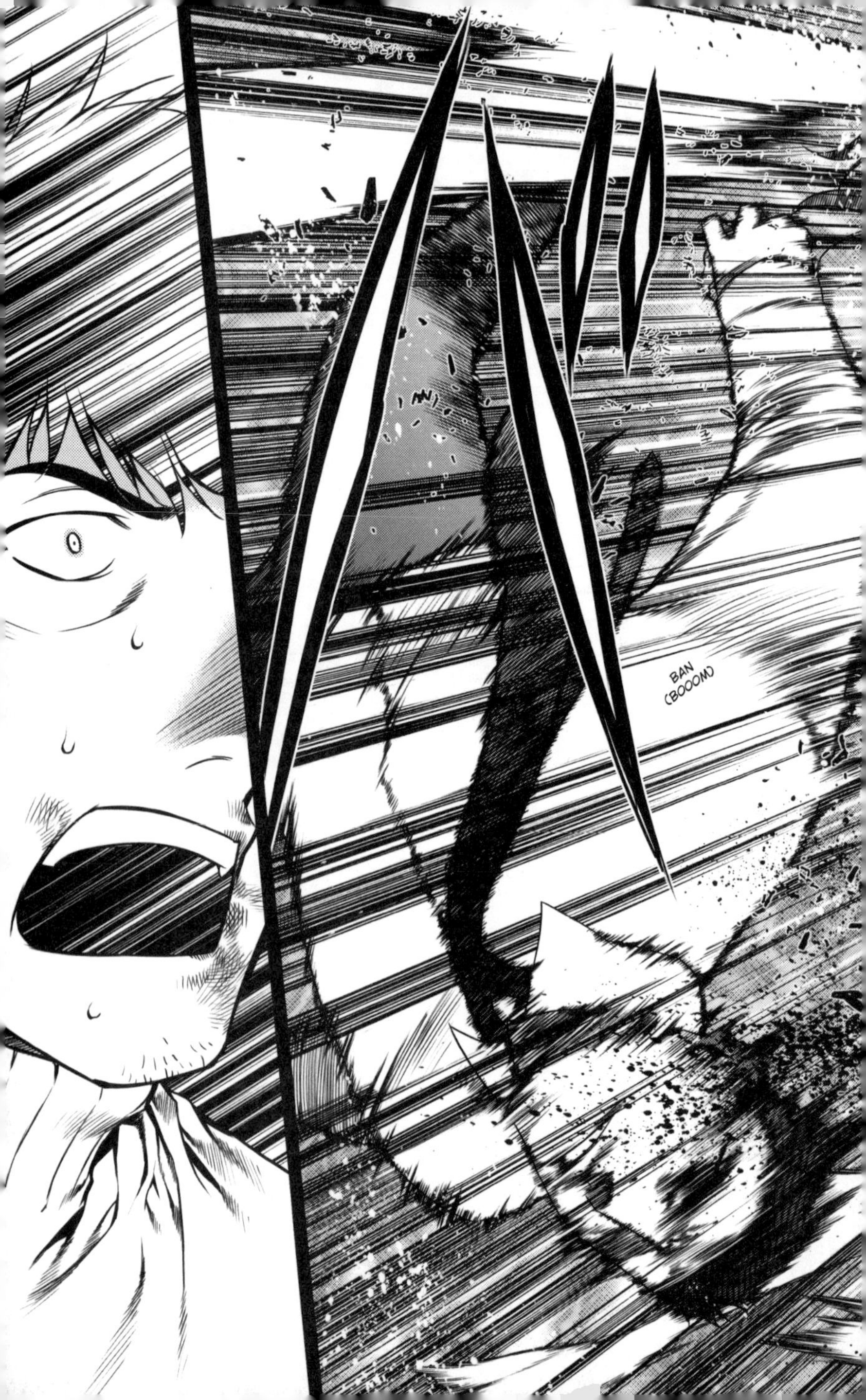
BAN
(BOOOM)

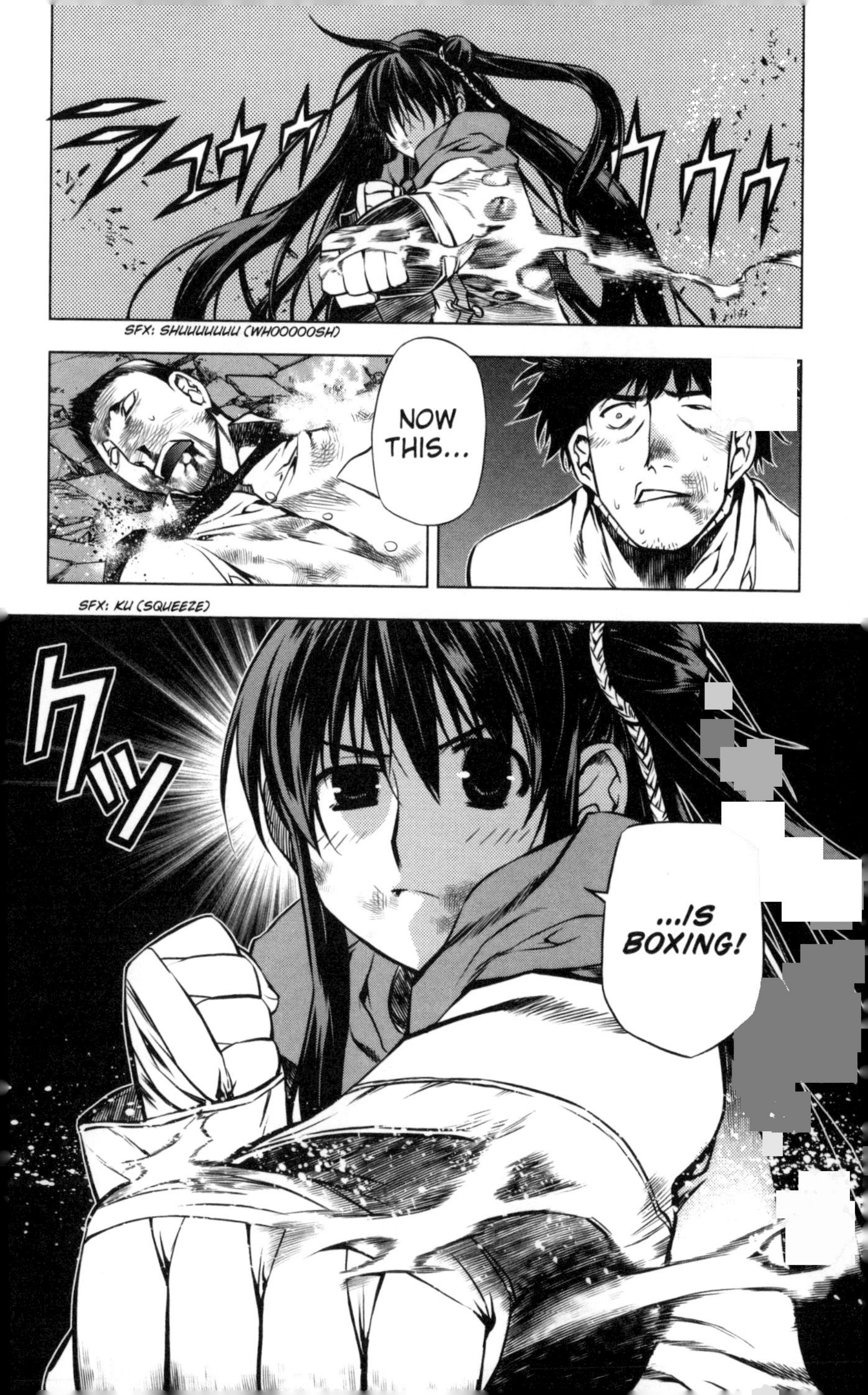
SFX: SHUUUUUUUU (WHOOOOOOSH)
NOW THIS...
SFX: KU (SQUEEZE)
...IS BOXING!

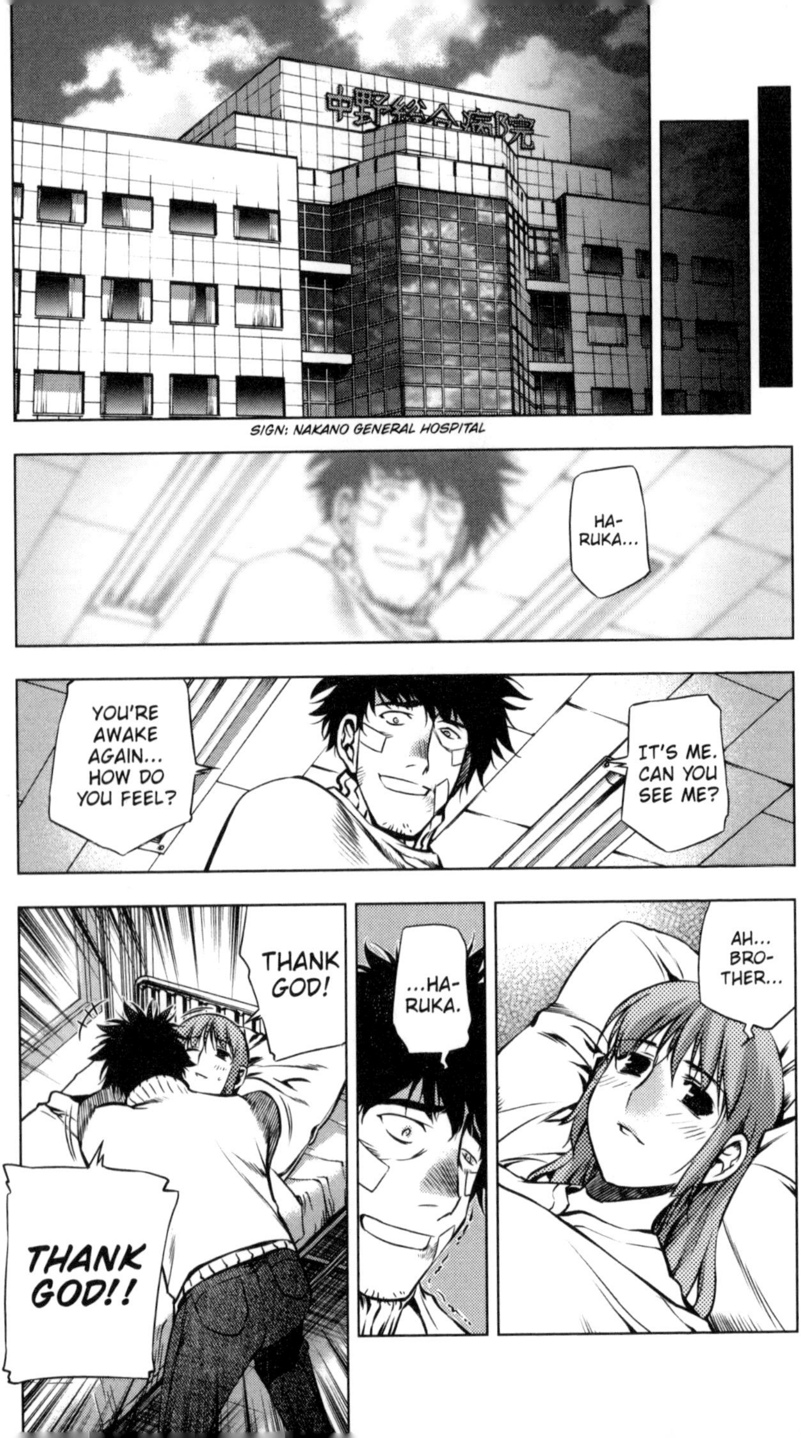
中野総合病院
SIGN: NAKANO GENERAL HOSPITAL
HA-RUKA...
IT'S ME. CAN YOU SEE ME?
YOU'RE AWAKE AGAIN... HOW DO YOU FEEL?
AH... BRO-THER...
...HA-RUKA.
THANK GOD!
THANK GOD!!

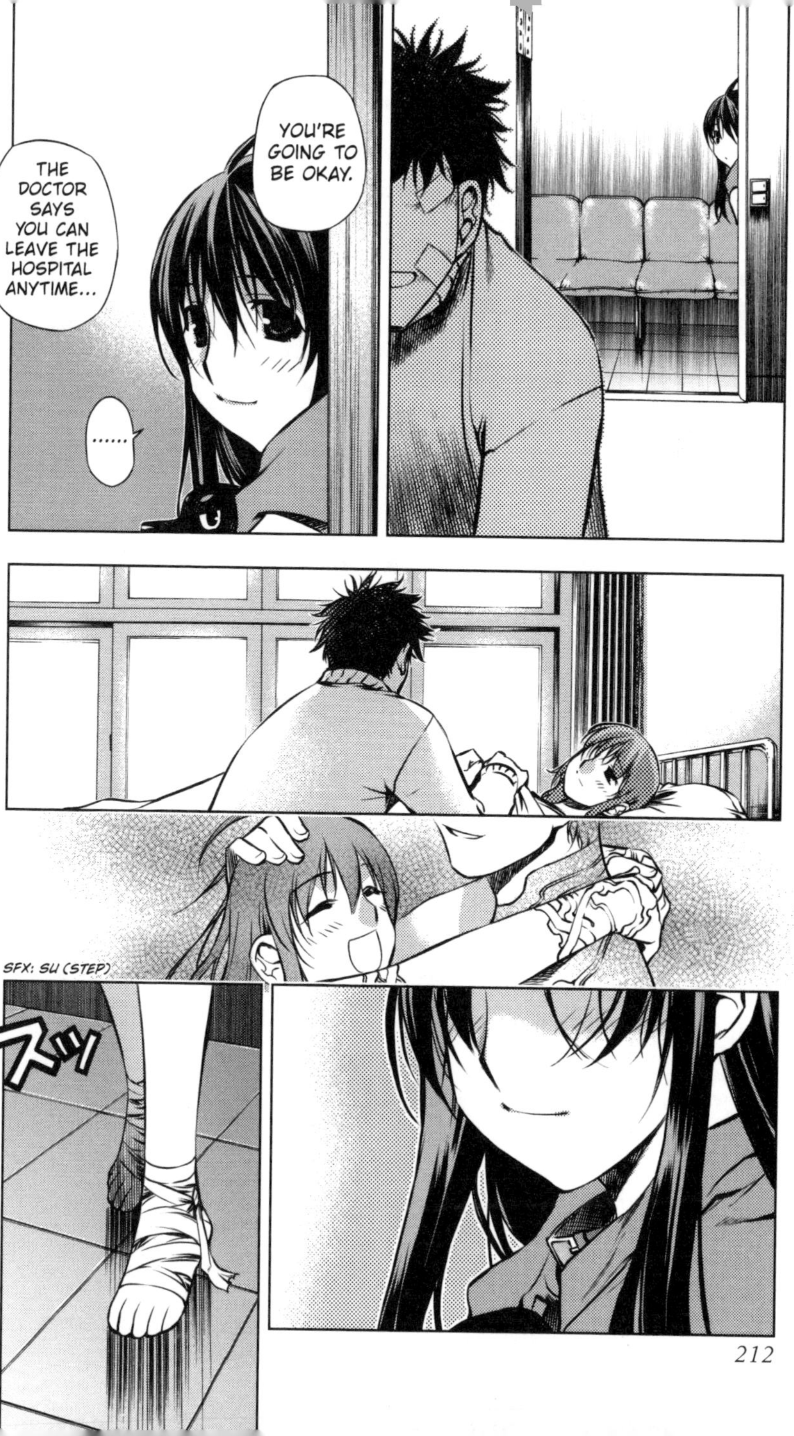
YOU'RE GOING TO BE OKAY.
THE DOCTOR SAYS YOU CAN LEAVE THE HOSPITAL ANYTIME...
......
ズッ
SFX: SU (STEP)

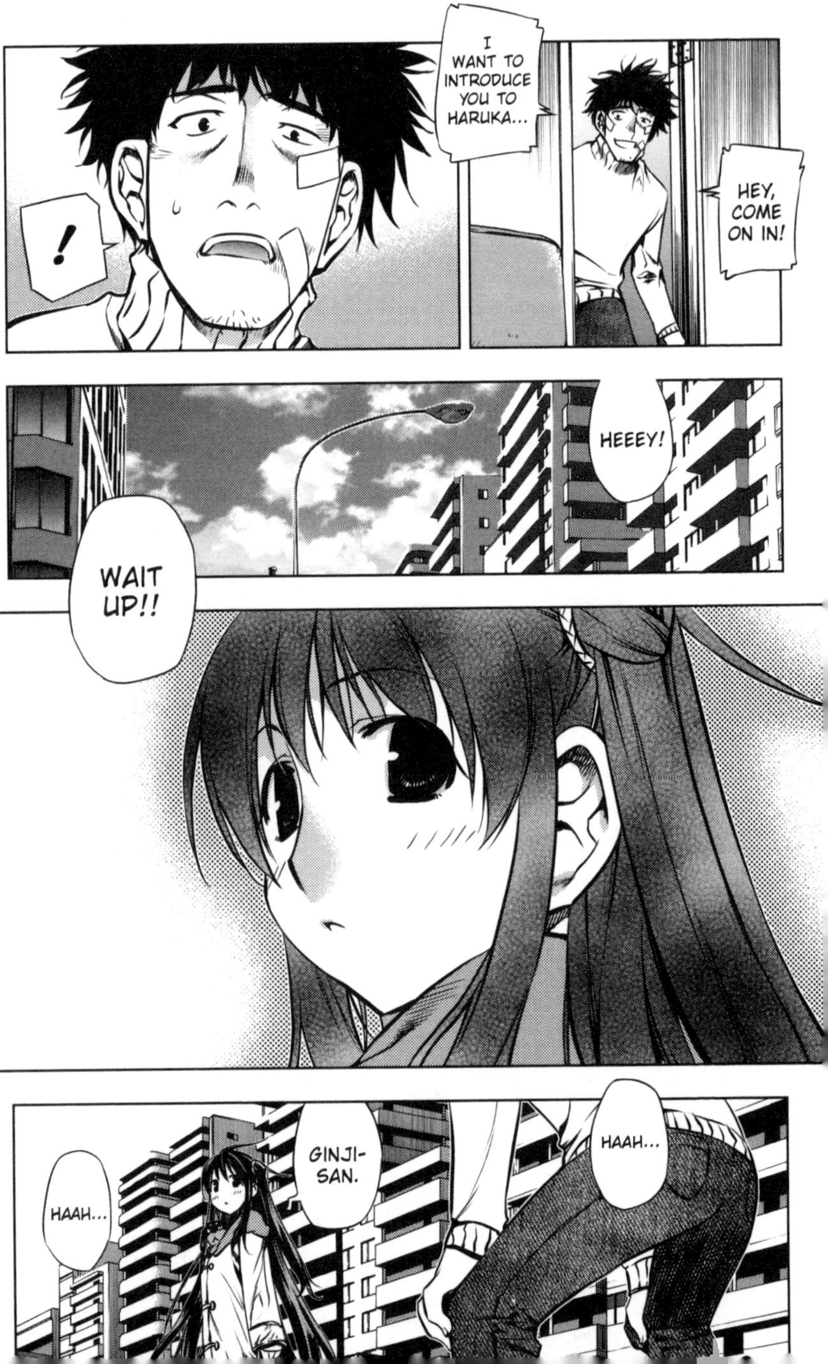
HEY, COME ON IN!
I WANT TO INTRODUCE YOU TO HARUKA...
!
HEEEY!
WAIT UP!!
HAAH...
GINJI-SAN.
HAAH...

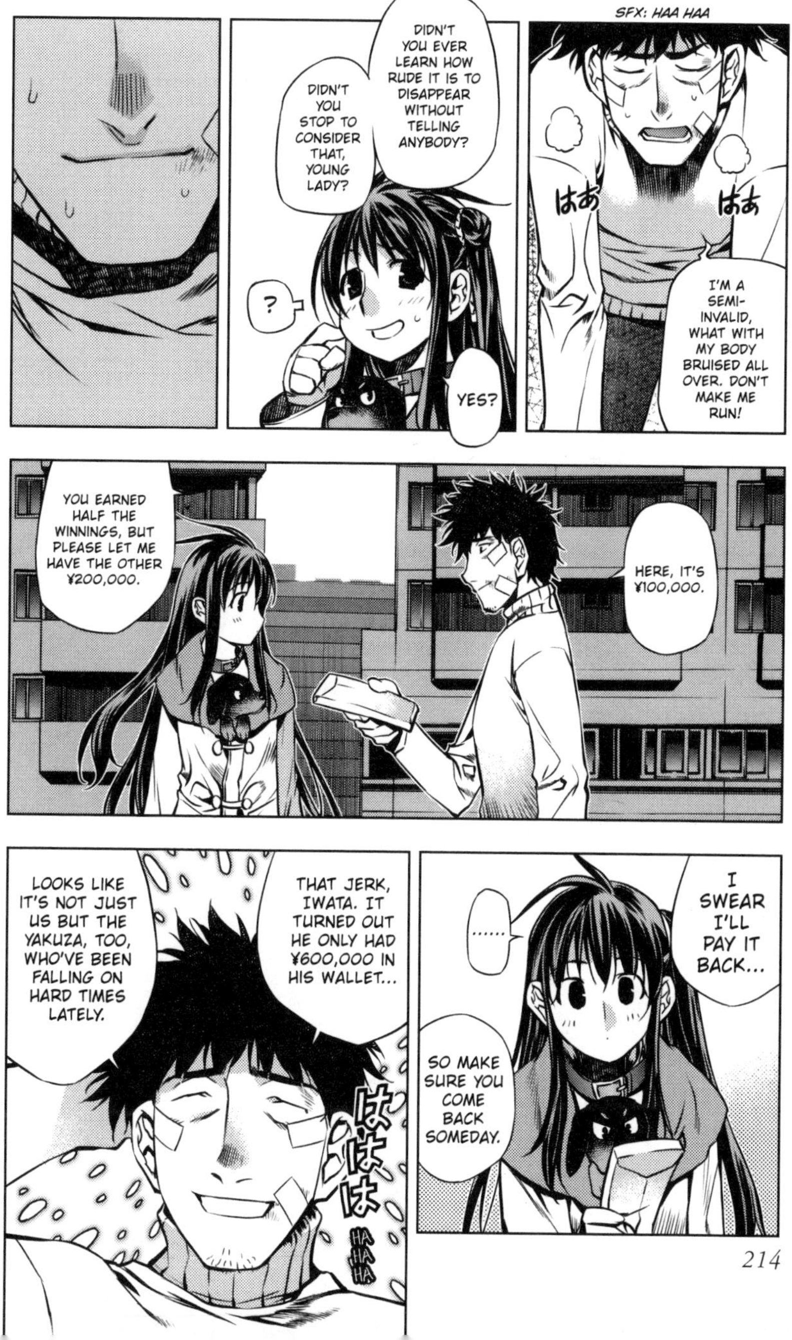
SFX: HAA HAA
はあ はあ
I'M A SEMI-INVALID, WHAT WITH MY BODY BRUISED ALL OVER. DON'T MAKE ME RUN!
DIDN'T YOU EVER LEARN HOW RUDE IT IS TO DISAPPEAR WITHOUT TELLING ANYBODY?
DIDN'T YOU STOP TO CONSIDER THAT, YOUNG LADY?
?
YES?
HERE, IT'S ¥100,000.
YOU EARNED HALF THE WINNINGS, BUT PLEASE LET ME HAVE THE OTHER ¥200,000.
I SWEAR I'LL PAY IT BACK...
......
SO MAKE SURE YOU COME BACK SOMEDAY.
THAT JERK, IWATA. IT TURNED OUT HE ONLY HAD ¥600,000 IN HIS WALLET...
LOOKS LIKE IT'S NOT JUST US BUT THE YAKUZA, TOO, WHO'VE BEEN FALLING ON HARD TIMES LATELY.
ははは
HA HA HA

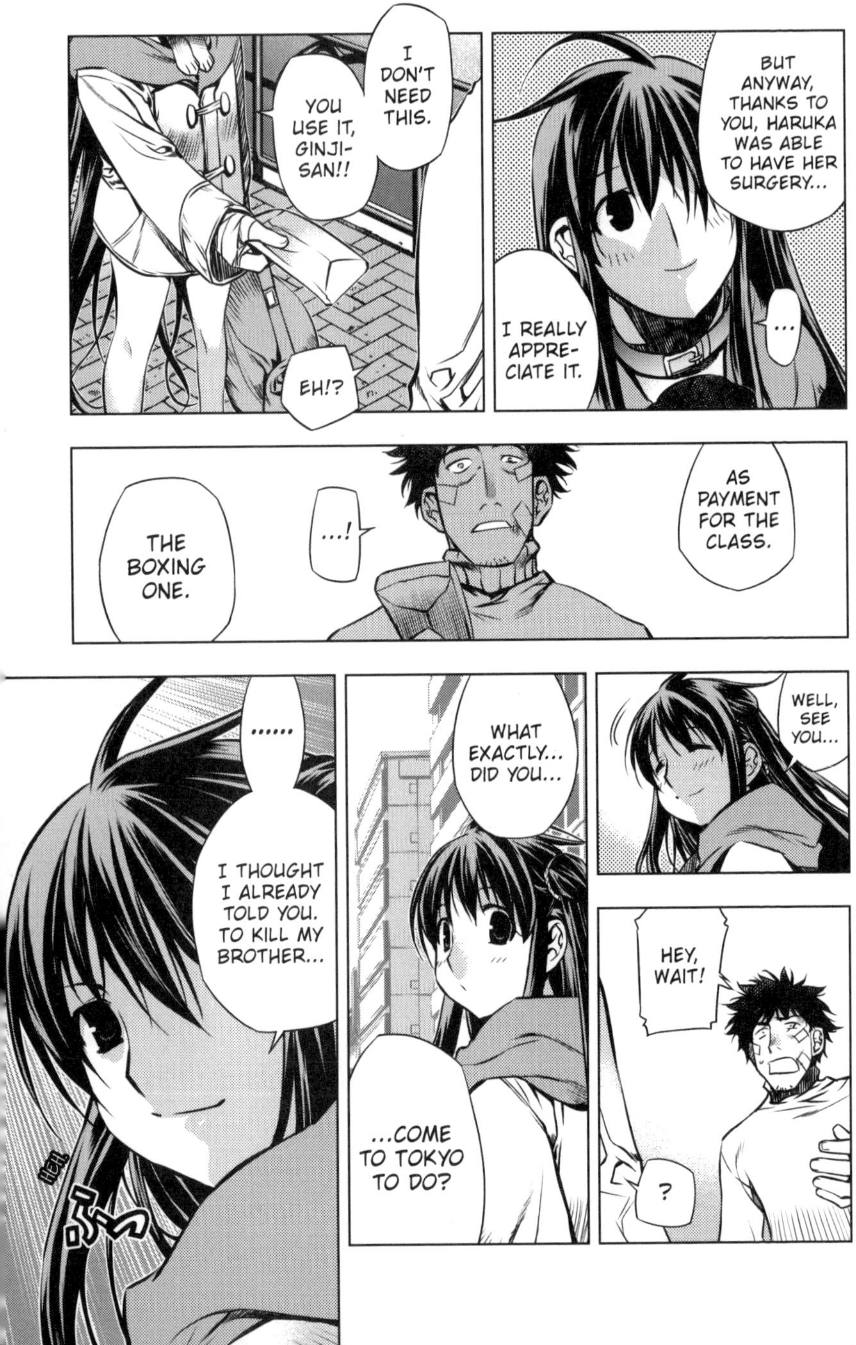
BUT ANYWAY, THANKS TO YOU, HARUKA WAS ABLE TO HAVE HER SURGERY...
...
I REALLY APPRECIATE IT.
I DON'T NEED THIS.
YOU USE IT, GINJI-SAN!!
EH!?
AS PAYMENT FOR THE CLASS.
...!
THE BOXING ONE.
WELL, SEE YOU...
HEY, WAIT!
?
WHAT EXACTLY... DID YOU...
...COME TO TOKYO TO DO?
......
I THOUGHT I ALREADY TOLD YOU. TO KILL MY BROTHER...
HEH
ふっ

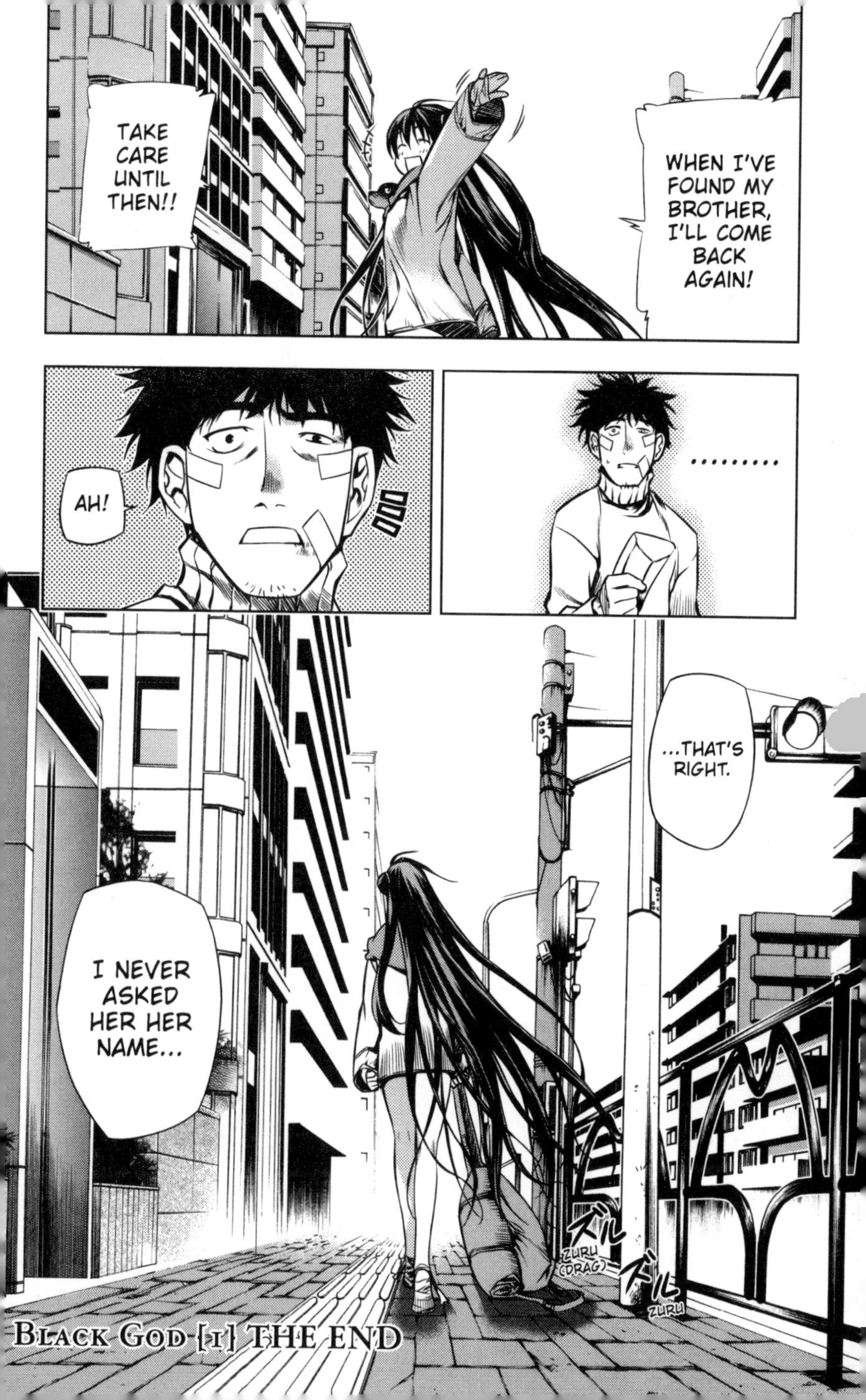
WHEN I'VE FOUND MY BROTHER, I'LL COME BACK AGAIN!
TAKE CARE UNTIL THEN!!
....
AH!
...THAT'S RIGHT.
I NEVER ASKED HER HER NAME...
ズル
ZURU (DRAG)
ズル
ZURU
BLACK GOD [1] THE END

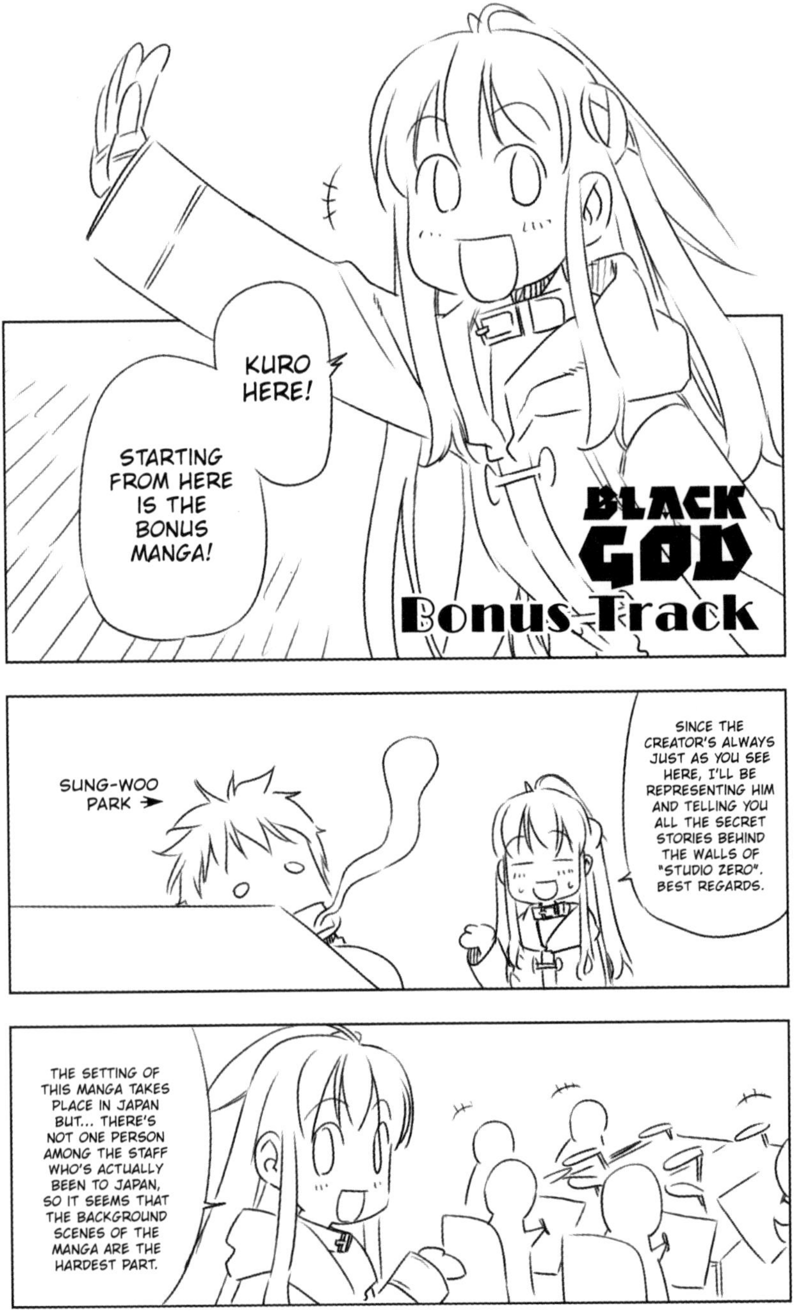
KURO HERE!
STARTING FROM HERE IS THE BONUS MANGA!
BLACK GOD
Bonus Track
SINCE THE CREATOR'S ALWAYS JUST AS YOU SEE HERE, I'LL BE REPRESENTING HIM AND TELLING YOU ALL THE SECRET STORIES BEHIND THE WALLS OF "STUDIO ZERO". BEST REGARDS.
SUNG-WOO PARK
THE SETTING OF THIS MANGA TAKES PLACE IN JAPAN BUT... THERE'S NOT ONE PERSON AMONG THE STAFF WHO'S ACTUALLY BEEN TO JAPAN, SO IT SEEMS THAT THE BACKGROUND SCENES OF THE MANGA ARE THE HARDEST PART.

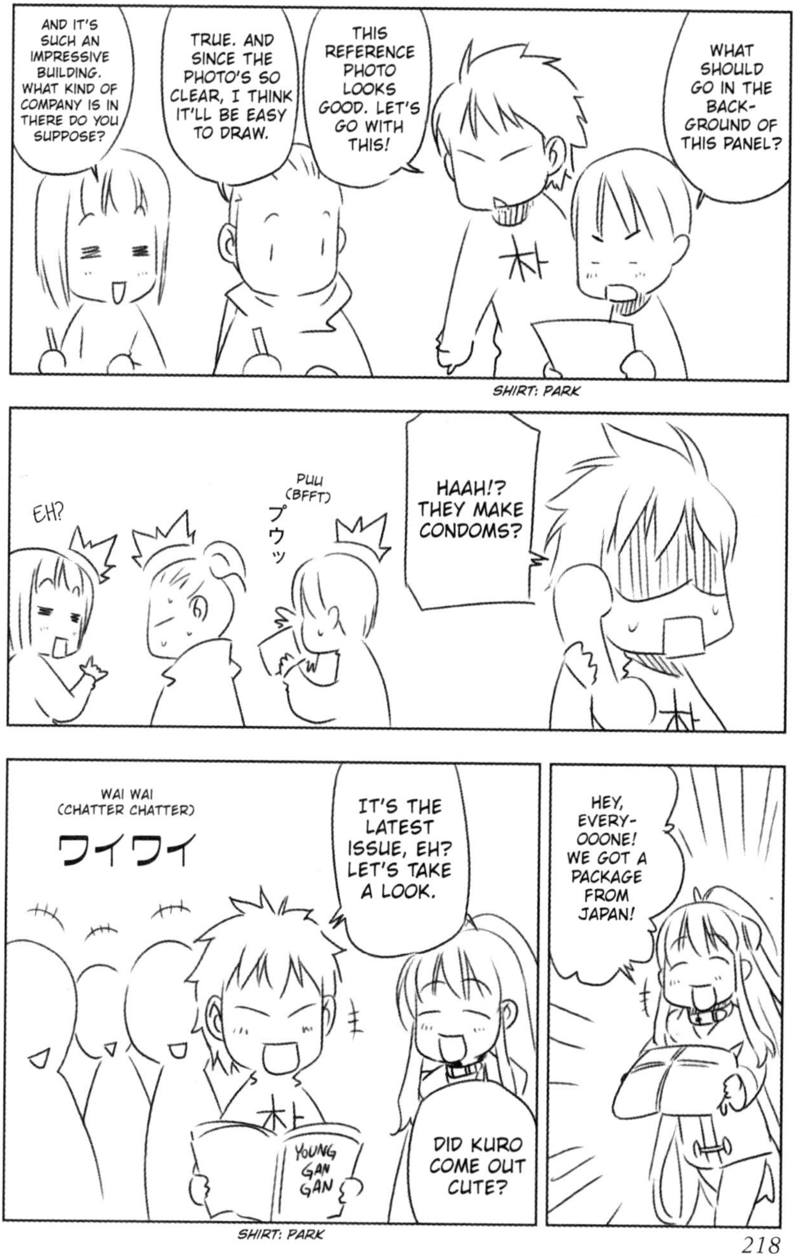
WHAT SHOULD GO IN THE BACK-GROUND OF THIS PANEL?
THIS REFERENCE PHOTO LOOKS GOOD. LET'S GO WITH THIS!
TRUE. AND SINCE THE PHOTO'S SO CLEAR, I THINK IT'LL BE EASY TO DRAW.
AND IT'S SUCH AN IMPRESSIVE BUILDING. WHAT KIND OF COMPANY IS IN THERE DO YOU SUPPOSE?
SHIRT: PARK
HAAH!? THEY MAKE CONDOMS?
PUU (BFFT)
プウッ
EH?
HEY, EVERY-OOONE! WE GOT A PACKAGE FROM JAPAN!
IT'S THE LATEST ISSUE, EH? LET'S TAKE A LOOK.
WAI WAI (CHATTER CHATTER)
ワイワイ
DID KURO COME OUT CUTE?
YOUNG GAN GAN
SHIRT: PARK

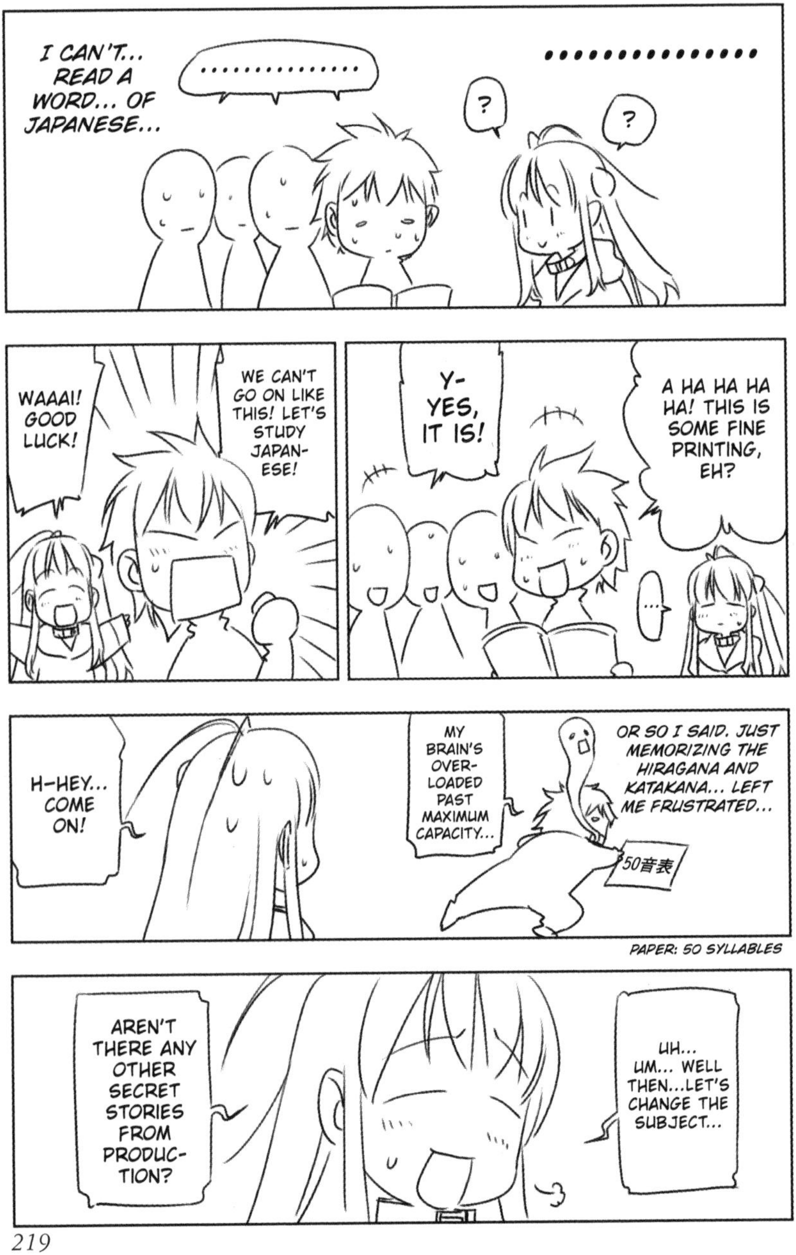
....
?
?
....
I CAN'T... READ A WORD... OF JAPANESE...
A HA HA HA HA! THIS IS SOME FINE PRINTING, EH?
Y-YES, IT IS!
...
WE CAN'T GO ON LIKE THIS! LET'S STUDY JAPANESE!
WAAAI! GOOD LUCK!
OR SO I SAID. JUST MEMORIZING THE HIRAGANA AND KATAKANA... LEFT ME FRUSTRATED...
MY BRAIN'S OVERLOADED PAST MAXIMUM CAPACITY...
50音表
H-HEY... COME ON!
UH... UM... WELL THEN...LET'S CHANGE THE SUBJECT...
AREN'T THERE ANY OTHER SECRET STORIES FROM PRODUCTION?
PAPER: 50 SYLLABLES

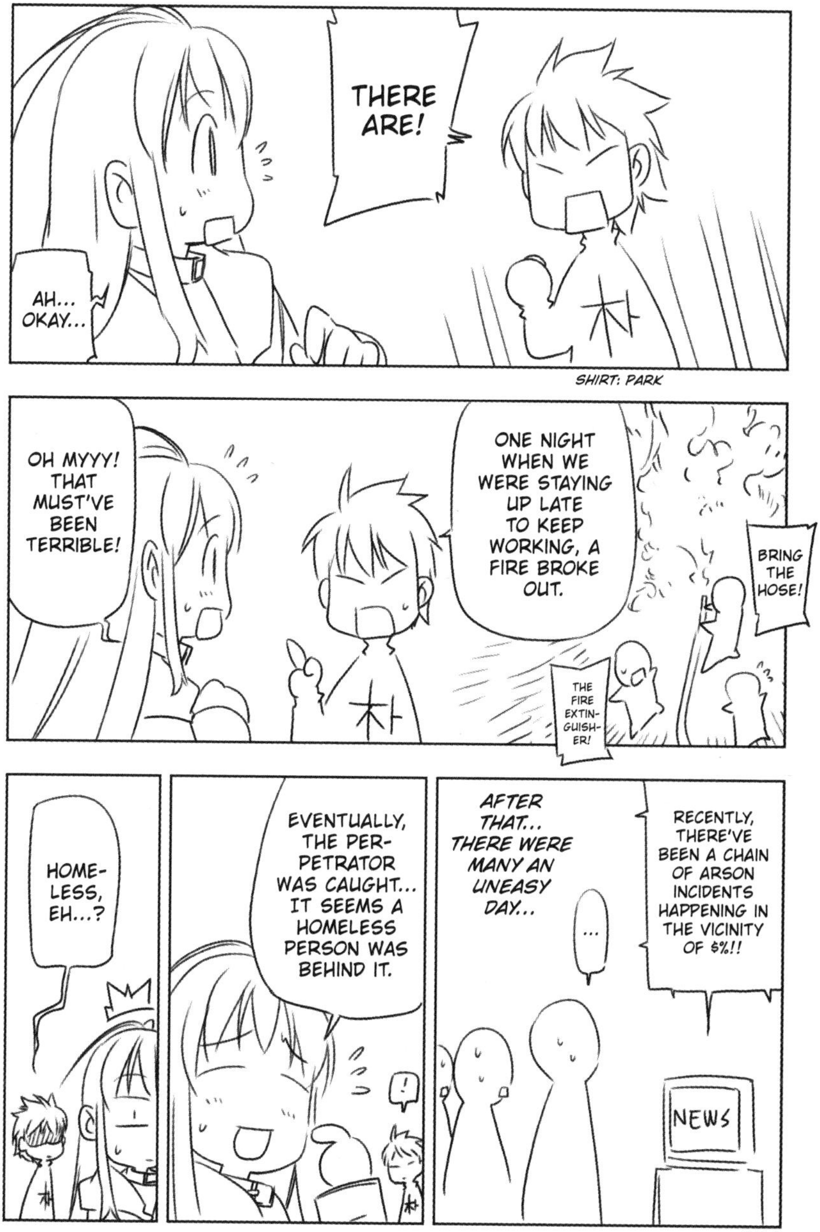
THERE ARE!
AH... OKAY...
SHIRT: PARK
ONE NIGHT WHEN WE WERE STAYING UP LATE TO KEEP WORKING, A FIRE BROKE OUT.
BRING THE HOSE!
THE FIRE EXTIN-GUISH-ER!
OH MYYY! THAT MUST'VE BEEN TERRIBLE!
RECENTLY, THERE'VE BEEN A CHAIN OF ARSON INCIDENTS HAPPENING IN THE VICINITY OF $%!!
AFTER THAT... THERE WERE MANY AN UNEASY DAY...
...
NEWS
EVENTUALLY, THE PER-PETRATOR WAS CAUGHT... IT SEEMS A HOMELESS PERSON WAS BEHIND IT.
!
HOME-LESS, EH...?

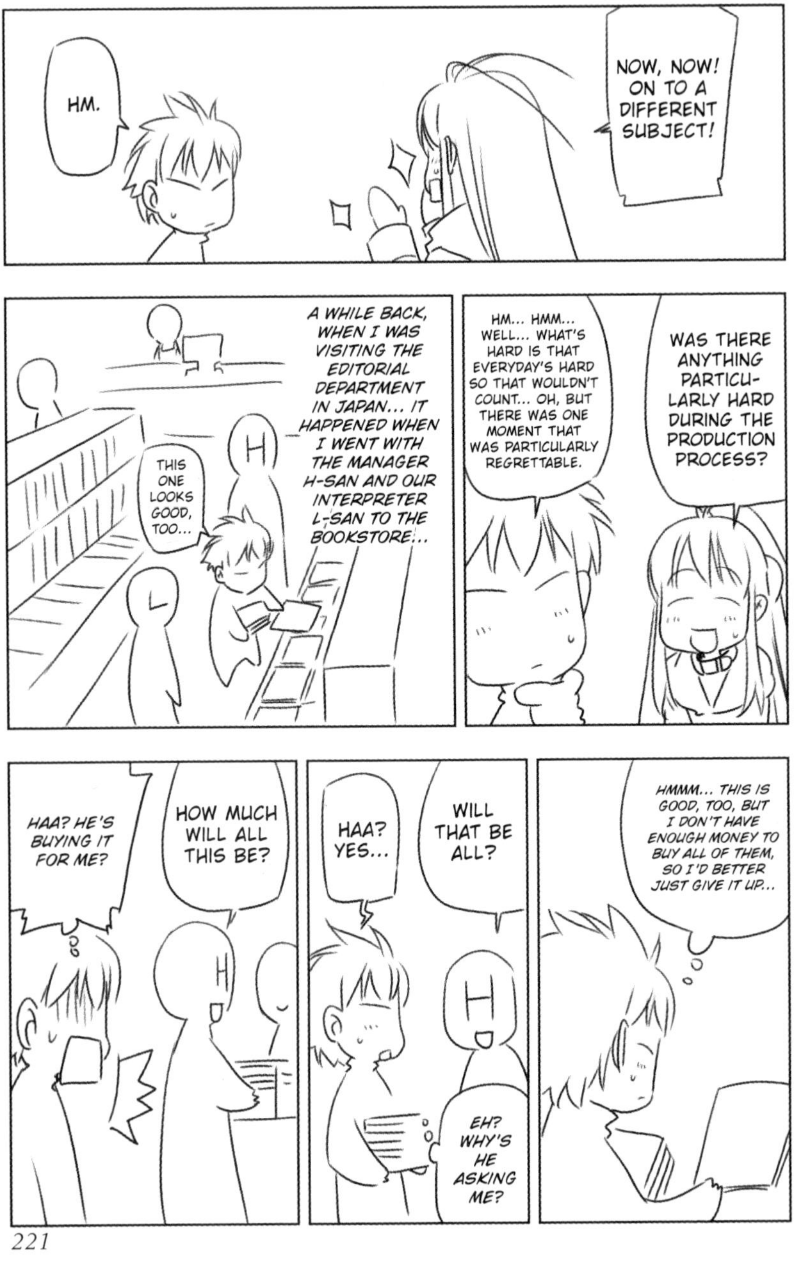
NOW, NOW! ON TO A DIFFERENT SUBJECT!
HM.
WAS THERE ANYTHING PARTICU-LARLY HARD DURING THE PRODUCTION PROCESS?
HM... HMM... WELL... WHAT'S HARD IS THAT EVERYDAY'S HARD SO THAT WOULDN'T COUNT... OH, BUT THERE WAS ONE MOMENT THAT WAS PARTICULARLY REGRETTABLE.
A WHILE BACK, WHEN I WAS VISITING THE EDITORIAL DEPARTMENT IN JAPAN... IT HAPPENED WHEN I WENT WITH THE MANAGER H-SAN AND OUR INTERPRETER L-SAN TO THE BOOKSTORE...
THIS ONE LOOKS GOOD, TOO...
HMMM... THIS IS GOOD, TOO, BUT I DON'T HAVE ENOUGH MONEY TO BUY ALL OF THEM, SO I'D BETTER JUST GIVE IT UP...
WILL THAT BE ALL?
HAA? YES...
EH? WHY'S HE ASKING ME?
HOW MUCH WILL ALL THIS BE?
HAA? HE'S BUYING IT FOR ME?

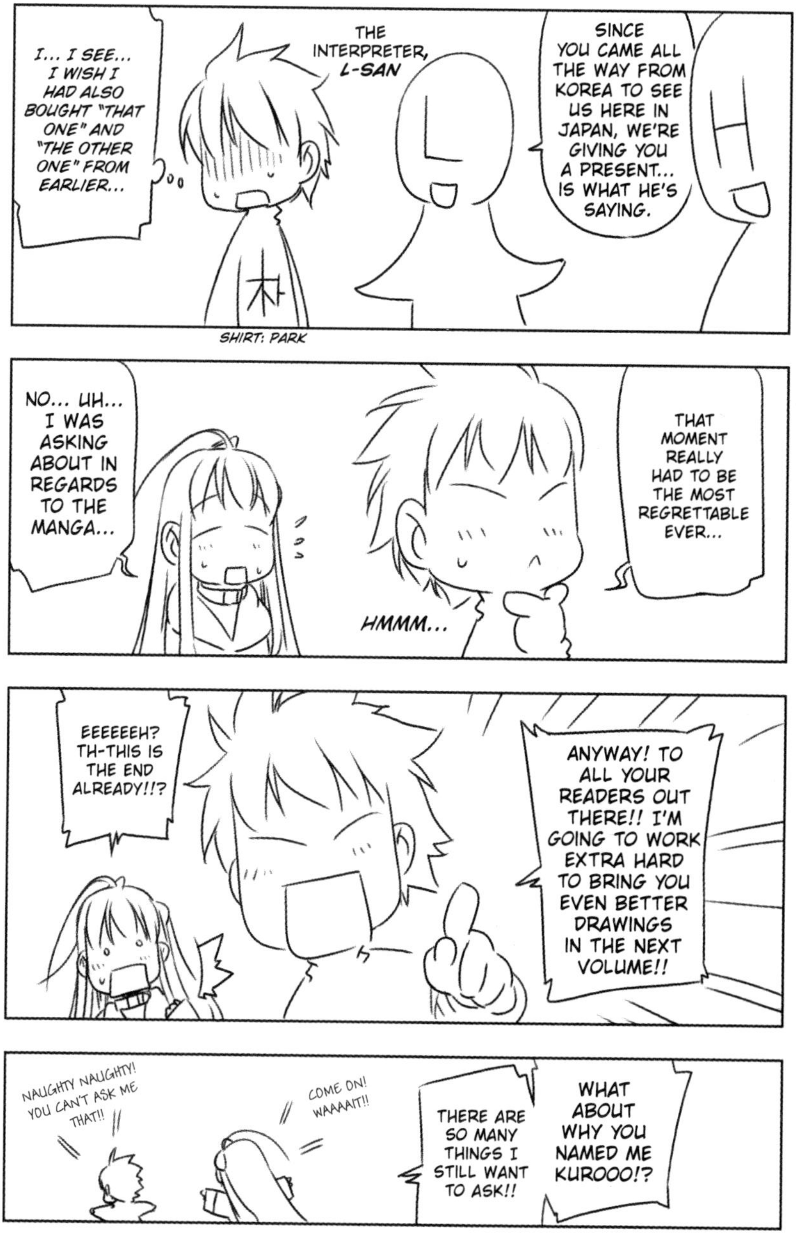
SINCE YOU CAME ALL THE WAY FROM KOREA TO SEE US HERE IN JAPAN, WE'RE GIVING YOU A PRESENT... IS WHAT HE'S SAYING.
THE INTERPRETER, L-SAN
I... I SEE... I WISH I HAD ALSO BOUGHT "THAT ONE" AND "THE OTHER ONE" FROM EARLIER...
SHIRT: PARK
THAT MOMENT REALLY HAD TO BE THE MOST REGRETTABLE EVER...
HMMM...
NO... UH... I WAS ASKING ABOUT IN REGARDS TO THE MANGA...
ANYWAY! TO ALL YOUR READERS OUT THERE!! I'M GOING TO WORK EXTRA HARD TO BRING YOU EVEN BETTER DRAWINGS IN THE NEXT VOLUME!!
EEEEEEH? TH-THIS IS THE END ALREADY!!?
WHAT ABOUT WHY YOU NAMED ME KUROOO!?
THERE ARE SO MANY THINGS I STILL WANT TO ASK!!
COME ON! WAAAAIT!!
NAUGHTY NAUGHTY! YOU CAN'T ASK ME THAT!!

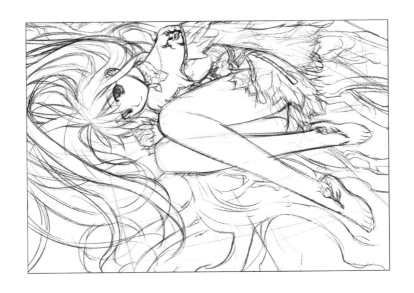

●Drawing staff（作画スタッフ）

Young-Shin Do　Yun-Hee Shin　Jin-Ju Jung
Do-Kyoung Kim　Myong-Ho Jo　Hyuck-Jin Kwon

——Studio zero——

●Manager（マネージャー）
Jin-Woo Park

●Project cooperator（企画協力）
Hyun-Seok Lee (warmania)

●Translator（翻訳）
Jong-Choul Jang (張綜哲)

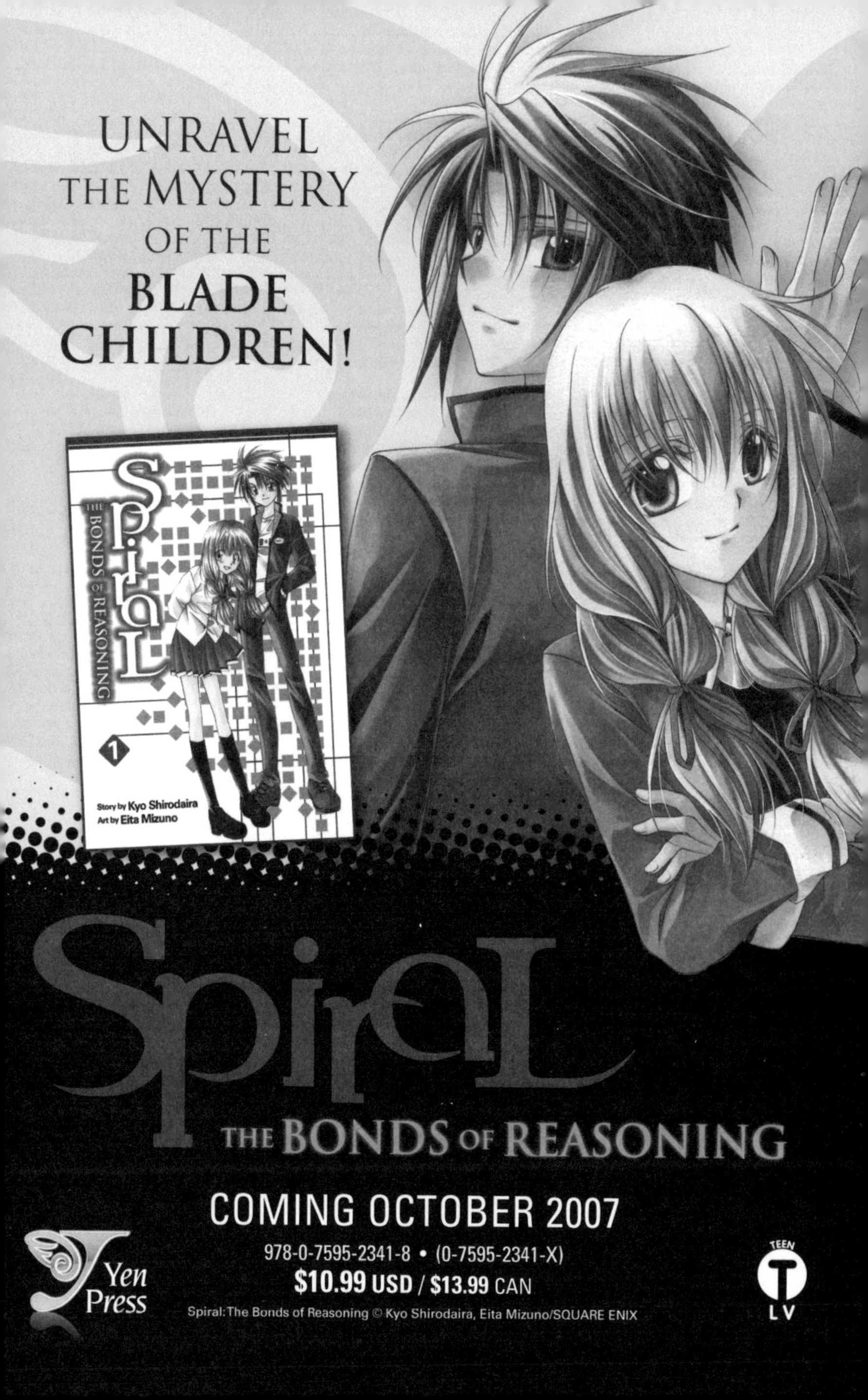
UNRAVEL THE MYSTERY OF THE BLADE CHILDREN!
Spiral THE BONDS OF REASONING
1
Story by Kyo Shirodaira
Art by Eita Mizuno
Spiral THE BONDS OF REASONING
COMING OCTOBER 2007
978-0-7595-2341-8 • (0-7595-2341-X)
$10.99 USD / $13.99 CAN
Yen Press
Spiral: The Bonds of Reasoning © Kyo Shirodaira, Eita Mizuno/SQUARE ENIX
TEEN T LV

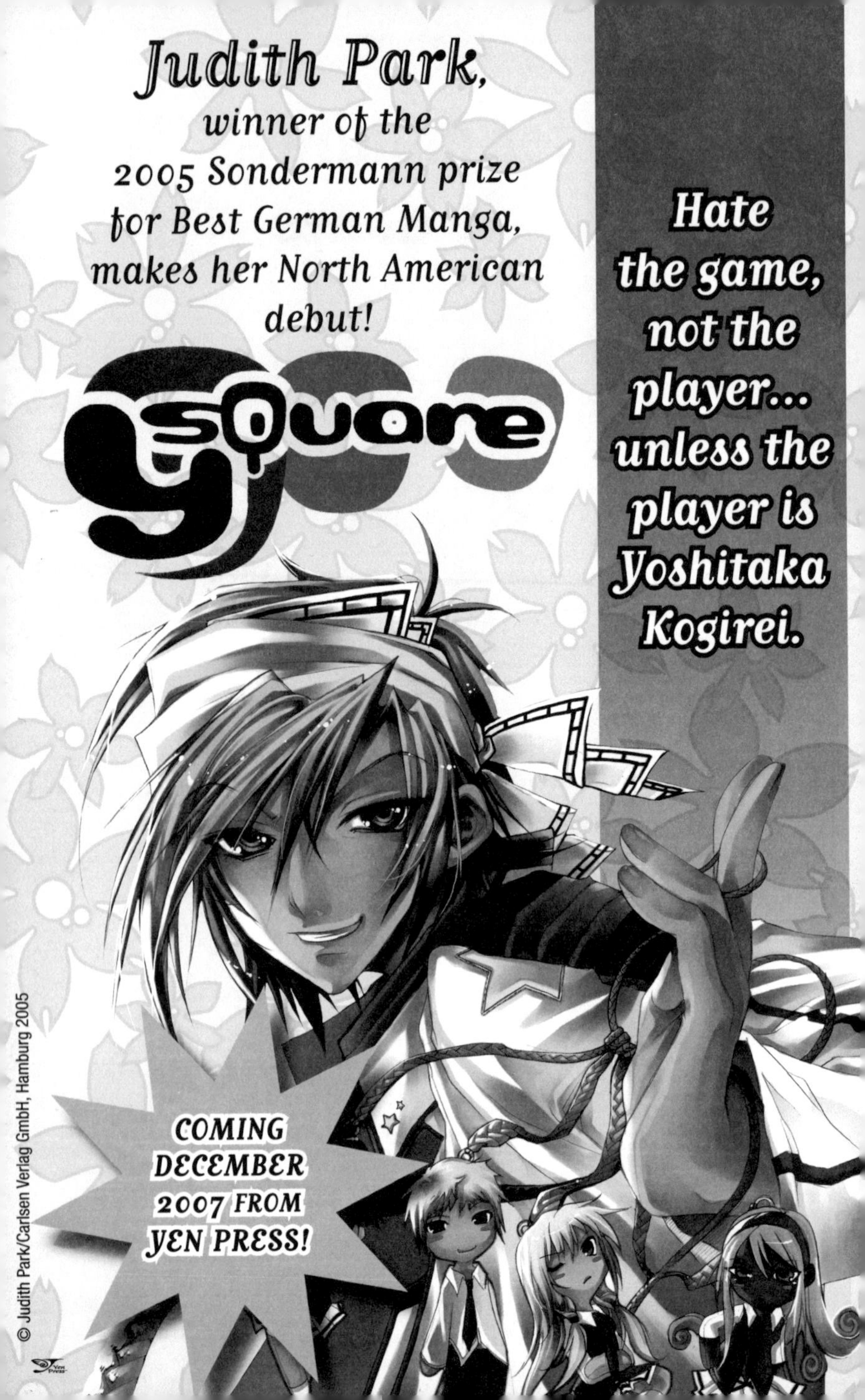
Judith Park,
winner of the
2005 Sondermann prize
for Best German Manga,
makes her North American
debut!
y square
Hate
the game,
not the
player...
unless the
player is
Yoshitaka
Kogirei.
COMING
DECEMBER
2007 FROM
YEN PRESS!
© Judith Park/Carlsen Verlag GmbH, Hamburg 2005
Yen Press

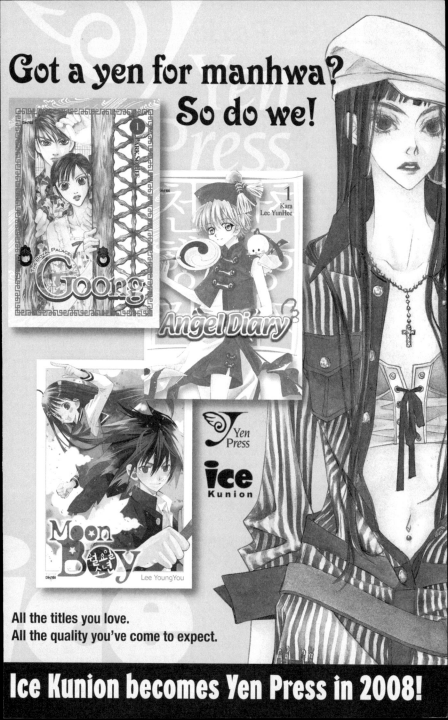

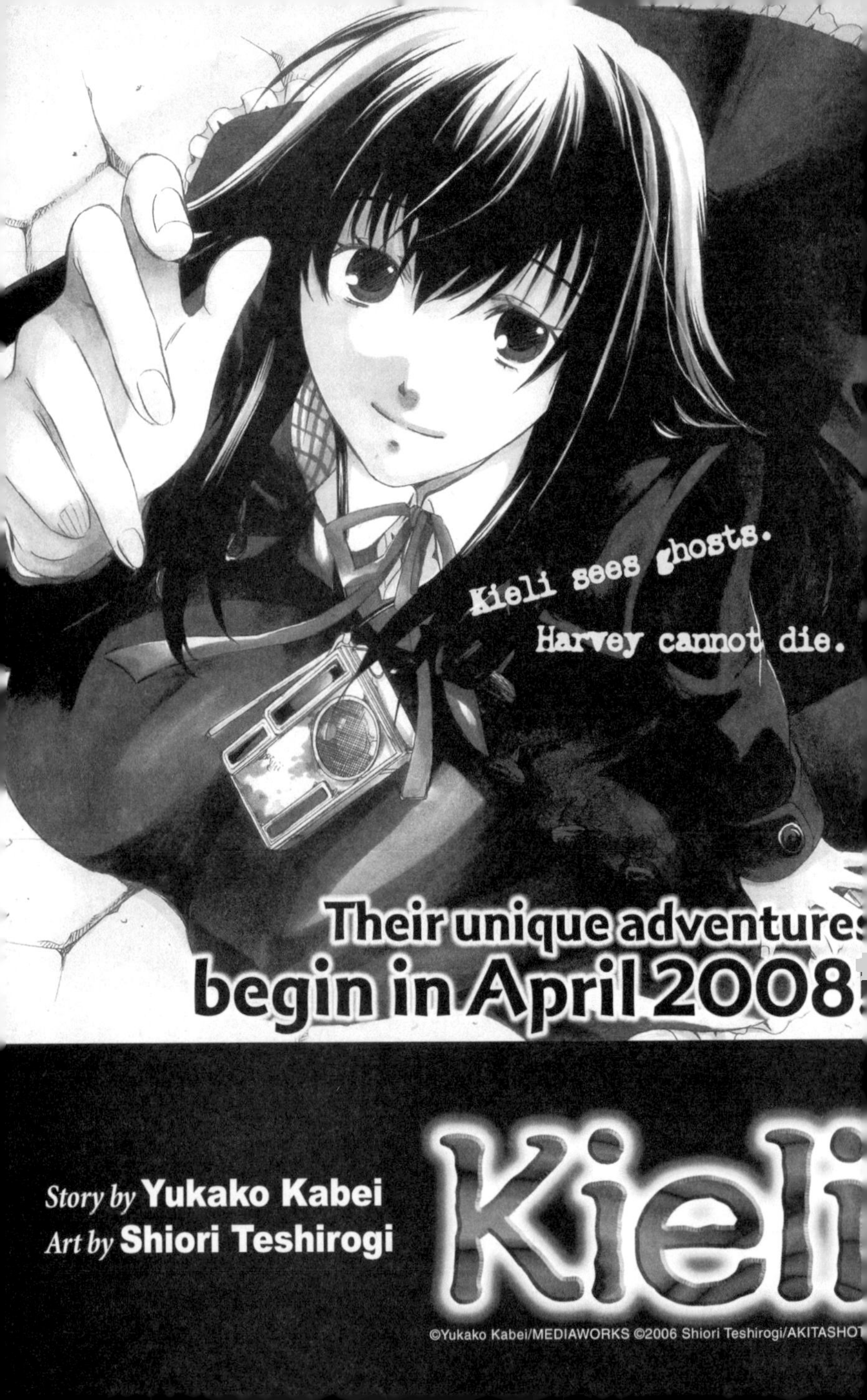
Kieli sees ghosts.
Harvey cannot die.
Their unique adventures
begin in April 2008
Story by Yukako Kabei
Art by Shiori Teshirogi
Kieli
©Yukako Kabei/MEDIAWORKS ©2006 Shiori Teshirogi/AKITASHO

BLACK

by Dall-Young Lim and

Translation: Christine Schilling
Lettering: Fawn Lau

BLACK GOD © 2005 Lim Dall Young, Park Sung Woo / SQUARE ENIX.
All rights reserved. First published in Japan in 2005 by SQUARE ENIX,
CO., LTD. English translation rights arranged with SQUARE ENIX CO.,
LTD. and Hachette Book Group USA through Tuttle-Mori Agency, Inc.

Translation © 2007 by SQUARE ENIX CO., LTD.

Yen Press
Hachette Book Group USA
237 Park Avenue, New York, NY 10017

Visit our web site at www.HachetteBookGroupUSA.com and
www.YenPress.com.

Yen Press is a division of Hachette Book Group USA, Inc.
The Yen Press name and logo is a trademark of
Hachette Book Group USA, Inc.

First Edition: October 2007

The characters and events in this book are fictitious. Any similarity
to real persons, living or dead, is coincidental and not intended by the
author.

10 9 8 7 6 5 4 3 2 1

WOR

Printed in the United States of America